A Selected Bibliography of German Literature in English Translation, 1956-1960

A second supplement to Bayard Quincy Morgan's
*A Critical Bibliography of German
Literature in English Translation*

by

MURRAY F. SMITH

The Scarecrow Press, Inc.
Metuchen, N.J.   1972

ISBN 0-8108-0411-5

Library of Congress Catalog Card No. 76-157727

PREFACE

When the possibility of continuing and updating Dr. B.Q. Morgan's translation bibliography as a dissertation was first brought to my attention by Dr. Hildegard Platzer Brownfield, the idea immediately caught and held my interest. Shortly thereafter, Dr. Harold von Hofe advised that Dr. Morgan be made aware of my intentions, since that field really was the latter's domain and therefore it was only proper to ask his permission. This particular advice turned out to be of inestimable value, serving as the basis for Dr. Morgan's full cooperation and thus preserving the validity of my research. Had he been unaware of my work, the publication of his second supplement would have superseded and thus negated this publication.

Not knowing Dr. Morgan personally, I wrote, somewhat hesitantly, rather expecting him to object to my "intrusion." Quite to my surprise, he not only welcomed my interest, but offered to restrict his new supplement (a work then already in the process of completion and intended to cover the period to 1960) to editions published prior to 1956, thus allowing me to prepare the ensuing five-year period through 1960.

Somewhat later Dr. Morgan again demonstrated his thoughtfulness by offering and subsequently sending all his previously collected post-1955 bibliographical entries. It was this kind gift that formed the nucleus for this publication and thus greatly aided in its successful completion. Without this help the task would have been far more difficult.

I regret that Dr. Morgan's death in February of 1967 prevents me from conveying my gratitude to him. I would, however, like to express my appreciation to both Dr. Brownfield and Dr. von Hofe for their contributions, as well as to Dr. John Spalek, whose guidance has been greatly appreciated.

CONTENTS

INTRODUCTION

The ever-increasing need and frequency of intellectual interchange among the various countries of our modern world is nowadays becoming more and more evident. Since translations are both a cause as well as a result of such interchange, sometimes providing the only bridge available to those who either desire or need to span the cultural and linguistic gap, a bibliography of translations should be a worthwhile contribution toward interrelating cultures and furthering intercultural exchange.[1]

The present compilation is a further extension of the pioneering work, A Critical Bibliography of German Literature in English Translation, 1481-1927, long the only work of its kind, at least in the field of German/English translation.[2] Through the recent publication of two additional supplements since the inception of this publication, the complete coverage of German literature for the period between 1481 and 1960 is assured.[3]

Although challenges are a natural part of any publication, the obstacles met in compiling this bibliography were, I believe, unique in both degree and kind. I had originally assumed that the many hours of scanning would pose the greatest problem. However, a much greater one was the resolving, or at least the correlating of innumerable discrepancies between sources, trying to create an intelligible method of recording such discrepancies, developing a research approach for each of the varied source formats, and especially the determining of more or less satisfactory coverage limits, a question referred to by Dr. B.Q. Morgan as "never satisfactorily answered."[4] However, to my surprise, by far the greatest of all these problems was the seemingly simple task of just distinguishing between the bona fide translation and the apparent or probable one. Since all such items either had to be included, at least to begin with, or disproved as scanning progressed, the problem arose at every turn, often in conjunction with that of scope.

1

Among other things, these problems and some of the pertinent as well as sometimes exceedingly intriguing details involved in facing and occasionally solving them will serve as the basis for the following pages of this introduction.

Sources and Format

As research sources, three main works were originally selected: (1) the Library of Congress Catalog, herein referred to as LC; (2) the UNESCO publication, Index Translationum, referred to as IT; and (3) the catalog of the British Museum. Since the latter work was not available to me for the 1956 period, I have drawn from another source which is based on the holdings of the British Museum as well as several other holdings in that country, the British National Bibliography. [5] This source has been abbreviated in the present bibliographical listing as B56 for the edition covering the 1956 publications, and so on to B61; for textual reference "BNB" will also be used.

The specific LC designations derive from the two five-year cumulative catalogs covering the periods 1953-1957 and 1958-1962, with resultant entries of LC57 or LC62. To the IT abbreviation is added the particular number of the volume, ranging from 1956 (IT9) to 1962 (IT14). Each of these abbreviations has been added at the end of every entry to indicate the origin of the material.

The internal sequence of data for the individual items has undergone various changes, the major one being the use of the English title rather than that of the German work as the basis for secondary alphabetizing when several works appear under the same author. Actually, there would be a greater advantage in using the German title since it would readily effect a natural grouping of works translated from the same German original, thus their relationship would be clear. Because such translations frequently are given dissimilar titles, especially when published in different countries, cataloging by English title often prevents this advantageous grouping and thus tends to obscure relationships. Nevertheless, faced with the lack of many German titles, I found it necessary to use those in English instead. Where known, the German title now appears in parentheses as the third element and is followed by the translator or the designation "Tr. Anon." Data pertaining to the edition, editor or illustrator, and the normal bibliographical facts of publication follow. Since pagination and size play an important part in determining whether a given edition represents a separate translation or the same one reissued, that information is also recorded, and the entry is completed with the source designation(s).

Whenever possible, i.e., when all the particulars of both agree, British and American editions of the same translation, although listed separately in the original sources, are combined into a single entry, since they represent only one translation. In cases where minor discrepancies in size or pagination exist, the figures derived from the BNB are enclosed in parentheses, as are any sizes obtained from that source unless corroborated by the LC. Major divergencies, especially those from the IT, are listed as separate entries, since they represent either different translations or serious errors. In either case a separate listing is justified.

In order to conserve space in the internal format, three adaptations have been incorporated: (1) for translations having several different editions, full information is given only in the initial entry, subsequent entries being introduced by the word "same" and beginning with the data which deviates from the foregoing entry; (2) commonly known publisher names are shortened to the (first) surname; and (3) the names London, New York, and New Jersey are rendered simply as L, NY, NJ, for the sake of brevity, as they appear so frequently.

It should also be noted that multiple editions of a single work are presented in their order of publication, when known. Unless the entry sequence is already established by the source work, two or more editions published the same year are arbitrarily listed by place of publication as follows: (1) a German-speaking area, (2) Great Britain, (3) United States, (4) other.

Initial General Research

The initial phase of research was begun by listing all entries found under the German literature headings in the LC title catalog, since this seemed the logical place to begin acquiring belles-lettres material, which was my intent. Because I had used the Morgan bibliography only as a belles-lettres reference work, my interpretation of the term "Literature," as used by Dr. Morgan, was overly narrow. I had also thought that most German authors were being translated and published almost as soon as the original was on the market. These two misconceptions led me to expect a plethora of translations of literature (in the restricted sense of the term). When the actual yield turned out to be much smaller than had been anticipated, I first assumed it was due to my inexperienced approach. Only later did it become clear that my premise was wrong and that relatively few translations of belles-lettres authors are undertaken.

Because presuming to know all German authors, especially the current ones, would have been even more naive, I was at that time unable to scan the LC author list on an item-by-item basis with any real hope of success. Even using the Morgan bibliography would have produced only a partial listing of possible authors, as many new authors have begun publishing since that work was first compiled.

Faced with this problem, I turned to the IT, thinking that it would provide the solution to my dilemma by presenting a broader coverage of countries and therefore both the desired translation quantity and the needed modernized author list. With this in mind, I began researching the IT by thoroughly covering the literature section under each country heading. Even this produced a disappointing amount of applicable translation entries. However, in spite of the restricted quantity produced, turning to the IT at this particular time was a fortuitous decision because for the novice this type of research is, at the outset, a tedious process which can be carried on only for short periods before fatigue sets in. Although the IT format did not completely alleviate this difficulty, it did effect a decrease by lessening the amount of reading necessary before an appropriate item was located. The IT is also far less complicated to deal with since it contains only translations. Thus scanning was less problematic in this source than it would have been in the LC at this period in my preparation.

Because Dr. Morgan provided me with his previously collected post-1955 bibliographical entries, I was able to continue, equipped with a recent, valid source against which to check my own research as it progressed, and a broader, more useful concept of the term "literature" as used by my predecessor in his own research. Moreover, I had a concrete nucleus upon which to build. In scanning the voluminous LC, I found this to be especially valuable since it provided me with accurate checkpoints to insure that important materials had not been missed. With it I could scan until a possible entry was located, then check in Dr. Morgan's listing to see if that work were recorded, or possibly any works preceding the newly found one. Thus the tedium inherent in scanning was greatly alleviated by having an attainable short-term goal at all times. This provided a sense of progressive accomplishment as well as relative security.

A second coverage of IT9, the first volume involving 1956 publications, was now undertaken--this time covering all categories in all countries. Having been overly expectant before, and thus restricting my search to an area which was too narrow, I now became overly thorough--a more productive although time consuming shortcoming, if such it be at all. It was still possible to save some time because of the asterisk affixed to all items not originating from the official language(s) of the country in which the translation was published. When scanning entries from those countries not directly concerned with English or German, I needed to direct my attention only to the asterisk and then note whether the particular entry also was derived from German. Thus a quick, yet thorough coverage was attained. The result was a much greater efficiency and yield than before.

After the completion of the six IT volumes, my attention turned to the much more involved task of scanning the 26-volume, five-year catalog of the Library of Congress (LC57). In this case, materials published before 1956 were disregarded, thus greatly reducing the quantity of items to be covered. As was already mentioned, having the Morgan research at hand also greatly lightened the burden since it had been drawn in large part from that catalog. The real problem came in trying to go beyond the 1957 date because there was as yet no five-year series, only the paper-bound volumes that are issued periodically, each with its own alphabetical listing. Because of this difficulty, I decided that a letter-by-letter search covering the entire period through 1961 would be best, rather than completing each volume. The D's had just been fully researched when the new five-year series of fifty volumes was received by the library. This new complication meant, of course, that it would be necessary for me to begin the 1958-1960 period anew to make certain that any new entries, added since the earlier periodical listings were compiled, would also be recovered.

In addition it meant choosing between complete coverage of that five-year span during the ensuing scanning, even though the 1961 and 1962 publications were not needed at present, or else partial coverage to fill the needs of the moment and a second scanning of those same fifty formidable tomes. I chose the first, although there was a certain regrettable amount of time loss in being thorough the first time. In my opinion it far outweighed the awesome task of replowing already spaded ground. The time "lost" in the year and a half in the LCs was more than compensated for by the tedium avoided. There was also a certain sense of accomplishment in "completing" an area. Necessary cross-checking more than assured reasonably thorough coverage without a forced rerun being planned in advance.

It might be added here, in retrospect, that the sense of accomplishment could have been much greater had the BNB been the second source rather than the third, as it turned out to be. Since that work lists alphabetically under each individual category, it prevents or at least greatly encumbers an alphabetical recovery. By leaving this source until last, I prevented myself from finishing any given section until all the research was completed. Not only was this frustrating in a sense, but it also added unnecessary indecision as well as error in the choice of both format and content of reference cards produced during research and the format of the final bibliographical listing itself. On the other hand it must be said that the BNB research was accomplished with few other complications as I had gained somewhat more skill and flexibility as a researcher, and most of the problems had been solved by that time, due in part to my previous contact with the BNB through cross-checking.

At this point some clarification ought to be added regarding an earlier statement concerning the paucity of translation. Having been plagued by the problem of lack of quantity at the very outset of my research, and finding the impression growing ever stronger that the same meager percentage of translation initially found in the belles-lettres area of the German materials extended not only to other areas within German but to all other languages as well, I felt obligated to make a somewhat deeper study of the problem to gain a more accurate basis for my conclusion. For this purpose materials were arbitrarily drawn from the LC. After various aspects of volumes forty-three and forty-seven were researched, several individual authors from other volumes were checked. The conclusion was apparent; less than 10 per cent of all German works listed have been translated (based on the entries of translations under those authors). Admittedly this rather minor percentage increased greatly in certain isolated cases such as Rudolf Bultmann or Berthold Brecht, who have many works in translation, in some cases several editions of a single work. However, the overall percentage remained very low, due to the large number of untranslated authors.

In volume forty-three, for example, the first 100 German authors were selected (pp. 1-38), and it was found that ninety-seven had no translations listed, while the remaining three had seven translations among them. No attempt was made in this case to check on the total number of German listings involved, but it becomes clear that only three per cent of the authors in that random sampling had been translated. To discover the approximate amount of works translated, volume forty-seven was thoroughly scanned, revealing some 500 German works. Since dissertations are less often translated, they were not included in the survey.[6] Of these 500 works only fifty had translations listed--exactly 10 per cent.

A further broad sampling was made by checking on listings under "Schmidt" in the LC. Here no distinction as to linguistic affiliation was made--only the assumption that most of them would be German authors. In this case, sixty columns of listings were found to contain only thirteen German-to-English translations, about one full column in all.

The next sampling pertained to individual authors, again arbitrarily selected in the course of the research. This produced the following calculations, in which the first figure in each case pertains to the number of German works listed for that author, the second to the amount of translations: Edith Stein, 2/2; Ludwig Anzengruber, 7/1; Albert Steffen, 10/1; Edzard B. Schaper, 27/2; Ernst Barlach, 16/1; Bettina Arnim, 7/0; Ruth Schaumann, 14/0. Goethe, of course, has a far greater number of translations--Faust alone has six--but Goethe has consistently been one of the most popular of the German authors in English translation.[7]

Some years ago it was generally expected that the newly opened field of machine translation would solve this problem of translation paucity, as well as other problems associated with translation. In November of 1966 the National

Research Council, headed by John R. Pierce of Bell Telephone Laboratories, Inc., reported on a special two-year study concerning the 19 million dollar, ten-year investment made by the National Science Foundation and others interested in "automatic language processing," as the process is called. The gist of the report was that little help could be expected in the near future from mechanical sources to alleviate the problems in translation. To put it in their words: "To date there has been no satisfactory machine translation of scientific texts, and none is expected soon."[8]

Surprisingly enough, even our logical expectations for at least a rapid if not accurate translation are destroyed by this report, since it notes that the machines are presently 21 per cent slower than their human counterparts, as well as 29 per cent harder to understand. Thus little help in solving the translation lack can be expected from mechanical translation, at least at present.

Individualized Research Procedures

Since each of the three sources uses a different basis for its cataloging system, the research procedure had to be individually adapted, according to the particular aspect of each work, which would either reveal the appropriate translation or at least permit non-applicable materials to be readily recognized and disregarded. In every case precautionary measures had to be taken to compensate for possible error, either on the part of the reference work or of the researcher. Each approach also had to be developed as research progressed, since the best system for the particular publication could be worked out only after sufficient acquaintance with its peculiarities had been gained.

After preliminary research revealed the special disposition employed by the IT, that of cataloging on the basis of the country in which a translation has been published, research problems with countries not directly concerned with German or English were basically eliminated by using the asterisk to quickly discover any applicable material.[9] It may be of interest that Israel published many translated German works, some in English (i.e., five for 1956-1960, then five in 1961 alone.) The listings of those countries vitally concerned with the two languages were thoroughly checked, namely Australia, Austria, Canada, Germany, Great Britain, Liechtenstein, Luxemburg, Switzerland, and the United States.

To be sure, the great majority of materials came from publishers in Great Britain and the United States, but the occasional contributions from other countries, sometimes listed
only under these sources, made it necessary, for the sake
of thoroughness, to research them carefully as well.

The special feature in the IT, besides the asterisk,
was the source-language designation at or near the end of
each entry, followed by the title of the work in the original
language. By scanning the whole entry quickly, and paying
particular attention to this part of the entry, materials were
readily retrieved and recorded. Entries lacking both of
these check-points were re-read for other possible clues such
as an author with a seemingly German name. When it
seemed they might be German, they were recorded, their
lack of language designation being carefully noted.

The normal alphabetical listing of the LC did not
permit the use of national areas as had the IT. Because of
this, and because of the vast coverage and rather small
print, the procedure for the LC had to be based more on
eliminating linguistically impossible items and carefully
checking all features of those remaining. Since there were
far fewer translations than originals, this was very time-
consuming. Nonetheless, at least some time was saved by
concentrating only on works with German or English titles.
Here as before, the author name that looked German, the
place of publication (when in a German-speaking area), the
word "translation" and the appended information had to be
checked in order to be relatively sure of not overlooking
pertinent items.

It might be mentioned that the checking of author
name later came to be done more out of curiosity than for
real verification of anything about the translation; this was
due to the surprising amount of apparently, sometimes obviously, non-German authors who nonetheless had written
German works.[10] Although these were frequently unpublished
dissertations which, for the present at least, were still untranslated, they still required investigation. It was only
through such persistent checking that Arno Wuest's translated
dissertation was discovered.[11]

Whenever German titles were found listed, extra care
had to be exercised in those areas in order to pick up possible "hidden" translations, i.e., those English translations
not identified as such by the aforementioned clues. The

rechecking resulting from this approach uncovered a number
of works and produced the listings of rather unusual author /
language combinations appended to this introduction.

Perhaps the most unusual feature of LC scanning was
the need to alternate scanning direction--down the first
column and up the next. This became necessary, or at least
advantageous, because of the great bulk of non-eligible items,
the lack of any context, and the resultant monotony. Alter-
nating the scanning direction created the desired illusion of
change.

As eligible items were recognized, they were recorded
either on three-by-five cards or on a list, depending on
whether they were repeat items, i.e., those previously carded, or new ones. New acquisitions were listed on sheets by
recording the page, column designation (a, b, c), author, and
partial title, followed by place of publication and year. Any
other important information, such as the German title listed
with another entry, was appended to this. Cards were later
typed from these lists, producing neat, readable references.

In contrast to both of the foregoing sources, the BNB
categorizes according to the content of each work and then
alphabetizes within each resultant area, thus greatly hamper-
ing, if not preventing any alphabetically-oriented recovery of
materials. Because of this system, the attempt at cross-
checking for carded translations already gleaned from the
other sources failed. This was partially due to the unwieldi-
ness of the mass of cards produced by this time, only a
part of which could be conveniently carried to the library at
one time. Since any few pages of items in the BNB spanned
the entire alphabet, a portion of the carded materials was
always insufficient. On the other hand, the prospect of
scanning each individual entry 26 times, once during the
search for each letter, was absurd. Thus it was that only
a sheet listing was made for all BNB entries, although many
had already been recorded on cards during cross-referencing.
From this, cards were once more typed, resulting in a
second group of neatly prepared references, especially
important in the case of the BNB because of numerous
deviations from LC practices in the area of pagination and
size measurement. By this is meant the apparent counting
of both sides of sheets, whether bearing printing or not, and
usage of the one-half centimeter. BNB editors obviously
intend these as steps toward greater accuracy, which they
well may be in the final analysis, but because the practice

causes inevitable deviations between BNB data and that listed
in other sources, it was an additional encumbrance for me,
forcing a choice between the dissimilar figures--options for
which I had no valid basis--or the inclusion of both.   The
latter choice seemed to be the more judicious, although it
necessitated a further adaptation (that of placing the BNB
data in parentheses except when it paralleled that found in
the LC), in order to maintain clarity regarding data origins.

It should be brought out here that, for the most part,
only the successful methods have been emphasized in the
foregoing.   The following are some of those that were dis-
carded as either unfruitful or unnecessary: adapting entries
during research to a preconceived format rather than repro-
ducing them exactly; combining the British and the American
editions of a work regardless of disparities; and attempting
to be all-inclusive by listing every type of available data,
such as size and publication details for the German originals,
the month of publication for British editions, the initial date
of issue for all reprints, and extensive locater lists for
editions held by university libraries in the United States.

Scope and Related Problems

As briefly mentioned earlier in this introduction, the
concept of scope varied greatly from that initially held (belles-
lettres only), to almost everything that could be regarded as a
proven translation from German to English.   Due to the time-
consuming aspect of that "proof," as well as to general
principles, several categories were dropped: (1) government
published tourist "propaganda" material such as Facts
About Germany and Facts About Austria, which are frequently
revised and which, conceivably, do not necessarily represent
translations;   (2) reports of international meetings which have
taken place in Europe (often the Germans speak in English,
the Russians in German, and so on, without recourse to
translation);   (3) instruction pamphlets on "How to Operate..."
etc.;   (4) most technical materials in scientific fields (although defining the term "technical" nowadays becomes exceedingly difficult);   and (5) most translations from German
when a third language has been the real origin.

This last area is by far the most problematic to work
with since such translations are frequently listed simply as,
"translated from the German," without indication of the
original language.   Only when discovered can such works be

eliminated, and even then it is done more or less arbitrarily, since a translation may (though it certainly shouldn't in most cases) have become an "original" by virtue of the license taken by the translator. Only a close comparison of the two would reveal this, of course. An example of such "creative" work is the English translation of Harald Steinert's Goldsucher...., a work of 387 pages, 21 cm., published in 1957. The so-called translated version, The Atom Rush, copyrighted in 1958, measures 183 pages and 23 cm. Can it be possible that a two-centimeter difference has absorbed all of those pages? Perhaps there has been, on the other hand, an error in recording, and the original had only 187 pages; or the translation 383 pages. Only by comparing the editions themselves would the actual facts be revealed that would warrant the result being regarded as an "original" work. This, of course, is only an example of possible changes in translation that happened to be seen and does not really represent a translation from a third language, yet the problem itself still holds.

As a more appropriate choice let us select Hugo Steinhaus' work Mathematical Snapshots, translated from a German work entitled Kaleidoskop der Mathematik. Actually the original title is in Polish and is called Kaleidoskop matematyczny. But without the texts to compare, who can say to what degree the translator has translated and to what degree created? In such circumstances the real authorship of the work becomes questionable. A case in point is that of Arnim Tuulse whose work, Burgen des Abendlandes (Vienna, 1958) is listed by BNB as the original from which Castles of the Western World, published in 1952, was translated.[12] LC states, however, that the German version comes from the Swedish original, Borgar i Vasterlandet, published in 1952 and translated into German by Gerhard Eimer. Who now is the "German" author, if indeed there be any? Had there been no such information in LC, this work would have been listed as a German work in the present bibliography. Such examples make one wonder how many more works belong to this category.

A second difficulty arises when the attempt is made to define the term "German." What makes a work a German original? Does an author born in Germany automatically merit that title although he may write in some other language or languages? Does he retain the title, once gained, for all works published, whether written in German or not, as long as he continues to write some works in that language, as a

number of authors now do? Would Werner von Braun, for
example, be referred to at present as a German author?
Would that hold for such an author's publications in all
cases even though prepared in English? Rudolf Bultmann,
for instance, gave lectures in English at Yale University
that do not purport to be anything but English originals.[13]
Should this be regarded as an English translation anyway?
Can Alfred Adler's book The Pattern of Life, 1931, be a
translation when it represents "case histories. . . from
Adler's practice in the USA"?[14] Would the work, Individual
Psychology of Alfred Adler, New York, 1959, be regarded
as one with the preface statement: "Because every word in
the main body of the work is Adler's. . ."?[15] Can it be
assumed that these words were German, or might they have
been English?

If it is assumed that all German-born writers retain
the right to being called German for translation purposes,
there is no problem in this regard, though new ones may be
created. The real question is whether this can be assumed.
And if this is used as the criterion, what is to be done with
the American or the Japanese or the Swede who writes an
original German language work? Can he also be a "German"
author or must he remain with his own ethno-linguistic
group? The acceptance of a C.F. Meyer, or more to the
point, perhaps, a Chamisso as definitely German already
sets the precedent for those who, by thereafter devoting
themselves to German, continue "in the faith" as it were.
But what of those who are only "visitors," so to speak, and
who use German for but one work or for merely a few?
Even beyond these questions, but closely allied to them nonetheless, is the group of German-language authors whose
works have found their way into English translation indirectly.
Such is the case with Rudolf G. Hegler's Crete and its
Treasures, which is an English translation of a German
original with French as the intervening step. Can this still
be listed as a translation from German?

Even when an author's eligibility for inclusion is not
in dispute, it may happen that a seemingly obvious case of
translation among his works turns out to be an English
original instead. Perhaps the best example of such a cir-
cumstance is to be found in a work by Max Born and Emil
Wolf, published in both London and New York, 1959, entitled
Principles of Optics. There is in existence a much earlier
German work by the same writers bearing the title Optik;
therefore the English edition seems to be a translation. Only

14

the reading of the introduction by Max Born reveals that,
due to the time lapse between the two editions and the vast
changes in the field of optics, "a translation was hardly appropriate; instead a substantially new book was prepared."[16]

A third problem still remains if and when the foregoing are solved: what percentage of a published work has
to involve translation before the work is eligible for inclusion
with full translations? Will the introduction suffice, or commentary?[17] Are a few articles enough--or half? The
previously mentioned Individual Psychology of Alfred Adler
states: "Nearly half of the selections were translated by the
editors."[18] This, to be sure, proves that it really was a
translation, as was asked in problem two, but is half
enough? I certainly think so, and for this reason the work
has been included in this bibliography.

A fourth problem in the interpretation of the term
"technical" confronts the researcher. Dr. Morgan mentions
in his earliest edition that he had limited his collecting to
"essays, travel and description, German history and
biography, history of German literature, history of Greece
and Rome, history and theory of art and music, aesthetics,
philosophy and . . . correspondence."[19] The reason given
for the choice was: "for their cultural advantage and the
aesthetic pleasure they afford."[20] Though this same basic
statement is repeated in the second supplement, the decision
is finally made that "non-technical works, in whatever field"
would be acceptable.[21] Having found the area of strict
"belles-lettres" far too small to merit a bibliography, I
decided that a listing of all works of general interest to the
average modern reader would be quite appropriate and helpful, but "technical" works would be disregarded. Then, after
having passed up a work on set theory, because it seemed too
restricted for general interest, I was informed by my ten-
year old daughter that they were learning about set theory in
her grade-school class.[22] With that I realized that I was
simply not qualified as a judge of what the "average" reader
might find worthwhile, particularly with the amazing rate of
change in our modern world. Who can tell at this point what
will be "too restricted" and what "average" will mean in a few
years? Following this rather disillusioning experience, I decided to record all substantiated translations to begin with, and
to decide later what, if any, should be excluded.

Thus the fifth problem was brought about, since anything acquired with great effort is not readily given up again.

So it was with these hard-won gains. Only very reluctantly have I dropped items, thinking they might be tomorrow's "group theory," so to speak. The result has been a very large, somewhat unwieldy bibliography of quite heterogeneous character that both observes and at the same time exceeds Dr. Morgan's admonition of "non-technical works, in whatever field."

At this point it occurs to me that a plausible solution to some of these problems might be found by later appending to this basic bibliography an additional one comprising third-language sources for which German has served as "mediator." This would both provide the materials and yet segregate them properly. The same could be done for technical translations. The first might form a particularly useful tool for the field of comparative literature. For example, it would indicate how often German has served in this capacity. How many works have become known to the English-speaking world only through the mediation of German? Does any specific type of material dominate this area?

The second appended listing might serve as an additional checklist for those source works that regularly publish bibliographies for technical fields.[23] Since my only information about such sources has been gleaned from LC scanning and not from direct contact, I have no idea how complete their listings are, therefore, I am not able to comment further on them at this time; and because the task at hand must take precedence, both of these projects must be relegated to the future.

To return to the unanswered question of inclusion, let me give particulars by way of outline and summary. I have included: (1) any work which has as its basis a German language work and has not gone through an intermediary language--this would include stories drawn from the Grimms but not "translated" as such; (2) any English translation which has resulted directly from a German-language source by an author of any ethnic background or linguistic group (by the same token I have excluded those works written in English, either by former German nationals or by German citizens still living in German language areas, when it can be demonstrated--usually by remarks in the preface--that no translation as such occurred;)[24] (3) a work with any amount of translation, save spot quotes, if demonstrably from a German original, since its possible worth to others is difficult for me to evaluate.

As to the dates of inclusion, it might here be mentioned that works not dated but that have not previously been
carried in the LC have been recorded here since they may
not have been known to Dr. Morgan. Also, works with in-
consistent dating have been listed if one of the datings fell
in my period. For example, Wilhelm Andersen's Towards a
Theology of Mission is listed in BNB as having been published in October 1955, which would cause its exclusion. LC,
however, lists that same London publication as 1956, so the
work has been added. This discrepancy occurs because of a
number of things, no doubt, one of them being the reporting
of a publication before it actually appears on the market. [25]

Major Problems

The minor physical problems of fatigue, brought on at
least in part, by the lack of context to entice the mind, have
already been sufficiently mentioned. The aggravation caused
by incessant need for correlation of discrepancies now re-
quires somewhat more detailed treatment here. Under this
category might be listed as the first element the BNB usage
of one-half centimeter designations which naturally always
vary from the LC size, sometimes by one and one-half
centimeters. The solution here was to include both, since I
had no way of knowing who was right. Of more consequence
was the IT practice of sometimes adding the Roman and the
Arabic numerals together, thus producing a page total which
is at variance with all other sources. [26] Since this is neither
their standard (nor even standardized) practice as far as I
know, it creates a real problem for the bibliographical researcher who wants to know whether a given entry represents
a new translation or just a reprint. A further difficulty would
be encountered by any researcher attempting to determine
relative size variance between original and translation. Should
such a task be undertaken, the IT would frequently mislead
rather than aid, and result in inaccurate conclusions. This
would be especially true in the case of translations, since the
introduction (recorded in Roman numerals) is often not a part
of the original work at all and therefore has no direct relationship to the size of the text (in Arabic numerals).

A somewhat more serious practice of that same work
is that of correcting previous errors of pagination, language
source, title, etc., by entering the data in its corrected
form without any indication that the information is the

corrected version of a former error. When this is not
known, and to some extent afterward as well, severe research problems may be brought about, to say nothing of the
subsequent constant need to verify all ensuing IT data which
greets the now-jaundiced eye of the researcher. As a case
in point, let us refer to a work by Tor Andrae, apparently
one of three German works he wrote, Mohammed, sein
Leben und sein Glaube, published in 1932. The translation,
Mohammed, the Man and His Faith, was recovered from
IT11, which gave the German title as Die Person Muhammeds
in Lehre und Glauben seiner Gemeinde, 1917.[27] Further research revealed the same translation title listed in IT13 as
having been translation from Mohammed, sein Leben und
sein Glaube.[28] No date was given. Because I was unaware
of the correction practice of the IT, it was necessary for me
to do rather extensive research to uncover the truth, since a
quick check of the Deutsches Bücherverzeichnis produced no
works by Tor Andrae between 1910 and 1930.

By checking the International Who's Who of 1937, I
found a listing of three works by Tor Andrae, the earliest of
which was Die Person M-- . . . , 1913.[29] My conclusion
was that the second entry must be incorrect, though the date
still bothered me. The 1938 edition of that same reference
work listed four titles for Andrae, the first a 1918 edition
of Die Person M-- . . . , noted as having been published
originally in 1913, and the last, Mohamed [sic.] His Life and
Faith, 1935. Now I wasn't even sure the IT listing was a
translation from German at all. This was seemingly con-
firmed during LC scanning because all other German works
by Andrae were listed as translations from Swedish. This
appeared far more reasonable because of the author's name.
In checking the LC covering the 1917 period to see if such a
German work might be listed there, I found a Spanish translation which had in turn been derived from the German, an
indication in just the opposite direction. In addition, a 1936
edition of the English version was also listed, but the final
piece of the puzzle was supplied by locating the 1936 copy of
the English translation in which was written: This volume is
a translation from the German of Professor Tor Andrae's
Mohammed, sein Leben und sein Glaube . . . Göttingen,
1932."[30] This, together with supporting proof gleaned by
checking the 1931-1935 Deutsches Bücherverzeichnis, finally
solved the problem as to correct German title. Had the IT
noted that their second entry was a correction of the first,
this added time expenditure could have been avoided. To be
sure, it is difficult to both record and correct all errors

encountered in research; yet for an annual publication, clarified correction within its own pages should pose no overwhelming problem. For example, the editors should include the item number and volume of the earlier incorrect listing in parentheses following the regular item number. This would serve the dual purpose of warning the researcher that a correction has been made as well as providing him with the reference number for easy comparison of the two entries.

In this compilation the source from which each item is derived is listed with every entry. Comparing sources will reveal any divergencies, most of which involve spelling errors.[31] When the author's name has been misspelled, both spellings are listed, however, the erroneous form carries a "see" reference rather than the full entry.

An additional point should perhaps be brought out here regarding the obvious importance of the editions themselves, where available. In many cases, as in that just presented, only the textual source can produce final clarification, to say nothing of other information. Dr. Morgan mentions his use of the translation collection being made at Pennsylvania State University by Professor Philip Allison Shelley. Although I have not yet had the opportunity to draw on that source, I do have great admiration and appreciation for such provisions being made, having faced the Andrae problem. It might also be mentioned here that if Dr. Morgan's most recent supplement covering this period had been published at the time, the research involved in this case would have been unnecessary since he lists the 1936 translation.

A third problem, one which I suppost is almost inescapable, is the incorrect listing of some author names, due possibly to typesetting errors. I say almost inescapable because each of the three works suffered from this to some extent. LC lists, for example, both Benno Zieser and Bruno Zeiser as the author of Road to Stalingrad. (The first seems to be the correct one.) IT10 presents the author of The Willing Flesh as Heinrich Willi (actually Willi Heinrich as the IT itself lists in four other entries in that same volume.)[32] Perhaps the epitome of error in author names is exemplified in the BNB entry which interchanges two entire names: the one is Wilhelm Andersen, The Bridges of God; the other, Donald Anderson McGavran, Towards a Theology of Mission, translated from the German. Actually, the two should be reversed.[33] Even this type of error is exceeded by IT12, this time with a translator name listed as Kathrine Schramm.[34]

Actually, the name derives from combining that of the translator, Kathrine Potts, with that of the illustrator, Ulrik Schramm. In this same vein we find names occasionally translated in the IT.[35] In other cases the name is respelled by the French compiler or typist.[36] Finally, the title itself is not always safe from error, as demonstrated by the IT listing which changed Aichinger's The Bound Man to The Round Man.[37]

Before going into detail on the last, and by far the greatest problem, that of recognizing many works that are bona fide translations, let me mention the most grueling though trifling task, that of trying to be consistent while drawing from three diverse sources. If, for example, original entries were made on the cards according to the presumed final format, they had to be rechecked later to make sure they still matched the final sequence of information. If they were typed according to the actual entry they represented, material had to be deleted and rearranged for the final entry. Even after that, the minor details of sequence of European, British, and American entries, uniform usage of comma or period after "same" entries, etc., created an endless aggravation, in no small part due to the constant proofreading necessary to insure correctness. The use of IBM computer cards has helped considerably through both ease of correction and rapid delivery of proof copy on short notice. To be sure, it is dismaying to find blank spaces replaced by asterisks on a print because of a sudden quirk in an old machine, but these are only occasional things.

Methods for Determing a Bona Fide Translation from German

Let us turn now to the final and most elusive task of all, that of recognizing a work which is a translation from German to English. What is the key revealing point about such a work? Can't we just look for authors who have German names and use that as our clue? Yes, but it remains just that, since, as shall be demonstrated shortly, many authors with German names do not write German works, though there may be German translations listed for those works. On the other hand, to a far greater degree than one would suppose, authors having non-German names write German originals, and many of them cannot be regarded as German by any criterion except their choice of language. Dr. Morgan oversimplifies, I am sure, his actual method of

checking when he tells us his approach "was to go through
each list from beginning to end, stopping at each name that
looked German, and examining the titles under it to see if
any were translations."[38] This is just the beginning and the
first key to a possible German to English translation, as I'm
sure he would admit. An expert often shows how he accomplished a deft maneuver better than he describes that same
maneuver to others. The key is probably closer akin to what
Germans call Fingerspitzengefühl, a feeling in the tips of the
fingers, based on years of experience, a vast memory bank
of which combinations are likely to produce results and
which are not.

     As a second clue, Dr. Morgan states that "if a given
writer has a German title in print, that proves he had a
German upbringing, a German education, and a German background and could be classed as permanently German."[39]
Based on this he then concludes: "Therefore, anything he
wrote came out of a German mind and might fairly be called
German."[40] This view can readily be ascribed to if we
alter it slightly to read "A German upbringing, and/or a
German education, and/or a German background." This
presumes that the German title mentioned is not an unan-
nounced translation, as has been the case here and there.
To the rest I can heartily subscribe.

     Doubtlessly it is one's knowledge of such a "German
title in print" (i.e., recognition and therefore acceptance of
an author as German) that makes it possible to recognize an
English work by such authors as Goethe and Schiller as a
translation from German, whether marked as such or not.
That same knowledge may also mislead, however, even in
the case of the well-known author, unless great pains are
taken to research any doubtful or seemingly erroneous bit
of data. Such a situation is exemplified in Heine's Religion
and Philosophy in Germany, a Fragment, listed in B60 as a
translation from German, but accompanied by the original
title De l'Allemagne. My "knowledge" interpreted the latter
as fallacious, since German works normally bear German
rather than French titles, and it is well known that Mme. de
Staël wrote De l'Allemagne. In addition, LC62 had already
supplied the "correct" German title, Zur Geschichte der
Religion und Philosophie in Deutschland. Although very certain that the French title was spurious, I nevertheless took
the time to locate both the 1959 edition of the translation,
and the original one of 1882. In the latter publication was
found the following:

In the French version of Heine's works, the book now translated appears as the first part of the two volumes entitled 'De l'Allemagne.' These volumes were carefully revised by Heine during the latter years of his life, but the later German editions had not the benefit of such revision. The French version, as finally revised by the author, must therefore be regarded as the definitive form in which he desired the work to appear. [41]

Confronted not only by this support of the French title, but also proof of a French version prior to that in German, I began to doubt that the translation information in the BNB was correct. The next page of the introduction revealed that "the actual translation, however, has been made rather from the German than from the French," which corroborated the complete BNB entry, as well as that in LC62. [42] The French title was the original one (according to publication sequence), while the German title was drawn from the actual work translated; thus I had both a French and a German title for Heine's work (each of which was correct on its own terms), some new knowledge about an author I thought I had known well, and reinforced proof of the importance of relying on research, not knowledge, when data appears to be dubious.

In the case of authors who are not known to the researcher and who do not appear to be German, clues other than those mentioned thus far must be used. In the case of Jacques Bloch and his work Frozen Shoulder, it was the combination of place of publication (Basle) and the name of the co-author (Fritz Fischer) that piqued my curiosity. I had almost passed over the work as not being a translation, since there was no indication that it was; that is, it had no statement mentioning translation, no footnote indicating a German source, and no other German title listed for the same author. As a last resort, I attempted an educated guess which I could test by research. Because of the names I guessed it was a translation, and the Deutsches Bücher-verzeichnis listed it as such. Of course, many such works have turned out to be original English works and not translations at all, but the pleasure of having located at least a few works that might otherwise have remained hidden, is well worth the necessary persistence and effort.

An additional clue may be that of subject matter, as was the case with a work by Netty (Railing) Radnanyi referred to as novelettes, (from the German Novellen).

Actually, the clue of subject matter may be just as mislead-
ing as helpful, as it was in the case of a work entitled The
Life of Ludwig van Beethoven, by a very non-German sound-
ing author named Alexander Wheelock Thayer. Neither LC
nor BNB gave any indication of this being a translation,
though IT 13 listed it as such. [43] Location of the work itself
produced the facts, but still only in part, because the work
available to me was not the Illinois University Press edition
of 1960, referred to in the IT, but a 1934 edition published
in New York by the Beethoven Association. It explains in
reference to the author that "he gave the first volume to the
world--and then in a foreign tongue." [44] This would seem,
then, to indicate a German original translated into English,
but on the following page we find that it is:

> ...not a translation of the German work but a
> presentation of the original manuscript, so far as
> the discoveries made after the writing did not mar
> its integrity, supplemented by the knowledge ac-
> quired since the publication of the first German
> edition, and placed at the service of the present
> editor by the German revisors of the second
> edition.

Thus a work originally written in English was published first
in German, a rather unique situation. Although the work was
now ineligible for inclusion on normal terms, it proved to
have some English translations of letters written by
Beethoven. I therefore chose to include it in the bibliography.
Note here that because of the German edition being published
first, the date cannot be used as a valid proof of translation,
as might otherwise be the case.

From the foregoing it would seem that a translation is
easily recognized if, and only if, the author is known to have
never written any works in English or the translation is cor-
rectly marked as such with full information. The latter instance doesn't occur as frequently as one would wish, and
the former presumes extensive knowledge both of the author's
life and of all his works.

All translations not recognized on the above mentioned
terms must be carefully scrutinized and checked for possible
German author or translator names (which may or may not
help), and English or a German title (especially if other
works by the same author have German or English titles), a
title covering a German-related topic, or a publisher in a

German-language area. All such works must be recorded or disproven, since one reference work may later reveal translation facts not given in previously researched sources and thus cause a second or third search for previous listings.

Conclusions

It would seem that several pertinent conclusions can be drawn at this point, the first one being in regard to the sequence for successful use of reference works. At least for compiling a bibliographical work of any scope, it is generally overly encumbering to leave a work which is arranged in any fashion other than strictly alphabetically until last, since that is the time when the greatest bulk of materials must be cross-checked. Had I researched the BNB as the second source rather than the last, it would not have been necessary to wait until the research in all sources was finished before any given section could be completed, which was both frustrating and unnecessary. It might also be mentioned that such a change would have permitted an earlier decision on the problem of format, because the difficulties occurring in a single section do not differ greatly from those encountered in the whole bibliography. Of course, no sequence would obviate the rather frequent cross-checking necessary; nor should it do so, since this is the one accurate way of insuring relative completeness and thoroughness.

The second conclusion pertains to the amount of works translated from German to English during the period 1956-1960. This seems to be at most some 10 per cent, based on rather extensive but arbitrarily selected surveys in LC62. That little help toward increasing that percentage can be expected at present, if at all, from the field of machine translation is also apparent.[45]

A related aspect of the preceding is the fact that not only is there a small percentage of translation, at least according to the LC, but that this too is restricted to an even smaller group of authors. This is borne out by the fact that many authors have no translations recorded at all.

A third conclusion must be drawn as to ethnolinguistic areas represented in German works in the present LC holdings; namely, that authors from nearly every such area are to be found among those who write German works of one kind or another. In part, this seems due to the international scope of students at German universities, demonstrated by the breadth of nationalities and cultures represented in those who write dissertations there.

The fourth and final conclusion concerns the now obvious difficulty encountered in attempting to recognize the bona fide German/English translation; the great variety of national origins represented among the names of "German" authors is partly responsible. Additional contributing factors are the increased shift of population in our modern western world and the greater opportunity for lecturing in English-speaking areas. One last factor should also be mentioned, namely the still-continuing but unfortunate practice of publishers neglecting to give credit to translators for their efforts and contributions. This naturally results in many translations not being marked as such. The translator ought to be given both credit and, where necessary, responsibility for his contribution toward intercultural exchange.

The question may reasonably be asked as to the real value of this bibliography now that it has been compiled. Even in the manuscript stage it has been of service to a professor of English inquiring about recent Faust translations, as well as to a graduate student of drama. The latter needed to know if Kaiser's Bürger von Calais had been previously translated. Since I knew it had not been translated prior to 1961, and no subsequent translation had been made, the student is now translating that work as a Master's thesis, with the possibility of future publication. It is hoped that many others will also be able to profit from the bibliographical information contained herein.

Notes

1. That this interchange has caused more than one unexpected interpretation is, I am certain, no surprise. Perhaps the best example in the literary field is that resulting from the choice of works translated in the cases of Goethe and Schiller, causing the former to be known in the English-speaking world as Germany's great dramatist (Faust) and the latter as its great author of poetry (Die Glocke and numerous other poems, many of which have been set to music.) That the works of these same two authors are regarded as purely romantic is also greatly the result of translation. The reversed equivalent of this

situation is exemplified in the unique impact of Shakespeare upon the German Storm and Stress authors, including Goethe and Schiller, due to the prose translation of his works by Wieland. It might be mentioned that this original impression was later altered by the Schlegel translation in verse.

2.   Originally compiled by Dr. B. Q. Morgan as A Bibliography of German Literature in English Translation (University of Wisconsin Studies, 1922), then enlarged and reissued in 1938. The 1922 edition will be referred to hereafter as Morgan I.

3.   The revised editions (New York: Scarecrow Press, 1965) covering to 1927 and then to 1955, will be referred to as Morgan II and Morgan III, respectively.

4.   Morgan, I, p. 9.

5.   Published annually in London by the Council of the British National Bibliography, Ltd.

6.   Arno Wuest's translated dissertation may be cited as one of the few.

7.   In Morgan II, p. 14, we find: ". . . Goethe and Schiller head the line, and Goethe so far outstrips the rest as almost to be in a class by himself."

8.   From a Washington (UPI) statement circulated nationally, on or about November 25, 1966.

9.   Discussed on p. 9 of this introduction.

10.   The reader is referred to the special listing of such authors at the end of this introduction.

11.   Previous reference to this author is made in footnote 6.

12.   B59, entry no. 5866.

13.   These are presented in his Jesus Christ and Mythology (New York, Scribners, 1958) and later, as a paperback (London, SCM Press, 1960).

14. Lewis Way, Adler's Place in Psychology (London: Allen and Unwin, 1950), p. 319, a supporting source for similar indications on p. 3 of the Adler work cited.

15. Heinz L. Ansbacher and Rowena R. Ansbacher, eds. 1st ed. (New York: Basic Books, 1956), p. v.

16. Principles of Optics, (London and New York, (1959)) p. v.

17. Erich Naumann's commentary on Apuleius' work Amor and Psyche was shown to be from a German original entitled Ein Beitrag zur seelischen Entwicklung des Weiblichen, so the work was included.

18. Ansbacher, p. vii.

19. Morgan, I, p. 10.

20. Ibid.

21. Morgan III, p. 7.

22. The work referred to is P. Aleksandrov's An Introduction to the Theory of Groups, which turned out to be from a Russian original although translated from Einführung in die Gruppentheorie.

23. Two might here be mentioned: (1) the United States Department of Commerce publication Technical Translations, superseding Translation Monthly published in Chicago by the John Crerar Library for the Special Libraries Association; (2) a work of scientific, technical and engineering translations, published by Morris D. Friedman, Inc., West Newton, Massachusetts.

24. A number of works by Paul Tillich fall in this category.

25. Morgan III, p. 13.

26. Cf. the Heinrich Wölfflin entry in LC 62 (xvi, 237p.) and that of IT9 (253 p.).

27. Item No. 7499. The LC published in 1958 lists this work as the author's inaugural dissertation at Uppsala.

28. Item No. 9180.

29. This may be an error since the dissertation was accepted in 1917 as noted earlier.

30. Mohammed, the Man and His Faith, New York: Scribner's Sons, 1936, p. 5.

31. Heinz Schröter's Stalingrad is such an example. LC62 lists "Bis zur letzten Patrone" as the continuation of the title of the New York edition, but spells it "...letzen..." for the London publication.

32. IT10, item No. 18874.

33. B55.

34. IT12, item 19477.

35. IT13, item 12533 makes Maurice out of Moriz.

36. IT11, item 7830 respells Bauer as Baueur.

37. IT9, item 5719.

38. Morgan I, p. 9.

39. Morgan III, p. 8.

40. Ibid., p. 9.

41. London, Trübner and Co., 1882, p. viii.

42. Ibid., p. ix.

43. Item 9353.

44. Thayer, p. viii.

45. A rather promising new approach to computer translation is presented by Eldon G. Lytle of Brigham Young University in his work A Grammar of Subordinate Structures in English, Mouton and Co., The Hague, 1971.

Authors whose names are apparently not German
but who have written German works
(Some dissertations may be in English with a German title)

Abdelasim, A. Letfy
Abd-Ellatif, Mohammed
    Ismael
Abd-Ru-Shin
Abir, Simbah
Acosta, Matthais
Adams, Alfons
Afifi, Mohamed Ahmed
Agouri, Elias Rene
Ahlsson, Lars Erik
Ahmed, Midhart Shams al-Din
Ahmed, Naseem
Ahmed, Sadullah
Ahn, Chang-su
Ahn, Yongpal
Ahsin, Niyazi
Alanne, Eero
Aldus, Rolf
Alewyn, Richard
Ali el-Sauaf, el-Sayed
Aliberti, Aline
Allam, Mohammed Aly
Allen, G.C.
Allison, Serge
Aloni, Jenny Rosenbaum
Alverdes, Kurt Hermann
Aman, Mohammed
Amery, Jean
Amzar, Dumitru
Anderson, Robert Ralph
Anderson, Walter
Andre de la Porte, Wicher
Andrejewski, Walter
Andriesson, Carl
Anton Andres, Angel
Antoni, Victor
Araki, Tadao Johannes

Archibald, James
Arifin, Sjahabuddin
Arigoni, Duilio
Arkosi, Zolten
Arquint, Caspar
Artik, Naci Erdogan
Arui, Armand
Asambuja
Ashein, Ivar
Asher, John
Askildsen, Arne
Atabay, Cyrus
Auburtin, Victor
Ayih, Michel

Badavi, Helmi
Bairy, Maurice A.
Balabanov, Aleksandur
    Mikhailov
Baljet, Jan Willem
Banerjee, Biswanath
Barbatti, Bruno
Barberis, Franco
Bardachzi, Karl
Barikian, Anahid
Bassiouni, Ahmed Abdel
    Hamid
Beathalter, Alfons
Beau, Horst
Benes, Renee
Berry, Margaret
Birkel, Suitbertus
Bochenski, Innocentius
Bothas, Dagmar
Brainard, Paul
Brown, William Greenwood
Brustgi, Franz Gustav

Calalan, Alain Jean
Chen, Yian-nian
Chow, Chung-Cheng

Dejka, Alois
Demelle, Joseph

Guggisberg, Charles Albert
  Walker
Guido, Glur

Hall, Robert
Hamed, Abdul Samad
Hamed, Mohamed
Hasumik, Toshimitsu

Inciarte, Fernando

Mathiopoulos, Basil P.
Mattle, Louis
Mesot, Jean
Michels, Robert
Millar, Lynn
Miller, A. G.
Miller, Arthur Maximilian
Miller, Fritz
Miller, Josef
Miller, Maria Luise
Milojcic, Vladimir
Minger, Charles
Mingotti, Anton
Mlinsek, Dusan
Montagu, Ruth (Freudmann)
Moor, Emmy
Moretti, August
Mourzsy, Abdel Wahab
Mras, Karl
Mrsic, Wilhelm
Mtwiejew, Aleksander
Muddathi, Ahmed
Murray, Joseph Pogtsa

Namglies, Ursula
Nasarski, Peter
Nicholston, Merickston
Nicolussi, Johann
Nikolov, Nikola

Nitobe, Inazo
Norwood, Lotte
Nouer-Weiding, Alfred
Novotny, Alexander
Nowikowa, Irene

Obraztsov, Nicholas
Ocana, Carmona Antonio
Oda, Shigeru
Ong-Oei, Tiauw Liong
Orelli, Marcus
Oudenrijn, Marcus
Ouvrier, Eugen
Ozolins, Eizens Adrians

Pachernegg, Joe
Pai, Soo-tong
Paintner, Kurt
Paleczek, Otto
Palmie, Friedrich
Panconcelli-Calzia, Guilo
Papakonstantinu, Konstantin
Parikh, Krishn akant
Parke, Kurt
Parker, Felix
Pasternack, Joachim
Paszkouski, Jerzy
Pavlin, Ivan
Payne, Albert
Perazzi, Gianni
Perrin, Charles
Petitpierre, Max
Petriconi, Hellmuth
Philippovich, Alexander
Philipps, Wilhelm
Pia, Hans Werner
Piatruchinski, Horst
Piiper, Johannes
Pilleri, George
Ping-Pong
Pink, Hans
Pink, Karl
Pirani, Marcello Stefano van
Pollock, Frederick
Platbarzdis, Aleksandrs
Polt, Robert, ed.
Popioloek, Kazimierz, ed.

Poraller, Curt
Porchet-Brauchli, Anna
Pospelowa, Galina
Primavesi, Luigi
Prokopositsch, Erich
Prokoptschuk, Gregor
Pross, Harry
Przywara, Erich
Pyrker, Johann Ladislav
Pzillas, Friedrich

Quade, Fritz and Eva
Quindt, William

Rabikauskas, Paul
Raineteau, Pedro Mendez
Rakintzis, Nikolaus Theodor
Raphaeli, Nachum
Re, Luciano
Refai, Eglal Mohammed
Reid, Hans
Renggli, Guido
Resai, Mohammed Ismail
Resetar, Milan
Rey, William Henry
Reznicek, Felicitas
Ri, Sok-Hang
Rich, Arthur
Ridder, Betsy
Riva, Guido
Rizzi, Silvio
Rock, C. V.
Roques de Maumont, Harald
   von
Ross, Stanley
Rossier, Jean
Rouselle, Edwin Arthur
Royal, Roland
Rusconi, Carlo
Ryan, Lawrence

Sabec, Drago
Saberi, Mohammed
Sadeghi, Mansur
Sagoschen, Josef Alois
Salathe, Rene

Salis, Jean Rodolphe de
Sandoz, Jean Daniel
Santas, Joannis
Santifaller, Leo
Santschi, Alfred
Saria, Balduin
Savio, Mario
Scamoni, Alexis
Scanzoni, Signe von
Seper, Mirko
Sganzini, Carlo
Shenfield, Arold
Sherhag, Richard
Silva Tarouca, Egbert
Silva-Vigur, Anil de
Simmat, William E.
Simojoki, Meikki
Simmonsson, Nels
Simson, William von
Single, Ernst
Sjöberg, Boris
Skold, Tryggve
Sloman, Ricardo
Stampa, Aribert
Stampa, Renato
Stephenson, Kurt
Sterling, Eleonore
Suball, Louis
Sundara, Raja Iyeneger, K. T.
Svane, Gunnar Olaf
Szarota, Elida Maria
Szczesny, Gerhard
Szigeti, Peter Rudolf
Szydzik, Stanis Edmund

Taygun, Hüseyin Fikret
Thomas, Charlotte
Thomasson, Bengt
Thomson, Erik
Thudichim, John Louis
   William
Ting, Wen-Chih
Tkalcic, Wilhelm
Tomita, Takemasa

Ujvary, Sandor

Valentini, Goffredo
Vallinheimo, Veera
Valtavuo, Toivi
Veen, Pieter J.
Viga, Diego
Villain, Jean
Virkkunen, Mirja

Walker, James
Wilson, Max
Wunderly, Charlie

Xochellis, Panagiotis

Yasamoto, Makoto
Yesudian
Yoshida, Tetsuro

BIBLIOGRAPHY

ABD-RU-SHIN, pseud. (i.e. Oskar Ernst Bernhardt, 1875-1941.)
In the light of truth, the grail message. Tr. anon.
Vomperberg, Austria: Bernhardt; Edinburgh, 1956. v2.
500p. (23.5cm.) [B56]

Same. Vomberberg, Austria: Bernhardt; L: Grail Foundation of Great Britain, 1959. v3. 523p. (23.5cm.)
24cm. [LC62, B59, IT12]

ABRAHAM, Karl, 1877-1925.
Clinical papers, and essays on psychoanalysis. Tr. & ed.
Hilda Abraham and others [i.e. D.R. Ellison, assisted by
Hilde Maas & Anna Hackle]. Pref. Ernest Jones. NY:
Basic, 1956. 336p. (Sel. papers, v2, Basic classics in
psychiatry.) [CBI]

Sel. papers, with introd. memoir by Ernest Jones (whole
of Abraham's more important . . . work except his
Traum und Mythus . . . and his study on Amenhotep.)
Trs. Douglas Bryan and Alix Strachey. NY: Basic, 1957.
527p. 22cm. (3rd American impression. The basic
classics in psychiatry, no. 4) [LC62]

ABSHAGEN, Karl Heinz, 1895-
Canaris. (C--, Patriot und Weltbürger.) Tr. Alan
Houghton Broderick. L: Hutchinson, 1956. 264p. 22cm.
[LC62, B56, IT9]

ACKEN, Bernard Van.
The holy eucharist, the mystery of faith and the sacrament of love. Tr. H.G. Strauss. Westminster, Md.:
Newman, 1958. 141p. 20cm. [LC62, IT11]

ACKERKNECHT, Erwin Heinz, 1906-
A short history of psychiatry. (Kurze Geschichte der
Psvchiatrie.) Tr. Sulammith Wolff. L, NY: Hafner, 1959.
98p. (22.5cm.) 23 cm. [LC62, B59, IT12]

ACKERMANN AUS BOEHMEN. See SAAZ, Johannes.

ADAM, August, 1888-
The primacy of love. (Der Primate der Liebe.) Tr.
Elisabeth Corathiel Noonan. Westminster, Md.: Newman,
1958. 217p. 21cm. [LC62, IT11]

ADAM, Karl, 1876-
The Christ of faith. The Christology of the church. (Der
Christus des Glaubens.) Tr. Joyce Crick. L: Burns,
1957. 364p. (22.5cm.) [LC62, B57, IT10]

Same. NY: Pantheon, 1957. 364p. 24cm. [LC62,
IT10]

Holy Marriage. (Die sakramentale Weihe der Ehe.)
Tr. anon. Collegeville, Minn.: Liturgical Pr., 1956.
20p. 18cm. [LC62]

The Roots of the Reformation, A lg. Pt. of One and holy
(Una sancta im katholischen Sicht.) Tr. Cicely Hastings.
L, NY: Sheed, 1957. 7-95p. 18cm. [LC62, B57, IT10]

ADAMS, George Ed. See STEINER, Rudolf.
The Michael Mystery.

ADAMS, Miriam.
Rumpelstiltskin, a play with music based on the Grimm's
fairy tale. Music by John Clements. L: Oxford U. Pr.,
1959. 47p. (17.5cm.) [LC62, B59]

ADENAUR, Konrad, 1876-1967.
World indivisible, with liberty and justice for all. Trs.
R. and C. Winston. Introd. Ernest Jackh. Ed. Ruth
Nanda Anshen. L: Allen 1956. 122p. (19.5cm.) 20cm.
(World Perspective series v5. no. 3.) [LC62, B56, IT9]

ADLER, Alfred, 1870-1937.
The individual psychology of A--A--, a systematic
presentation in selections from his writings. Tr., ed.
and annot., Heinz L. Ansbacher and Rowena R. Ansbacher. 1st ed. NY: Basic, 1956. 503p. 25cm.
[LC62]

Same. L: Allen, 1958. 504p. (23cm.) [B58]

The practice and theory of individual psychology.
(Theorie und-Praxis der Individual-Psychologie.) Tr. P.
Radin. Paterson, NJ.: Littlefield, Adams, 1959.

(Reprint) 352p. 20cm. [LC62, IT12]

ADLER, Marta.
My life with the gipsies. (Mein Schicksal waren die Zigeuner.) 1st Eng. ed. L: Souvenir, 1960. 204p. (22.5cm.) 23cm. [LC62, B60, IT14]

ADLON, Hedda.
Hotel Adlon, the life and death of a great hotel. (Hotel Adlon.) Tr. and ed., Norman Denny. L: Barrie, 1958. 256p. (22.5cm.) 23cm. [LC62, B58, IT11]

Same. 1st American ed. NY: Horizon, 1960. 22cm. [LC62, IT13]

ADOLF, Hugo. See Bernatzik, Hugo Adolf.

ADOX Fotowerke G. M. B. H. Dr. C. Schleussner.
The Adox guide to dental radiography. 1st Eng. ed. Frankfurt/Main, Adox Fotowerke. Dr. C. Schleussner, G. M. B. H. , 1957. 441. [LC62]

AESCHBACHER, Hans 1906- . See Fischli, Hans.
Hans Aeschbacher. Einleitung von Hans Fischli.

AGE OF ROCOCO. See Schoenberger, Arno.

AHLFELD, Hugo. Ed. See Licht, F. O.

AHRENS, Hans (George Ludwick August).
Safe explosives of high power. Tr. H. S. Eisner. Sheffield. S. M. R. E. , 1956. 26p. (24.5cm.) [B56]

AICHINGER, Ilse 1921- .
The bound man and other stories. (Der Gefesselte, erzählungen.) Tr. Eric Mosbacher. NY: Noonday, 1956. 100p. 22cm. [LC62, IT9]

Same. The bound man. Spender S. Coll., 1960.

ALBERS, Josef.
Drawings. (Zeichnungen.) Tr. Anon. NY: Wittenborn, 1956. 12 plates, 25 x 33cm. (Issued in portfolio.) [LC62]

Poems and drawings. Tr. anon. New Haven; Readymade, 1958. 1v. unp. 22 x 25cm. (500 copies, Ger. and Eng.) [LC62]

ALEKSANDROV, Pavel Sergeevic, 1896- .
An introduction to the theory of groups. (Einführung in
die Gruppentheorie.) Trs. Hazel Perfect and G. M. Peter-
sen. L: Blackie, NY: Hafner, 1959. 23cm. [LC62, B59,
IT12]

ALEXANDER, Edgar.
Adenauer and the new Germany, the chancellor of the vanquished. (Adenauer und das neue Deutschland. Einführ-
rung in das Wesen und Wirken des Staatsmannes.) Tr.
T. E. Goldstein, Pref. Alvin Johnson. Epilog K. Adenauer. NY: Farrar, 1957. 300p. 22cm. [LC62, IT10]

ALEXANDER, Franz (Gabriel) 1891- . And Hugo Staub.
The Criminal, the judge, and the public. A psychological analysis. (Der Verbrecher und seine Richter.) Tr.
of orig. ed. Gregory Zilboorg. Rev. ed. with new chapters F--A--. Glenco, Ill.: Free Pr., c1956. 239p.
22cm. [LC62]

ALEXANDROFF, P. See Aleksandrov, Pavel Sergeevic,
1896- .

ALLGEMEINE WOCHENZEITUNG DER JUDEN IN DEUTSCH-
LAND.
Fifteen years afterward. Documents about people who
dared love one another while terror ruled their nation.
By Karl Marx and others. (From Narben, Spuren.
Zeugen.) Tr. Anon. Dusseldorf: 1960. 47p. 21cm.
[LC62]

ALPHEN, Jan Van.
Rubber chemicals, by Jan Van Alphen in coop. with W. J.
K. Schoenlau and M. Van Den Tempel. (Gummichemi-
kalien.) Tr. anon. Amsterdam, NY: Elsevier, L:
Cleaver-Hume, 1956. 164p. (23.5cm.) 24cm. (Eng. and
Ger.) [LC62, B56, IT9]

ALT, Albrecht, 1883-1956.
The God of the fathers. Summarized in tr. by unknown
person in Union Theological Seminary. NY: N. D. 12p.
28cm. (Photocopy of TW.) [LC62]

ALTANER, Berthold, 1885- .
Patrology. (Patrologie. 5th ed. Basis for tr.) Tr.,
Hilda C. Graef. Freiburg, NY: Herder, 1960. 659p.
23cm. [LC62 IT13]

Same. Edinburgh, L: Nelson, 1960. 660p. (22.5cm.)
[B60, IT14]

ALTE NEWE ZEITUNG. See Rollenhagen, Georg.

ALTENBERG, Peter 1859-1919. (Orig. name Richard
Englander.)
Alexander King presents Peter Altenberg's Evocations of
love. Tr., Anon. NY: Simon, 1960. 175p. 29cm.
(Much of orig. pub. in Ger.) [LC62]

ALTHAUS, Paul August Wilhelm Hermann, 1888- .
The so-called kerygma and the historical Jesus.   (Das
so-genannte Kerygma und der historische Jesus.) Tr.
David Cairns.   Edinburgh, L: Oliver, 1959.   89p.
(22.5cm.) [LC62, B59, IT12]

The so-called kerygma and the chronological Jesus.
Trs., Marcy Punnet and Gustav-Adolf B. H. Pohlig.
Syracuse, NY: 1959. 321. 28cm. [LC62]

Fact and faith in the kerygma of today.   (Das sogenannte
kerygma und der historische Jesus.) Tr., David Cairns.
Philadelphia: Muhlenberg, 1959.   89p.   23cm.   [LC62]

ALVERDES, Paul, 1897- .
Little dream horses.   (Die Traum-Pferdchen) Tr., anon.,
picts. Beatrice Braun-Fock. NY: Sterling, 1958.   31p.
26cm. [LC62]

AMANN, Paul, 1884-1958.   See Mann, Thomas.
Letters to P--A--.

AMELUNG, Walther, 1894- .
Medical climatology, climatic health resorts in Germany.
(Medizinische klimatologie.) Bonn: Deutscher Bader-
verband, 1956.   15p. [LC62]

AMSTUTZ, Walter and Herdeg, Walter, eds.
(Das goldene Buch vom Engadine.) Trs., Henry Hoek,
Bernard Lemoine, Brian Lunn, and Emma Nater. Munich:
Bruckmann, 1957.   1v. (unp. chiefly illus.), 30cm.
(Pref. and text in Ger., Eng., Fr., Italian.) [LC62,
IT10]

ANASTASIA NIKOLAEVNA, Grand Duchess of Russia.
I am Anastasia.   (Ich, Anastasia erzäble.)   An autobiog-

ANASTASIA NIKOLAEVNA--
raphy with notes by Roland Krug von Nidda.   Tr. ,   Oliver
Coburn.   NY: Harcourt, 1959.   282p. 23cm.   [LC62]

I, Anastasia.   (Ich, Anastasia Erzähle.)   An autobiogra-
phy with notes by Roland Krug von Nidda.   Tr. ,   Oliver
Coburn.   L: Joseph, 1958.   282p.   (22. 5cm.)   23cm.
[LC62, B58]

ANDERS, Günther, 1902- .
Franz Kafka.   (Kafka, pro et contra.)   Trs. ,   Alun Steer
and A. K. Thorlby, eds. ,   Erich Heller and Anthony Thorlby.   L: Bowes, 1960.   110p.   18cm.   (18. 5cm.)   (Studies in modern European literature and thought.)   [LC62, B60]

Same.   NY: Hillary, 1960.   104p.   19cm.   [LC62]

ANDERSCH, Alfred, 1914- .
Flight to afar.   (Sansibar, oder der letzte Grund.)   Tr. ,
Michael Bullock.   L: Gollancz, 1958.   192p.   20cm.
(20. 5cm.)   [LC62, B58, IT11]

Same.   1st American ed.   NY: Coward-McCann, 1958. 18p.
21cm.   [LC62, IT11]

ANDERSEN, Wilhelm, 1911- .
Towards a theology of mission, a study of the encounter
between the missionary enterprise and the church and its
theology.   (Auf dem Wege zu einer Theologie der Mission.)
Tr. ,   Bishop Stephen Neill.   L: SCM, 1956.   64p.   22cm.
(IMC Research pamphlet no. 2.)   [LC62, B55, IT8]

ANDO, Hiroshige, 1797-1858.
Hiroshige.   (H--, Japanische Landschaftsbilder.)   Tr. ,
Marguerite Kay.   Introd. Werner Speiser.   Text Walter
Exner.   Edinburgh, L: Methuen, 1960.   112p.   (32. 5 x
32. 5cm.)   33cm.   [LC62, B61, IT13]

Same.   NY: Crown, 1960.   112p.   33cm.   [LC62]

ANDRAE, Tor, 1885-1947.
Mohammed, the man and his faith.   (Mohammed, sein Leben und sein Glaube.)   Tr. ,   Theophil Menzel.   L: Allen,
1956, 196p.   [LC62]

Same.   (German title error-It.)   NY: Barnes, 1957.
196p.   22cm.   [LC62, IT11]

Same. (Corrected German title-It.) NY: Harper, 1960.
194p. 21 cm. [LC62, IT13]

ANDREAE, Bernard. See Matt, Leonard V.
Ancient Roman sculpture. (Römische Bildwerke.)
Introd. Bernard Andreae. L: Longmans, c1960. (29cm.)
[LC62, B60]

Architecture in ancient Rome. Introd. Bernard Andreae.
Tr. anon. L: Longmans, 1960. 29cm. [LC62, B60]

ANDRES, Stefan, 1906- .
We are God's Utopia. (Wir sind Utopia.) Tr. Elita
Walker Caspari. Chicago: Regnary, 1957. 94p. [IT10]

ANDRESEN, Th.
Living in Scandinavia. (Wohnen in Skandinavien, ein Bild-
bericht über Siedlungen, Wohnhäuser, moebel und gerät
von T--A-- und bitten jordan.) Stuttgart: Hoffman, 1958.
120p. (chiefly illus.) 30cm. [LC62]

ANDRESSEN, Th. (See Andresen, Th.)

ANDRIST, Friedrich, ed.
Mares, foals, and foaling, a handbook for the small
breeder. (Geburten im Stall.) Tr. Anthony Dent. Fwd.
J. McCunn. Introd. Phylis Hinton. 2nd imp. L: Allen,
c1959. 56p. 19cm. [LC62]

ANLER, Ludwig, 1882- .
The pastoral companion. (A tr. and adapt. of Fr. Louis
Anler's Ger. work, Comes pastoralis.) Formerly ed.
Honoratus Bonzelet. 11th ed. rev. and ampl. Marcian J.
Mathis and Clement R. Leahy. Chicago: Franciscan
Herald, 1956. 419p. 20cm. [LC62]

ANNAHEIM, Hans, (and others)
Across the Alps, aerial views between Nice and Vienna.
(Flugbild der Alpen von der Cote d'Azur zum Wienerwald.)
Tr. B. M. Charleston. Berne: Kummerly, 1960. 54p.
31cm. (Dist. Rand McNally, Chicago) [LC62]

ANTHES, Rudolf, 1896- .
The head of Queen Nefretete. (Die Büste der Königin
Nofretete.) Tr. Kathleen Bauer. NY: Efron, 1958.
22p. 32cm. [IT11]

ANTIKE UHREN.
Antique clocks, a selection of the most beautiful clocks of the special show of antique clocks, which was effected on occasion of the Internal Congress for Chronometry, 1959, at Munich. (Eine Auswahl der schönsten Uhren aus der Sonderschau "antike Uhren.") Ulm: Verlag der neuen Uhrmacher Zeitung, 1960. 168p. (Ger., Eng., and Fr.) [LC62]

ANTZ, August.
Legends of the Rhineland, a journey through the land of the monks, knights, and rogues. (Rheinlandsagen) Tr. Kathlyn Rutherford. Illus. August Leo Thiel and Ernst Paul. Wittlich, Germany: Fischer, 1956. 99p. 8° [IT10]

ANZENGRUBER, Ludwig, 1839-1889.
The cross-makers, a comedy of rustic life. Trs. substituting Irish for the orig. Bavarian setting. Tr. B. Q. Morgan. n.p., 1958. 70l. unp. microf. of tw. Columbia U. [LC62]

APITZ, Bruno.
Naked among wolves. (Nackt unter Wölfen.) Tr. Edith Anderson. Ed. Kay Pankey. Berlin: Seven Seas, 1960. 415p. 19cm. (Seven Seas Bks. no. 7) [LC62]

Same. L: Collet's., 1960. 416p. (19cm.) [B61]

APULEIUS, Madaurensis. See Neumann, Erich.

ARBEITSGEMEINSCHAFT DEUTSCHER LANDWIRTE UND BAUERN.
White book on democratic land reforms, documents and reports on the expulsion and destruction of the established agricultural population in the Soviet zone of Germany. (Weissbuch über die demokratische Bodenreform.) Ed. Joachim von Kruse. Westberlin: Verl. für Internationalen Kulturaustausch, 1959. 143p. 24cm. (A pub. of the Assoc. of Ger. Farmers and Peasants) [LC62]

ARBEITSGRUPPE BILDBAND. Sindelfingen, Germany.
(Sindelfingen, ein Bericht. Idee, text und gestaltung Hans-Gottfried Kusch et al.) 1st ed. Sindelfingen: Rohm, 1958. 67p. (chiefly illus.) 26cm. (Caps. in Ger., Eng., and Fr.) [LC62]

ARBITRAL COMMISSION.
Arbitral commission on property, rights, and interests in Germany. (Entscheidungen der Schiedskommission für Güter, Rechte und Interessen in Deutschland.) Koblenz: Euler, 1958. 67 p. (chiefly illus.) 26cm. (caps. in Ger., Eng. and Fr.) [LC62]

ARCHITEKTUR WETTBEWERBE.
Students housing. (Studentenwohnheime.) Stuttgart: Kramer, 1960. 92p. 30cm. (Its sonderheft, Mai 1960. Text in Ger. and/or Eng.) [LC62]

ARENDT, Hannah.
Rahel Varnhagen, the life of a Jewess. (Rahel Varnhagen, Lebensgeschichte einer deutschen Judin aus der Romantik.) Trs. R. and C. Winston. L: East and West Lib., 1958. 222p. 24cm. (Pub. of Leo Beck Inst. of Jews from Ger.) [LC62, B58, IT11]

ARIELLI, Arc David and Braun, Werner. Photogs. Israel. (I--.) Tr. Gladys Wheelhouse. Introd. Erich Luth. Munich: Andermann, 1960. 61p., 30p. 12° [LC62]

ARNDT, Johann, 1555-1621.
Devotions and prayers. Sel. and tr. John Joseph Stoudt. Grand Rapids: Baker, 1958. 111p. 16cm. [LC62, IT12]

ARNET, Edwin, 1901- .
The book of Zurich. (Zürich, das Buch einer Stadt.) Bk. designed Hans Kasser, brief ABC of men and things in Zurich. Anglo-Zurich annals Max Wildi. 2nd ed. Zurich: Artemis, 1959. 71p. 20cm. [LC62]

ARNIM, Volkmar von.
The world tobacco economy. (Die Welttabakwirtschaft.) Geneva: Pub. under auspices of Internat. Union of Food and Drink Workers Assoc., 1958. 76p. 25cm. [LC62]

ARNOLD, Gottfried, 1666-1714.
Baptism among early Christians. (Wahre Abbildung der ersten Christen nach ihren lebendigen Glauben und heiligen Leben.) Tr. with introd. Donald E. Miller. n.p., 1956. 22p. 30cm. [LC62]

ARP, Hans. See Giedion-Welcker, Carola.

ARP, Hans--
Jean Arp.

ARS VENANDI IN AUSTRIA.
Die kunsthistorische Bearbeitung erfolgte durch Bruno
Grimschitz und Bruno Thomas. Wien: Druck und Verlag
der österreichischen Staatsdruckerei. c1959. (unp. chiefly illus. text in Ger., Fr., Italian, and Span.) [LC62]

ASIA MINOR. See Osward, Maxim.

AUERBACH, Erich 1892-1957.
Mimesis, the representation of reality in Western litera-
ture. (Mimesis, dargestellte Wirklichkeit in der abend-
ländischen Literatur.) Tr. Willard Trask. Garden City,
NY: Doubleday, 1957. 498p. no cm. (A107.) [LC62,
IT10]

Scenes from the drama of European literature, six essays. Tr. Ralph Manheim. NY: Meridian, 1959. 249p.
19cm. [LC62]

AUERBACH, Max, 1879- . See Schider, Fritz.

AUFSBERG, Lala et al. Photogs. See Beautiful Carinthia.
Beautiful Carinthia. A pictorial record. (Schönes Karn-
ten.) Tr. Oscar Konstandt. Introd. Herbert Strutz.
Innsbruck: Pinguin, 1960. 72p. 27cm. [LC62]

Same. L: Thorsons, 1960. 8p. (27.5cm.) [B60]

AUGUSTINY, Waldemar, 1897- .
The road to Lambarene, a biography of Albert Schweitzer.
(Albert Schweitzer und du.) Tr. William J. Blake. L:
Muller, 1956. 228p. (20.5cm.) 21cm. [LC62, B56,
IT9]

AUSTRIA.
The Austrian coaxial cable. Pub. to commemorate the
completion of the Vienna-Graz cable. (Das österreichische Koaxialkabel, Festschrift anlässlich der Inbetrieb-
nahme des letzten Teilabschnittes Wien-Graz.) 1st ed.
L: Standard Telephones and Cables, 1958. 24p. 26cm.
[LC62]

AUSTRIA. Bundesministerium für Handel und Wiederaufbau.
See Brieger, Theodor.

AUSTRIAN ALPS.
The Austrian Alps. (Österreichs Alpenstrassen vom
Bodensee bis zum Wienerwald.) Tr. Anon. L: Thames,
1958. 18p. (24.5cm.) (Beautiful highway series) [B58]

AUSTRIAN ASSOCIATION OF PROFESSIONAL SKI TEACHERS.
The new official Austrian ski system. (Österreichischer
Schilehrplan.) Tr. Roland Palmedo. Ed. The Austrian
Assn. of Professional Ski Teachers in collaboration with
the Federal Ministry of Education and others. NY:
Barnes, 1958. 29cm. 126p. [LC62, IT11]

AUSWÄRTIGES AMT. See Germany, Aswärtiges Amt.

AUTENRIETH, Georg Gottlieb Philipp, 1833-1900.
An homeric dictionary for use in schools and colleges.
Tr. Robert P. Keep. Rev. Isaac Flagg. New ed. Nor-
man: U. of Oklahoma Pr., 1958. 297p. 20cm. [LC62]

Same. With additions, corrections, and introd. by trans.
L: Macmillan, NY: St. Martin's, 1960. 377p. 19cm.
[B60]

BACK, Leo. See Baeck, Leo.

BACHMANN, Ingeborg, 1926- .
Selections in Rothenberg, 1959.

BAECK, Leo, 1873-1956.
God and man in Judaism. Tr. A. K. Dallas. Fwd.
Leonard G. Montefiore. L: Vallentine, c1958. 76, 1p.
19cm. [LC62]

Same. NY: Union of American Hebrew Congregations,
1958. 76p. 19cm. [LC62, IT13]

Judaism and Christianity, essays. Tr. and introd. Walter
Kaufmann. Philadelphia: J.P.S.A., 1958. 292p. 22cm.
[LC62, IT11]

BAEHR, Benedikt.
In silence with God. Tr. Elizabeth Corrthiel-Noonan.
[sic] Chicago: Regnery, 1956. 157p. [IT9]

BAHLSEN, Hans, 1901- .
Water, its use for commercial and household purposes.
(Das Wasser.) Tr. H--B--. Munich: Oldenbourg, 1956.

BAHLSEN, Hans--
139p. [LC62, IT9]

BALDASS, Ludwig von, 1887- .
Hieronymus Bosch. Tr. Anon. L: Thames, 1960. 242p.
33cm. (33.5cm.) [LC62, B60]

Same. NY: Abrams, 1960. 34cm. [LC62, IT13]

BALLERSTEDT, Kurt.
Eugen Rosenstock-Huessy and biography, including a medi-
tation by E--R--H-- entitled, Biblionomics. Tr. Robert
G. Heath. NY: 1959. 38p. 24cm. [LC62, IT12]

BALLREICH, Hans, ed. and Doehring, Karl et al.
Decisions of German superior courts relating to international law. (Höchstrichterliche Rechtsprechung in völkerrechtlichen Fragen.) Tr. Anon. (Ger., Eng., and Fr.)
Köln, Berlin: Heymann, 1956. 250p. 27cm. [LC62, IT9]

BALTHASAR, Hans Urs von, 1905- .
Elisabeth of Dijon, an interpr. of her spiritual mission.
(E-- von D-- und ihre geistliche Sendung.) Tr. and
adpt. A. V. Littledale. L: Harvill; NY: Pantheon, 1956.
11-126p. 22cm. (22.5cm.) [LC62, B56]

Science, religion and Christianity. (Die Gottesfrage des
heutigen Menschen.) Tr. Hilda Graef. L: Burns, 1958.
155p. (22.5cm.) 23cm. [LC62, B58]

Same. Westminster, Md.: Newman, c1958. 155p.
22cm. [LC62, IT12]

BAMM, Peter, pseud. (i.e. Emmrich, Kurt, 1897- .)
Early sites of Christianity. (Frühe Stätten der Christenheit.) Tr. Stanley Godman. NY: Pantheon, 1957. 255
illus. 22cm. [LC58, IT11]

Same. L: Faber, 1958. 240p. (22.5cm.) [LC58,
B58, IT11]

The Invisible flag, a report. (Die unsichtbare Flagge.)
Tr. Frank Herrmann. L: Faber, 1956. 229p. 23cm.
[LC58, B56, IT9]

Same. Tr. Anon. NY: Day, 1956. 250p. 21cm.
[LC62, IT9]

Same. Tr. Frank Herrmann. L: Muller; NY: New American Lib., 1958. 189p. (18.5cm.) [B58, IT12]

The Kingdoms of Christ from the days of the apostle to the Middle Ages. (Welten des Glaubens aus den Frühzeiten des Christentums.) Tr. and adapt. Christopher Holme. L: Thames; NY: McGraw, c1959. (1960.) 367p. (368p.) 25cm. [LC62, B60]

BANGE, Hans.
(Das Gladbacher Münster, die ehemalige Benediktiner-Abteikirche Sankt Vitus.) Tr. Anon. Gladbach: Kühlen, 1957. 59p. 17cm. (caps in Ger. and Eng.) [LC62]

BARAVALLE, Hermann von.
Rudolf Steiner as educator. Tr. Anon. Rev. ed. Englewood, NJ: St. George, 1960. 46p. [LC62]

BARCATA, Louis, 1906- .
Articles on communist China. Tr. from Austrian newspaper Die Presse, Jan. 4 and 6, 1959. Tr. Anon. NY: U.S.J.P.R.S. 1959. 101. [LC62]

BARGATZKY, Eugen.
(Baden-Baden.) Text und Gestaltung Eugen Bargatzky. Mit einem Vorwort von Kasimir Edschmid. Zweite verb. und erweiterte Auflage. (Ger., Fr., and Eng.) 179p. p.30-179 Illus. 26cm. [LC62]

BARLACH, Ernst, 1870-1938.
Two acts from the flood, a letter on Kandinsky. 8 sculptures, Brecht- notes on the Barlach exhibitions. Tr. Anon. Northampton: 1960. 39p. [LC62]

BARRAN, Fritz Richard.
(Der offene kamin.) Tr. Institut Hans Joachim Führer. Stuttgart: Hoffmann, 1957. 148p. 30cm. [LC62, IT10]

Same. 2nd ed. c1959. [LC62]

BARTH, Hans, 1904- .
The idea of order, contributions to a philosophy of politics. Trs. Ernest W. Hankamer and William M. Newell. Dordrecht: Reidel, 1960. 209p. 23cm. [LC62]

BARTH, Heinrich, 1821-1865.
The travels of Abdul Karim in Hausaland and Bornu.
Abr. and adpt. E. W. Allen. Illus. Caroline Sassoon.
Zaria North Regional Literature Agency, 1958. 80p.
20cm. [LC62]

BARTH, Karl, 1886- .
Anselm's proof of the existence of God in the context of
his theological scheme. (Anselm. Fides quaerens intel-
lectum.) Tr. Ian W. Robertson. L: SCM, 1960. (From
2nd Ger. ed.) 173p. (22.5cm.) 23cm. 1st Eng.
[LC62, B60, IT14]

Same. Richmond, Va.: John Knox, 1960. [LC62, IT14]

Christ and Adam. Man and humanity in Romans 5.
(Christus und Adam nach Römer 5.) Tr. T. A. Smail.
Edinburgh, L: Oliver, 1956. 45p. 22cm. [LC62, B56, IT9]

Same. NY: Harper, 1957. 96p. 20cm. [LC62, IT10]

Christmas. (Weihnacht.) 2nd. ed. Tr. Bernhard Citron.
Edinburgh, L: Oliver, 1959. 63p. (22.5cm.) 23cm.
[LC62, B59, IT12]

Church dogmatics. The doctrine of the word of God
(prolegomena to church dogmatics . . .) v.1, pt. 1-2.
(Kirchliche Dogmatik, pub. in 1927 as Die christliche
Dogmatik im Entwurf.) Authorized tr. G. T. Thomson.
Edinburgh: Clark, 1936-1956. 2v. 23cm. [LC62]

Church dogmatics vol.1, 2nd half vol., The doctrine of the
word of God (Die kirchliche Dogmatik, 1, Die Lehre von
Worte Gottes.) Trs. G. T. Thomson and Harold Knight.
Eds. G. W. Bromiley and T. F. Torrance. Edinburgh:
Clark, 1956. 905p. (22cm.) [B56]

Church dogmatics, vol.2, 1st half vol., The doctrine of
God. (Die kirchliche Dogmatik. Die Lehre von Gott.)
Trs. T. H. L. Parker, W. B. Johnston, Harold Knight,
and J. L. M. Clark, 1957. 699p. 22cm. (22.5cm.)
[LC62, B57]

Same. NY: Scribner, 1957. v, 22cm. [LC62]

Church dogmatics, vol.2, 2nd half vol. The doctrine of
God. (Die kirchliche Dogmatik, 2, die Lehre von Gott.)

Trs. G. W. Bromiley, J. C. Campbell, Iain Wilson, J. Strathearn McNab, Harold Knight, and R. A. Stewart. Edinburgh: Clark, 1958. 806p. (22cm.) [B58, IT11]

Church dogmatics. Vol. 3, pt. 2, The doctrine of creation. Tr. H. Knight and others. Eds. G. W. Bromiley and T. F. Torrance. Edinburgh: Clark, 1960. 661p. (22.5cm.) [B60, IT14]

Church dogmatics, vol. 4, pt. 1. The doctrine of reconciliation. (Die kirchliche Dogmatik, die Lehre von der Versöhnung.) Tr. G. W. Bromiley. Eds. G. W. Bromiley and T. F. Torrance. Edinburgh: Clark, 1956. 802p. (22.5cm.) [LC62, B57]

Same. NY: Scribner, 1956. V. [LC62, IT10]

Church dogmatics, vol. 4, pt. 2. The doctrine of reconciliation. (Die kirchlichte Dogmatik. Die lehre von der Versöhnung.) Tr. G. W. Bromiley. Eds. G. W. Bromiley and T. F. Torrance. Edinburgh: Clark, 1958. 867p. 22cm. (Pt. 1 and 2) [LC62, B58, IT11]

Community, state and church, 3 essays with introd. Will Herberg. Tr. Anon. NY: Doubleday, 1960. 193p. 18cm. [LC62, IT13]

The doctrine of creation. Vol. 3, pt. 1. (Die kirchliche Dogmatik. Die Lehre von der Schöpfung.) Trs. J. W. Edwards, C. Bussey, and Harold Knight. Eds. G. W. Bromiley and T. F. Torrance. Edinburgh: Clark, 1959. 428p. 22cm. (22.5cm.) [LC62, B59]

Dogmatics in outline. (Dogmatik im Grundriss.) (1st pub. 1949, reprint 1957.) Tr. G. T. Thompson. L: SCM, 1957. 155p. 22cm. [LC62]

Same. With a new fwd. by the author. Tr. G. T. Thompson. NY: Harper, 1959. 155p. 21cm. [LC62, IT12]

The epistle to the Romans. Tr. (from the 6th ed.) Edwyn C. Hoskyns. L, NY: Oxford U. Pr., 1957. 547p. 22cm. [LC62]

The faith of the church. Tr. Gabriel Vahanian. Ed. Jean-Louis Leuba. L: Collins, 1960. 160p. (22cm.) [B60]

BARTH, Karl--
Same. (From French.) NY: Meridian, 1958. 188p.
18cm. [LC62, IT11]

From Rousseau to Ritschl. (Die protestantische Theologie
im 19. Jahrhundert, 11 chaps.) Tr. Brian Cozens. L:
SCM, 1959. 435p. (22.5cm.) 23cm. [LC62, B59, IT
12]

God, grace, and gospel (gospel and law, the humanity of
God, evangelical theology in the 19th cent.) (Evangelium
und Gesetz. Die Menschlichkeit Gottes and evangelische
Theologie im 19. Jahrhundert.) Tr. James Strathearn
McNab. Edinburgh, L: Oliver, 1959. 74p. (21.5cm.)
[LC62, B59, IT12]

How to serve God in a Marxist land. (Briefe an einen
Pfarrer in der DDR.) Introd. Robert McAfee Brown. NY:
Association, 1959. 126p. 20cm. [LC62, IT12]

The humanity of God (content, Evangelical theology in the
19th century, the gift of freedom.) (Die Menschlichkeit
Gottes.) Trs. John N. Thomas and Thomas Wieser.
Richmond, Va.: John Knox, 1960. 96p. 21cm. [LC62,
IT13]

Protestant thought, from Rousseau to Ritschl. (Die protestantische Theologie im 19. Jahrhundert, 11 chaps.)
Tr. Brian Cozens. L: SCM, 1959. 435p. (22.5cm.)
23cm. [LC62, B59, IT12]

Same. Tr. Rev. H. H. Hartwell. NY: Harper, 1959.
435p. 22cm. [LC62, IT12]

A shorter commentary on Romans. (Kurze Erklärung des
Römerbriefes.) Tr. D. H. Van Daalen. L: SCM, 1959.
188p. (22cm.) [LC62, B59, IT12]

Same. Richmond, Va.: John Knox, 1959. 188p. 23cm.
[LC62]

The teaching of the church regarding baptism. Tr.
Ernest A. Payne. L: SCM, 1959. 64p. [LC62]

Word of God and the word of man. (Das Wort Gottes und
die Theologie.) Tr. with a new fwd. Douglas Horton.
NY: Harper, 1957. 327p. 21cm. [LC62]

BARTL, Franz and Boehrin, Julie.
Ravenna. Einleitung von F. W. Diechmann. (Text in Ger.,
Eng., and Fr.) Baden-Baden: Grimm, 1959. 2v. 31cm.
[LC62]

Same. L: Kimber, 1958. 190p. 23cm. [LC62]

BARTZ, Karl, 1900-1956.
The downfall of the German secret service. (Die Tragödie
der deutschen Abwehr.) Tr. Edward Fitzgerald. Introd.
Ian Colvin. L: Kimber, Toronto: Ryerson, 1956. 202p.
(22.5cm.) 23cm. [LC62, B56, IT9]

Swastika in the air, the struggle and defeat of the German
air force, 1939-1945. (Als der Himmel brannte.) 2nd ed.
Tr. Edward Fitzgerald. L: Kimber, 1956. 9-204p.
22cm. (22.5cm.) [LC62, B56, IT9]

BASILEIA. See Schmidt, Karl Ludwig and others.

BAUER, Carl.
Oberammergau and its surroundings. (Oberammergau und
Umgebung.) Tr. Edith Barr. Munich: Berg-Verlag.
Rudolf Rother, 1959. v. [LC62]

BAUER, Hans, 1904- .
Animals are quite different, a study of the relation between
mankind and the animals. (Tiere sind ganz anders.) Tr.
James Cleigh. L: Melrose, 1957. 208p. 22cm. (LC62,
B57, IT9]

BAUER, Josef Martin, 1901- .
As far as my feet will carry me. (So weit die Füsse
tragen.) Tr. Lawrence Wilson. L: Deutsch, 1957.
253p. (254p.) (21.5cm.) 22cm. [LC62, B57, IT10]

Same. NY: Random, 1957. 347p. 22cm. [LC62, IT10]

Same. L: Landsborough, 1959. 223p. (18cm.) [B59,
IT12]

BAUER, Paul, 1896- .
The siege of Nanga Parbat, 1856-1953. (Das Ringen um
den Nanga Parbat.) Tr. R. W. Rickmers. Pref. Sir
John Hunt. L: Hart-Davis, 1956. 211p. (22.5cm.)
[LC62, B56]

BAUER, Walter, (Felix) 1877- .
A Greek-English lexicon of the New Testament and other
early Christian literature. (Griechisch-Deutsches Wörterbuch zu den Schriften des Neuen Testaments und der
übrigen Urchristlichen Literatur.) Tr. and adpt. William
F. Arndt and F. Wilbur Gingrich. Cambridge: Cambridge
U. Pr.; Chicago: Chicago U. Pr., 1957. 909p. (25.5
cm.) 26cm. [LC62, B57]

BAUERMEISTER, Carl L. See Baurmeister, Carl Leopold.

BAUM, Julius, 1882- .
German cathedrals. (Zwölf deutsche Dome des Mittel-
alters.) Photos. by Helga Schmidt Glassner. L: Thames;
NY: Vanguard, 1956. 63p. 31cm. [LC62]

BAUMANN, Hans, 1914- .
Angelina and the birds. (Kleine Schwester Schwalbe.)
Tr. Katherine Potts. Illus. Ulrik Schramm. L: Oxford
U. Pr., 1959. 64p. (23.5cm.) 24cm. [LC62, B59,
IT12]

Same. NY: Watts, 1959. 62p. 25cm. [LC62, IT12,
13]

The Barque of the brothers, a tale of the days of Henry
the navigator. (Die Barke der Brüder.) Trs. I. and F.
McHugh. Illus. Ulrik Schramm. L: Oxford U. Pr.,
1958. 245p. (22.5cm.) [B58, IT11]

Same. NY: Walck, 1958. 245p. 23cm. [LC62, IT11]

The crochety crocodile. (Das gekränkte Krokodil.) Tr.
Katharine Potts. L: Oxford U. Pr., 1960. 64p. (23.5
cm.) [B60, IT13]

The dragon next door. (Penny. Das Geheimnis der
Dschunke vom freundlichen Ostwind.) Trs. I. and F. Mc
Hugh. L: Harrap, 1960. 95p. (19cm.) 20cm. [LC62,
B60, IT13]

Jackie the pit pony. (Hänschen in der Grube.) Tr. Anon.
L: Oxford, 1958. 52p. (23.5cm.) [B58, IT11]

Same. NY: F. Watts, 1958. 52p. [LC62]

The lion and the unicorn. (Das Einhorn und der Löwe.)

Tr. Katherine Potts. L: Oxford U. Pr., 1959. 49p.
(50p.) 23cm. (23.5cm.) [LC62, B59, IT13]

Son of Columbus. (Der Sohn des Columbus.) Trs. Isa-
bel and Florence McHugh. Illus. William Stobbs. L:
Oxford U. Pr., 1957. 248p. (22.5cm.) 24cm. [LC62,
B57, IT10]

Same. NY: Oxford, 1957. 254p. [IT10]

Sons of the Steppe, the story of how the conqueror Genghis
Khan was overcome. (Steppensöhne.) Trs. Isabel and
Florence McHugh. L: Oxford U. Pr., (1957.) 1958.
273p. (22.5cm.) 23cm. [LC62, B57, IT11]

The world of the Pharoahs. (Die Welt der Pharaonen Entdecker am Nil.) Trs. R. and C. Winston. Col. photos,
Albert Burges. L: Oxford U. Pr., 1960. 236p. (21.5
cm.) [B60]

Same. NY: Pantheon, 1960. 255p. 22cm. [LC62,
IT13]

BAUMANN, Hans. See French Alps.

BAUMBACH, Werner (Friedrich Wilhelm.)
Broken swastika, the defeat of the Luftwaffe. (Zu spät.)
Tr. Frederick Holt. L: Hale, 1960. 224p. (22.5cm.)
23cm. [LC62, B60, IT13]

The life and death of the Luftwaffe. (Zu spät.) Tr.
Frederick Holt. NY: Coward-McCann, 1960. 224p.
23cm. [LC62, IT13]

BAUR, Benedikt, 1877- .
Frequent confession. It's place in spiritual life. Instruction and considerations for the frequent reception of the
sacrament of penance. (Die häufige Beichte. Belehrungen,
Betrachtungen und Gebete für den öfteren Empfang des heiligen Bussakraments.) Tr. Patrick C. Barry. (From 7th
Ger. ed.) Langley Bucks, St. Paul, 1960. 5-271p.
(19.5cm.) [B60]

Same. 1959. [IT13]

Frequent confession of penance. Tr. from 7th Ger. ed.
P. C. Barry. L; Staten Isl., NY: St. Paul, 1960. 217p.

52

BAUR, Benedikt--
19cm. [LC62, IT13]

In silence with God. (Still mit Gott, Gedanken für die
Stunden der Einkehr.) Tr. (from 4th ed.) Elisabeth
Corathiel-Noonan. Chicago: Regnery, 1956. 157p. 22cm.
[LC62]

Same. 1960. 235p. 21cm. [LC62, IT13]

The light of the world. Liturgical meditations for week-
days and Sundays of ecclesiastical year. (Werde Licht.)
Tr. Edward Malone. (Rev. ed.) St. Louis: Herder,
1958-1959. 3v. 278p. 383p. 494p. 25cm. [LC62,
IT11]

Saints of the missal. (Werde Licht.) Tr. Raymond Mey-
erpeter. St. Louis: Herder, 1958. 2v. 20cm. [LC62,
IT11]

BAUR, Hans, 1897- .
Hitler's pilot. (Ich flog Mäechtige der Erde.) Tr. Edward Fitzgerald. L: Muller, 1958. 241p. 20cm.
(20.5cm.) [LC62, B58, IT11]

BAUR, (Johannes) Chrysostomus, 1876- .
John Chrysostomus and his time. Vol. 1. Antioch. (Der
heilige Johannes Chrysostomus in seiner Zeit.) Tr.
(from 2nd Ger. ed.) M. Gonzaga. L: Sands, 1959. 399p.
(22.5cm.) 23cm. [LC62, B60, IT13]

Same. Westminster, Md.: Newman, 1959-1960. 2v.
23cm. [LC62, IT13]

BAUER, Franz. See Schuler, Josef Egon, ed.
Interiors for contemporary living. An international survey
in color. (Das schöne Zuhause.) Introd. Cathrin Seifert.
Tr. Anon. Ed. Josef Egon. NY: Architectural, 1960.
204p. 27cm. [LC62]

BAURMEISTER, Carl Leopold.
Revolution in America. Confidential letters and journals,
1776-1784. Tr. and annotated Bernhard A. Uhlendorf.
L: Patterson; New Brunswick, NJ: Rutgers, 1957.
640p. (23.5cm.) 24cm. [LC62, B59, IT10]

BAWERK, Eugen Böhm von. See Böhm von Bawerk.

BEAUTIFUL CARINTHIA. See Aufsberg, Lala, et al.

BECHYNE, Jan, 1920- .
 Beetles. (Welcher Käfer ist das.) Tr. C. M. F. von
 Hayek. L, NY: Thames, 1956. 156p. 20cm. [LC62]

 Same. L: Thames, 1956. 158p. (20.5cm.) [B56, IT9]

BECKER, Hans, pseud.
 Devil on my shoulder. Trs. Kennedy McWhirter and
 Jeromy Potter. L: Landsborough, 1958. 192p. 18cm.
 [B58, IT11]

BECKER, Hans Joseph and Schlote, Wolfram.
 Contemporary Finnish houses. (Neuer Wohnbau in Finn-
 land.) Tr. Beate Brettar-Jung. Stuttgart: K. Kraemer,
 Zürich, Edinburgh: Girsberger, 1958. 120p. 27cm.
 [LC62]

BECKER, Karl, 1907- .
 O truly blessed night. A study of the theology of the
 Easter vigil. (Wahrhaft selige Nacht.) Tr. Ruth M.
 Bethell. St. Louis: Pio Decimo, 1956. 119p. 23cm.
 [LC57, IT9]

 Our father. A handbook for meditation. (Das heilige
 Vaterunser.) Tr. Ruth M. Bethell. Chicago: Regnery,
 1956. 334p. 22cm. [LC57, IT9]

BEDNARIK, Karl.
 The young worker today. A new type. (Der junge Arbeit-
 er von heute, ein neuer Typ.) Tr. Renee Tupholme.
 Glencoe, Ill.: Free Pr., 1956. 146p. 20cm. [LC62,
 IT9]

BEELITZ, Paul.
 The operation of the radiosonde service of the DDR during
 the international geophysical year. (Tr. from Radio und
 Fernsehen, no. 13, 1957, Berlin.) n.p., 1958. 121.
 36cm. [LC62]

BEERBOHM, Max.
 A social success. In Bently, the modern theatre. Vol. 6.
 1960.

BEETHOVEN, Ludwig van, 1770-1827.
 Fidelio . . . text by Joseph Sonnleithner and Georg

BEETHOVEN, Ludwig van--
Friedrich Treitschke. Eng. version Joseph Machlis.
NY: Ballantine, 1959. 42p. 23cm. [LC62]

Letters, journals and conversations. Ed., tr. and introd.
M. Hamburger. NY: Doubleday, 1960. 290p. 18cm.
[LC62, IT13]

New Beethoven letters. Tr. and annotated Donald W. Ma-
cardle and Ludwig Misch. Norman: U. of Oklahoma Pr.,
1957. 577p. 25cm. [LC62 IT10]

BEHL, Carl F. W., 1899- .
Gerhard Hauptmann, his life and work. (Gerhard Hauptmann, Überblick über Leben und Werk.) Tr. Helen Taubert. Würzburg: Holzner, 1956. 60 p. 20cm. [LC62,
IT9]

BEIN, Alex, 1903- .
Theodore Herzl, a biography. Tr. Maurice Samuel.
Philadelphia: J. P. S. A., 1956. 551 p. 22cm. [LC62, IT10]

Same. L: East and West Library, new ed., 1957. 551p.
22cm. [LC62, B57]

BEKESSY, Jean 1911- . See Habe, Hans, pseud.

BEKESY, Georg von.
Experiments in hearing. Tr. E. G. Wever. L, NY: Mc
Graw-Hill, 1960. 745p. (23.5cm.) [LC62, B60, IT13]

BELL, George.
Bear and forbear. A trifle. Adapted from Ger. L, NY:
French, n. d. 11p. 19cm. [LC62]

BEN-GAVRIEL, Moshe Yaacov. (Orig. Hoeflich, Eugen
1891- .)
Mahaschavi in peace and war. (Frieden und Krieg des
Bürgers Mahaschavi, part 1.) Tr. Basil Creighton. L:
Duckworth, 1958. 221p. (19.5cm.) [B58]

Same. 121p. [IT11]

Mahaschavi in peace and war. A novel. (From Hebrew
though orig. Ger.) Introd. Harry Golden. NY: Citadel,
1960. 224p. 21cm. [LC62, IT13]

BENARY-ISBERT, Margot.
  Blue mystery. (Ein blaues Wunder.) Trs. Richard and
  Clara Winston. Illus. Enrico Arno. NY: Harcourt, 1957.
  190p. 22cm. [LC62, IT10]

  Same. L: Macmillan, 1958. 190p. (20.5cm.) [B58, IT11]

  Castle on the border. (Schloss an der Grenze.) Trs.
  Richard and Clara Winston. NY: Harcourt, 1956. 277p.
  21cm. [LC62, IT9]

  Same. L: Macmillan, 1957. 278p. (279p.) (20.5cm.)
  21cm. [LC62, B57, IT10]

  The long way home. Trs. Richard and Clara Winston.
  NY: Harcourt, 1959. 280p. 21cm. [LC62, IT12]

  Same. L: Macmillan; NY: St. Martin's, 1960. 253p.
  (20.5cm.) [B60]

  Rowan Farm. (Der Ebereschenhof.) Trs. Richard and
  Clara Winston. L: Macmillan, 1959. 310p. (20cm.)
  [B59]

  The wicked enchantment. (Heiligenwald.) Trs. Richard
  and Clara Winston. L: Macmillan, 182p. (20.5cm.)
  [B56, IT9]

BENATZKY, Ralph, 1884- .
  White Horse Inn. A musical comedy. (Im weissen Roessl.)
  Adapted from Blumenthal and Kadelburg's play. Music
  Ralph Benatzky. Songs Robert Stolz. L: French, c1957.
  65p. (25cm.) [LC62, B57]

BENCKISER, Joh. A. G. M. B. H.
  Change and growth within five generations. 1823-1958.
  (Wandel und Werden fünf Generationen, 1823-1958.) 135
  years of history of John A. Benckiser Co. narrated K.W.
  Boetticher for 100th anniversary of existence of works at
  Ludwigshafen on Rhine. Ludwigshafen: Benckiser, 1958.
  60p. [LC62]

BENESCH, Otto, 1896- .
  Edvard Munch. Tr. Joan Spencer. L: Phaidon, 1960.
  143p. 27cm. (27.5cm.) [LC62, B60]

  Same. NY: Phaidon, 1960. 143p. 27cm. [LC62]

BENESCH, Otto.　See Schiele, Egon, 1890-1918.
Egon Schiele as a draughtsman by Otto Benesch.　Tr.
Anon.　Vienna: State Printing Office of Austria, 195-.
13p.　34cm.　[LC62]

Rembrandt.　(R--.)　Tr.　James Emmons.　Geneva:
Skira, 1957.　156p.　[IT11]

Rembrandt.　Biographical and critical study.　Tr.　James
Emmons.　NY: Skira, 1957.　153p.　[LC62, IT10]

Rembrandt as a draughtsman.　An essay.　L: Phaidon,
1960.　163p.　(164p.)　(27. 5cm.)　28cm.　[LC62, B60]

BENJAMIN, Israel Joseph, 1818-1864.
Three years in America.　1859-1862.　(Drei jahre in Amerika.)　Tr.　Charles Reznikoff.　Philadelphia: J. P. S. A.,
1956.　2v.　23cm.　[LC62, IT9]

BENN, Gottfried, 1886-1956.
The conquest.　(In Spender's coll. great German short
stories, 1960.)　Tr.　Christopher Middleton.

Primal vision.　Selected writings.　Ed. E. B. Ashton,
pseud. (i. e. , Ernst Basch).　NY: New Directions, 1960.
291p.　22cm.　[LC62, IT13]

Same.　Norfolk, Conn. :　Laughlin, 1960.　291p. [LC62]

BENSER, Walter
Photographing colour.　(Wir photographieren farbig.)　Tr.
Ursula Benser.　Drawings F. Bradley.　L: Fountain, 1959.
300p.　292p.　(22. 5cm.)　[B59, IT12]

Same.　292p.　23cm.　[LC62]

35mm. colour magic.　(Farbiges Photographieren in der
Praxis erlebt.)　Tr. F. Bradley.　Stuttgart: Diener,
1956.　200p.　23cm.　[LC62]

Same.　L: Fountain, 1956.　201p.　(203p.)　(22. 5cm.)
[LC62, B56, IT9]

BENTLEY, Eric (Russell), comp. and ed.
The classic theatre.　Vol. 2.　Five German plays.　(1)
Egmont, (2) Don Carlos, (3) Mary Stuart, (4) Penthesilea,
(5) Prince Friedrich of Homburg.　Trs. (1) M. Hamburger,

(2) James Kirkup, (3) Joseph Mellish, (4) Humphry Tre-
velyan, and (5) James Kirkup. NY: Doubleday; (L:
Mayflower), 1959. 511p. 18cm. [LC62, B60]

The modern theatre. Vol. 5. includes Danton's death.
(Dantons Tod.) Tr. John Holmstrom. Garden City, NY:
Doubleday, 1957. v. 18cm. [LC62]

The modern theatre. Vol. 6. Includes (1) Spring's awakening, (2) The underpants, (3) A social success, (4) The
measures taken. Trs. (1, 2 and 4) Eric Bentley, (3)
Anon. Garden City, NY: Doubleday, 1960. v. 18cm.
[LC62]

BENZ, Ernst, 1907- .
The present meeting between Christianity and the oriental
religions. Roma: Ismeo, 1957. 14p. 31cm. [LC62]

BERAN, H. E.
Austria. 160 photographs by Alfred Nawrath and others.
Introd. H. E. Beran. Tr. Anon. L: Thames; NY:
Studio, 1956. 24p. (27p.) (30.5cm.) [LC62, B56]

BERBER, Friedrich Joseph, 1898- .
Rivers in international law. (Die Rechtquellen des inter-
nat. Wassernutzungsrechts.) Tr. R. K. Batstone. L:
Stevens, 1959. 296p. 23cm. [LC62, IT12]

Same. NY: Oceana, 1959. 196p. [LC62, IT13]

. . . some methological considerations concerning the
study on the uses of the waters of international rivers.
Submitted to the members of the Committee of the International Law Association on the use of the waters of international rivers. München: Institut für Völkerrecht der
Ludwig-Maximilians-Universität, München, 1957. 11p.
23cm. [LC62]

BERCKHEMER, Fritz, 1890-1954.
The language of the rocks. Tr. Eleanor S. Salmon. NY:
Ungar, 1957. 119p. 27cm. [LC62, IT10]

BERENBROK, Hans Dieter, 1924- .
Defeat at sea, the struggle and eventual destruction of the
German navy, 1939-1945. (Kampf und Untergang der
Kriegsmarine.) Tr. C. D. Bekker. NY: Ballantine, 1957.
c1955. 184p. 18cm. [LC62]

BERENDT, Joachim Ernst.
Blues. München: Nymphenburger Verlagsbuchhandlung,
1957. 122p. 25cm. [LC62]

BERENS, Willy and Bettmann, Jürgen.
Düsseldorf and Duisburg. Original text Willy Berens and
Jürgen Bettman. Eng. version Mrs. H. S. B. Harrison.
L: Muller, 1960. 135p. 16cm. [B60]

Same. Geneva. NY: Nagel, 1960. 135p. 16cm.
[LC62]

BERLICHINGEN, Goetz von.
The autobiography. Ed. H. S. M. Stuart. Tr. Anon. L:
Duckworth, 1956. 192p. (22.5cm.) [B56]

BERLIN (West Berlin), Bürgermeister.
Berlin's special tasks. Statement by governing mayor.

Willy Brandt, made before the Berlin House of Representa-
tives on Jan. 15, 1959. Berlin-Schöneberg, Press and Information Agency of the Land of Berlin, 1959. 45p.
[LC62]

BERLIN (West Berlin). Büro für Gesamtberliner Fragen.
Berlin's importance for human relations between East and
West. Berlin: Der Senat von Berlin, Büro für Gesamt-
berliner Fragen, 1960. 19p. [LC62]

BERLIN (West Berlin). Der Senator für Bau- und Wohnungs-
wesen.
Result of the International city-planning competition. (Berlin, Ergebnis des Internationalen Städte Baulichen Ideen-
wettbewerbs.) Tr. Anon. Stuttgart: Krämer, 1960.
123p. 30 x 42cm. [LC62]

BERLIN (West Berlin). Der Senator für Inneres.
Eastern underground activity against West Berlin. Berlin:
Author, 1959. 71p. [LC62]

BERLINER BANK, A. G.
. . . Western Germany's external trade in the year 1955
. . . Tr. from our Foreign Trade Bulletin no. 3, March
24, 1956. Berlin-Charlottenburg, 1956. 7p. 29cm.
[LC62]

BERNARD, Denis F., 1915- .
The suspended man. (Mensch ohne Gegenwart.) Tr. Robert
Molloy. NY: Putnam, 1960. 248p. 21cm. [LC62, IT13]

BERNATZIK, Hugo Adolf, 1897-1953 and Bernatzik, Emmy,
1904- .
The spirits of the yellow leaves. (Die Geister der gelben
Blätter.) Tr. E. W. Dickes. L: Hale, 1958. 222p.
(22.5cm.) [LC62, B58, IT11]

Same. Hollywood-by-the-sea, Fla.: Transatlantic Art,
1958. 222p. [IT11]

BERNHARDI, Charlotte, (von Krusenstern)
Memoir of the celebrated Admiral John de Krusenstern,
the first Russian circumnavigator. Tr. Charlotte Bernhardi. Ed. Sir John Ross. L: Longmans, 1956. 75p.
23cm. [LC62]

BERNSTEIN, Elsa (Porges), 1866- . See Rosmer, Ernst,
pseud.

BERON, Richard, 1904- .
The Bible story, simply told. (Kinder- und Hausbibel.)
Tr. Isabel and Florence McHugh, with applications to daily
living, Alexander Jones. Chicago: Catholic Pr., 1959.
2v. 18cm. [LC62]

BERTALANFFY, Ludwig von 1901- .
Principles and theory of growth. Amsterdam: Elsevier,
1960. 137-259p. 25cm. [LC62]

Problems of life. An evaluation of modern biological and
scientific thought. (Das biologische Weltbild.) NY: Harper,
1960. 216p. 21cm. [LC62]

BERTHOLD, Will.
The sinking of the Bismarck. (Getreu bis in den Tod.
Sieg und Untergang der Bismarck.) Tr. Michael Bullock.
L, NY: Longmans, c1958. 190p. (191p.) (22.5cm.)
[LC62, B58, IT11]

Same. L: Transworld, 1960. 287p. 17cm. (16.5cm.)
[LC62, B60]

BERTHOLD, Will. See Gimpel, Erich. Spy for Germany.

BERTRAM, Werner.
A royal recluse, memories of Ludwig II of Bavaria. (Der
einsame König.) Tr. Margaret McDonough. Munich:
Herpich, 1958. 271p. [IT11]

BERTSCHE, Leopold.
Short addresses for nuns. (Directorium Sponsae.) Tr.
Marie Heffernan. Westminster, Md.: Newman, 1958.
[IV, IT12]

DER BESTRAFTE BRUDERMORD. See William Poel's
prompt-book of fratricide punished.

BETTEX, Albert W., 1906- .
The discovery of the world. (Welten der Entdecker.) Tr.
Daphne Woodward. L: Thames, 1960. 279p. 32cm.
[B60]

Same. L: Thames, 1960. 379p. [LC62]

BEYER, Victor.
Alsace. (Das Elsass.) Tr. Anon. Königstein im Taunus,
K. R. Langewiesche Nachfolger, Köster, 1960. 120p. 27cm.
[LC62]

BIANCHI-BANDINELLI, Ranuccio. See Borsig, Arnold von.

BICKEL, Lothar.
The unity of body and mind. (Innen und Aussen.) Tr.
Walter Bernard. NY: Philosophical Lib., c1959. 167p.
23cm. [LC62, IT13]

BIDDER, Irmgard, (Anita Albert)
Lalibela, the monolithic churches of Ethiopia. (Lalibela,
Monolithkirchen in Äthiopien.) Tr. Rita Grabham-Hort-
mann. Drawings Elfriede Fulda. L: Thames, 1959.
137p. 31cm. [LC62, B59, IT12]

Same. NY: Praeger, 1960. 136p. 31cm. [LC62,
IT13]

BIEHL, Max.
People's communes in China. (Aus Politik und Zeitge-
schichte, 21 Jan. 1959.) NY: U.S.J.P.R.S., 1959.
[LC62]

BIELER, Ludwig.
The grammarien's craft. (Extracted from Folia, vol. 10.
no. 2, 1958.) NY: Catholic Classical Assn., 1958. 42p.
23cm. [LC62]

BIEW, A. M.
The story of the British-trained scientist who invented the
Russian hydrogen bomb. (Kapitza, der Atom-Zar.) Tr.
James Cleugh. L: Muller, 1956. 288p. (20.5cm.)
21cm. [LC62, B56, IT9]

BIEZENO, Cornelis Benjamin, 1888- . and Grammel, Richard.
Engineering dynamics. (Technische Dynamik.) Tr. M. L.
Meyer. L: Blackie, 1954-1956. 4 vol. 27cm. [LC62, B56]

Same. Vol. 2. Elastic problems of single machine ele-
ments. L: Blackie, 1956. 527p. [B56]

THE BIG BOOK TO GROW ON.
Pictures by Janusz Grabianski. 1st Eng. lang. ed. NY:
Watts, 1960. 239p. 25cm. [LC62]

BIHALJI-MERIN, Oto, 1904- .
Byzantine frescoes and icons in Yugoslavia. L: Thames,
1960. 16p. (28.5cm.) [B60]

Lubarda, the battle of Kossovo. Tr. Peter Mijuskovic.
Belgrad: Yugoslavia, 1956. 15p. 34cm. [LC62]

Modern primitives: masters of naive painting. (Das naive Bild der Welt.) Tr. N. Guterman. L: Thames, 1961.
c1959. 290p. (21 x 25 cm.) [B61, LC62]

Same. NY: Abrams, 1961. c1959. 290p. (21 x 25cm.)
[LC62]

BIHLMEYER, Karl, 1874-1942.
Church history. Vol. 1, Christian antiquity. Tr. (from
13th ed.) Victor E. Mills, Paderborn, Schoeningh, 1958.
iv. 24cm. [LC62]

Same. Westminster, Md.: Newman, 1958. iv. 24cm.
[LC62, IT11]

BINSWANGER, Ludwig, 1881- .
Sigmund Freud. Reminiscences of a friendship. (Erinne-

BINSWANGER, Ludwig--
rungen an Sigmund Freud.) Tr. Norbert Guterman. NY:
Grune, 1957. 106p. 23cm. [LC62, IT11]

BIRCHER-BENNER, Maximilian-Oskar.
The prevention of incurable disease. 2nd ed. Tr. E. F.
Meyer. L: Clarke, 1959. 15-125p. [B60, IT13]

BIRNGRUBER, Silvester, 1941- .
Morals for lay people. (Laienmoral.) Tr. Walter Kane.
Foreword, Fr. Eugene Boylan. Chicago, Dublin: Scepter,
1960. 3-478p. 19cm. (19.5cm.) [LC62, B60, IT13]

BISCHOF, Werner and others, photogs., 1916-1954.
From Incas to Indios. (Indios.) Tr. James Emmons.
Paris: Delpire; NY: Universe, 1956. 25p. 29cm.
[LC62, IT9]

Incas to Indians. Photos Werner Bischof, Robert Frank and
Pierre Verger. Tr. James Emmons. Introd. Manuel Tunon
de Lara. Zürich: Conzett, 1956. 25p. 29cm. [LC62]

Same. L: Phot. Mag., 1956. 25p. 29cm. [LC62]

Same. L: Phot. Mag., 1957. 41p. (28.5cm.) [B57]

The world of Werner Bischof, a photographer's odyssey.
(Unterwegs.) Tr. Paul Steiner. Text Manuel Gasser.
NY: Dutton, 1959. unp. 29cm. [LC62, IT12]

BITTNER, Herbert.
Käthe Kollwitz, drawings. Tr. Anon. NY: Yoseloff,
1959. 35, 130p. 29cm. [LC62]

BITZIUS, Albert, 1797-1854. See Gotthelf, Jeremias, pseud.

BLANKENBURG, P. von, ed.
Studying agriculture, horticulture and forestry in the Universities of the Federal Republic of Germany, a guide.
(Das landwirtschaftliche, gartenbauliche und forstliche
Studium in der Bundesrepublik Deutschland, ein Studien-
führer.) Bad Godesberg: Agricultural and Home Economics Evaluation and Information Service, 1959. 69p. [LC62]

BLASER, Werner, 1924- .
Classical Dwelling houses of Japan. (Wohnen und Bauen in
Japan.) Eng. ver. D. Q. Stephenson. Teufen: Switzer-

land: Niggli, Tokyo: Kinokuniya, 1958. 78p. 18cm. [LC62]

Japanese temples and teahouses. (Tempel und Teehaus in Japan.) Eng. ver. D. Q. Stephenson. Basle: W. Blaser; NY: Dodge, 1957. 156p. 33cm. [LC62, IT10]

BEE BLESSING. In Loomis, C. G.

BLIEWEIS, Theodor and others.
The venture of marriage, a priest, a mother and a doctor speak to young people. (Wagnis der Ehe.) T--B--, Josefine Gangl, Dr. Albert Niedermeyer. Tr. Norman C. Reeves. Cork: Mercier, 1960. 98p. (18cm.) [B61]

BLINZLER, Joseph, 1910- .
The Jewish and Roman proceedings vs. Jesus Christ. Described and assessed from the oldest accounts. (Der Prozess Jesu.) Trs. Isabel and Florence McHugh. (From the 2nd rev. and enl. ed.) Westminster, Md.: Newman, 1959. 312p. 23cm. [LC62, IT12]

BLOCH, Ivan, 1872-1922. See Dühren, Eugen, pseud.

BLOCH, Jacques and Fischer, Fritz K.
Frozen shoulder. (Probleme der Schultersteife.) Tr. Anon. Basel: Geigy, 1960. 761p. 24cm. [LC62]

BLOCH, Markus Eliezer, 1723-1799.
Fishes. (Allgemeine Naturgeschichte der Fische.) Tr. Eva Mannering. L: Ariel, 1959. 15p. (39.5cm.) 40cm. [LC62, B59, IT12]

BLOEMERTZ, Gunther.
Freedom in love. (Dem Himmel am nächsten.) Tr. Mervyn Savill. L: Kimber, 1959. 159p. (20.5cm.) [B59]

Same. Tr. Robert Cohen and Alan Earney. L: Hamilton, 1959. 158p. (17.5cm.) [B59]

Same. L: Angus and Robertson, 1958. [B58]

BOCHENSKI, Innocentius M., 1902- .
Ancient formal logic. Tr. Anon. Amsterdam: North-Holland, 1957. 122p. 22cm. [LC62]

Contemporary European philosophy. (Europäische Philosophie der Gegenwart.) Trs. Donald Nicholl and Karl Asch-

BOCHENSKI, Innocentius M. --
enbrenner. Berkeley: California U. Pr.; L: Cambridge
U. Pr., 1956. 326p. 22cm. [LC62, B56, IT9]

A precis of mathematical logic. Tr. and ed. from French
and Ger., Otto Bird. Dordrecht, Holland: Reidel, 1959.
100p. 23cm. [LC62]

BOCHNER, Salomon, 1899- .
Lectures on Fourier integrals, with an author's supplement
on monotonic functions, Stieltjes integrals, and harmonic
analysis. (Monotone Funktionen, Stieltjessche Integrale und
harmonische Analyse.) Trs. Morris Tenenbaum and Harry
Pollard. Princeton, N.J.: Princeton U. Pr., Oxford U.
Pr., 1959. 333p. 26cm. (26.5cm.) [LC62, B60]

BOCK, Emil.
The apocalypse of St. John. (Apokalypse.) Auth. Eng.
tr. Alfred Heidenreich. L: Christian Community Pr.,
1957. 190p. (22cm.) [B57]

BODE, Wilhelm von, 1845-1929 and Kühnel, Ernst, 1882- .
Antique rugs from the Near East. (Vorderasiatische
Knüpf-Teppiche aus älterer Zeit.) Tr. Charles Grant Ellis.
NY: Heinman, 1959. (4th rev. ed.) 184p. 26cm.
[LC62, IT12]

BODELSEN, Merete (Christensen), 1907- .
Foreign artists in Denmark. (Exerpt from Festschrift
Hans Vollmer.) Leipzig: 1957. 45-86p. [LC62]

BODENHEIMER, Friedrich Shimon.
A biologist in Israel, a book of reminiscences. Tr. Anon.
From Ms. Jerusalem, biological studies, 1959. 502p.
[IT12]

BOEHLE, Bernd, 1906- .
Handy guide to Western Germany, a reference book for
travel in the German Federal Republic. (Das praktische
Reisebuch.) Trs. N. V. Timewell and H. H. Hoyer.
Gütersloh: Bertelsmann; NY: Sloane, 1956. 488p.
20cm. [LC62, IT9]

BOEHLE, Bernd, 1906- . and TOEPFFER, Joachim.
Where to stay in Germany. A Guide to 300 of her finest
hotels and restaurants. (Rast auf Reisen.) Trs. Moira
Lane and Herbert Rück. L: Stanford, 1958. 320p.
25cm. [LC62, B58, IT11]

BÖHM VON BAWERK, Eugen, Ritter, 1851-1914.
Capital and interest. A critical history of economic theory. (Kapital and Kapitalzins.) Tr., pref. and analysis, William Smart. NY: Kelley, 1957. 431p. 22cm. [LC62]

Capital and interest. Trs. George D. Huncke (Vol. 2) and Hans. F. Sennholz (vol. 3). South Holland, Ill.: Libertarian, 2v. 1959. 25cm. [LC62, IT12]

The exploitation theory, an extract. Trs. George D. Huncke and Hans F. Sennholz. South Holland, Ill.: Libertarian, 1960. 241-473p. 24cm. [LC62]

BÖHM, Theobald, 1794-1881.
The flute and flute-playing in acoustical, technical, and artistic aspects. 2nd Eng. ed., rev. and enl. Tr. Dayton C. Miller. NY: McGinnis, 1960. 197p. 20cm. [LC62]

BÖHME, Jacob, 1575-1624.
The Aurora. (Aurora oder die Morgenröte im Aufgang.) Tr. John Sparrow. Eds. Charles James Barker and D.S. Hehner. L: Watkins, 1960. 723p. 23cm. [LC62]

Dialogues on the supersensual life. Tr. William Law et al. Ed. Bernard Holland. NY: Ungar, 1958. 144p. 19cm. [LC62, IT11]

Six theosophic points and other writings. Tr. John Rolleston Earle. Ann Arbor: U. of Mich. Pr., (Woodthorpe, Nottingham, Hall), 1958. 208p. (20.5cm.) 21cm. [LC62, B58, IT11]

BÖHME, Jakob. See Hartmann, Franz.

BOEHMER, Heinrich, 1869-1927.
Martin Luther, road to reformation. (Der junge Luther.) Trs. John W. Doberstein and Theodore G. Tappert. L: Thames; NY: Meridian, 1957. 449p. 19cm. [LC62, IT10]

BOEHN, Max von, 1860-1932.
Dolls and puppets. Tr. Josephine Nicoll. With a note on puppets by George Bernard Shaw. Rev. ed. Boston: Branford, 1956. 521p. 22cm. [LC62, IT10]

BÖLL, Heinrich, 1917- .
Bread of our early years. (Das Brot der frühen Jahre.)
Tr. Mervyn Savill. L: Arco, 1957. 128p. (19cm.)
[LC62, B57, IT10]

The man with the knives. In Spender's coll. , 1960.

Tomorrow and yesterday. (Haus ohne Hüter.) Tr. Anon.
NY: Criterion, 1957. 250p. 21cm. [LC62, IT10]

The train was on time. (Der Zug war pünktlich.) Tr.
Richard Graves. (1st ed.) L: Arco, 1956. 142p.
(19.5cm.) [LC62, B56, IT10]

Same. NY: Criterion, 1956. 142p. 21cm. [LC62, IT10]

Traveller, if you come to Spa. (Wanderer. kommst du
nach Spa.) (1st ed.) Tr. Mervyn Savill. L: Arco,
1956. 199p. (19.5cm.) 20cm. [LC62, B56, IT9]

The unguarded house. (Haus ohne Hüter.) Tr. Mervyn
Savill. L: Arco, 1957, 254p. (255p.) 20cm. (20.5cm.)
[LC62, B57, IT10]

BOER, Friedrich, ed.
Igloos and totem poles. (So lebt man anderswo.) Tr. F. Mc-
Hugh. L: Lutterworth, 1959. 124 p. (21.5cm.) [B59, IT12]

BOER, Hans Alfred de.
The bridge is love, jottings from a traveller's notebook.
(Unterwegs notiert, Bericht einer Weltreise.) (1st Eng.
ed.) Tr. Anon. Fwd. Dr. Martin Niemoeller. L: Marshall, 1958. 255p. 22cm. [LC62]

Same. 256p. [IT11]

Same. Grand Rapids: Eerdmans, 1958. 255p. 23cm.
[LC62, IT11]

BOGER, Bert, photog.
Portrait of Spain. (Mit Kamera und VW in Spanien.) Tr.
Joan Schoenenberger. Text Anton Dietrich. Edinburgh,
L: Oliver, 1958. 138p. (27.5cm.) 28cm. [LC62,
B58, IT11]

BOHM, Ewald Bernhard, 1903- .
A textbook in Rorschach test diagnosis for psychologists,

physicians, and teachers. (Lehrbuch der Rorschach--
für Psychologen, Arzte und Pädagogen.) Trs. Anne G.
Beck and Samuel J. Beck. NY: Grune, 1958. 322p.
24cm. [LC62, IT11]

BOLLER, Willy.
Masterpieces of the Japanese colour woodcuts. (Meister
des japanischen Farbholzschnittes.) Tr. Anon. Boston:
Book and Art Shop, 1957. 187p. 37cm. [LC62]

Same. L: Elek, 1958. (2nd rev. ed.) 187p. (36.5cm.)
[B58, T11]

Same. NY: Crown, 1958. (2nd ed.) 187p. [IT11]

BOLLIGER, Hans.
Picasso for Vollard. Tr. Norbert Guterman. Introd.
Hans Bolliger. Ed. Milton S. Fox. NY: Abrams, 1956.
22p. 28cm. [LC62]

Picasso's Vollard suite. Tr. Norbert Guterman. Introd.
Hans Bolliger. L: Thames, 1956. 22p. (29cm.) [LC62,
B56]

BOLTZIUS, Johann Martin, 1703-1765.
Johann Martin Boltzius answers a questionnaire on Carolina and Georgia. Trs. Klaus G. Leowald, Beverly Star-
ika, and Paul S. Taylor. Williamsburg, Va.: c1957.
218-261p. 24cm. [LC62]

BOMAN, Thorleif.
Hebrew thoughts compared with Greek. (Das hebräische
Denken in Vergleich mit dem Griechischen.) Tr. Jules L.
Moreau. L: SCM, 1960. 224p. (22.5cm.) [B56]

Same. Philadelphia: Westminster, 1960. 224p. 23cm.
[LC62, IT13]

BONHOEFFER, Dietrich, 1906-1945.
The cost of discipleship. (Nachfolge.) Tr. R. H. Fuller.
Rev. Irmgard Booth. L: SCM, 1959. 285p. (22.5cm.)
[LC62, B59, IT12]

Same. NY: Macmillan, 1959. 285p. 23cm. (LC62,
IT13]

Creation and fall, a theological interpretation of Genesis

BONHOEFFER, Dietrich--
1-3. (Schöpfung und Fall.) Tr. John C. Fletcher. Rev.
staff of SCM, L: SCM, 1959. 96p. 21cm. (22cm.)
[LC62, B59, IT12]

Same. NY: Macmillan, 96p. 22cm. [LC62, IT12]

Letters and papers from prison. (Widerstand und Erge-
bung, Briefe und Aufzeichnungen aus der Haft.) Tr.
Reginald H. Fuller. L: SCM, 1956. 207p. 22cm. [LC62]

Same. L: Collins, 1959. 192p. (18cm.) [B59, IT12]

Life together. (Gemeinsames Leben.) L: SCM, 1958.
112p. 19cm. [LC62]

Temptation. (Versuchung.) Tr. Kathleen Downham. NY:
1956. 47p. 19cm. [LC62]

BONIN, Gerhardt von, 1890- .
Some papers on the cerebral cortex. Ed. and tr. (from
Fr. and Ger.) Gerhardt von Bonin. Springfield, Ill.:
Thomas, 1960. 396p. (23.5cm.) 24cm. [LC62, B60]

BONITZ, Hermann, 1814-1888.
The origin of the Homeric poems. Tr. Lewis R. Pack-
ard. NY: Harper, 1958. 119p. [IT11]

BORCHERT, Bernhard.
Oskar K. Kokoschka. (O--K--K--.) With an introd. and
note Bernhard Borchert. L: Faber, 1960. 24p. (30.5
cm) 31cm. [LC62, B60]

BORGNER, Hedwig.
Rathausplatz no. 16. Ed. and tr. Alfred Perles. L:
Arco, 1957. 196p. (22.5cm.) 23cm. [LC62, B57,
IT10]

BORN, Max, 1882- .
Atomic physics. (Moderne Physik.) Tr. John Dougall.
Rev. M--B-- with R. J. Blin-Stoyle. 6th ed. L:
Blackie, 1957. 445p. (22.5cm.) [B57, IT10]

Same. NY: Hafner, 1957. 445p. 23cm. [LC62]

Man and the atom. Introd. Victor F. Weisskopf. South-
hampton, Pa.: Society for Social Responsibility in Sci-

ence, 1957. 12p. [LC62]

The mechanics of the atom. (Vorlesungen über Atom-
mechanik.) Tr. J. W. Fisher. Rev. D. R. Hartree. NY:
Ungar, 1960. 317p. 24cm. [LC62, IT13]

Physics in my generation. A selection of papers. Tr.
Robert Oppenheimer and anon. L, NY: Pergamon, 1956.
232p. 23cm. [LC62]

BORNHÄUSER, Karl, 1868-1947.
The death and resurrection of Jesus Christ. (Die Leidins-
und Auferstehungsgeschichte Jesu.) Tr. A. Rumpus. L:
Independent, 1958. 264p. (22cm.) [B58, IT11]

Same. Bangalore: C. L. S. Pr., c1958. 264p. 22cm.
[LC62]

BORNHOEFFER, Dietrich. See Bonhoeffer, Dietrich.

BORNKAMM, Günther.
Jesus of Nazareth. (Jesu von Nazareth.) Trs. Irene and
Fraser McLuskey, with James M. Robinson. L: Hodder,
1960. 239p. (22.5cm.) 23cm. [LC62, B60]

Same. NY: Harper, 1960. 239p. 22cm. [LC62, IT13]

BORNKAMM, Heinrich, 1901- .
Luther's world of thought. (Luthers geistige Welt). Tr.
Martin H. Bertram. St. Louis: Concordia, 1958. 315p.
22cm. [LC62, IT11]

BOROVKA, Grigorii Iosifovich.
Scythian art. Tr. V. G. Childe. NY: Paragon, 1960.
111p. 21cm. [LC62]

BORSIG, Arnold von, 1899- . photog.
Tuscany. 200 photos by Arnold von Borsig. (Die Tos-
cana.) Introd. and notes by Ranuccio Bianchi-Bandinelli,
tr. Anon. L: Thames, 1956. 45p. (47p.) (30.5cm.)
31cm. [LC62, B56]

BORSIG, Tet. See Borsig, Arnold, 1899- .

BOSCH, H. See Linfert, Carl.

BOSCH, Hieronymus van Aken, died 1518.
The paintings. Complete ed. with introd., Carl Linfert. Tr.
Joan Spencer. L: Phaidon, 1959. 118p. 28cm. [LC62]

BOSCHMANS, R.
Balearic Islands. Introd. Gladys Wheelhouse. Munich:
Andermann, 1960. 60p. 17cm. [LC62]

BOSCHVOGEL, F. R., pseud. (i. e. Ramon, Frans.)
Mary is our mother. (Maria, meine Mutter.) Tr. Elisabeth Abbot. Illus. Godelieve Schatteman. L: Campion,
1959. 41p. (23.5cm.) [B59, IT12]

BOSS, Medard, 1903- .
The analysis of dreams. (Der Traum und seine Auslegung.)
Tr. Arnold J. Pomerans. L: Rider, 1957. 223p.
(23.5cm.) 24cm. [LC62, B57, IT10]

Same. NY: Philosophical Lib., 1958. 223p. 24cm.
[LC62, IT11]

BOSSE, Heinz und F. Hoelzel.
1958 Niederdollendorf Seminar. (Article in Kartograph-
ische Nachrichten, vol. 8, no. 3, 1958. 69-70p.)
Germany, NY: U.S.J.P.R.S., 1959. 41. 28cm. [LC62]

BOSSERT, Helmuth Theodor, 1889- .
Decorative art of Asia and Egypt. Tr. Anon. NY:
Praeger, 1956. 13p. 35cm. [LC62]

Same. L: Zwemmer, 1956. 15p. (34cm.) [B56]

BOVET, Theodore, 1900- .
A handbook to marriage and marriage guidance. (Die
Ehe, das Geheimnis ist gross.) Tr. Anon. Fwd. David
R. Mace. L: Longmans, 1958. 152p. [LC62, IT11]

Love, skill, and mystery, a handbook to marriage. (Die
Ehe, das Geheimnis ist gross.) Tr. Anon. Garden City,
NY: Doubleday, 1958. 188p. 22cm. [LC62]

BRAATEN, Carl E., 1929- .
Christ, faith and history. An inquiry into the meaning of
Martin Kaehler's distinction between the historical Jesus
and the Biblical Christ developed in its past and present.
(Der sogenannte historische Jesus und der geschichtliche,
biblische Christus, von Martin Kaehler.) Tr. Anon. n. p.,

1959. 2v. 28cm. [LC62]

BRACHVOGEL, Albert Emil, 1824-1878.
Friedemann Bach. (F--B--.) Tr. Emanuel W. Hammer.
NY: Pagent, 1960. 209p. 22cm. [LC62, IT13]

BRAHMS, Johannes, 1833-1897.
Johannes Brahms and Theodor Billroth. Letters from a
musical friendship. Tr. Hans Barkan. Norman: U. of
Okla. Pr., 1957. 264p. 24cm. [LC62, IT10]

BRAND, Joel.
Advocate for the dead, the story of Joel Brand. Tr. Constantine Fitzgibbon and Andrew Foster-Melliar. L:
Deutsch; Toronto: Collins, 1958. 222p. 22cm. [LC62]

Desperate mission, Joel Brand's story as told by Alex
Weissberg. (Geschichte von Joel Brand.) 1st pub. in
Hebrew, trs. Constantine Fitzgibbon and Andrew Foster-
Melliar. NY: Criterion, 1958. 310p. 22cm. [LC62,
IT11]

BRAND, Joel. See Weissberg, Alexander.

BRANDI, Karl, 1868-1946.
The Emperor Charles V, the growth and destiny of a man
and of a world empire. (Kaiser Karl V. Werden und
Schicksal einer Persönlichkeit und eines Weltreiches.) Tr.
C. V. Wedgewood. L: Cape, 1960. 655p. 22cm.
[LC62]

BRANDSTEDT, Börje.
Powder cutting and flame processing. (Pulverbrennschneiden und Pulverflämmen.) Tr. Anon. Höganäs Sweden:
Höganäs-Billesholmes, 1959. 143p. [LC62]

BRANDT, Max, 1890- .
Problems of cancer research and cancer control in the
Soviet Union. (Fragen der Krebsforschung und Krebsbekämpfung in der Sowjetunion.) Tr. Anon. Berlin:
1956. 264p. 30cm. [LC62]

BRANDT, Paul, 1875-1929. See Licht, Hans, pseud.

BRANDT, Willy, 1913- .
A message from Berlin, the Soviet Sea around us.
Berlin: Graphische Gesellschaft Grunewald, 1958. 24p.

BRANDT, Willy--
30 cm. [LC62]

My road to Berlin, as told to Leo Lania. (Mein Weg nach
Berlin, aufgezeichnet von L--L--.) L: Davies, 1960.
279p. (280p.) 22cm. (22.5cm.) [LC62, B60]

Same. Garden City, NY: Doubleday, 1960. 287p.
22cm. [LC62]

BRANTL, Klaus.
Lake Constance. Introd. Wilhelm von Scholz. Tr. Dorothy Plummer. Munich: Andermann, c1959. 59p. 18cm. [B60]

BRAUMANN, Franz.
Gold in the Taiga. (Gold in der Taiga.) Tr. Joyce Em-
erson. L: Oxford U. Pr., 1960. 202p. (22.5cm.)
[B60]

BRAUN, Hanns, 1893- .
The theatre in Germany. Tr. Walter Moss. Munich:
Bruckmann, c1956. 78p. 21cm. [LC62]

BRAUN, Heinrich.
Industrialisation and social policy in Germany. (Industrial-
isierung und Sozialpolitik in Deutschland.) Tr. Anon.
Köln: Heymann, 1956. 381p. 21cm. [LC62]

Same. Tr. Rudolf Lederer. [IT9]

BRAUN, Werner, photog.
Olive trees. Tr. Anon. Carmel ed. Teufen Ar: Niggli;
Haifa: Willy Verkauf, (L: Tiranti), 1958, 19p. (20.5
x 20.5cm.) [B58]

BRAUNBEK, Werner, 1901- .
The drama of the atom. (Forscher erschüttern die Welt.)
Oliver, 1958. 242p. (22.5cm.) 23cm. [LC62, B58]

The pursuit of the atom. (Forscher erschüttern die Welt.)
Trs. Brian J. Kenworthy and W. A. Coupe. NY: Emerson, 1959. 242p. 22cm. [LC62, IT12]

BRAUNFELS, Wolfgang.
Central Italy, Tuscany and Umbria. (Toskana, Umbrien.)
Tr. Salvator Attanasio. Baltimore: Helicon, 1959. 139p.
17cm. [LC62]

BRECHT, Bertolt, 1898-1956.
The Caucasian chalk circle. (Kaukasischer Kreidekreis.)
Trs. Eric and Maja Bentley. L: Oxford U. Pr., 1956.
109-191p. (21.5cm.) [LC62, B56]

Galileo. Eng. ver. Charles Laughton. n.p., n.d., TW.
Carbon, 831. 30cm. [LC62]

The good woman of Setzuan. (Royal Court Theater version.) Tr. Eric Bentley. NY: 1956. 1171. [LC62]

In the jungle of cities, the fight of two men in the gigantic
city Chicago. (Im Dickicht der Städte.) Tr. Gerhard
Nellhaus. NY: Columbia U. Microf. TW, 1957. 771.
(LC62]

A man's a man, the rebuilding of the handy man Galy
Gay in the army barracks of Kilkon at the dawn of the
20th century. (Mann ist Mann.) A comic play, and a Ms.
copy of "the baby elephant." Ed. in cooperation with S.
Dudow, et al. Microf. TW, 1957. 841. [LC62]

The measures taken. (Die Massnahme.) Tr. Eric Bentley. From Colorado Review, Ft. Collins, vol. 1, no. 1,
Winter 1956. n.p., 1956. 50-72p. [LC62]

Same. In Bentley, Eric. The modern theatre. Vol. 6,
1960.

Mother Courage and her children. (Mutter Courage und
ihre Kinder.) Trs. Eric Bentley and J. Kirkup. Microf.
of TW., 1957. [LC62]

On agreement. Tr. Lee Baxandall. Columbia U. Microf.
TW. 281. 1959. [LC62]

On Tao te Ching. (Zu Taoteking.) Tr. Anon. Lexington, Ky.: Anvil, 1959. 12p. [LC62, IT12]

Plays. The Caucasian circle. Trs. J. and T. Stern,
The Threepenny Opera, Trs. D.I. Vesey and E. Bentley,
The Trial of Lucullus, tr. H. R. Hays, The Life of Galileo, tr. D. I. Vesey. L: Methuen, 1960. (345p.) 21
cm. [LC62, B60]

Poems on the theatre. Tr. Anon. From Mainstream. Vol.
12, no. 10, Nov., 1959. NY: 1959. 17-31p. [LC62]

BRECHT, Bertolt--
Puntila. (Herr Puntila und sein Knecht Matti.) Tr. Ger-
hard Nellhaus. Columbia U. Microf. of TW, 1959. 471.
[LC62]

The rise and fall of the city of Mahagonny. (Aufstieg und
Fall der Stadt Mahagonny.) Tr. Guy Stern. NY: 1957
32p. 30 x 30cm. [LC62]

The rise of Arture Ui. Tr. Hoffman Reynolds Hays. NY:
Microf. of TW. 1957. 2,841. [LC62]

Saint Joan of the stockyards. Tr. Frank Jones. In From
the modern repertoire, series 3. Ed. E. R. Bentley. U.
of Denver Pr., 1956. [LC62]

Schweyk. A play in 8 scenes. Adapted, Alfred Kreym-
borg. NY: Microf. of TW. 1957. 901. [LC62]

Selected poems. Tr. and introd. H. R. Hays. NY:
Grove, 1959. 179p. 22cm. [LC62, IT12]

Same. L: Calder, 1960. 179p. (20.5cm.) [B60]

Three penny novel. (3 Groschenroman.) Tr. D. I. Vesey.
Verses tr. Christopher Isherwood. NY: Grove, 1956.
396p. 21cm. [LC62, IT9]

Same. L: Hanison, 1958. 396p. 22cm. [LC62, IT11]

Two plays, the good woman of Setzuan and The Caucasian
chalk circle. Trs. Eric Bentley and Maja Apelman. NY:
Grove, 1957. 192p. 21cm. [LC62, IT10]

Same. L: Calder, 1958. 192p. (20.5cm.) [B58]

BREIDENSTEIN, Hartwig, 1902- .
Beautiful Tyrol, a pictorial record containing sixty-five
superb photographs by A. Defner and others. (Schönes
Tirol.) Tr. Oscar Konstandt. St. Johann: Pinguin,
c1956. 72p. [LC62]

Salzburg and the Salzkammergut, a pictorial record . . .
descriptive text. Trs. Oskar Konstandt and Michael Theo-

bold. Introd. Hanns Jahn. Innsbruck: Pinguin; L: Thorsons, 1958. 7p. (27cm.) [B58]

Same. L: Thorsons, 1958. 63p. [IT11]

BREIDENSTEIN, Hartwig. See Busch, Harold. Germany.

BREMEN, INSTITUT FÜR SCHIFFAHRTSFORSCHUNG. Facts and figures about shipping, ship-building, seaports and seaborne trade. Bremen: 1959. 535p. [LC62]

BRENGELMANN, J. The effect of repeated electric shock on learning in depressives. Tr. Anon. Berlin: Springer, 1959. 52p. 26cm. [LC62]

BRENNECKE, Hans Joachim. The hunters and the hunted. (Jäger-Gejagte.) Tr. R. H. Stevens. 1st ed. NY: Norton, 1958. 320p. 21cm. [LC62, IT11]

Same. L: Burke, 1958. 320p. (22.5cm.) 23cm. [LC 62, B60, IT11]

Same. L: Transworld, 1960. 383p. (16.5cm.) [B60, IT13]

BRENNECKE, Hans J. See Krancke, T., joint author.

BRENTANO, Clemens. Selection in Flores' anthology, 1960.

BREUER, Josef and Freud, Sigmund. Studies in hysteria by Josef Breuer and S. Freud. Tr. A. A. Brill. Boston: Beacon, 1950. (prob. 1958.) 241p. [IT11]

Studies on hysteria. (Studien über Hysterie.) Trs. James and Alix Strachey. Reprint of vol. II. Hogarth, Inst. of Psycho-Anal., 1956. 335p. 22cm. (22.5cm.) [LC62, B57, IT11]

Same. Tr. Anon. L: Routledge, 1957. 311p. (22.5cm.) [B57]

BREUR, Josef and Freud, Sigmund--
Same. Trs. James Strachey, Anna Freud, assisted by
Alix Strachey and Alan Tyson. NY: Basic, 1957. 335p.
23cm. [LC62, IT10]

BREUR, Joseph.
Introduction to the theory of sets. Tr. Howard F. Fehr.
Englewood Cliffs, NJ: Prentice-Hall, 1958. 108p.
22cm. [LC62]

Same. L: Bailey, 1958. 108p. 22cm. [B58]

BRINITZER, Carl.
A reasonable rebel, Georg Christoph Lichtenberg.
(Georg Christoph Licthenberg, die Geschichte eines
gescheiten Mannes.) Tr. Bernard Smith. L: Allen,
1960. 3-204p. (22cm.) 23cm. [LC62, B60]

Same. NY: Macmillan, 1960. 203p. 23cm. [LC62,
IT13]

BRINKMANN, Roland, 1898- .
Geologic evolution of Europe. (Abriss der Geologie.)
Tr. John E. Sanders. Stuttgart: Enke; NY: Hafner,
1960. 161p. 25cm. [LC62]

BROCKELMANN, Carl, 1868-1956.
History of the Islamic peoples, with a review of events,
1939-1947. By Moshe Perlmann. Trs. Joel Carmichael
and Moshe Perlmann. NY: Capricorn, 1960. 582p.
[LC62]

BROD, Max, 1884- .
The adventures of the soldier Schwejk. (Die Abenteuer
des braven Soldaten Schwejk während des Weltkrieges.)
From the novel by Jaroslav Hasek. Tr. Julian Leigh.
Max Pallenberg touring version. NY: Rialto Service
Bureau, 19--. 111 l. 30cm. [LC62]

Frank Kafka, a biography. Trs. G. Humphreys Roberts
and Richard Winston. (2nd enl. ed.). NY: Schocken,
1960. 267p. 21cm. [LC62, IT13]

Heinrich Heine, the artist in revolt. (Heinrich Heine.)
Tr. Jos. Witriol. (Rev. from 2nd Ger. ed.) L: Valentine, 1956. 355p. (22.5cm.) 23cm. [LC62, B56, IT9]

Same. NYU Pr.: 1957. 355p. 22cm. [LC62, IT10]

Hush the gallant soldier, his adventures in 17 scenes,
after Jaroslav Haschek. (Die Abenteuer des braven
Soldaten Schwejk während des Weltkrieges.) Tr. Ruth
Langner. NY: Rialto Service Bureau, 19--. v. 30cm.
[LC57]

BRODA, Engelbert.
Radioactive isotopes in biochemistry, with a pref. by G.
de Hevesy. (Radioaktive Isotope in der Biochemie.) Tr.
Peter Oesper. Amsterdam, NY: Elsevier, 1960. 376p.
24cm. [LC62]

BROWN, Marvin Luther, ed.
American independence through Prussian eyes. A neutral
view of the peace negotiations of 1782-1783. Selections
from the Prussian diplomatic correspondence. Tr. and
ed., Marvin L. Brown. Durham, North Carolina: Duke
U. Pr.; L: Cambridge U. Pr., 1959. 216p. (23.5cm.)
[B59, IT12]

BRUCKMANN, Hansmartin.
New housing in Gt. Britain. (Neuer Wohnbau in England.)
Tr. Sylvia Roberts. Stuttgart: Krämer, 1960. 131p.
27cm. [LC62]

Same. NY: Universe, 1960. 131p. 27cm. [LC62,
IT13]

Same. L: Tiranti, c1960. 131p. 27cm. [LC62]

BRUCKNER, Ferdinand, pseud. (i.e. Tagger, Theodor,
1891- .)
Napoleon the first. Adpt. Sidney Kingsley. n.p., 19--.
iv. TW. (29cm.) [LC62]

BRUCKNER, Karl, 1906- .
The golden Pharaoh. (Der goldene Pharao.) Tr. Frances
Lobb. Illus. Hans Thomas. L: Burke, 1959. 221p.
(20.5cm.) [B59, IT12]

Same. NY: Pantheon, 1959. 190p. 22cm. [LC62, IT12]

BRUCKNER, Karl--
Viva Mexico. (V--M--.) Tr. Stella Humphries. L:
Burke, 1960. 190p. (20.5cm.) [B60]

BRÜCKNER, Christine, 1921- .
Gabrielle. (Ehe die Spuren verwehen.) Tr. Paul Selver.
L: Hale, 1956. 192p. 19cm. [LC62, B56, IT9]

Katarina. (Katharina und der Zaungart.) Tr. Mervyn
Savill. L: Hale, 1958. 192p. 19cm. [LC62, B58,
IT11]

BRUEGEL, Pieter the elder, d. 1569.
Hay-making. Tr. Till Gottheiner. Introd. Jaromir Sip.
Photogs. K. and L. Neubert. L: Produced by Artia for
Spring, c1960. iv. 28 x 36cm. [LC62]

Peter Bruegel the elder. (Das grosse Bruegel-Werk.)
Tr. and ed. Gustav Glück, L: Thames, 1958. 53p.
(29.5cm.) 30 x 35cm. [LC62, B58]

BRUIN, Paul and Geigel, Philipp.
Jesus lived here. (Hier hat Gott gelebt.) Tr. William
Neil. L: Harrap, 1958. 234p. (240p.) 29cm. [LC62,
B58, IT11]

Same. NY: Morrow, 1958. 234p. 29cm. [LC62, IT11]

BRUINSMA, Anne Hendrik
Multivibrator circuits. Introd. to robot technique.
(Multivibrator Schaltungen.) Tr. Anon. Eindhoven:
Philips, 1959. 65p. [LC62]

Same. Tr. E. Harker. L: Cleaver-Hume, 1959. 66p.
(21cm.) [B59]

Practical robot circuits. Electronic sensory organs and
nerve systems. (Roboterschaltungen.) Tr. E. Harker.
Eindhoven: Philips; L: Cleaver-Hume, 1959. 125p.
(21cm.) [B59]

BRUNNER, August, 1894- .
Towards a theology of the Christian life. (Eine neue
Schöpfung. Ein Beitrag zur Theologie des christlichen
Lebens.) Tr. Anon. NY: Philosophical Lib., 1956.
143p. 23cm. [LC62]

BRUNNER, Francis de Sales, 1795-1859.
Four historical booklets regarding the American province
of the most precious blood. Tr. Anon. Carthagena,
Ohio: Messenger, 1957. 304p. 23cm. [LC62]

BRUNNER, Josef. See Jud, Karl.
(Zug. Photographien.) (Fr., Italian, and Eng.) Tr. R.
A. Langford. Zug, Verlag der Offizin Zürcher. c1956.
unp. 22cm. [LC62]

BRUNNER, Heinrich Emil, 1889- .
Dogmatics. (Dogmatik.) Tr. Olive Wyon. L: Lutterworth, 1957. (2nd print.) 2v. 22cm. [LC62]

Faith, hope and love. Philadelphia: Westminster, 1956.
79p. 20cm. [LC57]

Same. L: Lutterworth, 1957. 79p. 20cm. [LC62]

I believe in the living God. (Ich glaube an den lebendigen
Gott.) Tr. John Holden. Phil.: Westminster, 1960.
160p. 20cm. [LC62, IT13]

The letter to the Romans. (Der Römerbrief.) Tr. H. A.
Kennedy. L: Lutterworth; Philadelphia: Westminster,
1959. 168p. (22.5cm.) 23cm. [LC62, B59, IT12]

The philosophy of religion from the standpoint of Protestant theology. (Religionsphilosophie evangelischer Theologie.) Trs. A. J. D. Farrer and Bertram Lee Woolf.
L: Clarke, 1958. 11-194p. (20.5cm.) 21cm. [LC62,
B58, IT11]

BRUNS, Ursula, 1922- .
Horse and rider. English adpt., Annelise Derrick.
Freiburg: Herder, 1957. 13p. 19cm. [LC62, IT10]

Same. L: Interbook, 1957. 15p. (19cm.) [B57]

The snow ponies. (Dick und Dalli und die Ponies.) Tr.
Katya Sheppard. Illus., Princess Marie Luise of Salm.
L: London U. Pr., 1960. 160p. (22cm.) [B60]

BRUNSWICK.
Tradition, ruins, rebuilding, a pictorial report all about
the rebuilding of a town. 3rd Eng. ed., Brunswick:
Waisenhaus, 1959. 126p. 26cm. [LC62]

BUBER, Martin, 1878- .
Eclipse of God. Studies in the relation between religion
and philosophy. (Gottesfinsternis.) Tr. Anon. NY:
Harper, 1957. 152p. 21cm. [LC62]

For the sake of heaven. (Gog und Magog.) Tr. Ludwig
Lewisohn. L: Mayflower, 1958. 316p. 21cm. [LC62]

Same. NY: Meridian, 1958. 316p. 21cm. [LC62, IT11]

Hasidism and modern man. Tr. Maurice Friedman. NY:
Horizon, 1958. 256p. 21cm. [LC62, IT11]

I and thou. (Ich und du.) Tr. Ronald Gregor Smith.
NY: Scribner, 1957. 119p. 19cm. [LC57]

Same. Edinburgh: Clark, 1958. 119 p. [LC62]

Same. With a postscript. NY: Scribner, 1958. 137p.
20cm. [LC62, IT11]

Same. Edinburgh: Clark, 1959. 137p. 19cm. [B60,
IT13]

Same. NY: Scribner, 1960. 137p. [IT13]

The legend of the Baal-Shem. (Die Legende des Baal-
Shem.) Tr. Maurice Friedman. L: Horowitz, 1956.
17-222p. (22.5cm.) [B56, IT9]

Moses, the revelation and the covenant. (Moses.) Tr.
Anon. NY: Harper, 1958. 226p. 21cm. [LC62]

The origin and meaning of Hasidism. Tr. Maurice
Friedman. NY: Horizon, 1960. 254p. 21cm. [LC62,
IT13]

Paths in Utopia. (Pfade in Utopia.) Tr. R. F. C. Hull.
Introd. Ephraim Fischoff. Boston: Beacon, 1958. 152p.
21 cm. [LC62]

Same. 177p. [IT11]

Pointing the way. Collected essays. Tr. Maurice Friedman. L: Routledge, 1957. 239p. (22.5cm.) 23cm.
[LC62, B57]

Same. 234p. [IT10]

Same. NY: Harper, 1957. 239p. 22cm. [LC62, IT10]

Tales of angels, spirits and demons. (Erzählungen von Engeln, Geistern und Dämonen.) Trs. David Antin and Jerome Rothenberg. NY: Hawk's Well, 1958. 61p. [LC62]

Tales of the Hasidim, the early masters. Tr. Olga Marx. L: Thames, 1956. 335p. (22.5cm.) [B56]

Tales of the Hasidim. Vol. 1. The early masters, Vol. 2. The later masters. (Die chassidischen Bücher.) Tr. Olga Marx. L: Thames, 1956. 2v. 21cm. [LC62]

The tales of Rabbi Nachman. (Retold by Martin Buber.) Tr. Maurice Friedman. NY: Horizon, 1956. 214p. 22cm. [LC62, IT9]

To hallow this life. An anthology. (Selections from vars. trs. and trans.) Israel and Palestine, the history of an idea. Tr. Stanley Goodman. NY: Harper, 1958. 174p. 22cm. [LC62]

The way of man, according to the teachings of Hasidism. (Der Weg des Menschen nach der chassidischen Lehre.) Tr. Anon. Fwd. M. Friedman. Wallingsford, Pa.: Pendle Hill, 1960. 32p. 19cm. [LC62]

Writings, selected. Selections from Israel and the world. Other selections, anon. Trs. Olga Marx and Greta Hart. Introd. Will Herberg. NY: Meridian, 1956. 351p. 19cm. [LC62, IT9]

BUCHHEIM, Lothar-Günther.
The graphic art of German expressionism. (Graphik des deutschen Expressionismus.) Tr. Anon. NY: Universe, 1960. 294p. 30cm. [LC62, IT13]

Picasso, a pictorial biography. (P--. Eine Bildbiographie.) Tr. Michael Heron. L: Thames, 1959. 143p. 24cm. [LC62, B59, IT12]

Same. NY: Viking, 1959. 143p. 24cm. [LC62, IT13]

BUCHNER, Alexander.
Mechanical musical instruments. Tr. Iris Urwin. L:
Batchworth, 1959. 111p. 34cm. [LC62, B59]

Musical instruments through the ages. (Musikinstrumente
im Wandel der Zeiten.) Tr. Iris Urwin. L: Spring,
1956. 38p. 34cm. [LC62]

Same. 1957. 44p. (34cm.) [B57]

BUCHNER, Ernst, 1892- .
Art treasures of the Pinokothek. (Die alte Pinakothek.)
Tr. Peter Gorge. NY: Abrams, 1957. 58p. 35cm.
[LC62, IT11]

Same. L: Thames, 1957. 58p. (34.5cm.) [B57]

Same. L: Thames, 1957. 46p. 35cm. [LC62]

German late Gothic painting. Tr. Peter Gorge. München: Hirmer, c1960. 35p. 19cm. [LC62]

BUDDENBROCK, Wolfgang von, 1884- .
The love-life of animals. (Das Liebesleben der Tiere.)
Tr. J. M. Chaplin. L: Muller, 1957. 207p. (22cm.)
[LC62, B57, IT10]

Same. NY: Crowell, 1958. 207p. 22cm. [LC62, IT11]

The senses. (Die Welt der Sinne.) Tr. Frank Gaynor.
Woodthorpe, Nottingham, Hall, 1958. 167p. (21.5cm.)
[B58, IT11]

Same. Ann Arbor: Mich. U. Pr., 1958. 167p. 22cm.
[LC62, IT11]

Same. Ann Arbor: Mich. U. Pr., 1960. 167p. [IT13]

BÜCHLER, Adolf, 1867-1939.
Studies in Jewish history. The Adolf Büchler memorial
volume. Ed. I. Brodie and J. Rabbinowitz. L, NY:
Oxford U. Pr., 1956. 279p. 84p. 23cm. [LC62]

BÜCHNER, Franz, 1895- .
Personality and nature in modern medicine. (Person und
Natur in der modernen Medizin.) Tr. Anon. NY:
Grune, 1958. 36p. 19cm. [LC62]

BÜCHNER, Georg, 1813-1837.
Danton's death. (Dantons tod.) In Bentley, E. R. ed.,
The modern theatre, vol. 5. NY: Doubleday, 1957.
69-160p. 23cm. [LC62]

Lenz. In Spender's coll. 1960.

Leonce and Lena. In Bentley, E. R. ed., from The modern repertoire. Vol. 3. Bloomington: Indiana U. Pr.,
1956. 1-37p. [LC62]

BÜDELER, Werner, 1928- .
Operation vanguard, earth satellite. (Projekt Vorhut.)
Tr. Alexander L. Helm. L: Burke, 1957. 9-128p.
(22.5cm.) 23cm. [LC62, B57, IT10]

Same. Rev. ed. NY: Roy, 1958. 128p. 23cm. [LC62]

The other worlds, telescopes, rockets, stars. (Tele-
skope, Raketen, Gestirne.) Tr. A. L. Helm. NY: Joseph
Elstein, 1956. 224p. [IT9]

BÜHLER, Charlotte. See Buhler, Charlotte M., 1893- .

BÜSCHER, Gustav, 1892- .
The boy's book of the earth beneath us. (Geheimnisvolle
Tiefen.) Trs. Joseph Avrach and Egon Larsen. L:
Burke, 1960. 144p. (25.5cm.) [B60]

BUHL, Hermann, 1924- .
Nanga Parbat pilgrimage. (8000 drüber und drunter.)
Tr. Hugh Merrick. L: Hodder, 1956. 360p. 23cm.
[LC62, B56, IT9]

Same. NY: Dutton, 1956. 318p. 22cm. [LC62, IT9]

BUHLER, Charlotte (Malachowski), 1893- .
From birth to maturity, an outline of the psychological
development of the child. Trs. Esther and W. Menaker.
L: Routledge, 1956. (7th imp.) 237p. 19cm. [LC62]

BULST, Werner.
The shroud of Turin. (Das Grabtuch von Turin. Forsch-
ungsberichte und Untersuchungen.) Trs. Stephen McKenna
and James J. Galvin, in cooperation with the Holy Shroud
Guild. Esopus, NY; Milwaukee: Bruce, c1957. 167p.
23cm. [LC62]

BULTMANN, Rudolf Karl, 1884- .
Existence and faith, shorter writings of Rudolf Bultmann.
Tr. and introd. Schubert M. Ogden. NY: Meridian,
1960. 320p. 19cm. [LC62, IT13]

Jesus and the work. (Jesus.) Trs. Louis Pettibone
Smith and Ermine Huntress Lantero. NY: Scribner,
1958. 226p. 21cm. [LC62, IT11]

Same. Jesus and the world. (Jesus.) NY: Scribner,
1960. 226p. [IT13]

Primitive Christianity in its contemporary setting. (Das
Urchristentum im Rahmen der antiken Religionen.) Tr.
Reginald Horace Fuller. L: Thames, 1956. 240p.
(22.5cm.) 22cm. [L C62, B56, IT9]

Same. NY: Meridian, 1956. 240p. 18cm. [LC62, IT9]

Same. L: Collins, 1960. 256p. 18cm. [LC62, B60]

Theology of the New Testament. (Theologie des Neuen
Testaments.) Tr. Kendrick Grobel. L: SCM, 1958-59.
Vol. 1. 1959. 2 Vol. 22cm. [LC62]

This world and beyond. (Marburger Predigten.) Tr.
Harold Knight. L: Lutterworth, 1960. 248p. 22cm.
(22.5cm.) [LC62, B60]

Same. NY: Scribner, 1960. 248p. 21cm. [LC62, IT
13]

BULZANO, (PROVINCE) ENTE PROVINCIALE PER IL TUR-
ISMO.
Skier's guide to the Dolomites, South Tyrol, Italy. (Ski-
führer durch das Tiroler Etschland, Südtirol.) Tr. Anon.
Bolzano, Arti Grafiche R. Manfrien, 1958. 398p. 16cm.
[LC62]

BUONARROTI, Michelangelo, 1475-1564. See Goldscheider,
Ludwig, 1896- .

BURCKHARDT, Jakob Christoph, 1818-1897.
The civilization of the Renaissance in Italy. (Die Zivili-
sation der Renaissance in Italien.) Introd. Benjamin Nelson, tr. Anon. NY: Harper, 1958. 2 Vol. V.1. 278p,
V.2. 279-516p. 21cm. [LC62, IT11]

Same. Garden City, NY: Phaidon, 1960. Complete and unabridged Eng. rendering of 2nd orig. ed. 462p. 19cm. [LC62]

Same. L: Phaidon, 1960. (From 2nd Ger. ed.) 1st ed. 6th printing. 462p. (19cm.) [B60]

Judgments on history and historians. (Historische Fragmente.) Tr. Harry Zohn. Boston: Beacon, 1958. 280p. 21cm. [LC62, IT11]

Same. Introd. H. R. Trevor-Roper. L: Allen, 1959. 258p. (259p.) 22cm. (22.5cm.) [LC62, B59, IT12]

BURCKHARDT, Titus.
An introduction to Sufi doctrine. Tr. D. M. Matheson. Lahore: Sh. Muhammad Ashraf, 1959. 155p. [LC62]

Siena, the city of the Virgin. Tr. Margaret McConough Brown. 1st Eng. ed., L, NY: Oxford U. Pr., 1960. c1958. 126p. 30cm. [LC62]

BUSCH, Fritz Otto, 1890- .
The drama of the Scharnhorst. (Tragödie am Nordkap.) Trs. Eleanor Brockett and Anton Ehrenzweig. L: Hale, 1956. 186p. (22.5cm.) 23cm. [LC62, B56, IT9]

Same. L: Hamilton, 1957. 154p. (18.5cm.) [B57, IT10]

The drama of the Scharnhorst, a factual account from the German viewpoint by Corvette Captain Fritz Otto Busch. Trs. Eleanor Brockett and Anton Ehrenzweig. NY: Berkley, 1958. 157p. [IT11]

The five Herods. (Was begab sich aber zu der Zeit.) Tr. E. W. Dickes. L: Hale, 1958. 192p. (22.5cm.) 23cm. [LC62, B58, IT11]

Holocaust at sea, the drama of the Scharnhorst. (Tragödie am Nordkap.) Trs. Eleanor Brockett and Anton Ehrenzweig. NY: Rinehart, 1956. 182p. 22cm. [LC 57, IT10]

The story of the Prince Eugen. (Schwerer Kreuzer Prinz Eugen.) Tr. Eleanor Brockett. L: Hale, 1960. c1958. 190p. (22.5cm.) [LC62, B60]

BUSCH, Harald, 1904- . and Lohse, Bernd, 1911- . , eds.
Art treasure of Germany. (Kleinodien. Auserlesene
Kunstwerke in Deutschland.) Tr. P. Gorge. Introd.
Rudolf Hagelstange. Commentaries on illus. Helmut
Domke. L: Batsford, 1958. 42p. (27.5cm.) 28cm.
[LC62, B58, IT11]

Beautiful Bavaria. Tr. Anon. Introd. Johann Lachner.
Explanatory text and picture cap. Harald Busch. 2nd ed.
L: Batsford, c1956. 160p. 27cm. [LC62, B56]

Same. 168p. (27cm.) [B56]

Same. 3rd ed. Frankfurt/Main: Umschau, 1956. 160p.
27cm. [LC62]

Germany, countryside, cities, villages and people. Tr.
Anon. Introd. Rudolf Hagelstange. Caps. Harald Busch.
Eds. Harald Busch and H. Breidenstein. Frankfurt/
Main: Umschau, 1956. 224p. 27cm. [LC62]

Same. NY: Hastings House, c1956. 244p. 27cm.
[LC62]

Gothic Europe. (Baukunst der Gotik in Europa.) Tr. P.
Gorge. Introd. Kurt Gerstenberg. Eds. Harald Busch
and Bernd Lohse. Commentaries Helmut Domke. NY:
Macmillan, 1958. xxiii, 27cm. [LC62]

Same. 223p. [IT12]

Same. L: Batsford, 1959. xxiii (xxiv p.) 27cm. [LC
62, B59]

Romanesque Europe. (Baukunst der Romantik in Europa.)
Tr. Peter Gorge. Introd. R. H. C. Davis. Ed. Harald
Busch and Bernd Lohse. Commentaries Helmut Domke.
L: Batsford, 1960. (27.5cm.) [LC62, B60]

Same. NY: Macmillan, 1960. 23p. 27cm. [LC62,
IT13]

U-boats at war. (So war der U-Boat Krieg.) Tr. L. P. R.
Wilson. L: Hamilton, 1956. 189p. (18.5cm.) [B56]

BUSONI, Ferruccio Benvenuto, 1866-1924.
The essence of music, and other papers. (Von der Einheit der musik. Later, Wesen und Einheit der Musik.)
Tr. Rosamond Ley. L: Rockliff; NY: Philosophical Lib.,
1957. 204p. 22cm. [LC62, B57, IT10]

BUXBAUM, Franz.
Cactus culture based on biology. Tr. Vera Higgins. L:
Blandford, 1958. 13-224p. 22cm. (22.5cm.) [LC62,
B58]

CAIRNCROSS, John. (compiler)
By a lonely sea. Tr. and poems. Tr. Anon. Fwd. Edmund Blunden. (Fr., Italian, Span., and Ger.) Hongkong: Hongkong U. Pr.; L: Oxford U. Pr., 1959. 92p.
(19cm.) [B59]

CAMPENHAUSEN, Hans Freiherr von, 1903- .
The fathers of the Greek church. (Die griechischen
Kirchenväter.) Tr. Stanley Godman. NY: Pantheon,
1959. 170p. 22cm. [LC62, IT12]

CARATHEODORY, Constantin, 1873-1950.
Theory of functions of a complex variable. (Funktionentheorie.) Tr. F. Steinhardt. 2nd Eng. ed. NY: Chelsea, 1958. 2v. 24cm. [LC62]

CARELL, Paul.
The foxes of the desert. (Die Wüstenfüchse. Tatsachenbericht.) Tr. Mervyn Savill. L: Macdonald, 1960.
370p. 23cm. (22.5cm.) [LC62, B60]

CARNAP, Rudolf, 1891- .
Introduction to symbolic logic and its applications.
(Einführung in die symbolische Logik.) Trs. William H.
Meyer and John Wilkinson. NY: Dover; L: Constable,
1958. 241p. (20.5cm.) 21cm. [LC62, B58]

The logical syntax of language, Tr. Amethe Smeaton.
(Countess V. Zepplin.) Paterson, NJ: Littlefield, 1959.
368p. [IT12]

CASPAR, Franz, 1916- .
Tupari. Tr. Eric Northcott. L: Bell, 1956. 224p.
22cm. [LC62]

CASPER, Max, 1880- .
Kepler. (Johannes Kepler.) Tr. and ed. C. Doris Hellman. L, NY: Abelard, c1959. 401p. 23cm. (23.5cm.)
[LC62, B59]

CASPARI, Karl Heinrich, 1815-1861.
The captivity of Jacob. (Christ und Jude.) A free rendering, anon. Columbus, Ohio: Book Concern, n.d. 302p. 19cm. [LC62]

CASSIRER, Ernst, 1874-1945.
Determinism and indeterminism in modern physics. Historical and systematic studies of the problem of causality. Tr. D. Theodor Benfey. Pref. Henry Margenau. New Haven: Yale U. Pr., 1956. 227p. 24cm. [LC62, IT9]

The philosophy of Ernst Cassirer. See Paul Arthur Schilpp, ed. Trs. R. W. Bretall and Paul Arthur Schilpp. 1st ed. NY: Tudor, 1958. 936p. 25cm. [LC62]

The philosophy of symbolic forms. The phenomenology of knowledge. (Philosophie der symbolischen Formen. Phaenomenologie der Erkenntnis.) Tr. Ralph Manheim. Introd. Charles W. Hendel. New Haven: Yale U. Pr.; L: Oxford U. Pr., Vol. 3. 1957. (501p.) 24cm. (24.5cm.)
[LC62, B58, IT11]

Same. 518p. [IT10]

The philosophy of the enlightenment. Trs. Fritz Kölln and James Pettegrove. Gloucester, Mass.: Peter Smith, 1959. 366p. 21cm. [LC62, IT12]

The Renaissance philosophy of man by Petrarca and others. Selections in trans., eds. Ernst Cassirer, Paul Oskar Kristeller and John Herman Randall, Jr. Chicago: U. of Chicago Pr., 1956. 404p. 21cm. [LC62]

Toward a logic of the humanities. (Zur Logik der Kulturwissenschaften.) Tr. with introd. Clarence Smith Howe. NY: Columbia U. thesis, c1960. 295l. 29cm. [LC62]

CATHOLIC CHURCH. Liturgy and ritual. Breviary, English. The divine office. (Ger. version of Officium divinum parvum. By Rev. Hildebrand Fleischmann.) Tr. Edward E. Malone. 1st ed. NY: Herder, 1959. 661p. 16cm. [LC62]

Same. Chicago: Franciscan Herald, 1959. 661, 141p.
16cm. [LC62]

CAWEIN, Madison Julius 1865-1914., tr.
The white snake and other poems. Tr. M--J--C--.
Louisville, Kentucky: Lost Cause, 1956. 3 (microprint)
cards 7.5 x 12.5cm. [LC62]

CELAN, Paul, 1920- .
Selections in Rothenberg, 1959.

CERAM, C.W., pseud. (i.e. Marek, Kurt W.)
Gods, graves, and scholars. The story of archaeology.
(Götter, Gräber und Gelehrte.) Tr. E. B. Garside. L:
Gollancz, 1956. 433p. 23cm. [LC62]

Same. NY: Knopf, 1959. 428p. 22cm. [LC62, IT13]

The march of archaeology. (Götter, Gräber, und Gelehrte
im Bild.) Trs. Richard and Clara Winston. NY: Knopf,
1958. 326p. 28cm. [LC62, IT11]

Narrow Pass, Black Mountain, the discovery of the Hit-
tite empire. (Enge Schlucht und schwarzer Berg.) Trs.
Richard and Clara Winston. L: Gollancz, 1956. 284p.
(22.5cm.) [LC62, B56, IT9]

A picture history of archaeology. (Götter, Gräber und
Gelehrte im Bild.) Trs. Richard and Clara Winston. L:
Thames, 1958. 360p. (23.5cm.) 24cm. [LC62, B58,
IT11]

The secret of the Hittites. The discovery of an ancient
empire. (Enge Schlucht und schwarzer Berg.) Trs.
Richard and Clara Winston. NY: Knopf, 1956. 281p.
22cm. [LC62]

CESCOTTI, Roderich.
Aviation dictionary. German-English/English-German.
(Luftfahrt-Wörterbuch.) 2nd ed. L: Ward, Lock, 1957.
448p. (15cm.) [B57]

CHAGALL, Marc, 1887- . See Meyer, Franz.
Writer on art.

CHAMISSO, Adalbert von, 1781-1838.
Peter Schlemihl. (Peter Schlemihls wundersame Ge-

CHAMISSO, Adelbert von--
schichte.) Tr. Leopold von Loewenstein-Wertheim. L:
Calder, 1957. 3-93p. (19.5cm.) [LC62, B57, IT10]

CHASE, Geoffrey Herbert, tr.
Poems from the German. Selected lyrics and ballads
from Heine, Goethe and others. Newly tr. into Eng.
verse. Fwd. L. A. Willoughby. Edinburgh, L: Black-
wood, 1959. 56p. (18.5cm.) 19cm. [LC62, B59]

CHMEL, Lucca and others, photogs.
Salzburg and the salzkammergut. A pictorial record con-
taining fifty-seven superb photographs by Lucca Chmel,
Stefan Kurckenhauser, Heinz Muller-Brunke and others.
Trs. Oscar Konstandt and Michael Theobold. Introd.
Hanns Jahn. Innsbruck: Pinguin; L: Thorsons, 1958.
7p. (27cm.) [B58]

CHOENZ, Selina.
A bell for Ursli. (Schellen-Ursli.) Tr. Anon. NY: Oxford U. Pr., 1957. 44p. 25cm. [LC62]

The snowstorm. (Der grosse Schnee.) Tr. Anon. NY:
Walck, 1958. unp. 25 x 33cm. [LC62]

CHORPENNING, Charlotte (Barrows).
Hansel and Gretel by the brothers Grimm. (full-length
play no. 14.) Chicago: Coach House, 1956. 63p. 22cm.
[LC62]

CHRISTALLER, Walter, 1893- .
A critique and tr. of (Die zentralen Orte in Süddeutschland.)
by Carlisle W. Baskin. Ann Arbor Univ. Microfilms,
1957. 458l. 25cm. [LC62]

CICHY, Bodo. See Relouge, Joseph Egon, ed.

CLAUSEWITZ, Karl von, 1780-1831.
On war. (Vom Kriege, hinterlassenes Werk.) Tr. J. J.
Graham. L: Routledge; NY: Barnes, 1956. 3v.
23cm. [LC62]

Principles of war. (Die wichtigsten Grundsätze des
Kriegsführens.) Tr. and ed. Hans W. Gatzke. Harris-
burg, Pennsylvania: Stackpole, 1960. 82p. 20cm.
[LC62]

CLEMEN, Wolfgang.
The development of Shakespeare's imagery. (Shakespeares Bilder, ihre Entwicklung und ihre Funktionen im dramatischen Werk.) Cambridge, Mass.: Harvard U. Pr., 1959. 236p. 23cm. [LC62]

Same. L: 1959. 236p. [LC62]

CLEMENTS, John, 1910- .
Rumpelstiltskin. A play with music. Based on the Grimm's fairy tale. L: Oxford U. Pr., c1959. 47p. 18cm. [LC62]

CLOSEN, Ludwig, Baron von, 1752-1830.
Revolutionary journal, 1780-1783. Tr. Evelyn M. Acomb. Chapel Hill: U. of N. Carolina Pr., 1958. 392p. 24cm. [LC62, IT11]

COAZ, Hans. See Schwarzenbach, Hans, 1911- .

COBBETT, William, 1763-1835.
Description of an old book printed in German by Gottlob Jungmann, Reading, 1797. The blood flag. (Die Blutfahne, by Peter Porcupine, pseud.) Tr. Joseph A. Donahoe. Delaware: Donahoe, 19--. 141. 15cm. [LC62]

CÖSTER, G.
Hessian soldiers in the American Revolution. Records of their marriages, and baptisms of their children in America. Tr. and abstracted Marie Dikore. Cincinnati: n.p., 1959. 25p. 26cm. [LC62]

COLDITZ, Heinz, and Lücke, Martin.
(Stalinstadt-neues Leben und neue Menschen.) Tr. Anon. (Russ., Eng., and Fr.) Berlin: Kongress, 1958. 165p. 29cm. [LC62]

COLERUS, Egmont, 1888-1939.
Mathematics for everyman, from simple numbers to the calculus. (Vom Einmaleins zum Integral.) Trs. B. C. and H. F. Brookes. NY: Emerson, 1957. 255p. 20cm. [LC62]

COLLATZ, Lothar, 1910- .
The numerical treatment of differential equations. 3rd ed. Tr. P. G. Williams. From supp. version of 2nd ed. Berlin: Springer, 1960. 568p. 25cm. [LC62]

COLM, Gerhard, 1897- .
A plan for the liquidation of war finance and the financial
rehabilitation of Germany. By Gerhard Colm and others.
(Reprinted from Zeitschrift für die gesamte Staatswissen-
schaft, 3 band, 2 heft, pp. 204-243, 1959.) Tüblingen:
Mohr, 1959. 41p. [LC62]

COMMITTEE FOR GERMAN UNITY, BERLIN. G. D. R. , 300
QUESTIONS.
300 answers. Committee for German unity. L: Collet's
1959. 232p. (20cm.) [B60]

COMMUNIST PARTY OF GERMANY.
The Karlsruhe trial for banning the communist party of
Germany. Extracts from the White paper on the Karls-
ruhe trial. Communist party of Germany. Tr. C. P.
Dutt. L: Lawrence, 1956. 127p. (18.5cm.) [B56]

CONRADI, F. W. , pseud. (i. e. Horster, Friedrich Wil-
helm Conrad.)
The book of exquisite conjuring, with supplements, cloth
painting, rag-pictures. H. W. Tagrey, tr. and Patter,
E. Harkewitz. Berlin: Horsterischer, n. d. 47p. 28cm.
[LC62]

CONRADIS, Heinz.
Design for flight. The Kurt Tank story. (Nerven, Herz
und Rechenschieber.) Tr. Kenneth Kettle. L: Macdonald, 1960. 246p. (22.5cm.) 23cm. [LC62, B60, IT13]

CONTE, Manfred.
Jeopardy. (Cassia und der Abenteurer.) Tr. Anon.
NY: Sloane, 1956. 214p. 22cm. [LC57]

Same. 278p. 21cm. [LC62, IT9]

CONZELMANN, Hans.
The theology of St. Luke. (Die Mitte der Zeit.) Tr.
Geoffrey Buswell. L: Faber, 1960. 3-255p. (22.5cm.)
23cm. [LC62, B60]

COREY, Lewis.
The social revolution in Germany. Including 2 articles on
socialism in Germany by Karl Liebknecht and Franz Mehring of the Sparticus group. Boston: The Revolutionary
Age, n. d. 108p. 22cm. [LC62]

CORTI, Egon Caesar, conte, 1886-1953.
The English empress. A study in the relations between
Queen Victoria and her eldest daughter, Empress Frederick [sic] of Germany. (Wenn. . . Sendung und Schicksal
einer Kaiserin.) Tr. Anon. L: Cassell, 1957. 406p.
23cm. [LC62]

COUDENHOVE-KALERGI, Richard (Nikolaus), Count.
From war to peace. (Vom Krieg zum Frieden.) Tr. Con-
stantine Fitzgibbon. L: Cape, 1959. 224p. (20.5cm.)
[B59, IT12]

COURANT, Richard, 1888- .
Differential and integral calculus. Tr. E. J. McShane.
2nd ed. L: Blackie, 1957. 1v. [LC62]

Same. NY: n.p. 2v. 1957. [LC62]

On the partial difference equations of mathematical physics. By R--C--., K. Friedrichs, and H. Lewy. Tr.
Phyllis Fox. NY: New York U., Institute of Mathematical Sciences, 1956. 76p. 28cm. [LC62]

CROSTA, Nicolas de, pseud. (i.e. Schlieben-Crosta, Trau-
gott von, 1900- .)
Blanche. (Bis aller Glanz erlosch.) Tr. Arnold J. Pomerans. L: Barrie, 1958. 381p. 20cm. (20.5cm.)
[LC62, B58, IT11]

CROY, Otto.
All about camera tricks. Tr. Anon. L, NY: Focal,
1959. 53p. 17cm. [LC62]

The complete art of printing and enlarging. L, NY:
Focal, 1956. 256p. 24cm. [LC62]

Same. L, NY: Focal, c1959. 256p. 23cm. [LC62]

The retina way. The Retina Photographer's Companion.
6th ed. L, NY: Focal, 1956. 303p. 22cm. [LC62]

Same. L, NY: Focal, 1957. 318p. 22cm. [LC62]

Retouching, corrective techniques in photography. 2nd ed.
L, NY: Focal, 1957. 199p. [LC62]

CULLMANN, Oscar.
Baptism in the New Testament. (Die Tauflehre des Neuen Testaments.) Tr. J. K. S. Reid. Illinois: Allenson, 1958. 84p. 22cm. [LC62]

Catholics and Protestants. A proposal for realizing Christian solidarity. (Katholiken und Protestanten.) L: Lutterworth, 1960. 62p. (16.5cm.) [LC62, B60, IT13]

The Christology of the New Testament. (Die Christologie des Neuen Testaments.) Trs. Shirley C. Guthrie and Charles A. M. Hall. L: SCM, Philadelphia: Westminster, 1959. 342p. (23.5cm.) 24cm. [LC62, IT12]

Early Christian worship. (Urchristentum und Gottesdienst, 2nd ed.) Trs. A. Stewart Todd and James B. Torrance. L: SCM, 1956. 124p. 22cm. [LC62]

The early church. Studies in early Christian history and theology. Trs. A. J. B. Higgins and S. Godman. L: SCM; Philadelphia: Westminster, 1956. 217p. 24cm. [LC62, B56, IT9]

Message to Catholics and Protestants. (Katholiken und Protestanten.) 1st Amer. ed. Tr. Joseph A. Burgess. Grand Rapids: Eerdmans, 1959. 57p. 20cm. [LC62, IT13]

Peter. Disciple, apostle, martyr. A historical and theological essay. (Petrus. Jünger, Apostel, Märtyrer. Das historische und das Theologische Petrusproblem.) Tr. Floyd V. Filson. NY: Meridian, 1958. 252p. 19cm. [LC62]

The state in the New Testament. NY: Scribner, 1956. 123p. 21cm. [LC62]

Same. L: SCM, 1957. (22.5cm.) 121p. [LC62, B57]

CUTLER, Ann.
The Trachtenberg speed system of basic mathematics. Trs. and adapts. Ann Cutler and Rudolf MacShane. Garden City, NY: Doubleday, 1960. 270p. 22cm. [LC62, IT13]

CZECH, Josef.
The cathode ray oscilloscope, circuitry and practical ap-

plications. (Der Elektronenstrahloszillograf.) Tr. G. E.
Luton. Eindhoven: Philips, NY: Interscience, 1957.
340p. 24cm. [LC62]

Same. Philips, L: Cleaver-Hume, 1957. 338p. (23.5
cm.) [B57]

CZEKANOWSKI, Jan.
Investigations in the area between the Nile and the Congo.
(Forschungen im Nil-Kongo-Zwischengebiet.) Tr. Frieda
Schütze. New Haven: n.p., 1959. 285p. 20cm.
[LC62]

DACH, S.
Selections in Loomis. C. G. Sel. 1958.

DAHRENDORF, Ralf or Ralph.
Class and class conflict in industrial society. (Soziale
Klassen und Klassenkonflikt in der industriellen Gesell-
schaft.) Tr., rev. and expanded R--D--. Stanford,
California: Stanford U. Pr., 1959. 336p. 25cm.
[LC62, IT12]

Same. L: Routledge, 1959. 336p. 25cm. [LC62,
IT12]

DA VINCI, Leonardo, 1452-1519. See Goldscheider, Ludwig, 1896- .

DAVIDSON, Arthur, tr.
Sundry sweet translations from European verse. L:
Davidson, 1958. 72p. 20cm. [LC62]

Davidson's miscellany of French and German lyrics. L:
n.p., 195-. 56p. [LC62]

DAWIHL, Walther, 1904- .
A handbook of hard metals. (Handbuch der Hartmetalle.)
Tr. Anon. NY: Philosophical Lib., 1956. 162p. 25cm.
[LC62]

DE BOER, Hans Alfred Carl. See Boer, Hans Alfred Carl
de.

DECKER, H.
The Italian lakes. (Oberitalienische Seen.) Tr. Anon.

DECKER, H. --
L: Thames, 1956. 20p. (80p.) (24.5cm.) 25cm.
[LC62, B56, IT9]

DECKER, Heinrich.
Romanesque art in Italy. (Italia Romanica. Die hohe
Kunst.) Tr. James Cleugh. L: Thames, 1959. 82p.
31cm. [LC62, B59, IT12]

Romanesque art in Italy. (Italia Romanica.) Tr. James
Cleugh. NY: Abrams, 1959. 82p. 32cm. [LC62,
IT12]

Venice. (Venedig.) Tr. Anon. L: Thames, 1957. 36p.
31cm. [LC62, B57]

Same. NY: Studio, 1957. 36p. 31cm. [LC62]

DECKERT, Kurt. See Guenther, Klaus.

DEER, Jozsef, 1905- .
The dynastic porphyry tombs of the Norman period in
Sicily. Tr. G. A. Gillhof. Cambridge: Harvard U. Pr.,
1959. 188p. 30cm. [LC62, IT13

DEFANT, Albert, 1884- .
Ebb and flow, the tides of earth, air, and water. (Ebbe
und Flut des Meeres der Atmosphäre und Erdfeste.) Tr.
A. J. Pomerans. L: Mayflower; Ann Arbor: Michigan U. Pr., 1958. 121p. (21.5cm.) 22cm. [LC62, B59]

DEGNER, Rotraud.
Cooking en voyage. (Camping Kochbuch.) Tr. Ruth
Michaelis-Jena. Edinburgh: Paterson, 1957. 105p.
(19cm.) [B57]

Salad days and ways. (Heiteres Rohkost-Brevier.) Tr.
Ruth Michaelis-Jena. Edinburgh: Paterson, 1957. 61p.
(19cm.) [B57]

DEHIO, Ludwig, 1888- .
Germany and world politics in the twentieth century.
(Deutschland und die Weltpolitik im 20. Jahrhundert.)
Tr. Dieter Pevsner. L: Chatto, 1959. 141p. (142p.)
(22cm.) 23cm. [B59, LC62]

Same. NY: Knopf, 1959. 141p. 23cm. [LC62]

DEICH, Friedrich, pseud. (i.e. Weeren, Friedrich August 1907- .)
The sanity inspector, a novel. (Windarzt und Apfelsinenpfarrer.) Tr. Robert Kee. L: Putnam, 1956. 200p. (20.5cm.) 21cm. [LC62, B56]

Same. NY: Rinehart, 1957. 275p. 22cm. [IT10]

DEISSMANN, Gustav Adolf, 1866-1937.
Paul, a study in social and religious history. Tr. William E. Wilson. NY: Harper, 1957. 323p. 21cm. [LC62]

DENK, Petr, compiler.
Ring O'Roses. A treasury for children. (Ringelreihen.) Tr. and adpt. Ingeborg Glaser. L: Dakers, 1958. 113p. 33cm. [D58, IT11]

DENNEBORG, Heinrich Maria, 1909- .
Grisella the donkey. (Das Eselchen Grisella.) Tr. Emile Capouya. NY: McKay, 1957. 138p. 22cm. [LC62, IT 10]

Jan and the wild horse. (Jan und das Wildpferd.) Tr. Emile Capouya. Illus. Horst Lemke. NY: McKay, c1958. 121p. 22cm. [LC62, IT12]

DENT, Anthony, compiler.
International modern plays. Tr. Anon. L: Dent; NY: Dutton, 1960. 304p. (19.5cm.) [B60]

DENT, Edward Joseph, 1876- , compiler.
The earliest compositions of Wolfgang Amadeus Mozart. By E--D-- and Erich Valentin in cooperation with H. J. Lauer. (Der früheste Mozart.) München: Deutsche Mozart-Gesellschaft, 1956. 50p. 22 x 30cm. [LC62]

DERFLER, Michael.
For the peace of Europe, the Austro-Yugoslavian discussion. (Um den Frieden Europas, die Österreichisch-Jugoslavischen Auseinandersetzungen.) Tr. Anon. Wien: n.p., 1957. 14p. [LC62]

DETMERS, Theodor.
The raider Kormoran. (Kormoran, der Hilfskreuzer.) Tr. Edward Fitzgerald. L: Kimber, 1959. 206p. (22.5cm.) [LC62, B59, IT12]

DEUTSCH, Otto Erich, 1883- ., ed.
Schubert. Memoirs by his friends. (S--. Die Erinner-
ungen seiner Freunde.) Trs. Rosamond Ley and John
Nowell. L: Black, 1958. 501p. (22.5cm.) 23cm.
[LC62, B58]

Same. NY: Macmillan, 1958. 501p. [LC62]

DEUTSCHER AKADEMISCHER AUSTAUSCHDIENST.
The foreign student in Germany, a study guide. (Aus-
ländischer Student in Deutschland. Ratgeber für Studium
und Aufenthalt.) Bonn: Bonner Universitätsbuchdruckerei,
1958. 376p. [LC62]

DEUTSCHER INDUSTRIE- UND HANDELSTAG.
Striving for balance in German economy. (Zum Problem
des Gleichgewichts zwischen Wirtschaftspolitik und Staats-
politik.) Tr. Anon. Bonn: n.p., 1958. 123p.
[LC62]

DEUTSCHER SPARKASSEN- UND GIROVERBAND.
The German savings Banks organisations. (Die Deutsche
Sparkassenorganisation.) Stuttgart: Deutscher Sparkassen-
verlag, 1960. 28p. [LC62]

DEUTSCHER VOLKSHOCHSCHULVERBAND.
The Volkshochschulen in the Federal Republic of Germany
and West Berlin. Bonn: Bearbeitet von Reinhard Wilke.
Bonn: 1956. 30p. 21cm. [LC62]

DEUTSCHES INDUSTRIEINSTITUT.
The West German economy. A handy guide to facts and
figures. (Taschenbuch für die Wirtschaft.) Tr. Anon.
Köln, Deutsche Industrieverlags-G.M.B.H., 1960. 641p.
11 x 16cm. (11 x 15.5cm.) [LC62, B60]

DEUTSCHLAND.
(D--, das Gesicht seiner Städte und Landschaften.) Text
Werner Lenz. Gütersloh: Bertelsmann, 1956. 240p.
24cm. (captions in English, Fr., and Ger.) [LC62]

DIBELIUS, Martin, 1883-1947.
Paul. (Paulus.) Tr. Frank Clarke. Philadelphia: Westminster, 1957. 172p. 19cm. [LC62]

Studies in the acts of the apostles. (Aufsätze zur Apos-
tolgeschichte.) Tr. Mary Ling. Ed. Heinrich Greeven.

L: SCM; NY: Scribner, 1956. 228p. (23.5cm.) 24cm.
[LC62, B56, IT9]

Same. NY: Scribner, 1956. 228p. 24cm. [LC62]

DIBELIUS, Otto (baptised 1880.)
Report to the Evangelical Church in Germany. NY: National Lutheran Council, 1958. 17p. 23cm. [LC62]

DIBOLD, Hans.
Doctor at Stalingrad. The passion of a captivity. (Arzt in Stalingrad.) Tr. H. C. Stevens. L: Hutchinson, 1958. 190p. (191p.) 22cm. [LC62, B58]

DIELMANN, Jakob Fürchtegott, 1809-1885. See Müller, Rolf.

DIEM, Hermann, 1900- .
Dogmatics. (Theologie als kirchliche Wissenschaft.) Tr. Harold Knight. Edinburgh, L: Oliver, 1959. 375p. (22.5cm.) 23cm. [LC62, B59, IT12]

Same. Philadelphia: Westminster, c1959. 375p. 23cm. [LC62, IT13]

Kierkegaard's dialectic of existence. (Die Existenzdialektik von Sören Kierkegaard.) Edinburgh, L: Oliver, 1959. 217p. (218p.) (22.5cm.) 23cm. [LC62, B59, IT12]

DIESEL, Eugen, 1889- , Goldbeck, Gustav, and Schildberger, Friedrich, jt. authors.
From engines to autos. (Vom Motor zum Auto.) Tr. Peter White. Chicago: Regnery, 1960. 302p. 22cm. [LC62, B60, IT13]

DIETMAN, V. A.
Selections in Loomis, C. G. 1958.

DIETRICH, Anton, See Boger, Bert, photog.

DIETRICH, Otto, 1897-1952.
The Hitler I knew. (12 Jahre mit Hitler.) Tr. Richard and Clara Winston. L: Methuen, 1957. 277p. (22.5 cm.) 23cm. [LC62, B57]

DIEUZAIDE, Jean.
Portugal. (Portugal.) Complete text Hans Seligo. Tr.

DIEUZAIDE, Jean--
G. A. Colville. (Ger., Eng., and Fr.) Munich: n.p.,
c1959. 62p. 18cm. [LC62]

DILLERSBERGER, Joseph, 1897- .
The gospel of St. Luke. (Lukas.) Tr. Anon. Cork:
Mercier, 1958. 558p. 23cm. [LC62, IT12]

Same. Westminster, Md.: Newman, 1958. 558p. 23cm.
[LC62]

DILTHEY, Wilhelm, 1833-1911.
Dilthey's philosophy of existence. (Gesammelte Schriften.)
Tr. Anon. L: Vision, c1957 (22.5cm) 1960. 74p. 23cm.
[LC62, B60]

Philosophy of existence. Introd. by Wm. Kluback and Martin
Weinbaum. L: Vision, 1957. 74p. (22.5cm.) 23cm. [LC62,
B60]

Same. NY: Bookman, 1957. 74p. 23cm. [LC62]

DIRKS, Walter and Hausmann, Manfred, jt. authors.
Germany in color. Tr. Anon. Photos. Kurt Peter Karfeld. Düsseldorf: Karfeld, 1956. v. 30cm. [LC62]

Same. NY: Studio, 1957. v. 30cm. [LC62]

DITZEN, Rudolf Wilhelm Friedrich. See Fallada, Hans,
pseud.

DOBBELSTEIN, Hermann.
Psychiatry for all. Tr. Norman C. Reeves. Cork:
Mercier, 1956. 124p. 18cm. [LC62]

DOCUMENTS ON THE EXPULSION OF THE GERMANS FROM
EASTERN-CENTRAL-EUROPE.
(Dokumentation der Vertreibung der Deutschen aus Ost-
Mitteleuropa.) Tr. Anon. Ed. Theodor Schieder. Bonn:
F. M. E. R. W. V., 1958. v. 24cm. [LC62]

DÖBLIN, Alfred, 1878-1957.
Alexanderplatz, Berlin. The story of Franz Biberkopf.
(Berlin, Alexanderplatz.) Tr. Eugene Jolas. NY: Ungar,
1958. 635p. 19cm. [LC62, IT11]

DÖNITZ, Karl, 1892- .
Memoirs, 10 years and 20 days. (10 Jahre und 20 Tage.)

Trs. R. H. Stevens and David Woodward. Cleveland: World, 1959. 500p. 23cm. [LC62, IT12]

Same. L: Weidenfeld, 1959. 500p. [IT12]

DÖRRIES, Hermann, 1895- .
Constantine and religious liberty. Tr. Roland H. Bainton. New Haven: Yale U. Pr., 1960. 141p. 21cm. [LC62, IT13]

DOHM, Christian Wilhelm von, 1751-1820.
Concerning the amelioration of the civil status of the mews. Tr. Helen Lederer. Ed. Ellis Rivkin. Cincinnati: H. U. C. -J. I. R., 1957. 841. 27cm. [LC62]

DOLLMANN, Eugen.
Call me coward. Tr. E. Fitzgerald (from ms). L: Kimber, 1956. 201p. (21.5cm.) 23cm. [LC62, B56, IT9]

DORMANN, Hans, 1923- .
Soldiers and no general. (Soldaten und kein General.) Trs. Robert Coben and Alan Earney. Sydney: Novak, 1958. 175, 165p. [IT11]

Same. L: Angus, 1958. 175p. 19cm. [LC62, B58, IT11]

Same. L: Hamilton, 1959. 158p. (17.5cm.) [B59]

DORNBERGER, Walter, 1895- .
V-2. (Der Schuss ins Weltall.) Trs. James Cleugh and Geoffrey Halliday. NY: Ballantine, 1958. 237p. [IT11]

Same. L: Hamilton, 1958. 192p. [B58, IT11]

DORRIES, Hermann. See Dörries, Hermann.

DREIKURS, Rudolf, 1897- .
Fundamentals of Adlerian psychology. (Einführung in die Individual-Psychologie.) Tr. Anon. (Pub. in London, 1935 as An introduction to individual psychology.) Jamaica: Know, 1958. 117p. 21cm. [LC62]

DREYER, Ernst Jürgen.
Selections in Rothenberg, 1959.

DROSTE-HÜLSHOFF, Annette Elizabeth, Freifrau von, 1797-1848
The Jew's beech. (Die Judenbuche.) Trs. Lionel and Doris Thomas. L: Calder, 1958. 80p. (19cm.) [LC 62, B58, IT11]

Selections in Flores. Anthol. 1960.

Selection in Loomis, C. G. 1960.

DRUDE, Paul Karl Ludwig, 1863-1906.
The theory of optics. Trs. C. Riborgmann and Robert A. Millikan. NY: Dover, 1959. 546p. 21cm. [LC62, IT12, IT13]

DUCRET, Siegfried.
Unknown porcelain of the 18th century. (Unbekannte Porzellane des 18. Jahrhunderts.) Tr. John Hayward. Frankfurt/Main: Woeller verlag, 1956. 142p. 25cm. [LC62]

DÜHREN, Eugen, pseud. (i. e. Bloch, Ivan, 1872-1922.) Sexual life in England, past and present. (Das Geschlechtsleben in England.) Tr. William H. Forstern. L: Arco, 1958. 664p. (22.5cm.) 23cm. [LC62, B58, IT11]

DÜRCKHEIM-MONTMARTIN, Karlfried, Graf von, 1896- .
The Japanese cult of tranquility. (Japan und die Kultur der Stille.) Tr. Eda O. Shiel. L: Rider, 1960. 106p. (107p.) (19cm.) 20cm. [LC62, B60]

DÜRRENMATT, Fr.
A dangerous game. (Die Panne.) Trs. Richard and Clara Winston. Illus. Rolf Lehmann. L: Cape, 1960. 95p. 21cm. [LC62, B60]

The judge and his hangman. (Der Richter und sein Henker.) Tr. Therese Pol. NY: Berkley, 1958. 143p. [IT12]

The pledge. (Das Versprechen, Requiem auf den Kriminalroman.) Trs. Richard and Clara Winston. L: Cape, 1959. 3-190p. (19.5cm.) [B59, IT12]

Same. 1st Am. ed. NY: Knopf, 1959. 183p. 21cm. [LC62, IT12]

Same. NY: New American Lib., 1960. 127p. [LC62, IT13]

Traps. (Die Panne.) Trs. Richard and Clara Winston. (1st Am. ed.), NY: Knopf, 1960. 114p. 21cm. [LC62, IT13]

The visit, a play in 3 acts. (Der Besuch der Alten Dame.) Adpt. Maurice Valency. NY: Random, 1958. 115p. 21cm. [LC62]

Same. NY: French, c1958. 108p. 19cm. [LC62]

DURES, A.
The writings. Tr. William M. Conway. L: Owen, 1958. 288p. 23cm. [LC62, B58, IT11]

Writings. Tr. W. Martin Conway. NY: Philosophical Lib., 1958. 288p. 23cm. [LC62, IT11]

DUKKER, Chrysostomus, 1927- .
The changing heart, the penance-concept of St. Francis of Assisi. (Umkehr des Herzens.) Tr. Bruce Malina. Chicago: Franciscan Herald, 1959. 156p. 22cm. [LC62, IT12]

DURNBAUGH, Donald F., comp. and tr.
European origins of the brethren. A source book on the beginnings of the Church of the Brethren in the early 18th cent. Elgin, Ill.: Brethren, 1958. 462p. 23cm. [LC62, IT11]

DUVOISIN, Roger (Antoine).
Fairy tales from Switzerland, The three sneezes, and other fairy tales. Tr. Anon. (1st ed.) L: Muller, 1958. 232p. (20.5cm.) [LC62, B58]

EBBINGHAUS, Hermann, 1850-1909.
Memory. A contribution to experimental psychology. Trs. Henry A. Ruger and Clara E. Bussenius. Providence: The Univ. Store, Brown U., 1956. 51p. 23cm. [LC62]

EBERHARD, Wolfram.
History of China. Tr. E. W. Dickes. 2nd ed. L: Routledge, 1960. 359p. (22.5cm.) [B60]

EBERMAYER, Erich and Meissner, Hans Otto.
Evil genius. The story of Joseph Goebbels. Tr. and
adpt. Louis Hagen. L: Hamilton, 1956. 207p. (18.5cm.)
[B56]

EBNER VON ESCHENBACH, Marie, Freifrau, 1830-1916.
Aphorisms. (Aphorismen.) Tr. G. H. Needler. Toronto:
Macheachern, c1959. 108p. 19cm. [LC62, IT13]

ECKARDT, Andre, 1884- .
Safo, the world writing system invented and elaborated by
A--E--. (Die neue Sinnschrift Safo als Einheitszeichen-
schrift der Völker.) Tr. Anon. Starnberg: Schraml,
1956. 22p. 21cm. [LC62]

ECKENER, Hugo.
My zeppelins. (Im Zeppelin über Länder und Meere.)
Tr. Douglas Robinson. L: Putnam, 1958. 216p.
(22.5cm.) 23cm. [LC62, B58, IT11]

ECKENER, Lotte.
Oberammergau, scene of the passion play. Tr. Leonard
F. Zwinger. Text Leo Hans Mally. Westminster, Md.:
Newman, 1960. 95p. 26cm. [LC62]

ECKHARDT, Meister. d. 1327.
Meister Eckhardt, an introduction to the study of his
works. Sel., annot. and tr. James M. Clark. L, NY:
Nelson, 1957. 267p. 22cm. (22.5cm.) [LC62, B57]

Meister Eckhardt. A modern tr. Raymond Bernard
Blakney. NY: Harper, 1957. 333p. 21cm. [LC62,
IT10]

Treatises and sermons. Tr. from Latin and Ger. James
M. Clark and John Vass Skinner. NY: Harper, 1958.
267p. 20cm. [LC62, IT11]

Same. L: Faber, 1958. 267p. 21cm. [LC62, B58,
IT11]

Meister Eckhardt speaks. A coll. of the teachings of the
famous German mystic. (M--E-- spricht.) Tr. Anon.
L: Blackfriars; NY: Philosophical Lib. 1957. 72p.
19cm. (18.5cm.) [LC62, B57, IT10]

EGGLER, Albert.
The Everest-Lhotse adventure. (Gipfel über den Wolken.)
Tr. Hugh Merrick. L: Allen; NY: Harper, 1957.
222p. (223p.) 23cm. [LC62, B57]

EGLI, Emil.
Europe from the air. (Flugbild Europas.) Tr. E. Osers.
Ed. Hans Richard Müller. Introd. Salvador de Madari-
aga. L: Harrap, 1959. 224p. (28.5cm.) [B58, IT12]

Same. NY: Funk, 1960. 223p. 29cm. [LC62, IT13]

EHEIM, Fritz and Winner, Gerhard, jt. authors.
History of the Fortress Wartenstein. (Geschichte der
Burg W--.) Tr. Carl Bayerschmidt. NY: Wrenner-
gren, 1958. 55p. [LC62, IT11]

EHRENBERG, Victor, 1891- .
The Greek state. (Der Griechische und der hellenist-
ische Staat.) Tr. Anon. Oxford: Blackwell; NY:
Barnes, 1960. 280p. 23cm. [LC62, IT13]

EHRHARD, Ludwig. See Erhard, Ludwig.

EHRLICH, Paul.
The collected papers of Paul Ehrlich. Comp. and ed. F.
Himmelweit. L: Pergamon, 1956. 653p. (25.5cm.)
[B56]

EIBL-EIBESFELD, Irenaeus.
Galapagos. Tr. Alan Houghton Broderick. L: MacGibbon, 1960. 192p. (22.5cm.) 23cm. [LC62]

Survey on the Galapagos Islands. Tr. Anon. Paris:
UNESCO, 1959. 31p. 28cm. [LC62]

EICHENDORFF, J. V.
Memoirs of a good-for-nothing. (Aus das Leben eines
Taugenichts.) Tr. B. Q. Morgan. NY: Ungar, 1960.
120p. 18cm. [LC62, IT13]

Selections in Flores, anthol. 1960.

Selections in Loomis, C. G. 1960.

EICHHORN, Franz.
The lost world of the Amazon. (In der grünen Hölle.)

EICHHORN, Franz--
Tr. Mervyn Savill. L: Souvenir, 1956. 188p. (22.5
cm.) [B56]

EICHMANN, Arnold Heinz.
Wilhelm Backhaus. Portraits Roger Hauert. Tr. Bar-
bara Wall. Geneva: Kister, c1958. 27p. 27cm.
[LC62]

Same. L: Rockliff, 1958. 31p. [B58]

EICHRODT, Walther, 1890- .
Man in the Old Testament. (Das Menschenverständnis des
Alten Testaments.) Trs. K. and R. Gregor-Smith. Chi-
cago: Allenson, 1956. 83p. 22cm. [LC62]

EID, Edward C., tr.
Mirror of the heart. Author unknown. Hauge Lutheran
Inner Mission Federation, 1959. [LC62]

EIMERT, Herbert, 1897- .
Electronic music. Tr. D. A. Sinclair. Ottawa: National Research Council of Canada, 1956. 4l. 27cm. [LC62]

The place of electronic music in the musical situation.
(Zur musikalischen Situation.) Tr. D. A. Sinclair. Ottawa: National Research Council of Canada, 1956. 14l.
28cm. [LC62]

Problems of electronic music notation. Tr. D. A. Sinclair. Ottawa: National Research Council of Canada,
1956. 9l. 28cm. [LC62]

EINSTEIN, Albert, 1879-1955.
Collected writings. Tr. Anon. NY: Readex Microprint,
1960. [LC62]

Einstein on peace. Eds. Otto Nathan and Heinz Norden.
Pref. Bertrand Russell. NY: Simon, 1960. 704p.
22cm. [LC62]

Essays in science. (From Mein Weltbild.) Tr. Alan
Harris. NY: Philosophical Lib., 1958. 125p. [IT11]

Ideas and opinions. (Mein Weltbild.) Tr. Sonja Barg-
mann. Ed. Carl Seelig et al. L: Redman, 1956. 377p.
23cm. [LC62, B56]

Investigations of the theory of the Brownian movement.
Ed. with notes by R. Fürth. Tr. A. D. Cowper. NY:
Dover, 1956. 119p. 21cm. [LC62]

The meaning of relativity. Tr. Edwin P. Adams. 1st
appendix Ernst G. Straus and 2nd appendix Sonja Barg-
mann. L: Methuen, 1956. 161p. 20cm. [LC62]

Relativity. The special and general theory. (Über die
spezielle und allgemeine Relativitaetstheorie.) Tr. Robert
W. Lawson. NY: Crown, 1956. 168p. 21cm. [LC62]

Same. L: Methuen, 1957. 165p. [LC62, B57]

Same. Gloucester, Mass.: Smith, 1959. 22cm. [LC62]

EINSTEIN, Albert. See Schilpp, Paul Arthur 1897- ., ed.
Albert Einstein, philosopher-scientist. Tr. Anon. 1st
Harper Torchbooks ed. NY: Harper, 1959. 2v. 781p.
21cm. [LC62]

EINSTEIN, Alfred.
Essays on music. Tr. Anon. 1st ed. NY: Norton,
1956. 265p. 23cm. [LC62]

Same. Pref. Ralph Leavis. L: Faber, c1958. 271p.
23cm. [LC62]

Mozart, his character, his work. Trs. Arthur Mendel
and Nathan Broder. 2nd ed. L: Cassell, 1956. 492p.
22cm.

Same. 1959. [LC62, B59]

A short history of music. (Geschichte der Musik.) Tr.
Eric Blom, et al. NY: Vintage, 1956. 205p. [LC62]

EIS, Egon, 1910- .
The forts of folly. The history of an illusion. (Illusion
der Sicherheit. Das Schicksal der grossen Bollwerke.)
Tr. A. J. Pomerans. L: Wolff; NY: Humanities, 1959.
271p. (22.5cm.) 23cm. [LC62, B58]

EKERT-ROTHOLZ, Alice Maria.
A net of gold. (Strafende Sonne-lockender Mond.) Trs.
R. and C. Winston. L: Cape, 1960. 415p. (20.5cm.)
21cm. [LC62, B60]

EKERT-ROTHOLZ, Alice Maria--
Same. NY: Viking, 1960. 437p. 22cm. [LC62, IT13]

The time of the dragons. (Wo Tränen verboten sind.)
Trs. Richard and Clara Winston. L: Cape, 1958. 476p.
(20.5cm.) 21cm. [LC62, B58, IT11]

Same. NY: Viking, 1958. 436p. 22cm. [LC62]

Same. 468p. 22cm. [LC62, IT11]

Same. NY: New American Lib., 1959. 479p. [IT12]

Same. L: Reprint Society, 1960. 404p. 20cm. [LC62]

ELDJARN, Kristjan, 1916- .
Ancient Icelandic art. (Alte isländische Kunst.) Tr.
Anon. Introd. and picture texts K--E--. Photos. Hanns
Reich, et al. München: Reich, c1957. 15p. 29cm.
[LC62]

ELERT, Werner, 1885-1955.
The Christian ethos. (Das christliche Ethos.) Tr. Carl
J. Schindler. Philadelphia: Muhlenberg, 1957. 451p.
24cm. [LC62]

ELLENBERGER, Hugo.
Vienna, metropolis on the Danube. (Wien, Weltstadt an
der Donau.) Tr. Dorothy Plummer. Vienna: Andermann, c1958. 61p. [LC62]

ELLENBERGER, Wilhelm, 1848-1929, et al.
An atlas of animal anatomy for artists. By W--E--. ,
H. Baum, and H. Dittrich. Tr. Helene Weinbaum. Ed.
Lewis S. Brown. 2nd ed. NY: Dover, 1956. 153p.
24 x 30cm. [LC62]

ELLERT, Gerhart, pseud. (i.e. Schmirger, Gertrud,
1900- .)
Knights of St. John. (Kreuzritter.) Tr. J. Brockett-
Pugh. Illus. A. Burgess Sharrocks. L: Lutterworth,
1958. 139p. 21cm. [LC62, B58, IT11]

ELTZBOCHER, Paul, 1868-192-.
Anarchism, exponents of the anarchist philosophy. (Der
Anarchismus.) Tr. Steven T. Byington. Ed. James J.
Martin. L: Freedom; NY: Libertarian, 1960. 272p.

109

(22.5cm.) 23cm. [LC62, B60, IT13]

EMERICUS A SANCTO STEPHANO, Father.
The great and little one of Prague. (Prägerisches Gross
und Klein.) Tr. Ludvik Nemec. Philadelphia: Reilly,
1959. 279p. 21cm. [LC62, IT13]

EMMRICH, Kurt, 1897- . See Bamm, Peter, pseud.

ENGELS, Fr.
The condition of the working class in England. (Die
Lage der arbeitenden Klasse in England.) Trs. and eds.
W. O. Henderson and W. H. Chaloner. Oxford: Black-
well; NY: Macmillan, 1958. 386p. 22cm. [LC62,
B58]

. . . on Marx's capital. Moscow: FLP House, 1960.
204p. 17cm. [LC62]

The origin of the family. Private property and the state.
(Der Ursprung der Familie.) Moscow: FLP House, 1959.
303p. [LC62]

The peasant war in Germany. (Der deutsche Bauern-
krieg.) Tr. Anon. Moscow: FLP House, 1956. 245p.
(247p.) (21cm.) 22cm. [LC62, B56]

Principles of communism. Tr. Paul M. Sweezy. Colom-
bo: 1956. 18p. 22cm. [LC62]

Socialism, utopian and scientific. Tr. Anon. Moscow,
FLP House, 1958. 126p. 17cm. [LC62]

ENGELS, Fr., joint author. See Marx, Karl.
The Holy family, or critique of critical critique. Moscow: FLP House, 1956. [LC62]

See Marx. Marx and Engels on Malthus. Sel. from the
writings of Marx and Engels dealing with the theories of
Thomas Ronald L. Malthus. Trs. Dorothea L. Meek and
Ronald L. Meek. New Delhi: Peoples Pub., 1956.
[LC62]

ENGESSER, Friedrich. See Geiger, Hermann, 1914- .
Geiger and the Alps. Lucerne: Bucher, 1958. [LC62]

ENKEL, Fritz.
The production of sound effects for radio. Tr. D. A.
Sinclair. Ottawa: National Research Council of Canada,
1956. 71. 28cm. [LC62]

ERANOS-JAHRBUCH.
Man and time by Henry Corbin, et al. Trs. R. Manheim
and R. F. C. Hull. NY: Pantheon, 1957. 414p. [LC62]

Same. L: Routledge, 1958. 414p. [LC62, B58]

The mysteries. Papers from the Eranos yearbooks.
Trs. R. Manheim and R. F. C. Hull. Ed. Joseph Campbell. L: Routledge, 1956. 476p. [B56]

Spiritual disciplines. Papers from the Eranos yearbooks.
By Rudolf Bernoulli, et al. Trs. Ralph Manheim and
R. F. C. Hull. NY: Pantheon, 1960. 506p. [LC62]

ERBEN, Walter.
Joan Miro. (J--M--.) Tr. Michael Bullock. L: Hum-
phries; NY: Braziller, 1959. 159p. (24.5cm.) 25cm.
[LC62, B59]

Marc Chagall (Der Maler mit den Engelsflügeln.) Tr.
Michael Bullock. L: Thames; NY: Praeger, 1957.
158p. (25.5cm.) 26cm. [LC62, B57]

ERDMANN, Kurt, 1901- .
Oriental carpets, an account of their history. (Der ori-
entalische Knüpfteppich, Versuch einer Darstellung seiner
Geschichte.) Tr. Charles Grant Ellis. L: Zwemmer,
1960. 78p. 28cm. [LC62]

Oriental carpets. An essay on their history. Tr.
Charles Grant Ellis. NY: Universe, 1960. 78p. 28cm.
[LC62]

ERFURT, Werner, pseud.
Moscow's policy in Germany. A study in contemporary
history. (Die sowjetrussische Deutschlandpolitik.) Tr.
Patrick Lynch. Esslingen: Bechtle, 1959. 138p. [LC
62]

ERHARD, Ludwig.
Prosperity through competition. (Wohlstand für alle.)
Trs. and eds. Edith Temple Roberts and John B. Wood.

L: Thames, 1958. 260p. (263p.) (22.5cm.) [LC62, B58]

Same. NY: Praeger, 1958. 260p. 23cm. [LC62]

Same. 2nd rev. ed. L: Thames, 1959. 260p. 23cm. [LC62]

Same. 3rd ed. L: Thames, 1960. 260p. 22cm. [LC62]

ERHART, Ludwig. See Erhard, Ludwig.

ERTL, Hans, 1908- .
Now up, now down, photographs of Bolivia. (Mal oben, mal unten, Bilder aus Bolivien.) Span. and Eng. tr. supervised by Dr. Franz A. Ressel. München: Bruckmann, 1958. 143p. 25cm. [LC62]

ESCH, Ludwig, 1883- .
New life in Christ. (Neue Lebensgestaltung in Christus.) Tr. W. T. Swain. Cork: Mercier, 1956. 294p. 22cm. [B58]

Same. Westminster, Md.: Newman, 1957. 294p. 22cm. [LC62]

ESCHENBACH, Wolfram von. See Wolfram von Eschenbach.

ESSEN. Villa Hügel. 5000 years art from India. Tr. Anon. Essen: 1959. 420p. 24cm. [LC62]

ESSER, Kajetan, 1913- .
The order of St. Francis, its spirit and its mission in the Kingdom of God. (Der Orden des heiligen Franziskus, seine geistige Gestalt und seine Aufgabe im Reiche Gottes.) Tr. Ignatius Brady. Chicago: Franciscan Herald, 1959. 60p. 19cm. [LC62]

EULENSPIEGEL.
The further adventures of Till Eulenspiegel. By Thomas Yoseloff. Based upon a Tr. Lillien Stuckey. NY: Yoseloff, 1957. 122p. 24cm. [LC62]

Till Eulenspiegel, the clown. (T--E--, zwölf seiner Geschichten frei nacherzählt.) Retold by Erich Kastner.

EULENSPIEGEL--
[sic] Trs. Richard and Clara Winston. Illus. Walter
Trier. NY: Messner, 1957. 70p. 27cm. [LC62]

EUROPEAN LEAGUE FOR ECONOMIC COOPERATION . . .
Topical talks of monetary policy in Europe. Tr. Anon.
Bruxelles: Imprimerie des Sciences, 1960. 14p. 22cm.
[LC62]

EUROPEAN ASSOCIATION FOR THE STUDY OF REFUGEE
PROBLEMS.
(Flüchtlingsprobleme in Berlin.) Tr. Anon. München,
1956. 59p. 26cm. [LC62]

THE EVANGELICAL CHURCH IN BERLIN AND THE
SOVIET ZONE OF GERMANY.
Tr. Patrick Lynch. Witten: Eckart Verlag, c1959. 51p.
21cm. [LC62]

EYCK, Erich, 1878- .
Bismarck and the German empire. A summary of the au-
thor's three-volume Bismarck. (Pub. in Ger.) Tr.
Anon. L: Allen, c1958. 327p. (22cm.) [LC62]

THE EZZO-SONG. (Ezzolied.) In Loomis, C. G. Selections. 1958.

FACHTAGUNG ELEKTRONISCHE RECHENMASCHINEN UND
INFORMATION-VERARBEITUNG.
Electronical digital computers and information processing.
(Elektronische Rechenmaschinen und Informationsver-
arbeitung.) Tr. Anon. Eds. A. Walter and W. Hoffmann.
Braunschweig: Vieweg, 1957. 229p. 30cm. [LC62]

FAHNING, Hans.
Hamburg, a banking centre. Tr. Anon. Hamburg:
Holler, 1956. 96p. [LC62]

THE FAIRY TALE BOOK, a sel. of 28 traditional stories
from Fr., Ger., Dan., Russ., and Japanese, by Hans
Christian Andersen et al. Tr. Marie Ponsot. NY: Simon, 1958. 156p. 34cm. [LC62]

FALLADA, Hans, pseud. (i.e. Ditzen, Rudolf Wilhelm
Friedrich.)
Little man, what now? (Kleiner Mann, was nun.) Tr.

Eric Sutton. NY: Ungar, 1957. 393p. 21cm. [LC62,
IT11]

That rascal, Fridolin. (Fridolin der freche Dachs.) Trs.
Ruth Michaelis-Jena and Arthur Ratcliff. Illus. Imre Hof-
bauer. L: Heinemann, 1959. 166p. (20.5cm.) 21cm.
[LC62, B59, IT12]

Same. NY: Pantheon 1959. 156p. 22cm. [LC62]

FANGER, Horst, 1919- .
A life for a life. (Wir selber sind das Rad.) Trs. Richard and Clara Winston. L: Hale, 1956. 190p. 19cm.
(19.5cm.) [LC62, B56, IT9]

FANNING, Robert Joseph, 1916- .
Kaethe Kollwitz. (K--K--.) Published in conjunction with
the Kollwitz exhibition in the Amerika Häuser in West
Germany. Tr. Anon. Karlsruhe: Müller, 1956. 137p.
24cm. [LC62]

FARBENFABRIKEN BAYER AKTIENGESELLSCHAFT.
Bayer pocket book for the plastic industry. Tr. Anon.
Leverkusen, 1959. 464p. 18cm. [LC62]

FAUST.
(Gustaf Gründgens. Faust in Bildern.) Tr. Rosemarie
Clausen. Braunschweig: Westermann, 1960. 77p. 33cm.
[LC62]

THE FEAR MAKERS, an anonymous novel. (Die Angstmach-
er.) (supposed author, Wilfrid Schilling.) Tr. Oliver
Coburn. L: Joseph, 1959. 296p. (20.5cm.) [LC62,
B59, IT12]

Same. NY: Doubleday, 1960. 312p. 22cm. [LC62]

FEDDERSEN, Martin, 1888- .
Chinese porcelain. (Chinesische Lackarbeiten, ein Brevier.)
Tr. Anon. Braunschweig: Klinkhardt, 1956. 46p. 20cm.
[LC62]

FEDERN, Paul, 1871-1950.
Ego psychology and the psychoses. (Ichpsychologie und
die Psychosen.) Tr. Anon. Ed. with introd. E. Weiss.
NY: Basic, 1960. 375p. [LC62]

FEGER, Robert.   See Liehl, Ekkehard.
Black Forest.

FELD, Friedrich, pseud.   (i.e. Rosenfeld, Friedrich,
1902- .)
The musical umbrella.   Tr. W. Kersley Holmes.   Illus.
Ferelith Eccles Williams.   L: Blackie, c1958.   92p.
(5-92p.)   (20.5cm.)   21cm.   [LC62, B58, IT11]

The runaway echo.   (Echo auf Reisen.)   Tr. W. Kersley
Holmes.   L: Blackie, 1960.   (5-92p.)   (20.5cm.)   [B60,
IT13]

The talking cat.   (Die Katze die alle Sprachen konnte.)
Tr. W. Kersley Holmes.   Illus. Norman Mommens.   L:
Blackie, 5-91p.   (23.5cm.)   [B60]

FELSKO, Elsa.
Portraits of wild flowers.   (Blumenatlas.)   Tr. Anon.
Oxford: Cassirer, 1959.   207p.   [IT13]

FERENCZI, Sandor and Rank, Otto.
(1) Sex in psycho-analysis, contributions to psychoanalysis.   (2) The development of psycho-analysis.   Auth. trs.
(1) Ernest Jones, (2) Caroline Newton.   NY: Dover,
1960.   288, 68p.   21cm.   [LC62]

FERNAN, J.   IT12 error.   See Fernau, Joachim.

FERNAU, Joachim.
Captain Pax.   A report on the terribleness and greatness
of men.   (Bericht von der Furchtbarkeit und Grösse der
Männer.)   Tr. Robert Kee.   L: Constable, 1960.   134p.
(135p.)   (19.5cm.)   20cm.   [LC62, B60]

Encyclopaedia of old masters.   Tr. Anon.   L: Thames,
1959.   334p.   [LC62, IT12]

FEUCHTWANGER, Lion, 1884-1958.
Jeptha and his daughter.   (Jefta und seine Tochter.)   Trs.
Eithne Wilkins and Ernst Kaiser.   L: Hutchinson, 1958.
271p.   (20.5cm.)   [B58, IT11]

Same.   NY: Putnam, 1958.   255p.   22cm.   [LC62, IT11]

Same.   NY: New American Lib., 1960.   221p.   [IT13]

Raquel, the Jewess of Toledo. (Die Judin von Toledo.)
Trs. Ernst Kaiser and Eithne Wilkins. L: Hutchinson,
1956. 414p. (415p.) (20.5cm.) 21cm. [LC62, B56,
IT9]

Same. NY: Messner, 1956. 433p. 21cm. [LC62,
IT9]

Same. NY: New American Lib., 1957. 379p. [IT10]

Same. NY: Signet Pocket Books, 1960.

This is the hour. A novel about Goya. Trs. H. T. Lowe-
porter and Frances Fawcett. NY: Heritage, 1956. 522p.
25cm. [LC62]

The widow Capet, a play in three acts. (Die Witwe
Capet.) Los Angeles: Pacific Press, 1956. 86p. 29cm.
[LC62]

FEUERBACH, Ludwig Andreas, 1804-1872.
The essence of Christianity. Tr. George Eliot. Introd.
essay Karl Barth. Fwd. H. Richard Niebuhr. NY:
Harper, 1957. 339p. 21cm. [LC62, IT10]

Same. Ed. and abridged E. Graham Waring and F. W.
Strothmann. NY: Ungar, 1957. 65p. 21cm. [LC62,
IT10]

FICHTE, Johann Gottlieb, 1762-1814.
The vocation of man. Tr. Anon. Ed. with introd. Rod-
erick M. Chisholm. NY: Liberal Arts, 1956. 154p.
21cm. [LC62]

FICHTENAU, Heinrich.
The Carolingian empire. (Das Karolingische Imperium.)
Tr. Peter Munz. Oxford: Blackwell, 1957. 196p.
22cm. (22.5cm.) [LC62, B57, IT10]

FIEBIGER, Josef, 1870- . See Trautmann, Alfred, 1884-
1952.
Fundamentals of the histology of domestic animals. Tr.
Anon. Tr. and rev. from 8th and 9th Ger. eds. NY:
Comstock, 1957. 25cm. [LC62, IT10]

FIEDLER, Konrad, 1841-1895.
On judging works of visual art. Trs. Henry Schaefer-

FIEDLER, Konrad--
simmern and Fulmer Mood. Berkeley: U. of California
Pr., 1957. 76p. 20cm. [LC62, IT11]

FIERZ, Markus, ed.
Theoretical physics in the twentieth century, a memorial
volume to Wolfgang Pauli. Ed. M--F--. and V. F.
Weisskopf. NY: Interscience, 1960. 328p. 24cm.
[LC62]

FILCHNER, Wilhelm, 1877- . Przybyllok, Erich and
Hagen, Toni.
Route-mapping and position-locating in unexplored regions.
Basel: Birkhauser; NY: Academic, 1957. 288p. 25cm.
[LC62, IT10]

FISCHER, Balthasar.
Questions the catechism didn't answer. 50 catechetical
instructions on the liturgy of the church. Tr. Anon.
Collegeville, Minn.: The Liturgical Pr., n.d. 114p.
18cm. [LC62]

FISCHER, Helen.
Peril is my companion. Tr. Eleanor Brockett. L:
Hale, 1957. 185p. (186p.) (22.5cm.) 23cm. [LC62,
B57, IT10]

FIRKEL, Eva.
Woman in the modern world. (Schicksalsfragen der Frau.)
Tr. Hilda C. Graef. L: Burns, 1956. 211p. 22cm.
[LC62]

Same. Chicago: Fides, 1956. 211p. 23cm. [LC62]

FISCHER, Edwin, 1886- .
Beethoven's pianoforte sonatas. (Ludwig van Beethovens
Klaviersonaten.) Trs. Stanley Godman and Paul Ham-
burger. L: Faber, 1959. 118p. [IT12]

FISCHER, Hans, 1909-1958.
Puss in boots, fairy tale adpt. from Charles Perrault.
(Der gestiefelte Kater.) Tr. Anon. NY: Harcourt,
c1959. unp. 29cm. [LC62, IT12]

FISCHER, Herbert, ed. (same as Hubert Fischer.)
An introduction to a Catholic catechism, its concepts,
usage and aims. (Einführung in den neuen Kathechismus.)

Tr. Bernard Adkins. Pref. Josef Andreas Jungmann. Introd. Clifford Howell. Freiberg: Herder; L: Burns, 1960. 169p. (20.5cm.) 21cm. [LC62, B60]

Same. NY: Herder, 1960. [LC62]

FISCHER, Klaus, 1919- .
Caves and temples of the Jains. Tr. Anon. 1st ed. Aliganj: World Jain Mission, 1956. 39p. 25cm. [LC62]

FISCHER, Ottokar.
Illustrated magic. Trs. and ed. June Mussey and Fulton Oursler. Introd. Fulton Oursler and Harry Kellar. n. p. 19--. 244l. [LC62]

FISCHER, Paul, 1906- .
Variegated foliage plants. (Buntblättrige Pflanzen.) Tr. and ed. Corry van Alphen. L: Blandford, 1960. 22cm. (22.5cm.) [LC62, B60]

FISCHLI, Hans, 1906- .
Hans Aeschbacher. Einleitung von Hans Fischli, avant-propo de Michel Seuphor (Fischli's foreword also in Eng.) Neuchatel: Editions du Griffon, 1959. 75p. 31cm. [LC62]

FITTKAU, Gerhard.
My thirty-third year, a priest's experience in a Russian work camp. (Mein dreiunddreissigstes Jahr.) Tr. Anon. NY: Farrar, 1958. 263p. 22cm. [LC62]

FLAIG, Walther, 1893- .
Along the Rhine. (Entlang dem Rhein. Strom und Strassen, Städte, Berge, Burgen.) Tr. Anon. Maps and sketches Lajos von Horvath. L, NY: Thames, 1957 23p. (24p.) 24cm. (24.5cm.) [LC62, B57, IT10]

Through the engadine. (Vom Engadin zum Comersee.) Tr. Anon. L: Thames, 1956. 19p. (20p.) (24cm.) [LC62, B56, IT9]

FLASCHE, Hans, 1911- .
Romance languages and literatures as presented in German doctoral dissertations, 1885-1950. (Die Sprachen und Literaturen der Romanen im Spiegel der deutschen Universitätsschriften, 1885-1950. Eine Bibliographie.) Added t. p. in Ger. and Fr. Issued also as Bd. 3 of Bonner

FLASCHE, Hans--
Beiträge zur Bibliotheks- und Bücherkunde.   Bonn:
Bouvier, 1958.   299p.   [LC62]

FLEMING, P.
Sel. in Loomis, C. G. Sel. 1958.

FLEMMING, Ernst Richard, 1866- .
Encyclopedia of textiles, decorative fabrics from antiquity
to the beginning of the 19th century including the Far East
and Peru. (Das Textilwerk.) Tr. Anon. Rev. introd.
Renate Jaques. L: Zwemmer, 1958. 306 plates. [LC
62, B58, IT11]

Same. Ed. and trs. Renate Jaques and Ernst Flemming.
Rev. new material added. NY: Praeger, 1958. 306p.
(29.5cm.) 30cm. [LC62, B58]

FLESCH, Karl, 1873-1944.
The memoirs. Tr. Hans Keller. L: Rockliff, 1957.
393p. 22cm. (22.5cm.) [LC62, B58, IT10]

Same. NY: Macmillan, 1958. 393p. [LC62, IT11]

The memoirs of Carl Flesch. Tr. Hans Keller. Ed.
Hans Keller in collaboration with C. F. Flesch. L: Rockliff, 1957. 393p. 22cm. (22.5cm.) [LC62, B58]

Same. NY: Macmillan, 1958. 393p. 22cm. [LC62]

Same. 406p. [IT11]

FLIESS, Wilhelm, 1858-1939. See Freud, Sigmund, 1856-
1939.
The origins of psychoanalysis. Letters, drafts and notes
to Wilhelm Fliess, 1887-1902. Tr. Anon. Garden City,
NY: Doubleday, 1957. [LC62, IT10]

FLOHN, Hermann.
The climate of the high mountains in Central Asia. (Be-
merkungen zur Klimatologie von Hochasien.) Tr. Anon.
(From Meteorologische Rundschau, vol. 9, no. 5-6, May-
June, 1956.) 131. 29cm. [LC62]

FLORA, Paul.
Viva vamp. A book of photographs in praise of vamps
from Mae West to Marilyn Monroe, from Marlene Dietrich

to Brigitte Bardot. Illus. Commentary Paul Flora. Poetical salute, Ogden Nash. NY: McKay, 1960. unp. 21cm. [LC62]

Flora's fauna. Cartoons and drawings by Paul Flora, Austrian wit and humor, pictorial. 1st Am. ed. Tr. Anon. Indianapolis: Bobbs-Merrill, 1959. unp. 27cm. [LC62]

FLORES, Angel, 1900- .
An anthology of German poetry from Hölderlin to Rilke in Eng. Tr. 1st ed. Garden City, NY: Doubleday, (L: Mayflower), 1960. 458p. (18.5cm.) 19cm. [LC62, B60, IT13]

Nineteenth century German tales. Tr. Anon. 1st ed. Garden City, NY: Doubleday, 1959. 390p. 19cm. [LC62, IT12]

FOCHLER-HAUKE, Gustav, 1906- .
Our world and its beginning. (Am Anfang schuf Gott Himmel und Erde.) Tr. W. H. Johnston. L: Oldhams, 1958. 352p. (25.5cm.) 26cm. [LC62, B59, IT12]

FOERSTER, Werner and Quell, Gottfried.
Bible keywords from Gerhard Kittel's (Theologisches Wörterbuch zum Neuen Testament.) Tr. Anon. Notes H. P. Kingdon. L: Black, 1958. 121p. (20.5cm.) [LC62, B58]

FOREL, F.
The unknown ally. The German expellees, a report. Tr. Anon. Göttingen, 1960. 15p. 19cm. [LC62]

FORSTER, Leonard Wilson, 1913- .
The Penguin book of German verse, with plain prose translations of each poem. Introd. and ed. L--F--. Hardmondsworth, Baltimore: Penguin, 1957. 466p. 18cm. [LC62, B57]

A 4-FIBEL.
Trs. Ted A. Woerner and John A. Bitzer. Huntsville, Ala.: Army Ballistic Missile Agency, Redstone Arsenal, 1957. 163l. 20 x 26cm. [LC62, IT13]

FOWKES, Robert Allen, 1913- . Ed. and tr.
(Literatur Auswahl, aus den Werken von Lessing, et al.)

120

FOWKES, Robert Allen--
NY: Cortina, 1960. 59p. 24cm. [LC62]

FRANCK, Klaus.
The works of Affonso Eduardo Reidy. Trs. Mary Hottinger and D. Q. Stephenson. Introd. S. Giedion. Text
Klaus Franck. L: Tiranti, 1960. 144p. (22.5 x 26.5
cm.) [B60]

FRANK, Bruno, 1887-1945.
Tempest in teapot, comedy in three acts. Tr. Julian
Leigh. n.p., n.d. TW. 120l. 28cm. [LC62]

FRANK, Wolfgang, 1909- .
The sea wolves. A war book. (Die Wölfe und der Ad-
miral.) Trs. R. O. B. Long and George Creasy. L:
World Distrib., 1957. 256p. (17cm.) [B57]

The sea wolves. The story of German U-boats at war.
(Die Wölfe und der Admiral.) Tr. R. O. B. Long. NY:
Ballantine, 1958. 220p. [IT11]

FRANK, Wolfgang, 1909- , and Rogge, Bernhard, 1901- .
The German raider Atlantis. (Schiff 16. Die Kaperfahrt
des schweren Hilfskreuzers.) Tr. R. O. B. Long. NY:
Ballantine, 1956. 154p. 21cm. [LC62, IT9]

Under ten flags. The story of the German commerce
raider Atlantis. (Schiff 16. die Kaperfahrt des schweren
Hilfskreuzers.) Tr. R. O. B. Long. L: Weidenfeld, 1957.
185p. 22cm. [LC62, IT9]

FRANKE, Herbert Werner, 1927- .
Wilderness under the earth. (Wildnis unter der Erde.)
Tr. Mervyn Savill. L: Lutterworth, 1958. 204p. 22cm.
[LC62, B58, IT11]

FRANKL, Paul, 1878- .
The Gothic, literary sources and interpretations through
eight centuries. Tr. Anon. Princeton, N.J.: Princeton
U. Pr., 1960. 916p. 25cm. [LC62]

Three articles on stained glass. Tr. Anon. Berlin:
n.p. 1956-1957. 3 pts. in 1 vol. 31cm. [LC62, IT10]

FRANKL, Viktor Emil.
The doctor and the soul, an introduction to logotherapy.

Trs. Richard and Clara Winston. NY: n.p. 1960. 279p.
[LC62, IT13]

From deathcamp to existentialism. A psychiatrist's path
to a new therapy. (Ein Psycholog erlebt das Konzentrationslager.) Tr. Ilse Lasch. Boston: Beacon, 1959.
111p. 22cm. [LC62, IT12]

FRAUENDORFER, Sigmund von.
Classification scheme of agricultural science. Tr. Anon.
3rd rev. enl. ed. L: Lockwood, 1960. 159p. 24cm.
[B60]

FREGE, Gottlob, 1848-1925.
The foundations of arithmetic. (Die Grundlagen der Arith-
mctik.) Tr. J. L. Austin. Oxford: Blackwell. 2nd rev.
ed., 1959. 119p. 22cm. [LC62]

Translations from the philosophical writings of G--F--.
Tr. Anon. Eds. Peter Geach and Max Black. 2nd ed.
Oxford: Blackwell, 1960. 244p. (22.5cm.) 23cm.
[LC62, B60]

FREIDANK.
Sel in Loomis, C. G. Sel. 1958.

FREIDIN, Seymour and Richardson, William, eds.
The fatal decisions by Werner Kreipe et al. Tr. Constan-
tine Fitzgibbon. Commentary Siegfried Westphal. Fwd.
S. L. A. Marshall. NY: Sloan, 1956. 302p. 22cm.
[LC62, IT9]

The fatal decisions. Six decisive battles of the second
world war from the viewpoint of the vanquished. Tr.
Constantine Fitzgibbon. Commentary Siegfried Westphal.
Introd. Cyril Falls. L: Joseph, 1956. 261p. (23.5cm.)
24cm. [LC62, B56]

FREIER DEUTSCHER GEWERKSCHAFTSBUND.
International forum of the Confederation of Free German
Trade Unions. Tr. Anon. Leipzig: 1960. 72p. [LC62]

FREIER DEUTSCHER GEWERKSCHAFTSBUND 5. KONGRESS,
BERLIN, 1959.
Speeches at the 5th FDGB Congress in Berlin from Oc-
tober 26/31, 1959. Walter Ulbricht and Hans Jendretzky.
Tr. Anon. n.p. 1960. 791. 30cm. [LC62]

THE FRENCH ALPS FROM MONT BLANC TO THE RIVIERA.
(Französische Alpenstrassen.) Tr. Anon. L, NY: Thames,
c1959. (20p.) (24.5cm.) [LC62, B59]

FREUD, Anna, 1895- .
The ego and the mechanisms of defense. (Das Ich und die
Abwehrmechanismen.) Tr. Cecil Baines. NY: Interna-
tional U. Pr., 1957. 196p. 22cm. [LC62]

Psychoanalysis for teachers and parents, introductory lec-
tures. (Einführung in die Psychoanalyse für Pädagogen.)
Tr. Barbara Low. Boston: Beacon, 1960. 119p. 21cm.
[LC62, IT13]

The psycho-analytical treatment for children. Technical
lectures and essays. Tr. Nancy Procter-Gregg. NY:
International U. Pr., 1959. 98p. 23cm. [LC62, IT13]

FREUD, Sigmund, 1856-1939.
An autobiographical study, inhibitions symptoms and anxiety.
The question of lay analysis, and other works. Tr. (under
gen. editorship) James Strachey in coll. with Anna Freud,
assis. Alix Strachey and Alan Tyson. Vol. 20. L: Hogarth, 1959. 22cm. [LC62, B60]

Beyond the pleasure principle. (Jenseits des Lustprinzips.)
Tr. James Strachey. NY: Bantam, c1959. 121p. [LC
62, IT12]

The case of Schreber. Papers on technique, and other
works. Tr. (under gen. editorship) James Strachey, in
coll. with Anna Freud, assis. Alix Strachey and Alan Tyson. Vol. 12. L: Hogarth, 1958. 373p. 22cm. (22.5
cm.) [LC62, B58]

Civilization and its discontents. (Das Unbehagen in der
kultur.) Tr. Joan Riviere. L: Hogarth, 1957. 144p.
23cm. [LC62]

Same. Garden City, NY: Doubleday, 1958. 105p. 19cm.
[LC62]

Collected papers. (Sammlung kleiner Schriften zu Neuro-
senlehre.) Authorized tr. under supervision Joan Riviere.
Trs. Alix and James Strachey. (Vol. III). Vol. V ed.
James Strachey. L: Hogarth, 1956. 5v. 25cm. [LC62]

Same. NY: Basic, 1959. 5v. 22cm. [LC62, IT12]

Delusion and dream, and other essays. Tr. Anon. Ed. and introd. Philip Rieff. Boston: Beacon, 1956. 238p. 21cm. [LC62, IT9]

Dreams in folklore by S--F-- and D. E. Oppenheim. Tr. A. M. O. Richards. L: Bailery; NY: International U. Pr., 1958. 111p. 21cm. [LC62, B58, IT11]

The ego and the id. Tr. Anon. L: Hogarth, 1957. 1v. [LC62, IT10]

Future of an illusion. (Zukunft einer Illusion.) Tr. W. D. Robson-Scott. Garden City, NY: Doubleday, 1957. 102p. 18cm. [LC62]

A general introduction to psychoanalysis. (Vorlesungen..) Tr. of rev. ed. Joan Riviere. Garden City: Permabooks, 1956. 480p. 18cm. [LC62]

Same. NY: Washington Square, 1960. 480p. [IT13]

A general selection from his works. Tr. Anon. Garden City: Doubleday, Anchor, 1957. 294p. 18cm. [LC62]

General selection from the works of Sigmund Freud. Ed. J. Rickman. NY: Liveright, 1957. 294p. 22cm. [LC62]

Group psychology and the analysis of the ego. Tr. James Strachey. Introd. Franz Alexander. Rev. ed. L: Hogarth, 1959. 85p. [LC62]

Same. NY: Bantam, 1960. 108p. [LC62]

An infantile neurosis and other works. Tr. and ed. James Strachey et al. Vol. 17. L: Hogarth, 1955. i.e. 1956. 303p. (22.5cm.) [B56]

The interpretation of dreams. Tr. and ed. James Strachey. NY: Basic, 1960. 692p. [LC62]

Jensen's "Gradiva" and other works. Tr. under editorship James Strachey, in coll. Anna Freud, assis. Alix Strachey and Alan Tyson. Vol. 9. L: Hogarth, 1959. 279p. 22cm. [LC62, B60]

FREUD, Sigmund--
Jokes and their relation to the unconscious. (Der Witz
und seine Beziehung zum Unbewussten.) Tr. and ed. James
Strachey. L: Routledge, 1960. 258p. 22cm. (22.5cm.)
[LC62, B60]

Same. NY: Norton, 1960. 258p. 22cm. [LC62, IT13]

Jokes and their relation to the unconscious. Tr. under
editorship James Strachey, in coll. with Anna Freud, assis.
Alix Strachey and Alan Tyson. Vol. 8. L: Hogarth, 1960.
258p. 22cm. [LC62]

Letters. Trs. T. and J. Stern. Sel. and ed. Ernst L.
Freud. NY: Basic, 1960. 470p. 25cm. [LC62, IT13]

Moses and the Monotheism. (Der Mann Moses und die
monothetistische Religion.) Tr. Katherine Jones. NY:
Vintage, 1957. 178p. 19cm. [LC62]

New introductory lectures on psycho-analysis. Tr. W. H.
J. Sprott. L: Hogarth, 1957. 239p. 23cm. [LC62]

On creativity and the unconscious. Papers . . . sel.
Benjamin Nelson. NY: Harper, 1958. 310p. 21cm.
[LC62]

On the history of the psychoanalytic movement. Tr. and
ed. James Strachey et al. Vol. 14. L: Hogarth, 1957.
374p. (22cm.) [B58]

The origins of psychoanalysis. Letters, drafts, and notes
to Wilhelm Fliess, 1887-1902. Trs. Eric Mosbacher and
James Strachey. Eds. Marie Bonaparte, Anna Freud,
Ernst Kris. Introd. Ernst Kriss. Garden City, NY:
Doubleday, 1957. 384p. 19cm. [LC62, IT10]

An outline of psycho-analysis. Tr. James Strachey. L:
Hogarth, 1959. 83p. 22cm. [LC62]

Psychopathology of everyday life. (Zur Psychopathologie
des Alltagslebens über Vergessen, Vergreifen, Alberglauben
und Irrtum.) Tr. S. S. Brill. L: Benn, 1956. 239p.
19cm. [LC62]

Same. NY: NAL, 1956. 168p. 18cm. [LC62]

Same. L: Collins, 1958. 180p. (18cm.) [B58]

The standard edition of the complete psychological works of S--F--. Tr. and ed. James Strachey in coll. with Anna Freud, assist. Alix Strachey and Alan Tyson. L: Hogarth and Institute of Psycho-Analysis, 1955-1960. 24v. 22cm. [LC62, B56, 58, 60]

Totem and taboo. (Totem und Tabu.) Authorized tr. James Strachey. L: Routledge, 1960. 172p. (22.5cm.) [B60]

Same. Tr. A. A. Brill. NY: Random, 1960. 207p. 19cm. [LC62, IT13]

FREUD, Sigmund. See Breuer, Josef. Studies on hysteria. Tr. Anon. L: Hogarth, 1956. [LC62]

Same. NY: Basic, 1957. [LC62]

FREUDENBERG, Walter.
The hide and skin markets of the world. (Die Häute- und Fellmarkte der Welt.) Tr. Anon. Ilford: Essex, 1959. 223p. [LC62]

FREYTAG, Heinrich.
The Contax way. The Contax photographer's companion. Tr. and adpt. Gerald R. Sharp. L, NY: Focal, 1956. (284p.) 287p. (21.5cm.) 22cm. [LC62, B57]

The Contaflex way. The Contaflex photographer's companion. L, NY: Focal, 1957. (310p.) 312p. (21.5cm.) 22cm. [LC62, B57, IT10]

Same. Tr. and adpt. Hans Wolff. L, NY: Focal, c1957. 309p. (21.5cm.) 22cm. [LC62, B58, IT10]

Same. 3rd ed. tr. and adapt. Hans Wolff. L: Focal, 1959, (1960). (311p.) 312p. (21.5cm.) [LC62, B59, IT13]

FREYTAG, Walter.
The Gospel and the religions. A biblical enquiry. (Das Rätsel der Religionen und die biblische Antwort.) Tr. Anon. L: SCM, 1957. 47p. (21.5cm.) 22cm. [LC62, B57]

FREYTAG, Walter--
Same. 1956. [IT10]

FRIEDENAU, Theo.
The constitutional state from two points of view. Theory
and practice of law in the democratic and totalitarian or-
bits. Tr. Anon. Ankara: Ankara U., n.d. [LC62]

Injustice becomes law. The present situation of the administration of justice in the Soviet zone of Germany.
n.p., n.d. 57p. 23cm. [LC62]

FRIEDENTHAL, Richard.
Leonardo da Vinci, a pictorial biography. (L--, eine
Bildbibliographie.) Tr. Margaret Shenfield. NY: Viking,
c1959. 143p. 24cm. [LC62, IT13]

Same. L: Thames, 1960. 143p. (144p.) 24cm. [LC
62, B60, IT13]

FRIEDLAENDER, Leo Cornelius, ed.
Vienna. (Wien.) Tr. Marianne Schön. Wien: Bergland
Verlag, 1956. 63p. 17cm. [LC62]

FRIEDLÄNDER, Max J., 1867-1958.
Early Netherlandish paintings from van Eyck to Bruegel.
(Die frühe niederlandische Maler von van Eyck bis Bruegel.) Tr. Marguerite Kay. L, NY: Phaidon, 1956.
425, 296p. (27.5cm.) [LC62, B56, IT9]

Same. NY: Phaidon, 1956. 141p. 24cm. [LC62, IT9]

On art and connoisseurship. Tr. Tancred Borenius.
Boston: Beacon, 1960. 284p. 21cm. [LC62, IT13]

FRIEDLÄNDER, Paul, 1882- .
Plato. (Platon.) An introduction. Tr. Hans Meyerhoff.
L: Routledge, 1958. 423p. (24.5cm.) [B58, IT11]

Same. NY: Pantheon, 1958. 423p. 25cm. [LC62, IT11]

FRIEDLAENDER, Walter F.
Mannerism and anti-mannerism in Italian painting, two essays. (from Repertorium für Kunstwissenschaft, XLVII,
1925, and Vorträge der Bibliothek, Warburg, XIII, 1929.)
Tr. Anon. NY: Columbia U. Pr.; L: Oxford U. Pr.,
1957. 89p. (23.5cm.) 24cm. [LC62, B57, IT10]

FRIEDRICH, Johannes, 1893- .
Extinct languages. (Entzifferung verschollener Schriften
und Sprachen.) Tr. Frank Gaynor. NY: Philosophical
Lib., n.d. 182p. 21cm. [LC62, IT10]

FRIEDRICH, Otto Andreas.
The Phoenix story on the 100th anniversay of the Phoenix
Gummiwerke A. G., 1856-1956. ("Ein Werk im Spiegel
der Weltwirtschaft" in "Hundertjahre Weltwirtschaft im
Spiegel eines Unternehmens." E. Samhaber und O. A. Friedrich, 1956.) Tr. Anon. Hamburg-Harburg: Phoenix-Gummi-
werke A. G., 1956. 47p. [LC62]

FRIEDRICH, Rudolf, 1909- .
Skiiing the new style or the old way, but skiing. (Modern
Skien oder altmodisch, aber Skien.) Tr. Anon. n.p.,
n.d. 99p. 21cm. [LC62]

FRIEDRICH, Werner Paul, 1905- .
English pronunciation. The relationship between pronunciation and orthography. Tr. R. A. Martin. L, NY: Longmans, (1958), 1959. 80p. (18.5cm.) 19cm. [LC62,
B58, IT11]

FRISCH, Karl von, 1886- .
Bees. Their vision, chemical senses and language. Tr.
Anon. NY: Cornell, 1956. 118p. [LC62]

Ten little housemates. (Zehn kleine Hausgennossen.) Tr.
Margaret D. Senft. Oxford, L, NY: Pergamon, 1960.
146p. 19cm. (19.5cm.) [LC62, B60]

FRISCH, Max, 1911- .
Homo Faber, a report. Tr. Michael Bullock. L, NY:
Abelard, c1959. 198p. (20.5cm.) 21cm. [LC62, B59,
IT12, 13]

I'm not Stiller. (Stiller.) Tr. Michael Bullock. L, NY:
Abelard, 1958. 363p. 21cm. [LC62, B58, IT11]

FRITZ, Egon. See Vietta, Egon, pseud.

FRITZ, Kurt von, 1900- .
Aristotle's contribution to the practice and theory of his-
toriography. Tr. Anon. Berkeley: U. of California Pr.,
1958. 490p. (24.5cm) [LC62, B58]

FRITZ, Rosemarie.
Foundations and development of the Chinese coal mining
industry. Tr. Anon. NY: U. S. J. P. R. S., 1958. 38p.
27cm. [LC62]

FROBENIUS, Leo.
The childhood of man. (Aus den Flegeljahren der menschheit.) Tr. A. H. Keane. NY: Meridian, 1960. 504p.
21cm. [LC62, IT13]

FROM LISBON TO CALICUT.
(Den rechten Weg auszufahren von Liszabon gen Kallakuth.)
Tr. Alvin E. Prottengeier. Commentary and notes John
Parker. 8p. 19-40p. 21cm. [LC62]

FUCHS, Georg, 1868- .
Revolution in the theater. Conclusions concerning the
Munich artists' theater. (Die Revolution des Theaters.)
Condensed and adpt. Constance Connor Kuhn. Ithica, NY:
Cornell U. Pr., (L: Oxford U. Pr.), 1959. 220p. 22cm.
(22.5cm.) [LC62, B59, IT12]

FUCHS, Peter.
The land of veiled men. (Im Land der verschleierten
Männer.) Tr. Bice Fawcett. NY: Citadel, 1956. 168p.
23cm. [LC62]

FÜLOEP-MILLER, Rene, 1891- .
The power and secret of the Jesuits. (Macht und Geheim-
nis der Jesuiten.) Trs. F. S. Flint and D. F. Tait. NY:
Braziller, 1956. 499p. 22cm. [LC62]

Same. L: Owen, 1957. 499p. 22cm. [LC62, B57]

The silver bacchanal. Trs. R. and C. Winston. NY:
Atheneum, 1960. 305p. 22cm. [LC62, IT10]

FUGGER, Wolfgang, 16th century.
Handwriting manual, entitled, A practical and well-ground-
ed formulary for divers fair hands. (Schreibbüchlein "Ein
nützlich und wolgegründet Formular mancherley schöner
Schriefften.") Tr. Frederick Plaat. Fwd. Harry Carter.
L, NY: Oxford U. Pr., 1960. (171p.) 16 x 20 cm. (16
x 21cm.) [LC62, B60]

FULDA, Edeltraud, 1916- .
And I shall be healed. A story of a miracle cure. (Und

ich werde genesen sein, Autobiographie.) Tr. John
Coombs. L: Heinemann, 1960. 289p. (290p.) (20.5
cm.) 21cm. [LC62, B60]

FUNCK-BRENTANO, Frantz, 1862-1947.
Cagliostro and Company. A sequel to the story of the
diamond necklace. Tr. George Maidment. NY: Brentano's. n. d. 256p. [LC62]

FÜRER-HAIMENDORF, Christoph von, 1909- .
Himalayan barbary. (Glückliche Barbaren, bei unbekann-
ten Völkern an der Nordostgrenze Indiens.) Tr. Anon.
NY: Abelard, (1955.) 1956. 241p. (22.5cm.) 23cm.
[LC62, B56]

FURTENBACH, Joseph, 1591 1667. See Serlio, Sebastiano,
1475-1552.
The Renaissance stage. Documents. Coral Gables, Fla.:
U. of Miami Pr., 1958. [LC62]

FUSCHELBERGER, R. Hans.
Translations of miscellaneous zoological literature. (Tr.
of portion of Das Hahnenbuch.) n. p., n. d., 121. 28cm.
[LC62]

GABLENTZ, Otto Martin von der. ed.
Documents on the status of Berlin. (The selection is
based on the more comprehensive Ger. ed., Dokumente
zur Berlin-Frage, 1944-1959.) Tr. Anon. Pref. Willy
Brandt. n. p., n. d. 239p. 25cm. [LC62]

GAISER, Gerd.
The falling leaf. (Die sterbende Jagd.) Tr. Paul Findlay.
L: Collins, 1956. 256p. (21cm.) [B56, IT9]

The final ball. (Schlussball.) Tr. Marguerite Waldman.
NY: Pantheon, 1960. 254p. 22cm. [LC62, IT13]

The game of murder. Tr. H. M. Waidson. In Spender's
coll. 1960.

The last dance of the season. (Schlussball.) Tr. Marguerite Waldman. L: Collins, 1960. 255p. (20.5cm.)
21cm. [LC62, B60, IT13]

The last squadron. (Die sterbende Jagd.) Tr. Anon.

GAISER, Gerd--
NY: Pantheon, 1956. 251p. 21cm. [LC62, IT9]

Same. Tr. Paul Findlay. L: Collins, 1960. 253p.
(18cm.) [B60]

GALINSKY, Hans, ed.
The frontier in American history and literature. Essays
and interpretations by H--G-- and others. (Die neueren
Sprachen. Beiheft 7) Tr. Anon. Frankfurt/Main: Die-
sterweg. 1960. 112p. 21cm. [LC62]

GALLAND, Adolf, 1912- .
The first and the last. The rise and fall of the German
fighter forces, 1938-1945. (Die Ersten und die Letzten.)
Tr. Mervyn Savill. L: Transworld, 1957. 415p. (16.5
cm.) [B57]

Same. NY: Ballantine, 1957. 280p. 18cm. [LC62,
IT10]

GANTNER, Anton., jt. ed. See Strache, Wolf, 1910- . ed.
Principality of Liechtenstein.

GANTNER, Joseph, 1896- , and Pobe, Marcel, 1907- . ed.
The glory of romanesque art. (Gallia romanica.) Tr.
Marie Heynemann. NY: Vanguard, 1956. 80p. 31cm.
[LC62, IT9]

Romanesque art in France. L: Thames, 1956. 80p.
30cm. (31cm.) [LC62, B56, IT9]

GANZ, Paul, 1872- . See Holbein, Hans the younger,
1497-1543.
The paintings of Hans Holbein. (H--H--. Die Gemälde.)
Text, Paul Ganz. Introd., tr. R. H. Boothroyd. Catalogue Marguerite Kay. Enl. ed. L: Phaidon, 1956.
297p. 31cm. [LC62]

GARBE, Richard von, 1857-1927.
India and Christendom. The historical connections between
their religions. (Indien und Christentum.) Tr. Lydia G.
Robinson. La Salle, Ill.: Open Court, 1959. 310p.
21cm. [LC62, IT13]

GARDI, Rene.
Tambaran. An encounter with cultures in decline in New

Guinea. (Tambaran. Begegnung mit untergehenden Kulturen auf Neuguinea.) Tr. Eric Northcott. n. p. , n. d. 201p. 24cm. [LC62, B60]

GARF-KHITTEL, Gita. See Graf-Khittel, Gita.

GARTMANN, Heinz, 1917- .
Man unlimited. Technology's challenge to human endurance. (Stärker als der Technik.) Trs. Richard and Clara Winston. L: Cape, 1957. 221p. (20.5cm.) [LC62, B57]

Same. NY: Pantheon, 1957. 213p. 22cm. [LC62]

The men behind the space rockets. (Träumer, Forscher, Konstrukteure.) Trs. Eustace Wareing and Michael Glenny. L: Weidenfeld; NY: McKay, 1956. 185p. 22cm. [LC62, B56]

Rings around the world. Man's progress from steam engine to satellite. (Sonst stünde die Welt still. Das grosse Ringen um das Neue.) Tr. Alan G. Readett. NY: Morrow, 1959. 366p. 22cm. [LC62, IT12]

Science as history, the story of man's technological progress from steam engine to satellite. (Sonst stünde die Welt still.) Tr. Alan G. Readett. NY: Morrow, 1959. 366p. 23cm. [LC62, B60]

Same. L: Hodder, 1960. 348p. 23p. [LC62, B60]

GASSNER, John (Waldhorn), 1903- .
A treasury of the theatre. From Aeschylus to Turgenev. Tr. Anon. Rev. ed. NY: Simon, 1959. V. [LC62]

A treasury of the theatre, from Henrik Ibsen to Eugene Ionesco. Tr. Anon. 3rd ed. NY: Simon, 1960. 1275p. 26cm. [LC62]

Twenty best European plays on the American stage. Tr. Anon. NY: Crown, 1957. 733p. 25cm. [LC62, IT10]

GASSNER, John. See Thompson, Stith, 1885- .

GASSER, Manuel. See Bischof, Werner Adalbert, 1916-1954. The world of Werner Bischof, a photographer's odyssey. (Unterwegs.) Tr. Paul Steiner. Text M--G--. NY:

GASSER, Manuel--
Dutton, 1959. unp. 19cm. [LC62, IT12]

GATZ, Konrad, ed.
Decorative designs for contemporary interiors. Tr. Anon.
NY: Architectural. 1956. 239p. 31cm. [LC62]

Same. L: Owen, 1960. 240p. (29.5cm.) [B60]

GEBHARDT, Hertha Antonie Mathilde von.
The girl from nowhere. (Das Mädchen von irgendwoher.)
Ed. and tr. James Kirkup. L: U. of London Pr., 1958.
176p. 22cm. [B58, IT11]

Same. NY: Criterion, 1959. 190p. [LC62, IT12]

Love from Nicky. (Absender Nikolaus Stuck.) Trs. and
adpt. Oliver Coburn and Ursula Lehrburger. L: Burke,
1960. 124p. (20cm.) [B60]

GEIGER, Rudolf, 1894- .
The climate near the ground. (Das Klima der bodennahen
Luftschicht.) Tr. Milroy N. Stewart et al. L: Oxford
U. Pr., 1957. 494p. (21.5cm.) 22cm. [B58, IT11]

Same. Cambridge: Harvard U. Pr., 1957. 494p. 22cm.
[LC62, IT10]

GEIGER, Wilhelm, 1856-1943.
Culture of Ceylon in mediaeval times, and bibliography of
W. Geiger's writings on Ceylon and Sinhalese language
and literature. Tr. Anon. Ed. Heinz Bechert. Wiesbaden: Harrassowitz, 1960. 286p. 25cm. [LC62]

GEIGY CHEMICAL CORPORATION. GEIGY PHARMACEUTI-
CALS.
200 years Geigy. (Zweihundert Jahre Geigy.) Tr. B. H.
de C. Ireland: Basel, 1958. 125p. 24cm. [LC62]

GEIRINGER, Karl, 1899- .
Musical instruments, their history in western culture from
the stone age to the present day. Tr. Bernard Miall.
Ed. W. F. H. Blandford. 2nd ed. NY: Oxford U. Pr.,
1959. 340p. 22cm. [LC62]

Symbolism in the music of Bach, a lecture. Tr. Anon.
Washington: n.p. 1956. 111, 16p. 23cm. [LC62]

GEISENHEYNER, Max, 1884- . See The Rhine, heart of
Europe.

GENTZ, Friedrich von, 1764-1832.
Three revolutions. The French and American revolutions
compared. John Quincy Adams, reflections on the Russian revolution. Tr. Stefan T. Possony. Chicago: Regnery, 1959. 144p. 17cm. [LC62]

GEORGE, Stefan.
Selections in Flores, anthology. 1960.

GERLACH, Heinrich.
The forsaken army. (Die verratene Armee.) Tr. Richard
Graves. L: Weidenfeld, 1958. 383p. (384p.) (20.5cm.)
21cm. [LC62, B58, IT11]

Same. NY: Harper, 1959. 383p. 22cm. [LC62, IT12]

Same. L: Transworld, 1960. 444p. (16.5cm.) [LC62,
B60, IT13]

GERLACH, Richard Hans Wilhelm Ferdinand, 1899- .
Pictures from Yemen. (Sonne über Arabien. Bilder aus
dem Yemen.) Tr. Anon. Leipzig: n.p., n.d. 29p.
31cm. [LC62]

GERMAN ANTIGUERRILLA OPERATIONS IN THE BALKANS,
1941-1944.
Historical study. The material for this study was obtained from German military records. The work of pre-
paring the study was done by Major Robert M. Kennedy of
the office of the chief of military history. Tr. Anon.
n.p., n.d. 82p. 24cm. [LC62]

GERMAN COLONIZATION SOCIETY, Charleston, South Carolina.
German colony protocol. Minute book of the German colonization society. Tr. B. E. Schaeffer. n.p., n.d. unp.
22cm. [LC62, IT13]

GERMAN P.O.W. CAMP PAPERS.
German P.O.W. camp papers. Arrangement of papers
is alphabetical by place of camp. Numbering arbitrarily
assigned. Papers are from camps chiefly in the U.S.
Tr. Anon. n.p., 19--. 22-37cm. [LC62]

THE GERMAN RHINE.
The German Rhine.   Thirty picturesque views of the Rhine
including Heidelberg, Wiesbaden and Frankfurt.   With in-
teresting descriptions.   Tr. Anon.   n. p. ,   n. d.   unp.
(22 x 28cm.)   [LC62]

GERMANY, Auswärtiges Amt.
Documents on German foreign policy, 1918-1945.   Vol. 1,
Jan. 30-Oct. 14, 1933.   Tr. Anon.   L: H. M. S. O. ,   1957.
962p.   (24. 5cm.)   [B58]

Same.   Vol. 2, Oct.   14, 1933-June 13, 1934.   L: H. M.
S. O. ,   1959.   929p.   24cm. [B59]

Same.   Vol. 3, June 14, 1934-Mar. 31, 1935.   L: H. M.
S. O. ,   1959.   1157p.   (24. 5cm.)   [B59]

Same.   Vol. 6, The last months of peace.   March-August,
1939.   L: H. S. M. S. O. ,   1956.   1149p.   (24. 5cm.) [B56]

Same.   Vol. 7, The last days of Peace.   Aug.   9-Sept. 3,
1939.   L: H. M. S. O. ,   1957.   670p.   (24. 5cm.)   [B57]

Same.   Vol. 9, The war years, March 18-June 22, 1940.
L: H. M. S. O. ,   1956.   792p.   [B56]

Same.   Vol. 10, The war years, June 23-August 31, 1940.
L: H. M. S. O. ,   1957.   615p.   (24. 5cm.)   [B57]

GERMANY.   DEMOCRATIC REPUBLIC, 1949.
The compulsory collectivization of independent farms in the
Soviet zone of occupation in Germany.   (Bundesministerium
für gesamtdeutsche Fragen.)   Tr. Anon.   Bonn: 1960.
121p.   [LC62]

Constitution of the German Democratic Republic.   Tr.
Anon.   Berlin: Verlag die Wirtschaft, 1957.   47p.   21cm.
[LC62]

East German statistical yearbook, 1955.   Tr. Anon.
Berlin: 1956.   585p.   27cm.   [LC62]

The German Democratic Republic and the Arab people's
struggle for liberty.   Tr. Anon.   Berlin: n. d.   23p.
[LC62]

German refugees and conditions in the Soviet zone of Germany. A government declaration delivered by Federal Minister for All-German Affairs Ernst Lemmer at the opening session of the German Bundestag in Berlin on Oct. 1, 1958. (Bundesministerium für Gesamtdeutsche Fragen.) Tr. Anon. Washington, 1958. 19p. [LC62]

Government declaration on the development of agricultural production cooperatives. Tr. Anon. n. p., 1960. [LC62]

Injustice the regime. Documentary evidence of the systematic violation of legal right in the Soviet zone of Germany, 1954-1958. (Bundesministerium für Gesamtdeutsche Fragen.) Tr. Anon. Berlin: Verlag für Internationalen Kulturaustausch. n. d. 196p. [LC62]

Law on the second five-year plan for the development of the people's economy in the German Democratic Republic for the years 1956-1960. (Die Wirtschaft. Special supplement, 10 Jan. 1958.) Tr. Anon. NY: U. S. J. P. R. S., 1958. 38p. 27cm. [LC62]

Law on the seven year plan for the development of the national economy of the German Dem. Rep. from 1959 to 1965. Adopted by the People's Chamber on Oct. 1, 1959. Tr. Anon. n. p. 1960. 80p. 21cm. [LC62]

Regulations for the postal and telecommunications system of the German Democratic Republic. (Gesetzblatt der Deutschen Demokratischen Republik, no. 27, May 11, 1959. 365-408p.) Tr. Anon. NY: U. S. J. P. R. S., 1959. 137p. 27cm. [LC62]

The Soviet zone of Germany, the facts. (Bundesministerium für Gesamtdeutsche Fragen.) Tr. Anon. Bonn: 1960. 31p. 21 x 10cm. [LC62]

Translation and glossary of 1957 statistical yearbook of the German Democratic Republic. Tr. Anon. NY: U. S. J. P. R. S., 1959. 733p. 27cm. [LC62]

GERMANY, FEDERAL REPUBLIC, 1949.
Action against the Communist Party of Germany. Reprint of documents for hearings initiated by petition of the Federal Government to establish the unconstitutionality of the Communist Party of Germany before the first Senate of the Federal Constitutional court. Washington, D. C.: 1957. 371 l. 27cm. [LC62]

136

GERMANY. FEDERAL REPUBLIC--
After ten years, a European problem, still no solution.
(Zehn Jahre nach der Vertreibung.) Tr. Anon. Frank-
furt/Main: Wirtschaftsdienst, 1957. 48p. [LC62]

Same. 64p. 24cm. [LC62]

The anti-semitic and Nazi incidents, from 25 Dec. 1959
until 28 Jan. 1960. White paper of the Federal Republic
of Germany. Tr. Anon. Bonn: 1960. 79p. 21cm.
[LC62]

Care and help for the expellees, refugees, immigrants,
evacuees, war victims, returnees, prisoners of war,
homeless foreigners, political refugees from abroad, re-
patriated persons, emigrants, by the Federal Ministry for
Expellees, Refugees and War Victims. Tr. Vivian Stran-
ders. Bonn: 1956, 55p. 24cm. [LC62]

Same. Tr. Anon. Bonn: n.d. 68p. 24cm. [LC62]

Bundesministerium für Ernährung, Landwirtschaft und
Forsten. Catalogue of technical schools, colleges and
other educational institutes for agriculture, wine growing,
horticulture, and forestry, with a review of the vocation-
al training system in agriculture, the rural people, universities, and the rural youth organizations of agricultural schools. Tr. Anon. Bad Godesberg: n.d. 184p.
[LC62]

Bundesministerium für Wohnungsbau. From the building
of houses to the development of terms. The period from
1949 to 1959 passed in review. Tr. Anon. Bad Godesberg: 1960. 18p. [LC62]

Germany and the Jews since 1945. Cover title, A moral
obligation. Tr. Anon. Washington, D.C., Pr. and Information Office: German Embassy, 1960. 18 p. [LC62]

Bundesministerium für Wirtschaftlichen Besitz Des Bundes.
Germany, 1958. Eng. ver. Walter Moss. Ed. Bernhard
Woischnik. Godesberg: Verlag für Publizistik, 1958.
64p. 35cm. [LC62]

Bundesministerium für Wohnungsbau. Housebuilding and
finance of housing in the Federal Republic of Germany.
Tr. Anon. n.p., n.d. 21cm. [LC62]

In the heart of Germany--in the twentieth century. Bonn:
1960. 47p. 22cm. [LC62]

State visit by the President of the Federal Republic of
Germany, Theodor Heuss to Washington, D. C. June 4-6,
1958. (Botschaft U. S.) Tr. Anon. n. p. , n. d. 38cm.
[LC62]

The ten years, 1949-1959, the Federal Republic of Ger-
many. (Botschaft, U. S.) Tr. Anon. Washington, D. C.
Pr. Office: German Embassy, 1959. 127p. 28cm.
[LC62]

To keep Berlin free. (Botschaft U.S.) Tr. Anon.
Washington, D. C.: 1959. 16p. [LC62]

The trends of agriculture research development in Germany. (Bundesministerium für Ernährung, Landwirtschaft und forsten.) Tr. Anon. n.p. n.d. 38cm.
[LC62]

GERMANY. GERMAN EMPIRE, 1871- .
Bismarck and the Hohenzollern candidature for the Spanish throne. The documents in the German diplomatic
archives. Tr. Isabella M. Massey. Fwd. G. P. Gooch.
Ed. and introd. Georges Bonnin. L: Chatto, 1957.
311p. (312p.) (25. 5cm.) 26cm. [LC62, B58]

German foreign ministry archives 1917-1920. A selection. Tr. Anon. Ann Arbor: Michigan U. Faculty Research Project no. 100, 1956. [LC62]

Germany and the revolution in Russia, 1915-1918.
Documents from the archives of the German foreign ministry. Tr. Anon. Ed. Z. A. B. Zeman. L, NY: Oxford U. Pr. , 1958. 157p. 22cm. [LC62, B58]

GERMANY, REICHSGERICHT.
Decisions of the German Supreme Court relating to inter-
national law. (Die Entscheidungen des Deutschen Reichsge-
richts in völkerrechtlichen Fragen.) Ed. Günther Jänicke.
Tr. Anon. Berlin: Heymann, 1931-1960. 2v. 26cm.
[LC62]

GERMANY, VOLKSKAMMER. See Germany, Democratic
Republic, 1949- .

GERNSHEIM, Helmut and Alison.
The recording eye. A hundred years of great events as
seen by the camera, 1839-1939. (Hundert Jahre Photographie.) Tr. Anon. NY: Putnam, 1960. 254p. [IT13]

GERSTÄCKER, Friedrich Wilhelm Chr.
Germelshausen. Tr. Alexander Gode von Aesch. Great
Neck, NY: Barron's. 1958. 51p. [IT11]

GERSTER, Georg.
Sahara. Tr. Stewart Thomson. L: Barrie, 1960. 302p.
(22.5cm.) [B60]

GERSTNER, Karl and Markus Kutter.
The new graphic art. (Die neue Graphik.) Tr. Dennis
Q. Stephenson. L: Tiranti, 1959. 247p. (24cm.)
[B59, IT12]

GESELL, Silvio, 1862-1930.
The natural economic order. (Die natürliche Wirtschafts-
ordnung.) Tr. Philip Pye. L: Owen, 1958. 452p.
(22cm.) [B59, IT12]

GIEDION, Siegfried, 1888- .
Architecture, you and me, the diary of a development.
(Architektur und Gemeinschaft, Tagebuch einer Entwicklung.) Tr. Anon. Cambridge: Harvard U. Pr., 1958.
221p. (21cm.) 22cm. [LC62, B58]

Space, time and architecture, the growth of a new tradition. Tr. Anon. 3rd ed. enl. Cambridge: Harvard U.
Pr., 1956. 778p. 25cm. [LC62]

GIEDION, Siegfried, 1888- . See Reidy, Affonso Eduardo.

GIEDION-WELKER, Carola.
Constantin Brancusi. Trs. Maria Jolas and Anne Leroy.
NY: Braziller, 1959. 240p. 31cm. [LC62, IT12]

Contemporary sculpture. (Moderne Plastik.) Trs. Mary
Hottinger-Mackie and Sonja Marjasch. L: Faber, 1956.
327p. (26cm.) [B56, IT9]

Jean Arp. (Hans Arp.) Tr. Norbert Guterman. NY:

Abrams, c1957. 122p. 30cm. [LC62, IT11]

Same. L: Thames, 1958. 122p. 30cm. [LC62, B58, IT11]

GIEGEL, Phillipp, jt. author. See Bruin, Paul.

GIERKE, Otto Friedrich von, 1841-1921.
Natural law and the theory of society, 1500 to 1800. With a lecture on the ideas of natural law and humanity by Ernest Troeltsch. (Das deutsche Genossenschaftsrecht. v. 4, 5 subsections.) Tr. Ernest Barker. Boston: Beacon, 1954. 423p. 21cm. [LC62]

Same. Cambridge: U. Pr., 1958. 423p. 24cm. [LC62]

Political theories of the Middle Ages. (Die publicistischen Lehren des Mittelalters. A section of v3 of Das deutsche Genossenschaftsrecht.) Tr. Frederic William Maitland. Cambridge: U. Pr., 1958. 197p. 24cm. [LC62]

Same. Boston: Beacon, 1958. 197p. 21cm. [LC62, IT11]

GILBERT, Mark, ed.
Wisdom of the ages, fourteen hundred concepts of 200 everyday subjects by 400 great thinkers of 30 nations extending over 5000 years. Tr. Anon. L: Heinemann, 1956. 431p. 18cm. [LC62]

GIMPEL, Erich, 1910- . With Berthold, Will.
Spy for Germany. (Spion für Deutschland.) Tr. Eleanor Brockett. L: Hale, 1957. 238p. 22cm. (22.5cm.) [LC62, B57]

Same. L: Hamilton, 1959. 224p. (18cm.) [B59, IT12]

GIRGENSOHN, Herbert, 1887- .
Teaching Luther's catechism. Vol. 1 the ten commandments. The creed, the Lord's prayer. (Kleiner Katechismus.) Tr. John W. Doberstein. Philadelphia: Muhlenberg, 1959. 310p. [IT12]

Teaching Luther's catechism. Baptism, confession, the supper. (Kleiner Katechismus.) Tr. John W. Doberstein. Philadelphia: Muhlenberg, 1960. 130p. [IT13]

GIRNUS, Wilhelm.
On the idea of the socialist university. Address at the
meeting of Chancellors in Berlin on June 14, 1957. (Zur
Idee der sozialistischen Hochschule, Rede auf der Rektor-
enkonferenz zu Berlin am 14. Juni 1957.) Tr. Alfred
Heber. Rev. Joan Becker. Berlin: Deutscher Verlag
der Wissenschaften, c1957. [LC62]

GLAS, Norbert.
How to look at illness. Tr. Anon. L: New Knowledge,
1956. 49p. 18cm. [LC62, B56]

GLASER, Hugo, 1881- .
The road to modern surgery. The advances in medicine
and surgery during the past hundred years. (Aufstieg der
Heilkunde.) Tr. Maurice Michael. L: Lutterworth, 1960.
223p. (224p.) 23cm. [LC62, B60]

GLASSER, Otto, 1895- .
Dr. W. C. Röntgen. 2nd ed. Tr. Anon. Springfield:
n. d. 169p. 22cm. [LC62]

Medical physics. Tr. Anon. 3v. 28cm. [LC62]

Physical foundations of radiology. 2nd ed. rev. and enl.
Tr. Anon. NY: Hoeber, 1957. 581p. 20cm. [LC62]

GLEIT, Maria, pseud. (i. e. Gleitsmann, Herta.)
Child of China. (Sa Tu Sai führt Krieg.) Tr. E. F.
Peeler. L: Oxford U. Pr., 1958. 188p. (20cm.)
[B58, IT11]

GLEITSMANN, Herta. See Gleit, Maria, pseud.

GLÜCK, Gustav, 1871- .
Peter Brueghel the elder. (Das grosse Brueghel-Werk.)
Tr. and ed. Gustav Glück. L: Thames, 1958. 53p.
(29.5cm.) 30 x 30cm. [LC62, B58, IT11]

GÖPEL, Erhard.
Munich. A picture book. (München.) Eng. ver. L. W.
Sayers. Photos. Peter Keetman. Text E--G--. Lindau:
Thorbecke, c1960. 95p. [LC62]

Same. L: Tiranti, 1960. 88p. (24cm.) [B60]

GOERING, Reinhard.
Sea fight, a tragedy. Trs. June Falcone and Bayard
Quincy Morgan. Microf. of TW. Columbia University,
1958. 2, 9-1301. [LC62]

GÖRLITZ, Walter, 1913- .
History of the German general staff, 1657-1945. Tr. Brian Battershaw. Introd. Walter Millis. NY: Praeger,
508p. 22cm. [LC62]

GÖRRES, Ida Friederike Coudenhove, 1901- .
The hidden face. A study of St. Therese of Lisieux.
(Das Senfkorn von Lisieux.) Trs. Richard and Clara Win-
ston. NY: Pantheon, 1959. 428p. 22cm. [LC62,
IT12]

GOERTZ, Lisa.
I stepped into freedom. Tr. Anon. L: Lutterworth,
1960. 82p. (18.5cm.) [LC62, B60]

GOES, Albrecht, 1908- .
The burnt offering. (Das Brandopfer.) Tr. Michael Ham-
burger. L: Gollancz, n.d. 94p. 19cm. [LC62, B56,
IT9]

Same. NY: Pantheon, n.d. 92p. 21cm. [LC62, IT9]

GOETHE, Johann Wolfgang von, 1749-1832.
Egmont, a tragedy in five acts. Tr. Anon. Ed. H. M.
Waidson. Oxford: Blackwell, 1960. 110p. 19cm. [LC
62]

Same. Tr. Willard R. Trask. Great Neck, NY: Barron's,
1960. 120p. 19cm. [LC62, IT13]

Elective affinities. (Die Wahlverwandtschaften.) Tr. Anon.
NY: Collier, n.d. 384p. 21cm. [LC62]

Faust. Tr. Philip Wayne. Baltimore: Penguin, 1958-
1959. 2v. 19cm. [LC62, IT13]

Same. Tr. John Shawcross. L: Wingate; NY: Daub,
1959. 9-448p. (22.5cm.) [LC62, B59, IT12]

Same. NY: Daub, 1959. 448p. [IT12]

Faust 1. Tr. B. Q. Morgan. NY: Liberal Arts, 1957.

142

GOETHE, Johan Wolfgang von--
155p. 21cm. [LC62, IT10]

Same. A new American version based upon a tr. C. F.
MacIntyre. NY: New Directions, 1957. 188p. 22cm.
[LC62, IT10]

Faust. Part 1. (Faust.) Tr. Bertram Jessup. NY:
Philosophical Lib., 1958. 224p. 19cm. [LC62, B58,
IT11]

Faust. (Pt. 2) (F---. II) Tr. Philip Wayne. L: Harmondsworth: Penguin, 1959. (288p.) 18cm. [LC62,
B59, IT12]

From Lake Garde to Sicily with Goethe. With orig. drawings. (Italienische Reise.) Tr. John Garrett. L: Macdonald, 1960. 115p. (117p.) (30.5cm.) [LC62, B60]

Great writings of Goethe. Ed. Stephen Spender. L, NY:
1958. 278p. (19cm.) [LC62, B58]

Iphigenia in Tauris, a play. Eng. ver. Roy Pascal.
Microf. Columbia U., c1958. 52l. [LC62]

Kindred by choice. (Wahlverwandtschaften.) Tr. H. M.
Waidson. L: Calder, 1960. 290p. [LC62]

Letters from Goethe. (Briefe.) Trs. Marianne V. Herz-
feld and C. A. Melvil Sym. Edinburgh: Edinburgh U. Pr.,
NY: Nelson, 1957. 574p. 23cm. [LC62, B57]

Poems of Goethe, sequel to Goethe the lyrist. Tr. E. H.
Zeydel. Chapel Hill: U. of North Carolina Pr., 1957.
126p. 23cm. [LC62, IT10]

Selection in Chase, G. H. Tr. poems from the German.

Selection in Hoegler, R. G.

Selections in Kerenyi, C. Greece in colour, 1957.

Selections in Willoughby, L. A.

Stella, A drama for lovers. Tr. B. Q. Morgan. n. p. ,
1958. Microf. Columbia U. [LC62]

The sufferings of young Werther. (Die Leiden des jungen
Werther.) Tr. B. Q. Morgan. L: Calder; NY: Ungar,
1957. 160p. 19cm. (19.5cm.) [LC62, B57, IT10]

Torquato Tasso, a play. (T--T--.) Trs. and introd. Ben
Kimpel and T. C. Duncan Eaves. Fayetteville: U. of Ar-
kansas, 1956. 76p. 23cm. [LC62, IT9]

The urfaust. (Urfaust.) Tr. Douglas M. Scott. Great
Neck, NY: Barron's. 1958. 71p. [LC62, IT11]

Wilhelm Meister's apprenticeship. Tr. Thomas Carlyle.
NY: Printed for the members of the Limited Editions
Club, 1959. 567p. 28cm. [LC62, IT12]

Same. NY: 1962. 542p. 18cm. [LC62]

GOETHE, Rudolf, 1880- . et al.
We are now Catholics. (Bekenntnis zur katholischen
Kirche.) Tr. Norman C. Reeves. Westminster, Md. :
Newman, 1959. 223p. 23cm. [LC62, IT12]

GOETSCH, Wilhelm, 1887- .
The ants. Tr. Ralph Manheim. Ann Arbor: U. of Michigan Pr., 1957. 169 p. (21.5cm.) 22cm. [LC62, B57]

Same. Ann Arbor: U. of Michigan Pr.; L: Mayflower,
1960. (169p.) 173p. (21.5cm.) 22cm. [LC62, B59,
IT13]

GÖTTINGER ARBEITSKREIS.
German Eastern territories, a manual and book of refer-
ence dealing with the regions east of the Oder and Neisse.
Ed. Göttingen Research Committee. (Ostdeutschland.)
Trs. Helen Taubert and Anni Mückenheim. Würzburg:
Holzner, 1957. 197p. 22cm. [LC62]

The German Eastern territories beyond Oder and Neisse in
the light of the Polish press. Ed. The Göttinger Research
Committee. Würzburg, Holzner, 1958. 112p. 21cm. [LC62]

GOGARTEN, Friedrich, 1887- .
The reality of faith. The problem of subjectivism in theology. (Die Wirklichkeit des Glaubens.) Trs. Carl Mi-

GOGARTEN, Friedrich--
chalson, et al. Philadelphia: Westminster, 1959. 192p.
21cm. [LC62, IT12]

GOLDBACH, Otto, 1908- .
Far side. (Die Rückseite des Mondes. Originally Der
Mond und die Enstehung der Erdkontinente.) Tr. Anon.
Dortmund-Aplerbeck, Verlagsbuchhandlung O. Goldbach,
1958. 241. 30cm. [LC62]

GOLDBECK, Gustav. See Diesel, Eugen, 1889- ., jt.
authors.

GOLDBRUNNER, Josef.
Cure of mind and cure of soul. (Personale Seelsorge.)
Tr. Stanley Godman. L: Burns; NY: Pantheon, 1958.
127p. 21cm. [LC62, B58, IT11]

Individuation, a study of the depth of psychology of C. F.
Jung. Tr. Stanley Godman. L: Hollis; NY: Pantheon,
1956. 204p. 22cm. [LC62]

Teaching the Catholic catechism with the religion workbook. Tr. Bernhard Adkins. NY: Herder, 195-. 18cm.
[LC62]

Teaching the Catholic catechism with the religion workbook. Vol. I. God and our redemption. (Katechismus-
unterricht mit dem Werkheft.) Tr. Bernard Adkins.
L: Burns, Freiburg, NY: Herder, 1959. 108p. 18cm.
(18.5cm.) [LC62, B59]

Same. Vol. 2. The church and the sacraments. L:
Burns. 1960. [B59, IT12]

THE GOLDEN COAST.
Naples, Pompeii, Sorrento, Capri, Amalfi, Paestrum.
(Die goldene Küste.) Tr. Anon. L, NY: Thames, 1958.
20p. (24.5cm.) 25cm. [LC62, B58]

THE GOLDEN GEOGRAPHIC ENCYCLOPEDIA.
Adpt. and ed. Theodore Shabad and Peter M. Stern.
(From Westermann Bildkarten Lexicon.) Tr. Anon. NY:
Simon, 1958. 228p. 25cm. [LC62]

GOLDSCHEIDER, Ludwig, 1896- .
The left arm of Michelangelo's "Notte." Tr. Anon

Milano, Annali, 1955. 18p. 17cm. [LC62]

Leonardo da Vinci. Life and work, paintings and drawings. Newly annotated. L: Phaidon, 1959. 192p. 31cm. [LC62]

GOLDSCHEIDER, Ludwig, 1896- . See Buonarroti, Michelangelo, 1475-1564.
Michelangelo, paintings, sculptures, architecture. Tr. Anon. 3rd ed. NY: Phaidon, 1959. [LC62]

GOLDSCHEIDER, Ludwig, 1896- . See Rembrandt, Hermanszoon van Rijn, 1606-1669.
Paintings, drawings and etchings. Tr. Anon. L: Phaidon, 1960. [LC62]

Same. Garden City, NY: Phaidon, n.d. [LC62]

GOLDSCHEIDER, Ludwig, 1896- . See Vermeer, Johannes, 1632-1675.
Paintings, complete ed. Tr. R. H. Boothroyd. L: Phaidon; NY: Distributed by Garden City Books, 1958. [LC62]

GOLDSTONE, Jean Stock.
Mary Stuart, a play in six scenes. By Jean Stock Goldstone and John Reich. (Derived from Fr. Schiller's Maria Stuart.) NY: Dramatists Play Service, 1958. 86p. 30cm. [LC62]

GOLDTHWAIT, John Turner, 1921- .
Tr. of Kant's "Observations on the feeling of the beautiful and sublime." Microf. Ann Arbor: Michigan, Thesis, Northwestern U., 1957. [LC62]

GOLLWITZER, Helmut.
The dying and the living Lord. (Jesu Tod und Auferstehung.) Tr. Olive Wyon. L: SCM; Philadelphia: Muhlenberg, 1960. 123p. (18.5cm.) 19cm. [LC62, B60, IT13]

GOLLWITZER, Helmut, ed., Kuhn, Käthe ed., and Schneider, Reinhold, ed.
Dying we live. The final messages and records of some Germans who defied Hitler. (Du hast mich heimgesucht bei Nacht.) Tr. Reinhard C. Kuhn. L: Harvill, 1956. 224p. (22.5cm.) [B57, IT9]

Same. New ed. L: Collins/Fontana, 1958. 253p. 18cm. [LC62, B58, IT11]

GOLLWITZER, Helmut--
Dying we live. The final messages and records of the
resistance. (Du hast mich heimgesucht bei Nacht.) Tr.
Reinhard C. Kuhn. NY: Pantheon, 1956. 285p. 24cm.
[LC62, IT9]

GORE, Frederick. See Neuwirth, Arnulf, 1912- .
Abstract art. (Abstraktion.) L: Methuen, 1956. 19p.
18cm. [LC62]

Same. NY: Crown, 1959. 19p. 19cm. [LC62]

GOTTFRIED VON STRASSBURG.
Tristan. Tr. A. T. Hatto. Tr. entire for the 1st time
with surviving fragments of the Tristan of Thomas. Harmondsworth, Baltimore: Penguin, 1960. 374p. (18.5
cm.) 19cm. [LC62, B60, IT13]

GOTTHELF, Jeremias, pseud. (i.e. Bitzius, Albert, 1797-
1854.)
The black spider. (Die schwarze Spinne.) Tr. H. M.
Waidson. L: Calder; NY: McClelland, 1958. 135p.
(19.5cm.) [B58, IT11]

Selections in Loomis, C. G. Prose. 1960.

GRAEF, Heinz, 1901- .
(Düsseldorf, Stadt am Strom.) Tr. S. M. Armetage.
Text and caps. in Ger., Eng. and Gr. Düsseldorf, Droste
verlag. 1959. 8p. 31cm. [LC62]

GRAEFE, Franz.
The approaching social order of the mothers and masters.
(Die kommenden Ordnungen der Mütter und Meister.) Tr.
Paul F. Kaemmerer. Melbourne: Hallcraft, 1960. 80p.
20cm. [LC62]

GRAF-KHITTEL, Gita.
Austria, music and theater. (Österreich, Musik und
Theater.) Tr. Oscar Konstandt. L: Thorsons, 1958.
104p. (27cm.) [LC62, B58, IT11]

GRASS, Günter, 1927- .
Selections in Rothenberg, 1959.

GREGOR, Manfred, 1929- .
The bridge. (Die Brücke.) Tr. Rob. S. Rosen. NY:

Random, 1960. 215p. 22cm. [LC62, IT13]

GREGOR SMITH, Ronald. See Smith, Ronald Gregor.

GRESSIEKER, Hermann.
Royal gambit, a drama in five acts. Tr. and adpt.
George White. NY: French, c1959. 70p. 19cm. [LC62]

GREWE, Wilhelm Georg, 1911- .
A peace treaty with Germany. An analysis. Tr. Anon.
Washington, Pr. and Information Office: German Embassy.
22p. [LC62]

Same. (Tr. of article in Europa-Archiv, v. 14, no. 910,
Oct. 1959.) Frankfurt/Main: 1959. 35p. [LC62]

GRILLPARZER, Franz, 1791-1872.
Hero and Leander, a tragedy in five acts. Tr. B. Q.
Morgan. n. p., Microf. Columbia U., 1958. [LC62]

Medea, tragedy in five acts. Tr. Arthur Burkhard.
Yarmouthport, Mass.: Register, 1956. 120p. 23cm.
[LC62, IT9]

GRIMM, Jakob Ludwig Karl, 1785-1863, and Grimm, Wilhelm Karl, 1786-1859.
Fairy tales. Retold by Amabel Williams-Ellis. Illus.
Fritz Wegner. L: Blackie, 1959. 344p. (22.5cm.)
23cm. [LC62, B59]

Fairy tales. Tr. Anon. Eds. M. W. and G. Thomas. Illus.
Shirley Hughes. L: Hutchinson, 1960. 96p. 18.5cm. [B60]

Fairy tales. Tr. Anon. L: Ward, Lock, 1958. 3-193p.
(18cm.) [B58]

Favorite fairy tales told in Germany. (Kinder- und Hausmärchen.) Tr. Virginia Haviland. Illus. Susanna Suba.
Boston: Little, 1959. 82p. 25cm. [LC62, IT12]

The fisherman and his wife. Tr. Anon. Illus. Madeleine Gekiere. NY: Pantheon, c1957. unp. 26cm.
[LC62]

German folk tales. See the Grimms' German folk tales.

The good-for-nothing. Tr. Anon. Drawings Hans Fischer.

148

GRIMM, Jakob Ludwig Karl--
NY: Harcourt, 1957. unp. 19 x 31cm. [LC62]

Grimms' fairy tales, based on tr. of Margaret Hunt. Rev.
James Stern. Complete ed. with 212 illus. Josef Scharl.
L: Routledge, 1959. 869p. 23cm. [LC62]

The Grimms' German folk tales and religious tales concerning children. (Kinder- und Hausmärchen and Kinder-
legenden.) Trs. Francis P. Magoun, Jr., and Alexander
H. Krappe. Carbondale: Southern Ill. U. Pr., Nottingham, Hall, 1960. 679p. 21cm. [LC62, B60]

Grimms' other tales. A new selection by Wilhelm Hansen.
Trs. and eds. Ruth Michaelis-Jena and Arthur Ratcliff.
L: Golden Cockerel, 1956. 160p. 25cm. [LC62]

Hansel and Gretel. Tr. Anon. Illus. Kay Lovelance
Smith. Chicago: Rand, 1960. 21p. 21cm. [LC62]

My book of Hansel and Gretel. Tr. Anon. Illus. Nardini.
NY: Maxton, 1960. unp. 33cm. [LC62]

My book of Snow-White and the seven dwarfs. Tr. Anon.
Illus. Nardini. NY: Maxton, 1960. unp. 33cm. [LC62]

New tales from Grimm. Trs. Ruth Michaelis-Jena and
Arthur Ratcliff. Edinburg, L: Chambers, 1960. 146p.
(22.5cm.) [B60]

Rapunzel. With pictures Felix Hoffmann. Tr. Katya Sheppard. L: Oxford U. Pr., 1960. 31cm. [LC62]

Selections in Loomis, C. G. Prose. 1960.

The shoemaker and the elves. Tr. Wayne Andrews. NY:
Scribner, 1960. unp. 26cm. [LC62, IT13]

The sleeping beauty. (Dornröschen.) Tr. Peter Collier.
L: Oxford U. Pr., 1959. (32p.) 30cm. (30.5cm.)
[LC62, B59, IT12]

Same. NY: Harcourt, 1960. unp. 30cm. [LC62, IT13]

Snow White and other stories. Retold Shirley Goulden.
NY: Grosset. 1957. 60p. 35cm. [LC62]

Tales from Andersen and Grimm. Told by W. K. Holmes.
Illus. Barbara Freeman. L: Blackie, 1958. 160p.
26cm. [LC62]

The wolf and the seven little kids. (Der Wolf und die
sieben Geisslein.) Tr. Anon. L: Oxford U. Pr., 1958.
32p. (21.5 x 30.5cm.) 22 x 31cm. [LC62, B58, IT11]

Same. NY: Harcourt, 1959. unp. 22 x 31cm. [LC62,
IT12]

GRIMM, Jakob Ludwig Karl, 1785-1863. See Chorpennig,
Charlotte.
Hansel and Gretel. Chicago: Coach House, 1956. 63p.
22cm. [LC62]

GRIMM, Jakob Ludwig Karl, 1785-1863. See Jonson, Marian.
Snow White and the seven dwarfs. Chicago: Coach House,
1957. [LC62]

GROCK, pseud. (i.e. Wettach, Charles Adrien, 1880- .
Grock, king of clowns. (Nit m-ö-ö-ö-glich.) Tr. Basil
Creighton. Ed. Ernst Konstantin. L: Methuen, 1957.
221p. (22.5cm.) [LC62, B57]

GRÖTTRUP, Irmgard.
Rocket wife. (Die Besessenen und die Mächtigen im Schatten der roten Rakete.) Tr. Susi Hughes. L: Deutsch,
1959. 188p. (21.5cm.) 22cm. [LC62, B59, IT12]

GROHMANN, Will, 1887- .
The art of Henry Moore. Tr. Michael Bullock. L:
Thames, 1960. 279p. 28cm. [LC62, B60]

Same. NY: Abrams, 1960. 279p. 28cm. [LC62]

Art since 1945. (Neue Kunst nach 1945.) Tr. Anon.
NY: Abrams, 1958. 374p. [LC62]

Expressionists. Tr. Anon. NY: Abrams, 1957. unp.
17cm. [LC62]

Paul Klee, drawings. Tr. Norbert Guterman. L:
Thames, 1960. 176p. (29cm.) [B60]

Same. NY: Abrams, 1960. 447p. 30cm. [LC62,
IT13]

GROHMANN, Will--
Wassily Kandinsky, life and work. (W--K--, Leben und Werk.) Tr. Norbert Guterman. L: Thames, 1958. 428p. [IT12]

Same. NY: Abrams, 1958. 428p. 30cm. [LC62]

Same. L: Thames, 1959. 428p. 30cm. (30.5cm.) [LC62, B59]

GROPIUS, Walter, 1883- .
The new architecture and the Bauhaus. Tr. P. Morton Shand. Introd. Frank Pick. L: Faber, 1956. 112p. [LC62]

Same. Boston: Branford, n.d. 112p. 21cm. [LC62]

Scope of total architecture. Three articles. (Architektur, Wege zu einer optischen Kultur.) Tr. Anon. 1st ed. L: Allen, 1956. (171p.) 185p. 20cm. (22.5cm.) [LC62, B56]

GROSSMANN, Gustav, 1893- .
The formula for success. The Grossman method of self-rationalization. (Sich selbst rationalisieren.) Tr. Tatiana Anderton. L: Thorsons, 1957. 271p. (22.5cm.) 23cm. [LC62, B57, IT10]

Same. Westport, Conn.: Associated Booksellers, 1958. 270p. 23cm. [LC62, IT11]

GROTEWOHL, Otto, 1894- .
Memorandum on the threat to peace represented by the armament policy of West Germany. Tr. Anon. Berlin: 1958. [LC62]

Towards a peaceful democratic and socialist Germany. (Auf dem Wege zu einem friedlichen demokratischen und sozialistischen Deutschland.) Tr. Anon. Berlin: Deutscher Zentralverlag, 1960. 119p. 27cm. [LC62]

The treaty of friendship and cooperation with the People's Republic of China. Tr. Anon. Berlin: Die Wirtschaft, 1956. 19p. 21cm. [LC62]

GRÜNEBAUM, Ernst.
Memoirs. Trs. Edith A. Simons and Norbert Guterman.
Scarsdale, NY: Grunebaum, 1960. 182p. 29cm. [LC62]

GRÜNEWALD, Mathias 16th century.
Grünewald, by Nikolaus Pevsner and Michael Meier. Includes the artist and his works. (Das Werk des Mathis
Gothardt Neithardt.) Tr. Peter Gorge. L: Thames.
42p. (43p.) (31.5cm.) [LC62, B58]

Same. NY: Abrams, 1958. 42p. 31cm. [LC62]

GRUENIG, Phillipp.
The dobermann pinscher. History and development breed-
ing, care, and management. Tr. Maximilian von Hoegen.
NY: Judd, 1959. 337p. 24cm. [LC62]

GRYPHIUS.
Selections in Loomis, C. G. 1958.

GRZIMEK, Bernhard.
Doctor Jimek, I presume. (Flug ins Schimpansenland.)
Tr. R. H. Stevens. L: Thames, (1955.) 1956. 224p.
22cm. (22.5cm.) [LC62, B55, IT8]

Same. NY: Norton, 1956. 247p. 22cm. [LC62, IT9]

No room for wild animals. (Kein Platz für wilde Tiere.)
Tr. R. W. Stevens. L: Thames, 1956. 250p. 22cm.
(22.5cm.) [LC62, B56, IT9]

Same. NY: Norton, 1957. 271p. 22cm. [LC62, IT10]

Serengeti shall not die. By B-- and Michael Grzimek.
Trs. E. L. and D. Rewald. Introd. Alan Moorehead. L:
Hamilton, 1960. 344p. 24cm. [LC62, B60]

A study of the game of the Serengeti Plains, by B-- and
Michael Grzimek. (From Zeitschrift für Säugettierkunde.)
Tr. Anon. Berlin: Verlag Naturkunde, 1960. 16p.
24cm. [LC62]

GRZIMEK, Michael, 1934-1959, jt. author. See Grzimek,
Bernhard.

GUARDINI, Romano, 1885- .
Before Mass. Tr. Elinor Castendyk Briefs. L: Long-

GUARDINI, Romano--
mans, 1957. 203p. (17.5cm.) [B57]

The conversion of Augustine. (Die Bekehrung des Heiligen
aurelius Augustinus.) Tr. Elinor Briefs. L: Sands,
1960. 258p. 22cm. [LC62]

Same. Westminster, Md.: 1960. 258p. [LC62, IT13]

The end of the modern world, a search for orientation.
Trs. Jos. Theman and Herbert Burke. NY: Sheed, 1956.
133p. 20cm. [LC62, IT9]

Same. L: Sheed, 1957. 133p. (19.5cm.) 20cm.
[LC62, B57]

The faith of modern man. Tr. Charlotte E. Forsyth.
NY: Pantheon, 1959. 166p. [LC62]

Jesus Christus, meditations. (Jesus Christus, geistliches
Wort.) Tr. Peter White. Chicago: Regnery, 1959. 111p.
21cm. [LC62, IT12]

Same. L: Burns, 1960. 111p. 19cm. (19.5cm.)
[LC62, B60]

The living God. Tr. Stanley Godman. NY: Pantheon,
1957. 112p. 21cm. [LC62]

(1) The living God. (2) The rosary of Our Lady. Trs.
(1) Stanley Godman; (2) H. von Schuecking. L: Longmans, Green, 1957. 200p. (17.5cm.) [B57]

The Lord. (Der Herr.) Tr. Elinor Castendyk Briefs.
L, NY: Longmans, 1956. 535p. 23cm. [LC62, B56]

The Lord's prayer. (Das Gebet des Herrn.) Tr. Isabel
McHugh. L: Burns, 1958. 124p. (125p.) 21cm.
[LC62, B58, IT11]

Same. NY: 1958. 124p. 21cm. [LC62, IT11]

Prayer in practice. (Vorschule des Betens.) Tr. Prince
Leopold of Loewenstein-Wertheim. L: Burns, 1957.
228p. (19.5cm.) [B57]

Same. NY: Pantheon, c1957. 228p. 22cm. [LC62]

Prayers from theology. (Theologische Gebete.) Tr.
Richard Newnham. (BNB-Newham.) NY: Herder; Edinburgh, L: Nelson, 1959. 61p. (62p.) 19cm. [LC62,
B59, IT12]

Sacred signs. (Von heiligen Zeichen.) Tr. Grace Branham. Drawings Wm. V. Cladek. St. Louis: Pio Decimo, 1956. 106p. 19cm. [LC62, IT9]

The way of the cross of our Lord and savior Jesus Christ.
(Der Kreuzweg unseres Herrn und Heilandes.) Tr. Anon.
With woodcuts Michael Biggs. Chicago: Scepter, 1959.
77p. 19cm. [LC62]

Same. Dublin: Scepter, 1959. 77p. [IT12]

GUDERIAN, Heinz, 1888-1954.
Panzer leader. (Erinnerungen eines Soldaten.) Tr. Constantine Fitzgerald. L: Harborough, 1957. 223p.
(18cm.) [B58]

GÜNTHER, Herbert, lecturer at University of Vienna.
Philosophy and psychology in the Abhidharma. Tr. Anon.
Lucknow: Buddha Vihara, 1957. 405p. 19cm. [LC62]

GÜNTHER, Klaus, 1907- . and Deckert, Kurt.
Creatures of the deep sea. (Wunderwelt der Tiefsee.)
Tr. E. W. Dickes. NY: Scribner; L: Allen, 1956.
222p. (223p.) (22.5cm.) 23cm. [LC62, B56, IT9]

GÜNTHER.
Selections in Loomis, C. G. 1958.

GUENTHER, Konrad, 1874- .
Nature and revelation. Tr. and adpt. Sigrid Munro. Ilfracombe: Stockwell, 1960. 144p. 19cm. [LC62]

GUGGISBERG, Charles Albert Walter.
Game animals of eastern Africa. Tr. Anon. 2nd rev.
ed. Nairobi: Patwa News Agency, 1956. 64p. 17cm.
[LC62]

GURLITT, Willibald, 1889- . See Bach, Johann Sebastian.
Johann Sebastian Bach, the master and his work. (J--
S--B--, Meister und sein Werk.) Tr. Oliver C. Rupprecht. St. Louis: Concordia, n.d. 149p. 19cm.
[LC62, IT10]

HAAB, Armin.
Mexican graphic art. (Mexikanische Graphik.) English
version C. C. Palmer. Teufen, Switz.: Niggli; NY:
Wittenborn, 1957. (126p.) 128p. (24cm.) [LC62, B57]

HAAB, Armin and Stocker, Alex.
Lettera, a standard book of fine lettering. (Standardbuch
guter Gebrauchsschriften.) Tr. Anon. 2nd ed. L: Niggli, 1958. 128p. 24cm. [B58]

Same. 3rd ed. Teufen, Switzerland: Niggli; NY: Hastings, 1960. 128p. 24cm. [LC62]

HAACK, Hermann.
Oriental rugs. (Echte Teppiche.) Trs. George and Cornelia Wingfield Digby. Newton, Mass.: Branford, 1960.
76p. 26cm. [LC62, IT13]

Same. L: Faber, 1960. 3-76p. (25.5cm.) 26cm.
[LC62, B60, IT13]

HAAPE, Heinrich, and Hentshaw, Dennis, jt. authors.
Moscow tram stop, a doctor's experiences with the German spearhead in Russia. Tr. Anon. L: Collins, 1957.
384p. (21.5cm.) 22cm. [LC62, B57]

HABE, Hans, pseud. (i.e. Bekessy, Jean, 1911- .)
Agent of the devil. (Im Namen des Teufels, Aufzeichnungen eines Geheimkuriers.) Tr. Ewald Osers. L: Harrap, 1958. 388p. (20.5cm.) 21cm. [LC62, B58, IT11]

Same. L: Transworld, 1959. 349p. (19.5cm.) [B59,
IT12]

All my sins. Autobiography. (Ich stelle mich. Meine
Lebensgeschichte.) Tr. E. Osers. L: Harrap, 1957.
400p. 22cm. [LC62, B57, IT10]

The devil's agent. Tr. Ewald Osers. NY: Fell, 1958.
388p. 21cm. [LC62]

Same. NY: Fell, 1958. 406p. 22cm. [LC62, IT11]

Off limits. A novel of occupied Germany. (Roman der
Besatzung Deutschlands.) Tr. Ewald Osers. L: Harrap,
417p. 22cm. [LC62, IT9]

Same. Sydney: Australian Pub. Co., 1956. 428p. [LC62, IT9]

Same. NY: Fell, 1957. 466p. 11cm. [LC62]

Walk in darkness. Tr. Richard Hanser. L: Hamilton, 1956. 315p. (18.5cm.) [B57]

HABSBURG, Erzherzog Otto V. See Otto, Archduke of Austria.

HABERLER, Gottfried.
Prosperity and depression. Tr. Anon. 3rd ed. L: Allen, 1958. 521p. (22.5cm.) [B58]

Same. 4th ed. L: Allen; Cambridge: Harvard U. Pr., 1958. 520p. 23cm. [LC62]

A survey of international trade theory. (Aussenhandel Theorie.) Tr. W. M. Blumenthal. Rev. and enl. G--H--. Princeton: 1958. 68p. [LC62]

The theory of international trade with its applications to commercial policy. Trs. Alfred Stonier and Frederic Benham. L: Hodge, 1958. 408p. 26cm. [LC62]

HÄNDLER, Gerhard.
German painting in our time. (Deutsche Maler der Gegenwart.) Tr. I. Schrier. Berlin: Rembrandt, c1956. 43,201p. 27cm. [LC62]

HÄRUNG, Bernhard, 1912- .
The sociology of the family. Tr. Meyrick Booth. Cork, Ireland: Mercier, 1959. 144p. [LC62]

HAFTMANN, Werner. See Klee, Paul, 1879-1943.
Emil Nolde. Tr. N. Gutermann. L: Thames; NY: Abrams, 1959. 44p. 96p. 33cm. [LC62, IT13]

Same. L: Thames, 1960. 140p. (33cm.) [B60]

The inward vision, watercolors, drawings, writings by Paul Klee. Tr. Norbert Guterman. L: Thames, c1958.

HAFTMANN, Werner--
61p. (33.5 x 31cm.) [LC62, B58]

Painting in the twentieth century. (Malerei im 20. Jahrhundert.) Tr. Ralph Manheim. L: Humphries, 1960. 2v. [LC62]

HAGELSTANGE, Rudolf.
Greece. (Griechenland.) Introd. Konrad Adenauer and Hermann Hesse. Tr. Anon. Book designed Detlef Michael Noack. 136p. 28cm. [LC62]

HAGELSTANGE, Rudolf. See Busch, Harald, 1904- .
Germany, countryside, cities, villages, and people.
(Deutschland, Landschaft, Städte, Dörfer und Menschen.)
Introd. R--H--. Frankfurt/Main: Umschau, c1956.
[LC62]

Same. 14th ed. NY: Hastings House, c1956. [LC62]

HAGEMANN, Otto.
The new face of Berlin. A book of pictures. (Das neue Gesicht Berlins. Ein Bildbuch.) Tr. Patrick Lynch.
Berlin-Grunewald: Arani, c1957. 13p. 139p. of illus.
22 x 23cm. [LC62]

Same. 3rd ed. c1959. 128p. [LC62]

HAGENBECK, Lorenz, 1882- .
Animals are my life. (Den Tieren gehört mein Herz.)
Tr. Alec Brown. L: Lane, 1956. 254p. (22.5cm.)
23cm. [LC62, B56]

HAHN, Albert 1889- .
Common sense economics. (Wirtschaftswissenschaft des gesunden Menschenverstandes.) Tr. Anon. NY, L:
Abelard, 1956. 244p. 23cm. [LC62, IT9]

HALLGARTEN, George Wolfgang Felix.
Devils or saviours. A history of dictatorship since 600 B.C. (Dämonen oder Retter. Eine kurze Geschichte der Diktatur seit 600 vor Christus.) Tr. Gavin Gibbons. L: Wolff, 1960. 343p. (22.5cm.) 23cm. [LC62, B60]

HALPERIN, Ernst, 1916- .
The triumphant heretic. (Der siegreiche Ketzer. Titos Kampf gegen Stalin.) Tr. Ilsa Barea. L: Heinemann,

1958. 324p. (21.5cm.) 22cm. [LC62, B58, IT11]

HAMANN, Johann Georg, 1730-1788. See Smith, Ronald Gregor.
A study in Christian existence. L: Collins, 1960. 270p. 22cm. [LC62, B60]

HAMEL, Johannes.
A Christian in East Germany. Writings gathered from several different sources. (Christ in der DDR.) Trs. Ruth and Charls C. West. NY: Association; L: SCM, 1960. 126p. (19.5cm.) 20cm. [LC62, B60, IT13]

HAMEL, Joseph, 1788-1869. See Barth, Karl, 1886- .
How to serve God in a Marxist land. NY: Association, 1950. [LC62]

HAMMERSCHLAG, Heinz Erich.
Hypnotism and crime. (Hypnose und Verbrechen.) Tr. J. Cohen. L, NY: Rider, 1956. 148p. 19cm. [LC62, B56]

Same. Hollywood: Wilshire, 1957. 148p. 22cm. [LC62, IT10]

A HANDBOOK OF THE LITURGY. (Handbuch der Liturgik für Katechetenlehrer.) Tr. H. E. Winston. NY: Herder, 1960. 316p. [IT13]

HANDRICK, Helmut.
The last paradise. (Das letze [sic] Paradis.) Tr. Elizabeth Guild. Edinburgh, L: Oliver, 1957. 158p. (30.5 cm.) [B57]

Same. Philadelphia: Chilton, 1959. 158p. 31cm. [LC 62, IT12]

HANFSTAENGEL Eberhard, 1886- .
Royal castles in Bavaria. Linderhof, Herren-Chiemsee: Neuschwanstein. Tr. Anon. München: Bruckmann, 1958. 40p. 17cm. [LC62]

HANHART, Rudolf.
Appenzell peasant art. (Appenzeller Bauernmalerei.) Eng. ver. Dennis Quibell Stephenson. Fwd. Christoph Bernoulli. Teufen: Niggli, 1959. 132p. (23.5 x 24cm.) 24cm. [LC62, B59, IT12]

HANHART, Rudolf--
Same. L: Tiranti, 1959. 132p. [IT12]

Same. NY: Hastings House, 1959. 132p. 24cm.
[LC62]

HANNAK, Jacques.
Emanuel Lasker, the life of a great chess master. (E--
L--.) Tr. Heinrich Fraenkel. L: Deutsch; NY: Simon,
1959. 320p. (22.5cm.) 23cm. [LC62, B59, IT12]

HANSLICK, Eduard, 1825-1904.
The beautiful in music. (Vom musikalisch-schoenen.)
Tr. Gustav Cohen. NY: Lap., 1957. 127p. 21cm.
[LC62]

HAPSBURG, Erzherzog Otto V. See Otto, Archduke of Austria.

HARDENBERG, Friedrich Freiherr von, 1772-1801. See
Novalis, pseud.

HARDT, Karl, S. J., ed.
We are now Catholics. Tr. Norman C. Reeves. Cork,
Ireland: Mercier, 1958. 165p. [LC62, IT12]

Same. Tr. Anon. Westminster, Md.: Newman, 1959.
[LC62]

HARDT, Karl, ed. See Goethe, Rudolf.

HARLAN, Walter, 1867-1931.
The Nuremberg egg. Drama in four acts. Tr. Bayard
Quincy Morgan. Microf. TW. at Columbia U.: 1958.
471. [LC62]

HARLINGHAUSEN, C. Harald and Merleker, Hartmuth.
Germany, travel guide. (Deutschland.) Tr. and adpt.
Donald M. Christie. Geneva, Paris: Nagel; NY:
Praeger, 1956. 744p. 684p. [LC62, IT9]

HARNACK, Carl Gustav Adolf von, 1851-1930.
History of dogma. (Lehrbuch der Dogmengeschichte.)
Tr. Niel Buchanan. (From 3rd Ger. ed.) NY: Russell,
1958. v2. 23cm. [LC62, IT11]

Outlines of the history of dogma. Tr. Edwin Knox Mit-

chell. Introd. Phillip Rieff. Boston: Beacon, 1957. 25,
567p. 21cm. [LC62, IT10]

Same. Boston: Starr King; L: Benn, 1960. 567p.
(21.5cm.) [B60]

What is Christianity? (Das Wesen des Christentums?)
Tr. Thomas Bailey Saunders. 1st Harper Torchbook ed.
NY: 1957. 301p. 21cm. [LC62, IT10]

Same. Introd. W. R. Mathews. 5th ed. L: Benn, 1958.
210p. (22.5cm.) [B58, IT10]

HARPE, Werner von.
Eastern Germany under Polish administration. Wuerzburg:
1960. 235p. 25cm. [LC62]

HARPRECHT, Klaus.
The East German rising. 17th June 1953. (Der Aufstand.)
By Stefan Brant (pseud.). Tr. and adpt. Charles Wheeler.
Fwd. John Hynd. NY: Praeger, 1957. 202p. 23cm.
[LC62]

HARRER, Heinrich, 1912- .
Seven years in Tibet. (Sieben Jahre in Tibet.) Tr.
Richard Graves. Introd. Peter Fleming. L: Hart-Davis,
c1957. 320p. [LC62, IT10]

Same. NY: Dutton, 1959. 314p. [IT12]

The white spider, history of the Eiger's north face.
(Spinne.) Tr. Hugh Merrick. L: Hart, 1959. 240p.
(23.5cm.) [B59, IT12]

The white spider, the story of the north face of the Eiger.
(Spinne.) (IT has Die weisse Spinne.) Tr. Hugh Merrick.
NY: Dutton, 1960. 240p. 24cm. [LC62, IT13]

Same. L: Hart, 1960. 240p. 24cm. [LC62]

HARRER, Heinrich. See Norbu, Thubten Jigme.

HARSDOERFFER.
Selections in Loomis, C. G. 1958.

HARTLAUB, Gustav Friedrich, 1884- .
Impressionists in France. Milan: Uffici, 1956. 95p.

HARTLAUB, Gustav Friedrich--
33cm. [LC62]

HARTLMAIER, Paul.
Golden lion, a journey through Ethiopia. (Amba ras, eine
Reise durch das Kaiserreich Athiopien.) Tr. F. A. Voigt.
L: Bles, 1956. (15-189p.) 186p. 22cm. (22.5cm.)
[LC62, B56]

HARTMANN, Emil. See Oechelhaeuser, Adolf von, 1852-
1923.
Heidelberg castle. Eng. text Louis de Branges de Bour-
cia. Based on 7th Germ. ed. rev. and added to by Emil
Hartmann and Aloys Wannemacher. Heidelberg: Hoern-
ing, 1956. [LC62]

HARTMANN, Franz.
Personal Christianity. The doctrines of Jakob Boehme.
Introd. and notes F--H--. NY: Ungar, 1957 or 8.
336p. 21cm. [LC62]

Same. 1960. [LC62]

HARTMANN, Heinz, 1894- .
Ego psychology and the problem of adaptation. (Ichpsychologie und Anpassungs problem.) Tr. David Rapa-
port. L: Imago; NY: International U. Pr., 1958.
121p. (22.5cm.) 23cm. [LC62, B59, IT11, 12]

Psychoanalysis and moral values. NY: International U.
Pr., 1960. 121p. 21cm. [LC62]

HARTMANN VON AUE.
Selections in Loomis, C. G. 1958.

HARTUNG, Fritz, 1883- .
Enlightened despotism. (Der aufgeklärte Absolutismus.)
Eng. version H. Otto. Rev. G. Barraclough. 32p. (34p.)
(21.5cm.) 22cm. [LC62, B57]

HARVEY, Wilfred.
Master luck. Adpt. from Grimms' fairy tales. Tr.
Anon. L: Harvey, private circulation, 1958. 25p.
(22.5cm.) [B59]

HARWERTH, Willi, 1894- .
A B C book. Tr. Anon. A note about this reproduction,

Philip Hofer. Meriden, Conn.: Meriden Gravure for Harvard, 1956. unp. 14cm. [LC62]

HASENCLEVER, Walter, 1890-1940.
Antigone. Tragedy in five acts. Tr. Winifred Smith. (From 7th ed.). NY: Microf. TW. at Columbia U., 1957. 571. [LC62]

The human race. (Die Menschen.) Tr. George Wellwarth. TW. n.p. 1958. 261. [LC62]

The magnificent Hugo. A comedy in three acts. American adpt. Louis S. Bardoly. NY: Hart Steno, c1960. 25, 40, 291. 29cm. TW. [LC62]

HASS, Frederick Wilhelm, 1818-1890.
A translation and copy of records from our grandfather, The Rev. F. Wilhelm Hass, by Sophia and Alma Hass. Galesville, Wis.: n.d. 17p. 22cm. [LC62]

HASS, Hans.
Diving to adventure. Harpoon and camera under the sea. Tr. Barrows Mussey. L: Jarrolds, 1956. 236p. 22cm. [LC62]

I photographed under the seven seas. (Ich tauchte in den 7 Meeren.) Tr. James Cleugh. L: Jarrolds, 1956. 163p. (164p.) 26cm. [LC62, B56]

Men and sharks. Tr. Barrows Mussey. L: Jarrolds, 1957. 232p. 22cm. [LC62]

We come from the sea. (Wir kommen aus dem Meer.) Tr. Alan Houghton Brodrick. L: Jarrolds, 1958. 238p. 22cm. [LC62]

Same. L: Jarrolds, 1958. 2997. (22cm.) [B58, IT11]

Same. Garden City, NY: Doubleday, 1959. 288p. 24cm. [LC62, IT12]

HASS, Sophia. See Hass, Frederick Wilhelm.

HASSE, Helmut, 1898- .
Prime numbers. Tr. of the first chapter. (Proben mathematischer Forschung in allgemeinverständlicher Behandlung.) Trs. Serge Kunitsky and W. H. Meyer.

HATJE, Gerd, ed. See New German architecture.
New German architecture. L: Architectural, 1956.
[LC62]

HAUFF, Wilhelm, 1802-1827.
Dwarf long nose. (Der Zwerg Nase.) Tr. Doris Orgel.
NY: Random, 1960. 60p. 24cm. [LC62, IT13]

HAUPT-BATTAGLIA, Heidi.
Let's embroider. (Wir sticken weiter.) Tr. Anon.
Rev. Eng. ed. L: Batsford, 1960. 200p. 26cm.
[LC62]

HAUPTMANN, Gerhart Johann Robert, 1862-1946.
The beaver coat. A thieve's comedy in four acts.
(Der Biberpelz.) Tr. Bayard Quincy Morgan. n. p.,
1958. 661. Microf. TW. at Columbia U. [LC62]

The heretic of Soana. (Der Ketzer von Soana.) Tr. B.
Q. Morgan. Introd. Harold von Hofe. NY: Ungar, 1958.
192p. 19cm. [LC62, IT11]

Same. L: Calder, 1960. 124p. (18.5cm.) [LC62,
B60]

The weavers. A drama of the eighteen forties. (Die
Weber.) Tr. with notes Bayard Quincy Morgan. n. p.,
1958. 89, 31. Microf. TW. at Columbia U. [LC62]

The weavers. Hannele. The beaver coat. (Die Weber
hanneles Himmelfahrt. Der Bibenpelz.) Trs. Horst
Frenz and Miles Waggoner. Introd. Horst Frenz. 218p.
19cm. [LC62]

HAUPTMANN, Gerhart. See Sinden, Margaret J., 1915- .
Gerhart Hauptmann, the prose plays. Tr. Anon.
Toronto: U. of Toronto Pr.; L: Oxford U. Pr., 1957.
238p. 22cm. [LC62, B58]

HAUPTVERBAND DER ÖSTERREICHISCHEN BUCHHÄNDLER.
The Austrian book. Tr. Anon. Vienna: 1960. 94p.
18cm. [LC62]

HAUSDORFF, Felix, 1868-1942.
Set theory. (Mengenlehre.) Trs. John R. Aumann, et al.

(From 3rd ed.) NY: Chelsea, 1957. 352p. 24cm.
[LC62, IT10]

HAUSER, Arnold, 1892- .
The philosophy of art history. (Philosophie der Kunstge-
schichte.) Tr. Anon. L: Routledge, 1959. 428p. 22cm.
[LC62]

Same. NY: Knopf, 1959. 410p. 22cm. [LC62, IT12]

HAUSER, Walter. See Matt, Leonard V.
St. Francis of Assisi. (Franz von Assisi.) Tr. Sebastian Bullough. L: Longmans; Chicago: Regnery, 1956.
106p. 25cm. [LC62]

HAUSMANN, Manfred. See Dirks, Walter.

HAUSMANN, Manfred, 1898- . See Karfeld, Kurt Peter.
Germany in color. Tr. Anon. NY: Studio, 1957.
[LC62]

HAY, Florence Huntley, 1913- .
Snow White and the seven dwarfs. Rhymed and illus.
Florence Huntley Hay for Mary Kay Stolz on her seventh
birthday, June 1957. Adpt. from Grimms' tales. Tokyo:
Radiopress, n.d. 48p. 29cm. [LC62]

HAYDE, Bertyl, ed.
A big book to grow on. (Das grosse Buch, für unsere
Kleinen.) Tr. Anon. L: Dobson; NY: Watts, 1960.
240p. (24.5cm.) [B61]

HAYDN, Joseph, 1732-1809.
Collected correspondence and London notebooks. Compiled
and tr. Howard Chandler Robbins Landon. L: Barrie,
1959. 367p. [LC62]

Same. Fair Lawn, NJ: Essential, 1959. 367p. 23cm.
[LC62, IT12]

HAYEK, Heinrich von, 1900- .
The human lung. (Die menschliche Lunge.) Tr. Vernon
E. Krahl. NY: Hafner, 1960. 372p. 26cm. [LC62,
IT13]

HEBBEL, Friedrich, 1813-1863.
Agnes Bernhauer. A German tragedy in five acts. (A--

HEBBEL, Friedrich--
B---.) Tr. Bayard Quincy Morgan. Microf. TW. at Columbia U., 1958. 105l. [LC62]

The Nibelungs. A German tragedy in three parts. Tr.
into Eng. verse Bayard Quincy Morgan. Microf. TW. at
Columbia U., 1958. 3231. [LC62]

Selections in Loomis, C. G. 1960.

HEBEL, Johann Peter, 1760-1826.
Francisca, and other stories. Trs. Clavia Goodman and
Bayard Quincy Morgan. Lexington, KY.: Anvil, c1957.
106p. 16cm. [LC62, IT10]

HECK, Fritzlutz.
Animal Safari. (Grosswild in Etoschaland.) Tr. Oliver
Coburn. L: Methuen, 1956. 212p. (22.5cm.) 23cm.
[LC62, B56, IT9]

HEGEL, George Wilhelm Friedrich, 1770-1831.
Encyclopedia of philosophy. (Encyclopedia der philosoph-
ischen Wissenschaften im Grundrisse.) Tr. Gustav Emil
Mueller. NY: Philosophical Lib., 1959. 287p. 19cm.
[LC62, IT12, 13]

Hegel, an annotated selection. Ed. Wanda Orynski. Tr.
Anon. L: Owen, 1960. 361p. (19.5cm.) [LC62, B60]

Hegel. Highlights, an annotated selection. Trs. J. Sibree and J. B. Baillie. Ed. Wanda Orynski. NY: Philosophical Lib., 1960. 361p. 20cm. [LC62, IT13]

The philsophy of history. (Vorlesungen über die Philosophie der Geschichte.) Tr. J. Sibree. NY: Dover, 1956.
457p. 21cm. [LC62, IT9]

Philosophy of right. (Grundlinien der Philosophie des
Rechts.) Tr. with notes, T. M. Knox. Oxford: Clarendon, 1958. 382p. 23cm. [LC62]

Selections. Trs. Josiah Royce, J. B. Baillie, and W.
Wallace. Ed. J. Loewenberg. NY: Scribner, c1957.
468p. 17cm. [LC62]

HEGEMANN, Otto.
The new face of Berlin. A book of pictures. Tr. Patrick

Lynch. Berlin: Arani, c1957. 22 x 23cm. [LC62]

HEHNER, D. S. , ed. See Böhme, Jakob, 1575-1624.
The aurora. Tr. Anon. L: Watkins, 1960. [LC62]

HEICHELHEIM, Fritz Moritz, 1901- .
An ancient economic history, from the palaeolithic age.
The migrations of the German, Slavic, and Arabic na-
tions. (Wirtschaftsgeschichte des Altertums.) Tr. Anon.
Rev. ed. Leiden: Sijthoff, 1958. v. 25cm. [LC62,
IT11]

HEIDEGGER, Martin, 1889- .
Essays in metaphysics. Identity and difference. (Identi-
tät und Differenz.) Tr. Kurt F. Leidecker. NY: Philosophical Lib., 1960. 82p. 19cm. [LC62, IT13]

Same. Tr. Anon. Introd. Werner Brock. Chicago:
1960. 369p. 17cm. [LC62]

Existence and being. Trs. D. Scott, R. F. C. Hull and
A. Crick. 2nd ed. L: Vision, 1956. 399p. 19cm.
[LC62]

An introduction to metaphysics. (Einführung in die Metaphysik.) Tr. Ralph Manheim. New Haven: Yale U. Pr.,
1959. 214p. 22cm. (22.5cm.) [LC62, B60, IT12]

Kant and the problem of metaphysics. Tr. , introd. and
notes James Spencer Churchill. (TW. ms.) Bloomington,
Indiana: n. d. 331p. [LC62]

The question of being. (Über die Linie.) (Ger. and Eng.)
Trs. William Kluback and Jean T. Wilde. NY: Twayne,
1958. 109p. 23cm. [LC62, IT12]

Same. L: Vision, 1959. 109p. (22.5cm.) [B59]

What is philosophy. (Was ist das--die Philosophie.) Trs.
W. Kluback and Jean T. Wilde. L: Vision, 1958. 397p.
21cm. [LC62, B58]

Same. NY: Twayne, 1958. 97p. 21cm. [LC62, IT11]

HEIDGEN, Heinz
The diamond seeker. The story of John Williamson.
(Diamantensucher in Tanganjika.) Trs. I. and F. McHugh.

HEIDGEN, Heinz--
  L: Blackie, 1959. 139p. (140p.) 21cm. (21.5cm.)
  [LC62, B59, IT12]

HEILER, Friedrich, 1892- .
  Prayer. (Das Gebet.) Trs. Samuel McCombs and J. Edgar Park. L: Oxford U. Pr., 1958. 376p. [IT12]

  Prayer, a study in the history and psychology of religion.
  Tr. and ed. Samuel McComb with J. Edgar Park. NY:
  Oxford U. Pr., 1958. 376p. 21cm. [LC62]

  Same. (Die Menschheit betet.) L: Oxford U. Pr., 1958.
  376p. 21cm. [B59]

HEIM, Karl, 1874- .
  Christian faith and natural science. (Der christliche
  Gottesglaube und die Naturwissenschaft, I, Grundlegung.)
  Tr. N. Horton Smith. NY: Harper, 1957. 256p. 21cm.
  [LC62]

  Jesus the Lord. The sovereign authority of Jesus and
  God's revelation in Christ. (Der evangelische Glaube und
  das Denken der Gegenwart. (2) Jesus der Herr.) Tr. D.
  H. Van Daalen. Edinburgh, L: Oliver, 1959. 192p.
  22cm. (22.5cm.) [LC62, B59, IT12]

  Jesus the world's perfecter. The atonement and renewal
  of the world. (Der evangelische Glaube und das Denken
  der Gegenwart. (3) Jesus der Weltvollender.) Tr. D. H.
  Van Daalen. Edinburgh, L: Oliver, 1959. 234p. (22.5
  cm) 23cm. [LC62, B59, IT12]

HEIMER, Franz Carl, librettist.
  Abu Hassan. Music by C. M. Weber. Eng. ver. David
  Harris. L: Oxford, 1959. 27p. (18cm.) [B59]

HEIMERAN, Ernst, 1902- .
  Paint a black horse. (Der schwarze Schimmel.) Tr.
  Leila Berg. L: Methuen, n.d. 34p. (22.5cm.) [B58,
  IT11]

HEINE, Heinrich, 1797-1856.
  Bittersweet poems of H--H--. Tr. Joseph Auslander. Mt.
  Vernon, NY: Peter Pauper, 1956. 60p. 19cm. [LC62,
  IT9]

(Die Lorelei.) Eng. ver. Mark Twain. Berkeley Heights,
NJ: Oriole, 1956. 9l. 18cm. [LC62]

Heinrich Heine, a biographical anthology. Ed. Hugo Bie-
ber. Tr. and selected Moses Hadas. Philadelphia: J. P.
S. A. , 1956. 452p. 24cm. [LC62, IT9]

Poems. Selected and tr. Louis Untermeyer. NY: Heritage, 1957. 297p. 25cm. [LC62, IT10]

The poetry and prose of Heinrich Heine. Selected, ed.
and introd. Frederic Owen. New tr. Aaron Kramer.
Prose newly tr. F--O--. Poetry tr. Louis Untermeyer.
NY: Citadel, 1959. 874p. 21cm. [LC62]

Religion and philosophy in Germany. A fragment. (Zur
Geschichte der Religion und Philosophie in Deutschland.)
Tr. John Snodgrass. Introd. Ludwig Marcuse. Boston:
Beacon, 1959. 177p. 21cm. [LC62, IT12]

Same. L: Mayflower, 1959. 177p. (20cm.) [B60]

Selection in Chase, G. H. Tr. poems from the German.

Selections in Flores, Anthol. 1960.

Selections in Loomis, C. G. 1960.

The sword and the flame. Selected prose. Based on tr.
Charles G. Leland. Ed. and introd. Alfred Werner.
NY: Yoseloff, 1960. 584p. 24cm. [LC62, IT13]

HEINISCH, Paul, 1878- .
Christ in prophecy. (Christus der Erlöser im Alten Testa-
ment.) Tr. William G. Heidt. Collegeville, Minn. :
Liturgical Pr. , c1956. 279p. 24cm. [LC62, IT9]

History of the Old Testament. Tr. W. Heidt. Collegeville, Minn. : Liturgical Pr. , 1956. 455p. 23cm.
[LC62]

Same. Rev. and supplemented. Liturgical Pr. , 1957.
457p. 24cm. [LC62]

Theology of the Old Testament. (Theologie des Alten Testaments.) Tr. William E. Heidt. Collegeville, Minn. :
Liturgical Pr. , 1957. 476p. 24cm. [LC62, IT13]

HEINKEL, Ernst, 1888- .
He 1000. (Stürmisches Leben.) Tr. Mervyn Savill. Ed.
Jürgen Thorwald. L: Hutchinson, 1956. 287p. 24cm.
[LC62, IT9]

Stormy life. Memoirs of a pioneer of the air age.
(Stürmisches Leben.) Tr. Anon. Ed. Jürgen Thorwald.
NY: Dutton, 1956. 256p. 22cm. [LC62, IT9]

HEINRICH, Willi.
Crack of doom. (Der goldene Tisch.) Tr. Oliver Coburn.
NY: Farrar, 1958. 313p. 22cm. [LC62, IT11]

Same. NY, Montreal: Bantam, 1959. 313p. [IT12]

The cross of iron. (Das geduldige Fleisch.) Trs. Richard
and Clara Winston. Indianapolis: Bobbs-Merrill, 1956.
456p. 22cm. [LC62, IT9]

Same. NY: Bantam, 1957. 437p. [IT10]

Mark of shame. A novel. (Die Gezeichneten.) Tr. Sigrid Rock. L: Weidenfeld, 1959. 316p. (20.5cm.) [B59,
IT12]

Same. NY: Farrar, 1959. 316p. 22cm. [LC62, IT12]

Same. NY, Montreal: Bantam, 1959. 313p. [IT12]

Same. L: Transworld, 1960. 284p. (16.5cm.) [B60]

The savage mountain. (Der goldene Tisch.) Trs. Oliver
Coburn and Ursula Lehrburger. L: Weidenfeld, 1958.
320p. (20.5cm.) 21cm. [LC62, B58, IT11]

Same. L: Transworld, 1959. 319p. (16.5cm.) [B59,
IT12]

The willing flesh. (Das geduldige Fleisch.) Trs. Richard
and Clara Winston. L: Weidenfeld, 1956. 478p. (20.5
cm.) [LC62, B56, IT9]

Same. Slightly abr. ed. L: Transworld, 1957. 368p.
(16cm.) [B57, IT10]

HEINRICH VON VELDEKE.
Selection in Loomis, C. G. 1958.

HEINROTH, Oskar, 1871-1945. and Katharina.
The birds. (Aus dem Leben der Vögel.) Tr. Michael
Cullen. Ann Arbor: U. of Michigan Pr., 1958. 181p.
22cm. [LC62]

Same. 178p. [IT11]

Same. L: Faber, 1959. 175p. 21cm. [B59]

Same. Ann Arbor: U. of Mich. Pr., 1960. 81p.
[IT13]

HEISENBERG, Werner, 1901- .
The physicist's conception of nature. (Das Naturbild der
heutigen Physik.) Tr. A. J. Pomerans. L: Hutchinson;
NY: Harcourt, 1958. 192p. (19cm.) 20cm. [LC62,
B58, IT11]

Physics and philosophy. The revolution in modern science.
(Physik und Philosophie.) Tr. Anon. L: Allen, 1959.
176p. (22.5cm.) 23cm. [LC62, B59]

HEISSENBUETTEL, Helmut, 1921- .
Selections in Rothenberg. 1959.

HELFRITZ, Hans, 1902- .
The Yemen. (Glückliches Arabien.) Tr. Michael Heron.
L: Allen, 1958. 180p. (3-181p.) (22.5cm.) [LC62,
B58, IT11]

HELLER, Erich, 1911- .
The disinherited mind. Essays in modern German literature and thought. (Enterbter Geist, Essays über neue
Dichter und Denker.) Tr. Anon. L: Bowes; NY: Farrar, 1957. 306p. 21cm. [LC62]

Same. NY: Meridian, 1959. 306p. 18cm. [LC62]

HELMS-BLASCHE, Anna.
(Bunte Tänze, wie wir sie suchten und fanden.) Tr. Anon.
Leipzig: Hofmeister, 1957. 173p. 30cm. [LC62]

HENGSTENBERG, Ernst Wilhelm, 1802-1869.
Christology of the Old Testament and a commentary on the
Messianic predictions. Trs. Theodor Meyer and James
Martin. Pref. Merrill F. Unger. Grand Rapids: Kregel,
1956. 4v. 23cm. [LC62, IT9]

HENRY, Nancy.
The pot of fat. This play is founded on Grimms' story
The cat and mouse as friends. L: Philip, 28p. (20.5
cm.) 21cm. [LC62, B56]

Red riding hood. A play for puppets or children, founded
on the old story. L: Philip, 1956. 26p. (20.5cm.)
21cm. [LC62, B56]

Snow White and Rose-Red. A play for puppets or children
founded on a story by the brothers Grimm. L: Philip,
1956. 30p. (20.5cm.) 21cm. [LC62, B56]

The turnip. A play for puppets or children founded on a
story by the brothers Grimm. L: Philip, 1956. 23p.
(20.5cm.) 21cm. [LC62, B56]

HENTSHAW, Dennis, jt. author. See Haape, Heinrich.
Moscow tram stop. A doctor's experiences with the Ger-
man spearhead in Russia. Tr. Anon. L: Collins, 1957.
[LC62]

HENZE, Anton and Filthaut, Theodor.
Contemporary church art. (Kirchliche Kunst der Gegen-
wart.) Tr. Cecily Hastings. Ed. Maurice Lavanoux.
L, NY: Sheed, 1956. 64, 128p. 29cm. [LC62, B57,
IT9]

HERAMBOURG, Peter, 1661-1720.
Saint John Eudes, a spiritual portrait. Tr. Ruth Hauser.
Ed. and annotated Wilfried E. Myatt. Introd. Edward A.
Ryan. Westminster: Newman, 1960. 318p. 23cm.
[LC62]

HERBERSTEIN, Sigmund, Freiherr von, 1486-1566.
Commentaries on Muscovite affairs. Ed. and tr. Oswald
P. Backus. Lawrence, Kan.: U. of Kansas, 1956. 153p.
22cm. [LC62]

HERBERTS, Kurt.
The complete book of artist's techniques. (Die Maltechni-
ken.) Tr. Anon. L: Thames; NY: Praeger, 1958.
351p. (21.5 x 21.5cm.) [LC62, B58, IT11]

HERING, Richard.
Dictionary of classical and modern cookery and practical
reference manual for the hotel, restaurant, and catering

trade. Vocabulary in Eng., Fr., Ger., Italian, and
Span. Tr. Walter Bickel. (11th rev. ed.) Giessen:
Pfanneberg, 1958. 852p. 20cm. [LC62]

HERLIN, Hans, 1925- .
Udet. A man's life. (Udet--eines Mannes Leben.) Tr.
Mervyn Savill. L: Macdonald, 1960. 22cm. (22.5cm.)
[LC62, B60]

HERMANN, Lazar, 1896- . See Brandt, Willy, 1913- .
My road to Berlin. Garden City, L: Davies; NY:
Doubleday, 1960. [LC62]

HERMANN, Lazar, 1896- . See Lania, Leo, pseud.

HERRIGEL, Eugen, 1884-1955.
The method of Zen. (Der Zen-Weg.) Tr. R. F. C. Hull.
Ed. Hermann Tausend. NY: Pantheon, 1960. 124p.
21cm. [LC62, IT13]

Same. L: Routledge, 1960. 102p. (19cm.) [B60,
IT13]

Zen in the art of archery. (Zen in der Kunst des Bogen-
schiessens.) Tr. R. F. C. Hull. Fwd. D. T. Zuzuki.
L: Routledge, 1956. 107p. [LC62]

HERRIGEL, Gustie Luise.
Zen in the art of flower arrangement. (Der Blumenweg.)
Tr. R. F. C. Hull. L: Routledge; Newton Centre,
Mass.: Bradford, 1958. 124p. 19cm. [LC62, B58,
IT11]

HERRLIGKOFFER, Karl Maria.
Nanga parbat. Trs. and additions Eleanor Brockett and
Anton Ehrenzweig. L: Hamilton, 1956. 1957. 208p.
(18.5cm.) [B57]

HERRMANN, Lazar. See Lania, Leo, pseud. (i.e. Hermann, Lazar, 1896- .)

HERRMANN, Paul, 1905- .
The great age of discovery. (Zeigt mir Adams Testament.)
Tr. Arnold J. Pomerans. NY: Harper, 1958. 507p.
25cm. [LC62, IT11]

The world unveiled. (Zeigt mir Adams Testament.) Tr.

HERRMANN, Paul--
Arnold Pomerans. L: Hamilton, 1958. 507p. (25.5cm.)
[B58]

The world unveiled, the story of exploration from Colum-
bus to Livingstone. (Zeigt mir Adams Testament.) Tr.
A. J. Pomerans. L: Hamilton, 1958. 507p. 26cm.
[LC62, IT11]

HERTLING, Ludwig Freiherr von, 1892- and Kirschbaum,
Engelbert, 1902- .
A history of the Catholic Church. Tr. Anselm Gordon
Biggs. Westminster, Md.: Newman, 1957. 643p. 23cm.
[LC62, IT10]

Same. Rev. ed. L: Darton, 1960. 274p. (19cm.)
[LC62, B56]

Same. L: Owen, 1958. 645p. (22cm.) [B58]

The Roman catacombs and their martyrs. (Die römischen
Katakomben und ihre Märtyrer.) Tr. M. Joseph Costelloe.
Milwaukee: Bruce, c1956. 224p. 22cm. [LC62, IT9]

HERTZ, Heinrich Rudolph, 1857-1894.
The principles of mechanics, presented in a new form.
Trs. D. E. Jones and J. T. Walley. Pref. H. von Helm-
holtz. Introd. Robert S. Cohen. NY: Dover, 1956.
46, 217p. 21cm. [LC62, IT9]

HERZER, Ludwig and Lohner, Fritz.
The land of smiles. (Das Land des Lächelns.) Tr. Christopher Hassal. L: Glocken, 1959. [IT13]

HERZL, Theodor, 1860-1934.
Complete diaries. Ed. Raphael Patai. Tr. Harry Zohn.
NY: Herzl, 1960. 5v. 1961p. 22cm. [LC62]

Diaries. (Tagebücher, 18??-1904.) Tr. Marvin Loewen-
thal. NY: Dial, 1956. 494p. 24cm. [LC62, IT9]

Same. L: Gollancz, 1958. 494p. (22.5cm.) 24cm.
[B58]

Herzl speaks his mind on issues, events, and men. Tr.
Anon. Ed. Herbert Parzen. NY: Herzl, 1960. 104p.
17cm. [LC62]

The Jewish state. An attempt at a modern solution of the Jewish question. (Der Judenstaat.) Tr. I. M. Lask, based on orig. tr. S. D. Avigor. Introd. essay, B. Locker. New ed. Tel-Aviv: Newman, 1956. 156p. [LC62, IT9]

Old-new land. Novel. (Altneuland.) Tr. Paul Arnold. Haifa: Haifa, 1960. 218p. 28cm. [LC62]

Same. 220p. [IT13]

HESS, Manfred.
Paint film defects, their causes and cure. (Häufige Anstrichmängel und Anstrichschäden.) Tr. Anon. Reprint with rev. L: Chapman, 1958. 543p. 23cm. [LC62]

HESS, Moses, 1812-1875.
Rome and Jerusalem. (Rom und Jerusalem.) Tr. Maurice J. Bloom. NY: Philosophical Lib., 1958. 89p. 22cm. [LC62, IT11]

HESSE, Hermann, 1877- .
Demian. (D--.) Tr. W. J. Strachan. L: Owen, Vision, 1958. 184p. 19cm. [LC62, B58, IT11]

Goldmund. (Narziss und Goldmund.) Tr. Geoffrey Dunlop. L: Owen, Vission, 1959. 287p. (19cm.) 20cm. [LC62, B59, IT12]

The journey to the East. (Die Morgenlandfahrt.) Tr. Hilda Rosner. L: Owen, Vision, 1956. 93p. 19cm. [LC62, B56, IT9]

Same. NY: Noonday, 1957. 118p. 22cm. [LC62, IT10]

Magister Ludi. (Das Glasperlenspiel.) Tr. Mervyn Savill. NY: Ungar, 1957. 502p. 22cm. [LC62, IT10]

The prodigy. (Unterm Rad.) Tr. Walter J. Strachan. L: Owen, Vision, 1957. 188p. 19cm. [LC62, B57, IT10]

Siddhartha. (S--.) Tr. Hilda Rosner. L: Owen, 1956. 167p. 19cm. [LC62]

Same. NY: New Directions, 1957. 153p. [LC62, IT10]

HESSE, Hermann--
Same.   Calcutta, etc., Rupa, 1958.   130p.   [IT11]

Steppenwolf.   (S--.)   Tr. Basil Creighton.   NY: Ungar,
1957.   309p.   19cm.   [LC62, IT10]

Same.   1960.   [IT13]

HESSLER, Bertram.
The Bible in the light of modern science.   (Die Bibel in
dem Spannungsfeld der modernen Naturwissenschaften.)
Tr. Sylvester Saller.   Chicago: Franciscan Herald, 1960.
87p.   19cm.   [LC62, IT13]

HETTES, Karel.
Old Venetian glass.   Photo.   Werner Forman.   Tr. Ota
Vojtisek.   L: Spring, 1960.   46p.   (28cm.)   [B60]

HEUSS, Theodor, 1884- . et al.
Four essays on Germany.   n. p.   Intercultural, 1957.   24p.
[LC62]

HEYDTE, Friedrich August, Baron von der 1907- .
Daedalus returned, Crete, 1941.   Tr. William Stanley
Moss.   L: Hutchinson, 1958.   185p.   (186p.)   22cm.
[LC62, B58, IT10]

Return to Crete.   Tr. W. Standley Moss.   L: World,
1959.   159p.   (17cm.)   [B59, IT12]

HEYM, Georg.
The autopsy.   Ed. and tr. M. Hamburger.   In Spender's
Coll.   1960.

HICKETHIER, Alfred.
Hickethier colour system.   (Farbenordnung Hickethier.)
Tr. Otto M. Lilien.   Hannover: Osterwald, 1956.   99p.
25cm.   [LC62]

HIEBEL, Friedrich, 1903
Novalis, German poet, European thinker, Christian mys-
tic.   (A condensed version, in Eng. of Novalis, der
Dichter der Blauen Blume.)   Tr. Anon.   2nd ed., rev.
Chapel Hill: U. of North Carolina Pr., 1959.   126p.
24cm.   [LC62]

HILBERT, David, 1962-1943. and Cohn-Vossen, S.
The foundations of geometry. (The original formed the
first part of Festschrift zur Feier der Enthüllung des
Gauss-Weber-Denkmals in Göttingen, Grundlagen der
Geometrie.) Tr. E. J. Townsend. LaSalle, Ill.: Open
Court, 1959. 143p. 19cm. [LC62]

Geometry and the imagination. (Anschauliche Geometrie.)
Tr. P. Nemenyi. NY: Chelsea, 1956. 375p. 23cm.
[LC62]

HILDEBRAND, Dietrich V., 1889- .
Liturgy and personality. (Liturgie der Persönlichkeit.)
Tr. Anon. Baltimore: Helicon, 1960. 131p. 23cm.
[LC62, IT13]

Transformation in Christ. On the Christian attitude of
mind. (Die Umgestaltung in Christus.) Tr. Anon. Baltimore: Helicon, 1960. 406p. 23cm. [LC62]

HILDEBRAND, Dietrich V. and Jourdain, Alice M.
Graven images, substitutes for true morality. Tr. Anon.
NY: McKay, 1957. 204p. 21cm. [LC62]

HILLMANN, Willibrord, 1912- .
Children's Bible. (Bilderbibel.) Tr. Lawrence Atkinson.
Illus. Johannes Grüger. Baltimore: Helicon, 1959. 92p.
21cm. [LC62, IT13]

Same. L: Burns, 1959. 95p. (21cm.) [B59, IT13]

HILPISCH, Stephanus, 1894- .
Benedictinism through changing centuries. (Das Benedikt-
inertum im Wandel der Zeiten.) Tr. Leonard J. Doyle.
Collegeville, Minn.: St. John's Abbey, 1958. 172p.
23cm. [LC62, IT13]

History of Benedictine nuns. (Geschichte der Benediktin-
erinnen.) Tr. M. Joanne Muggli. Ed. Leonard J. Doyle.
Collegeville, Minn.: St. John's Abbey, 1958. 122p.
23cm. [LC62, IT13]

HILS, Karl.
Crafts for all, a natural approach to crafts. (Weren [sic]
für alle.) Fwd. Herbert Read. Tr. Anon. Newton
Centre, Mass.: Branford, 1960. 168p. 25cm. [LC62,
IT13]

HILS, Karl--
Same. L: Routledge, 168p. (24.5cm.) [B60, IT13]

The toy, its value, construction and use. (Spielsachen
zum Selbermachen.) Tr. Edward Fitzgerald. L: Ward,
1959. 72p. (21cm.) [LC62, B59, IT12]

HINTERHOFF, Eugene.
Disengagement. (Pläne für ein militärisches Auseinander-
rücken der Weltmächte in Deutschland.) Tr. Anon. Fwd.
Sir John Slessor. L: Atlantic, Stevens, n.d. 445p.
23cm. [LC62]

HIRMER, Max. Illus. See Lullies, Reinhard, 1907- .

HIRMER, Max. See Lange, Kurt.

HIRMER, Max. See Marinatos, Spyridon.

HIRMER, Max. See Rice, David Talbot, 1930- .

HIRSCH, Samson Raphael, 1808-1888.
Judaism eternal, selected essays from the writings of S--
R--H--. Tr. and annotated with introd. and a short biography I. Grunfeld. L: Soncino, 1956. 2v. (Vol. 1,
270p. vol. 2, 315p.) 23cm. [LC62, B57]

HIRSCHBERGER, Johannes.
The history of philosophy. (Die Geschichte der Philosophie.)
Tr. Anthony N. Fuerst. Milwaukee: Bruce, 1958-1959.
2v. 23cm. [LC62, IT11]

HIRSCHFIELD, Victor, 1860-1940. See Lehar, Franz, 1870-
1948.
The merry widow. (Die lustige Witwe.) New book and
lyrics Phil Park. L: Blocken, 1958. 78p. (19.5cm.)
20cm. [LC62, B58]

HOCH, Dorothee.
Healing and salvation. (Heil und Heilung.) Tr. John
Hoad. L: SCM, 1958. 48p. 22cm. [LC62, B58, IT11]

HOCHWAELDER, Fritz, 1911- .
The public prosecutor, play in three acts. (Der öffent-
liche Ankläger.) Tr. Kitty Black. L: French, 1958.
4, 63p. (21.5cm.) 22cm. [LC62, B58, IT11]

HOEFLICH, Eugen. See later name, Ben-Gavriel, Moshe
Yaacov, 1891- .

HOEGLER, R. G. See Kerenyi, C., 1897- .

HÖHNEL, Ludwig, Ritter von, 1857-1942.
Count Teleke and the discovery of Lakes Rudolf and Stef-
anie. (Zum Rudolf- und Stephaniesee.) Tr. Anon. Ed.
C. G. Richards, in association with the East African Literature Bureau. L: Macmillan, 1960. 85p. (18.5cm.)
19cm. [LC62, B60]

HÖLDERLIN, Friedrich, 1770-1843.
Antigone. Libretto. Eng. music Carl Orff. Poem F--
H--. Tr. William Ashbrook. Terre Haute, Ind.: n.p.,
1960. 341. [LC62]

Selected poems, the German text. Tr., introd. and notes
J. B. Leishman. 2nd ed. rev. and enl. NY: Grove,
1956. 156p. 22cm. [LC62]

Selections in Flores, Anthol, 1960.

Selections in Kerenyi, C. Greece in colour. 1957.

Selections in Loomis, C. G. 1960.

Selections in Loomis, C. G. Prose. 1960.

HÖLLERER, Walter, 1922- .
Selections in Rothenburg, 1959.

HÖRNING, Bernd.
Soviet helminthology, literature survey for the years
1946-1953. Berlin: Brandt, 1957. 135p. 30cm. [LC
62]

HOESS, Rudolf (Franz Ferdinand), 1900-1947.
Commandant of Auschwitz. (Kommandant in Auschwitz.)
Tr. C. Fitzgibbon. L: Weidenfeld, 1959. 252p. (22.5
cm.) 23cm. [LC62, B59, IT13]

Same. C-- of A--, autobiography. Cleveland: World,
1960. 285p. 22cm. [LC62, IT13]

HOFER, Ernst.
Arctic Riviera, a book about the beauty of Northeast
Greenland. Tr. Anon. Berne: Kümmerly, 1957. 125p.
(30.5cm.) 31cm. [LC62, B58]

HOFER, Walther, 1920- .
Neutrality as the principle of Swiss foreign policy. Tr.
Mary Hottinger. Zürich: Schweizer Spiegel, 1957. 40p.
19cm. [LC62, IT10]

HOFINGER, Johannes.
The art of teaching Christian doctrine, the good news and
its proclamation. Tr. Anon. Notre Dame, Ind.: U. of
Notre Dame Pr., 1957. 278p. 24cm. [LC62]

HOFINGER, Joahnnes, et al.
Worship, the life of the missions. Tr. Mary Perkins
Ryan. Notre Dame, Ind.: U. of Notre Dame Pr., 1958.
342p. 24cm. [LC62, IT11]

HOFFER, Paul.
Guide for religious administrators. Tr. Gabriel J. Rus.
Milwaukee: Bruce, 1959. 171p. 22cm. [LC62, IT12]

HOFFMANN, Edith, 1907- . See Neumayer, Heinrich,
1905- .
Expressionism, with 24 illus. chosen by Heinrich Neumayer. Tr. Anon. L: Methuen, 1956. [LC62]

Same. NY: Crown, 1958. [LC62]

HOFFMANN, Ernst Theodor Amadeus, 1776-1822.
The king's bride. (Die Königsbraut.) Tr. Paul Turner.
L: Calder, 1959. 89p. 19cm. [LC62, B59, IT12]

Tales of Hoffmann. (Erzählungen.) Tr. Anon. Ed.
Christopher Lazare. NY: Grove, 1959. 509p. 21cm.
[LC62, IT13]

Same. L: Calder, 1960. 509p. (20.5cm.) 21cm.
[LC62, B60, IT13]

HOFFMANN, Hans, 1923- .
The theology of Reinhold Niebuhr. (Die Theologie Reinhold Niebuhrs im Lichte seiner Lehre von der Sünde.) Tr.
Louise Pettibone Smith. NY: Scribner, 1956. 269p.
22cm. [LC62, IT9]

HOFFMANN, Heinrich, 1856-1900.
Struwwelpeter, or, Merry stories and funny pictures.
(S---.) Tr. Anon. L: Blackie, 1960. (26cm.) [B60]

HOFFMANN, Herbert Daniel.
The date of the Panagurishte treasure. (Reprinted from
Archäologisches Institut des Deutschen Reiches--Abteilung
Rom.) Tr. Anon. Heidelber: Kerle, 1959. 121-141p.
26cm. [LC62]

HOFFMANN, Hilde.
Old man winter comes to town. (Der Winter und die
Kinder.) Tr. Anon. Illus. Beatrice Braunfock. NY:
Watts, 1960. unp. 31cm. [LC62, IT13]

HOFFMANN, Hubert. Scc Ncw Gcrman architecture.
New German architecture. L: Architectural; NY:
Praeger, 1956. [LC62]

HOFFMANN, Walther Gustav, 1903- .
The growth of industrial economics. (Rev. and expanded
version of Stadien und Typen der Industrialisierung.) Tr.
W. O. Chaloner. Manchester, Eng.: Manchester U. Pr.,
1958. 183p. (22cm.) 23cm. [LC62, B59, IT11]

Same. NY: Oceana, 1959. 196p. [IT12]

HOFMANN, Hans, 1923- . ed.
Making the ministry relevant. Tr. Anon. NY: Scribner,
1960. 169p. 21cm. [LC62]

The ministry and mental health. Tr. Anon. NY: Association, 1960. 251p. 26cm. [LC62]

HOFMANN, Johann Christian Konrad von, 1810-1877.
Interpreting the Bible. (Biblische Hermeneutik.) Tr.
Christian Preus. Minnesota: Augsburg, 1959. 236p.
22cm. [LC62, IT12]

HOFMANN, Joseph Ehrenfried, 1903- .
Classical mathematics, concise history of the classical era
in mathematics. (Geschichte der Mathematik.) Tr. Henrietta D. Midonick. NY: Philosophical Lib., 1960. 159p.
22cm. [LC62, IT13]

Same. L: Vison, 1960. 159p. (22cm.) [LC62, B60]

HOFMANN, Joseph Ehrenfried--
The history of mathematics. Trs. Frank Gaynor and
Henrietta D. Midonick. NY: Philosophical Lib., 1957.
V. 21cm. [LC62, IT10]

HOFMANN, O.
From Peking to Canton, surveying and mapping observations. (Articles from Vermessungstechnik, Vol. VI, nos.
2 and 4.) Tr. Anon. NY: U. S. J. P. R. S., 1958. 12p.
27cm. [LC62, IT12]

HOFMANN, Werner, 1928- .
Caricature, from Leonardo to Picasso. Tr. M. H. L.
L., Calder, 1957. 150p. 29cm. [LC62, B57, IT10]

Same. NY: Crown, 150p. 29cm. [LC62, IT10]

HOFMANN VON HOFMANNSWALDAU.
Selections in Loomis, C. G. 1958.

HOFMANNSTHAL, Hugo Hofmann, Edler von, 1874-1929.
Death and the fool. A short play in verse. Tr. Bayard
Quincy Morgan. 211. Microf. TW. at Columbia U.
19cm. [LC62, B60]

Selections in Flores, Anthol. 1960.

Selections in Loomis, C. G. 1958.

A tale of the cavalry. Tr. James Stern. In Spender's
Coll. 1960.

The woman without a shadow. (Die Frau ohne Schatten.)
Orig. libretto in Ger. with Eng. tr. by Publicity Dept.,
Decca Record Co. L: Decca Record Co., 1957. (4),
98p. (14 x 21. 5cm.) [B57]

HOFMEYER, Hans.
Garibaldi's ski-boat. Tr. Anon. L: Deutsch, 1960.
156p. 19cm. [LC62, B60]

The skin is deep. Tr. Anon. L: Secker, 1958. 238p.
(20. 5cm.) 21cm. [LC62, B58]

HOFNER, Herbert H. See Oesterle, Manfred.
Spain in three days. (Die Entdeckung Spaniens durch
Amerika.) Tr. Anon. Mühlacker: Stieglitz, 1958. 72p.
19 x 29cm. [LC62]

HOHENBERG, Markgraf V.
Selections in Loomis, C. G. 1958.

HOLBEIN, Hans, 1497-1543. The younger. See Ganz, Paul.
The paintings of Hans Holbein. (H--H--, die Gemälde.)
Text. Paul Ganz. Introd. tr. R. H. Boothroyd. Catalogue Marguerite Kay. Enl. ed. L: Phaidon, 1956.
297p. 31cm. [LC62]

HOLBEIN, Hans, 1497-1543. The younger. See Dance of
death.
Dance of death. (Holbeins Bilder des Todes.) Tr. Anon.
Berlin: Evangelische Verlags-anstalt, 1957. [LC62]

HOLIDAYS IN HEIDELBERG, an English guide to the town,
castle and environs. Tr. Anon. 10th rev. ed. Heidelberg: Brausdruck, 195-. 76p. 17cm. [LC62]

HOLL, Karl, 1866-1926.
The cultural significance of the reformation. Trs. Karl
and Barbara Hertz and John H. Lichtblau. NY: Meridian,
1959. 191p. 19cm. [LC62, IT12]

HOLM, Walter Andreas.
How television works. (Wege zum Fernsehen.) Tr. A. F.
Monypenny. L: Cleaver-Hume, 1958. 315p. 21cm.
[LC62, B58, IT11]

HOLSTEIN, Friedrich von.
The Holstein papers. Tr. Anon. Eds. Norman Rich and
M. H. Fisher. Cambridge: Cambridge U. Pr., 1957.
404p. (25.5cm.) [B57]

HOLTHUSEN, Hans Egon, 1913- .
The crossing. (Das Schiff.) Trs. Robert Kee and Susie
Hughes. L: Deutsch, 1959. 253p. (20.5cm.) [LC62,
B59, IT12]

HOMBURG, Ernst Christoph.
Selections in Loomis, C. G. 1958.

HOMEYER, Heinz von.
The radiant mountain. Tr. Elinor Castendyk. Chicago:
Regnery, 1957. 219p. 22cm. [LC62, IT10]

HONEGGER-LAVATER, Gottfried, 1917- .
Konolyi (Mrs. Arthur Barnwell). Text Gottfried Honegger-

HONEGGER-LAVATER, Gottfried--
Lavater. Eng. text Henry A. Frei. (Also Fr. and Italian.) Zurich, 1958. 75p. 39cm. [LC62]

HOOFT, Willem Adolph Wisser.
Rembrandt and the gospel. (Rembrandts Weg zum Evangel-
ium.) Trs. K. Gregor Smith. Eng. ed. rev. W--A--
W--H--. L: SCM, 1957. 128p. (22.5cm.) [B57]

HOPE, Ludvig, 1871-1954.
Spirit and power. Tr. Iver Olson. Minneapolis: Hague
Lutheran Innermission Federation, 1959. 197p. 24cm.
[LC62]

HOPHAN, Otto.
Mary, our most blessed lady. (Maria, unsere hohe liebe
Frau.) Tr. Berchmans Bittle. Milwaukee: Bruce; L:
Paterson, 1959. 374p. 24cm. [LC62, B60, IT12]

HORBACH, Michael, 1924- .
The betrayed. (Die verratenen Söhne.) Tr. Robert Kee.
NY: Coward, 1959. 239p. 21cm. [LC62, IT12]

Same. NY: Berkely, 1960. n.p. [IT13]

The great betrayal. (Die verratenen Söhne.) Tr. Robert
Kee. L: Lane, 1958. 240p. (19cm.) [B58, IT11]

Same. L: Bodley Head, 1958. 239p. 19cm. [LC62]

HORN, Siegfried H., 1908- .
Seventh Day Adventist Bible dictionary. With contributions
by other writers. With atlas. Tr. Anon. Washington:
Review and Herald, 1960. 1199p. 25cm. [LC62]

The spade confirms the book. Tr. Anon. Washington:
Review and Herald, 1957. 256p. 23cm. [LC62]

HORNSTEIN, Erika von, 1913- .
Russians in my home. Tr. Ingrid Enway Gunvaldsen. L:
Angus, 1960. 222p. (20.5cm.) 21cm. [LC62, B60]

HORSTER, Friedrich Wilhelm Conrad. See Conradi, F.W.,
pseud.

HUBER, Hans, 1901- .
How Switzerland is governed. Tr. Mary Hottinger.

Zürich: Schweizer Spiegel, 1960. 64p. [LC62]

HUBER, Heinz.
    The new apartment. Tr. Chris Holme. In Spender's
    Coll. 1960.

HUBER, Leo Fritz, ed.
    Fame. Famous portraits of famous people by famous
    photographers. Tr. Anon. L, NY: Focal, 1960. 159p.
    31cm. [LC62, B60]

HUBER, Siegfried.
    The realm of the Incas. (Im Reich der Inkas.) Tr. M.
    Savill. L: Hale, 1959. 212p. (22.5cm.) 23cm. [LC
    62, B59, IT13]

HÜBNER, Walter Georg Willy, 1917- . Jt. author.
    The practical anodising of aluminum by W--G--H--H--
    and A. Schiltknecht. 1st Eng. ed. Tr. Winifred Lewis.
    L: Macdonald, 1960. (330p.) 334p. 23cm. [LC62,
    B60]

HÜRLIMANN, Martin, 1897- .
    Asia. Introd. essay, historical notes. Tr. Anon. L:
    Thames, 1957. 262p. 31cm. [LC62, B57]

    Same. NY: Studio, 1957. 262p. 31cm. [LC62]

    Same. L: Thames, 1958. 262p. 31cm. [LC62]

    Athens. (Athen, Aufnahmen und Bilderläuterungen.) Tr.
    Anon. Historical notes. Introd. Rex Warner. NY:
    Studio, 1956. 118p. 26cm. [LC62]

    Same. Tr. Anon. Introd. Walter Herwig Schuchlardt.
    Zürich: Atlantis, 1956. 136p. 26cm. [LC62]

    Eternal France. Tr. Anon. L: Thames, 1957. 59p.
    31cm. [LC62]

    Europe. (Europa, Bilder seiner Landschaft und Kultur.)
    Tr. Anon. L: Thames, 1957. 71p. 32cm. [LC62]

    Same. NY: Studio, 1958. 71p. 32cm. [LC62]

    France. Historical notes, with an appreciation Paul Val-
    ery. Rev. and enl. ed. (published also with title,

HÜRLIMANN, Martin--
Eternal France.) Tr. Anon. L: Thames, 1957. 59p.
(30.5cm.) 31cm. [LC62, B57]

Same. NY: Studio, 1957. v. 32cm. [LC62]

Germany. Introd. Essay, historical notes. Tr. Anon.
Freiburg im Breisgau: Atlantis, n.d. 221p. 32cm.
[LC62]

Same. Zürich: Atlantis, c1956. 221p. [LC62]

Same. L: Studio, 1957. 248p. [LC62]

Same. Introd. Essay Stewart Thomson. Historical
notes Michael Meier. L: Thames, 1957. 251p. (31.5
cm) [LC62, B56]

Same. NY: Studio, 1957. 251p. 32cm. [LC62]

Istanbul. (Istanbul-Konstantinopel.) Tr. Anon. L:
Thames; NY: Studio, 1958. 154p. (25.5cm.) 26cm.
[LC62, B58]

Same. L: Thames, 1958. 154p. (25.5cm.) [LC62,
B58]

Italy. Introd. Essay, historical notes. New and enl. ed.
Tr. Anon. L: Thames, 1956. 250p. 31cm. [LC62]

Journey through the Orient. (Wiedersehen mit Asien.)
Tr. Isobel Nielson. Text and photos. M--H. -- Introd.
Sacheverell Sitwell. NY: Viking, 1960. 339p. 25cm.
[LC62]

London. Historical notes. Introd. Eric Walter White.
L: Thames; NY: Studio, 1956. 117p. 26cm. [LC62]

Moscow and Leningrad. (Moskau und Leningrad.) Tr.
Daphne Woodward. L: Thames, 1958. 135p. (136p.)
(25.5cm.) 26cm. [LC62, B58]

Same. NY: Studio, 1958. 135p. 25cm. [LC62, IT12]

Paris. Introd. and historical notes. 4th ed. Tr. Anon.
NY: Thames, 1957. 116p. 26cm. [LC62]

Same. L: Thames, 1958. 116p. 26cm. [LC62]

Rome. (Rom in 100 Bildern.) Tr. Anon. 2nd ed. L: Thames, 1957. 144p. (25.5cm.) 26cm. [LC62, B57]

Same. L: Thames, 1957. 144p. 26cm. [LC62]

Spain. Introd., essay and notes. Tr. Anon. n.p., n.d. 224p. 31cm. [LC62]

Switzerland. Introd., essay and historical notes. Rev. and enl. ed. Tr. Anon. L: Thames, 1956. IV. 31cm. [LC62]

Same. NY: Studio, 1956. 247p. 31cm. [LC62]

Same. 3rd ed. rev. and enl. Tr. Anon. NY: Viking, 1960. 1v. [LC62]

Traveller in the Orient. Tr. Isobel Nelson. Introd. Sacheverell Sitwell. L: Thames, 1960. 339p. (340p.) 25cm. [LC62, B60]

226 pictures in photogravure, 6 colour plates, introd. essay, historical notes. Rev. and enl. ed. Tr. Anon. NY: Studio, 1956. 247p. 31cm. [LC62]

HÜRLIMANN, Martin, 1897- . See Meyer, Peter. English cathedrals. Introd. M--H--. Descriptive text Geoffrey Grigson. Tr. Anon. L, NY: Thames, 1956. 47p. (31.5cm.) 32cm. [LC62, B56]

HÜTTINGER, Eduard.
Degas. Tr. Ellen Healy. NY: Crown, 1960. 92p. 29cm. [LC62, IT13]

HUGGLER, Max, 1903- .
Ten colour collotypes after watercolours. Tr. Robert Allen. Sel. and introd. M--H--. Boston Bk. and Art, 1959. 9, 9p. 51cm. [LC62]

HUMBOLDT, Alexander V.
Political essay on the kingdom of New Spain, Book 1. Tr. Henslet C. Woodbridge. Lexington: U. of Kentucky Lib., 1957. 72p. 28cm. [LC62, IT10]

HUMMEL, Innocentia Sister, 1909-1946. Illus. See Seemann, Margaret, 1893-1949.
The Hummel-book. Tr. Lola Ch. [sic] Eyetel. 7th ed. Stuttgart: Fink, (Label, NY: Heinman.), 1960. 64p. 24cm. [LC62]

HUNCK, Josef Maria.
India's silent revolution. A survey of Indo-German co-operation. (Indiens lautlose Revolution. Möglichkeiten und Grenzen einer deutsch-indischen Zusammenarbeit.) Tr. C. A. Brunton. Düsseldorf: Verlag Handelsblatt, 1958. 172p. 23cm. [LC62, IT12]

HUSSERL, Edmund, 1859-1938.
Cartesian meditations. An introduction to phenomenology. (Cartesianische Meditationen.) Tr. Dorion Cairns. The Hague: Nijhoff, 1960. 157p. 25cm. [LC62]

Ideas. General introduction to pure phenomenology. Tr. W. R. Boyce Gibson. L: Allen; NY: Macmillan, 1958. 465p. 23cm. [LC62]

Philosophy as a strict science. (Philosophie als strenge Wissenschaft.) Tr. Quentin Lauer. Reprint from Cross Currents, n. p. , 1956. V. 26cm. [LC62]

HUTTER, Clemens M.
Wedeln, the new Austrian skiing technique. (Wedeln. Schilauf in Österreich.) Tr. Anon. NY: Hanover House, 1960. 93p. 22cm. [LC62, IT13]

HUTTERER, Franz, 1925- .
Jascha. (Treue findet ihren Lohn.) Tr. Joyce Emerson. L: U. of London Pr., 1959. (1960.) 112p. (22cm.) [LC62, B60]

Trouble for Tomas. (Treue findet ihren Lohn.) Tr. Joyce Emerson. NY: Harcourt, 1959. 121p. 21cm. [LC62, IT12]

ILGENSTEIN, Anna Kalterfeld, 1880- .
The morning star of Wittenberg. (Der Morgenstern von Wittenberg.) Tr. Lydia Regehr. Washington: Review, 1956. 191p. 23cm. [LC62]

INDUSTRIEKURIER.
China, a promising market. (China, ein interessanter
Absatzmarkt.) Tr. Anon. Düsseldorf, 1958. 12p. [LC62]

INSTITUT ZUR ERFORSCHUNG DER UDSSR.
Berlin. A compilation of analytical and critical materials.
Verantwortlich für den Inhalt, A. I. Lebed. Munich, 1959.
101p. 29cm. [LC62]

Biographic directory of the USSR. Compiled by the Insti-
tute for the Study of the USSR. Tr. Anon. Ed. Waldimir
S. Merzalow. NY: Scarecrow, 1958. 782p. 23cm.
[LC62]

First comprehensive historical and tourist guide book to
the Holy City of Russians, Moscow, with detailed enumera
tion of historical and religious treasures in fourteen sug-
gested excursions. Tr. Anon. 1st ed. Frankfurt/Main:
Possev Verlag, 1956. 56p. 21cm. [LC62]

Forty years of the Soviet regime. A symposium of the
Institute for the study of the USSR. Tr. Anon. Ed. Oliver
J. Frederickson. Munich, 1957. V. 164p. 24cm.
[LC62]

Genocide in the USSR. Studies in group destruction. Eds.
Nikolai K. Deker and Andrei Lebed. Tr. Anon. Ed.
Oliver J. Frederiksen. Munich, 1958. 280p. 24cm.
[LC62]

Same. NY: Scarecrow, 1958. 280p. [LC62]

Institute publications, 1951-1956. Consolidated table of
contents. Tr. Anon. Munich, 1957. 36p. 24cm.
[LC62]

Institute publications, 1951-1958. Tr. Anon. Munich,
1959. 62p. 24cm. [LC62]

Problems of Soviet foreign policy. A symposium of the
Institute for the Study of the USSR. Tr. Anon. Ed. Oliver J. Frederiksen. Munich, 1959. 141p. [LC62]

Problems of Soviet internal policy, a symposium of the
Institute for the Study of the USSR. Tr. Anon. Ed. Oliver J. Frederiksen. München, 1960. 140p. [LC62]

INSTITUT ZUR ERFORSCHUNG DER UDSSR. --
Religion in the USSR. Tr. Anon. Eds. Boris Iwanow and
James Larkin. Munich, 1960. 236p. 24cm. [LC62]

Report on the Soviet Union in 1956. A symposium based
on the proceedings of the Seventh Institute Conference at
the Carnegie International Center, New York, April 28-29,
1956. Tr. Anon. Ed. Jaan Pennar. Munich, 1956.
218p. 24cm. [LC62]

Soviet society today. A symposium of the Institute for the
Study of the USSR. Tr. Anon. Ed. Oliver J. Frederiksen. München, 1958. V. 143p. 24cm. [LC62]

The Soviet Twenty-first Party Congress, Moscow, Jan. 27
to February 5, 1959. A compilation of analytical and
critical materials. Munich, 1959. 87p. 30cm. [LC62]

Soviet youth, twelve komsomol histories. Ed. Nikolai K.
Hovak-Deker. Tr. and ed. Oliver J. Frederiksen.
Munich, 1959. 256p. 24cm. [LC62]

Youth in the Soviet Union. A collection of article. Verantwortlich für den inhalt, A. I. Lebed. Tr. Anon.
Munich, 1959. 90p. 24cm. [LC62]

INTER NATIONES.
There's music in Germany, 1956. Published in coopera-
tion with the German section of the International Music
Council. Tr. Anon. Bonn, 1956. 111p. 21cm. [LC62]

There's music in Germany, 1960. Ed. Inter Nationes in
cooperation with the German section of the International
Music Council. Tr. Anon. Bonn, 1960. 62p. 21cm.
[LC62]

IPSER, Karl.
Vatican art. With 160 illus. (Die Kunstwerke des Vati-
kans.) Tr. Doireann MacDermott. L: Allen, 1957.
198p. (25cm.) [LC62, B57, IT10]

JACOB, Arthur, 1886- .
Magnesium, the fifth major plant nutrient. (Magnesia,
der fünfte Pflanzenhauptnährstoff.) Tr. Norman Walker.
L: Staples, 1958. 159p. 22cm. (22.5cm) [LC62,
B58, IT11]

JACOBI, Hermann Georg, 1850-1937.
(Das Ramayana.) Tr. S. N. Ghosal. Baroda: Oriental
Institute, 1960. 104p. [LC62]

JACOBI, Jolan. ed. See Paracelsus, 1493-1541.
Selected writings. 2nd ed. NY: Pantheon, 1958. [LC62]

JACOBI, Joland Jolande.
Complex, archetype, symbol in the psychology of C. G.
Jung. (Komplex, Archetypus, Symbol in der Psychologie
C. G. Jungs.) Tr. Ralph Manheim. L: Routledge; NY:
Pantheon, 1959. 236p. 21cm. [LC62, B59, IT12]

JACOBS, Karl E.
Berlin. Tr. Gladys Wheelhouse. Introd. Jürgen Graf.
Munich: Andermann, c1960. 61p. 17cm. [LC62]

JACOBSEN, Hermann, 1898- .
A handbook of succulent plants. (Handbuch der sukkulenten Pflanzen.) Tr. Hildegard Raabe. L: Blanford, 1960.
3v. 25cm. [LC62, B60]

Succulent plants. Description, cultivation, and uses of succulent plants, other than cacti. (Handbuch der sukkulenten
Pflanzen.) Tr. Vera Higgins. L: Benn, 1959. 293p.
26cm. [LC62]

JACOBSEN, Maxim.
Violin gymnastics. Physical exercises for the advanced
student. Tr. Anon. (Ger., Eng., and Fr.) L: Bosworth,
1960. 63p. (25cm.) [B60]

JAEGER, Hans, 1899- .
The reappearance of the swastika. Neo/Nazism and Fas-
cist International, comprehensive survey of all organizations, leaders, cross-connections, and their ideological
background. Tr. Anon. L: Gamma, 1960. 62p. 33cm.
[LC62, B60]

JAEGER, Werner Wilhelm, 1888- .
Aristotle. Fundamentals of his development. Tr. Richard
Robinson. 2nd ed. Oxford: Clarendon, 1960. 475p.
23cm. [LC62]

The theology of the early Greek philosophers. Tr. E. S.
Robinson. Oxford: Clarendon, 1960. 259p. [LC62]

JAENICKE, Günther, ed.
Decisions of the German Supreme Court relating to public
international law . . . 1929-1945 . . . including the German Reich. (Entscheidungen des Deutschen Reichsgerichts
in völkerrechtlichen Fragen.) Tr. Anon. Köln: Heymann,
1960. 535p. [LC62]

JAENICKE, Günther, ed. See Germany, Reichsgericht.

JAENICKE, Wolfgang Albert, 1881- .
Right and freedom for Silesia, Tr. Anon. Göttingen, 1959
21 p. 19cm. [LC62]

JAHNKE, Eugen, 1863-1921.
Tables of higher functions. (Funktionentafeln mit Formeln
und Kurven.) Tr. Anon. NY: McGraw, 1960. 318p.
26cm. [LC62]

JANUS, Horst.
Nature as architect. (Baumeister natur.) Tr. Jane
Bannard Greene. NY: Ungar, 1957. 119p. 27cm.
[LC62, IT10]

JASPERS, Karl, 1883- .
The idea of the university. (Die Idee der Universität.)
Trs. Harald A. T. Reiche and H. F. Vanderschmidt.
Boston: Beacon, 1959. 135p. 21cm. [LC62, IT12]

Same. L: Owen, 1960. 149p. 22cm. [LC62, B60,
IT13]

Man in the modern age. (Die geistige Situation der Zeit.)
Trs. Eden and Cedar Paul. Garden City, NY: Doubleday,
1957. 230p. [LC62]

Reason and existence. Five lectures. (Vernunft und Ex-
istenz.) Tr. William Earle. L: Paul, 1956. 157p.
22cm. (22.5cm.) [LC62, B56]

Same. 2nd ed. (From Ger. 3rd ed.) NY: Noonday,
1959. 157p. [LC62]

Truth and symbol. (Von der Wahrheit.) Trs. Jean T.
Wilde, William Kluback, and William Kimmel. L: Vision;
NY: Twayne, 1959. 79p. (22.5cm.) 23cm. [LC62, B60,
IT12, 13]

Way to wisdom, an introd. to philosophy. Tr. Ralph Manheim. New Haven, Conn.: Yale U. Pr., 1960. 208p. [IT13]

JASPERS, Karl, and Bultmann, Rudolf.
Myth and Christianity. (Die Frage der Entmythologisierung.) Tr. Anon. NY: Noonday, 1958. 116p. 21cm. [LC62, IT10]

JEDIN, Hubert, 1900- .
Ecumenical councils of the Catholic Church, an historical outline. (Kleine Konziliengeschichte.) Tr. Ernest Graf. Freiburg: Herder; Edinburgh, L: Nelson, 1960. 254p. (18.5cm.) [B60, IT13]

Same. NY: Freiburg, Herder, 1960. 253p. 19cm. [LC62, IT13]

A history of the Council of Trent. (Geschichte des Konzils von Trient.) Vol. 1. Tr. Ernest Graf. 1st Eng. ed. L, NY: Nelson, 1957. 618p. 25cm. [LC62, B57, IT10]

Same. NY: Nelson, 1957. 629p. [IT10]

Same. St. Louis: Herder, 1957. V. 25cm. [LC62]

JELLINEK, Paul.
The practice of modern perfumery. (Praktikum des modernen Parfümers.) Tr. A. J. Krajkeman. L: Hill, 1956. 219p. 23cm [LC62]

JEREMIAS, Joachim, 1900- .
The eucharistic words of Jesus. NY: Macmillan, 1956. 195p. [LC62]

Infant baptism in the first four centuries. (Die Kindertaufe in den ersten vier Jahrhunderten.) Tr. David Cairns. L: SCM; Philadelphia, 1960. 111p. (112p.) (22.5cm.) 23cm. [LC62, B60]

Jesus' promise to the nations. (Jesu Verheissung für die Völker.) Tr. S. H. Hooke. L: SCM, 1958. 84p. 22cm. [LC62, B58]

Same. Naperville, Ill.: Allenson, 1958. 84p. 22cm. [LC62, IT13]

JEREMIAS, Joachim--
The parables of Jesus. (Die Gleichnisse Jesus.) Tr. S.
H. Hooke. NY: Scribner, 1956. 176p. [LC62]

Same. L: SCM, 1958. 178p. 23cm. [LC62]

Unknown sayings of Jesus. (Unbekannte Jesusworte.) Tr.
Reginald H. Fuller. L: S. P. C. K.; NY: Macmillan,
1957. 110p. (19cm.) 20cm. [LC62, B57, IT10]

JEREMIAS, Joachim, 1900- . See Zimmerli, Walther,
1907- .
The servant of God. Tr. Anon. L: SCM; Naperville,
Ill. : Allenson, 1957. [LC62]

JETZINGER, Franz.
Hitler's youth. (Hitlers Jugend.) Tr. Lawrence Wilson.
L: Hutchinson, 1958. 200p. 22cm. [LC62, B58, IT10]

JOEDICKE, Jürgen.
A history of modern architecture. (Geschichte der modernen Architektur.) Tr. James C. Palmes. IT12-Palmer.
L: Architectural, 1959. 243p. (26.5cm.) 27cm. [LC
62, B59, IT12]

Same. NY: Praeger, 1959. 243p. 26cm. [LC62, IT12]

JOHANNES VON SAAZ, ca. 1360-1414. See Saaz, Johannes
von.

JOHNEN, Wilhelm.
Battling the bombers. (Duell unter den Sternen.) Tr. M.
Savill. NY: Ace, 1958. 192p. [IT11]

Duel under the stars. A German night fighter pilot in the
Second World War. (Duell unter den Sternen.) Tr. Mervyn
Savill. L: Kimber, 1957. 202p. (22.5cm.) 23cm.
[LC62, B57]

JONE, Heribert, Father. (Secular name Joseph Jone, 1885-)
Moral theology. Tr. Urban Adelman. Westminster, Md. :
Newman, 1956. 610p. [LC62]

Same. Westminster, Md. : Newman, 1959. 610p. 17cm.
[LC62]

JONES, Ernest, 1879- .
Sigmund Freud. Four centenary addresses. Tr. Anon.
NY: Basic; L: Book Centre, 1956. 150p. (21.5cm.)
[B56]

JONSON, Marian.
Snow White and the seven dwarfs. Chicago: Coach
House, 1957. 54l. 28cm. [LC62]

JOOS, Georg, 1894- . With Ira M. Freeman.
Theoretical physics. (Lehrbuch der theoretischen Physik.)
Tr. Anon. L: Blackie, 1958. 885p. (22.5cm.) 23cm.
[LC62, B58]

JOY, Charles R., ed. See Schweitzer, Albert, 1875- .

JUD, Karl. See Brunner, Josef.
(Zug. Photographien.) (Fr., Italian, and Eng.) Tr. R.
A. Langford. Zug: Verlag der Offizin Zürcher, c1956.
unp. 22cm. [LC62]

JÜNGER, Ernst, 1895- .
The glass bees. (Gläserne Bienen.) Trs. Louise Bogan
and Elizabeth Mayer. NY: Noonday, 1961. c1960.
149p. 21cm. [LC62]

JÜNGER, Friedrich George, 1898- .
The failure of technology. (Die Perfection der Technik.)
Tr. Anon. Chicago: Regnery, 1956. 189p. 18cm.
[LC62]

JUILFS, J. See Weizsäcker, Carl Friedrich Freiherr von,
1912- .
Contemporary physics. Tr. Arnold J. Pomerans. L:
Hutchinson, 1957. 150p. (22cm.) [LC62, B57]

Same. L, NY: Hutchinson, 1957. [LC62]

The rise of modern physics. NY: Braziller, 1957.
150p. 22cm. [LC62]

JUNCKERSTORFF, Kurt.
Modern management of enterprises. Tr. Anon. The
Hague: Nijhoff, 1960. 81p. 25cm. [LC62]

JUNG, Carl Gustav, 1875- .
Aion, researches into the phenomenology of the self.

194

JUNG, Carl Gustav--
Vol. 9, pt. 2, coll. works. (A---. Untersuchungen zur
Symbolgeschichte.) Tr. R. F. C. Hull. L: Routledge,
c1959. (xi, 333p.) 344p. (24cm.) [LC62, B57]

Same. NY: Pantheon. 2v. 24cm. [LC62, IT12]

Answer to Job. (Antwort auf Hiob.) Tr. R. F. C.
Hull. L: Routledge, 1958. 194p. [LC62]

Same. NY: Meridian, 1960. 223p. 19cm. [LC62,
IT13]

The archetypes and the collective unconscious. Vol. 9,
pt. 2, coll. works. (Mostly from Von den Wurzeln des
Bewusstseins.) Tr. R. F. C. Hull. L: Routledge;
NY: Pantheon, 1959. 462p. 24cm. [LC62, B59, IT12]

Basic writings. Tr. Anon. Ed. with introd. Violet
Staub de Laszlo. NY: Modern Lib., 1959. 552p. 19cm.
[LC62]

Collected works. V. 1. Psychiatric studies. V. 3. The
psychogenesis of mental disease. V. 5. Symbols for the
transformation. V. 7. Two essays on analytical psychology. V. 8. The structure and dynamics of the psyche.
V. 9. pt. 1, the archetypes and the collective unconscious.
Pt. 2, Aion. Researches into the phenomenology of the
self. V. 11. Psychology and religion, West and East.
V. 12. Psychology and alchemy. V. 16. The practice
of psychotherapy. V. 17. The development of personality.
Tr. R. F. C. Hull. NY: Pantheon, 1960. 24cm. [LC
62, B56, IT13]

The collected works. (8) The structure and dynamics of
the psyche. Tr. R. F. C. Hull. L: Routledge, 1960.
(588p.) 596p. 24cm. [LC62, B60, IT13]

Flying saucers, a modern mythos etc. (Ein moderner
Mythus.) Tr. R. F. C. Hull. L: Routledge, 1959.
184p. (19cm.) [LC62, B59, IT12]

Same. NY: Harcourt, 1959. 186p. 21cm. [LC62,
IT12]

The integration of the personality. Tr. Stanley M. Dell.
L: Routledge, 1956. 1v. [LC62]

Modern man in search of a soul. Tr. W. S. Dell and Cary F. Baynes. NY: Harcourt, 1957. 244p. 19cm. [LC62]

Psyche and symbol. A selection from the writings. Trs. Cary Baynes and R. F. C. Hull. Garden City, NY: Doubleday, 1958. 363p. 19cm. [LC62]

Psychiatric studies. Tr. R. F. C. Hull. L: Routledge; NY: Pantheon, 1957. 269p. 24cm. [LC62]

Same. L: Routledge, 1957. 261p. (24cm.) [B57]

The psychogenesis of mental disease. Vol. 3, coll. works. Tr. R. F. C. Hull. L: Routledge, 1960. 312p. [LC62]

Same. NY: Pantheon, c1960. 312p. 24cm. [LC62]

Psychological types or, The psychology of individualization. Tr. H. Goodwin Baynes. L: Routledge, 1959. 7-654p. 23cm. [LC62]

Psychology and religion. Vol. 11, Coll. works. Tr. R. F. C. Hull. L: Routledge; NY: Pantheon, 1958. 699p. (24cm.) [LC62, B58, IT11]

Same. New Haven: Yale U. Pr., 1960. 131p. 20cm. [LC62]

The psychology of interpersonal relations. Tr. Anon. L: Chapman; NY: Wiley, 1958. 322p. (23.5cm.) [B58]

Psychology of the unconscious. A study of the transformations and symbolism of the libido. (Wandlungen und Symbole der Libido.) Tr. Beatrice M. Hinkle. NY: Dodd, 1957. 566p. 22cm. [LC62, IT12]

The structure and dynamics of the psyche. Vol. 8. Coll. works. Tr. R. F. C. Hull. NY: Pantheon, 1960. 596p. 24cm. [LC62, IT13]

Same. L: Routledge, 1960. 588p. 24cm. [B60]

Symbols of transformation. An analysis of the prelude to a case of schizophrenia. Vol. 5. Coll. works.

JUNG, Carl Gustav--
(Symbole der Wandlung.) Tr. R. F. C. Hull. L: Routledge. 567p. 24cm. (24.5cm.) [LC62, B57]

Two essays on analytical psychology. (Über die Psycho-
logie des Unbewussten. Die Beziehungen zwischen dem
Ich und dem Unbewussten.) Tr. R. F. C. Hull. NY:
Meridian, 1956. 347p. 19cm. [LC62, IT9]

The undiscovered self. (Gegenwart und Zukunft.) Tr.
R. F. C. Hull. Boston: Little, 1958. 113p. 20cm.
[LC62, IT11]

Same. Tr. Anon. L: Routledge, c1958. 113p. 12mo.
[LC62, IT11]

Same. NY: New American Lib., 1959. 125p. [IT12]

JUNG, Emma.
Animus and anima. Two essays. (Ein Beitrag zum Prob-
lem des Animas.) Tr. C. F. Baynes. (Die Anima als
Naturwesen.) Tr. H. Nagel. NY: Analytical Psychology
Club of NY, 1957. 94p. 23cm. [LC62]

JUNGE, Werner, 1905- .
African jungle doctor. (Bolahun, als deutscher Arzt unter
schwarzen Medizinmännern.) Tr. Anon. L: Hamilton,
1956. 190p. (18.5cm.) [B56, IT9]

JUNGK, Robert, 1913- .
Brighter than a thousand suns. The moral and political
history of the atomic scientists. (Heller als tausend
Sonnen.) Tr. James Cleugh. L: Gollancz, 1958.
350p. (22.5cm.) [LC62, B58, IT11]

Same. NY: Harcourt, 1958. 269p. 21cm. [LC62,
IT11]

Same. Subtitle. A personal history of the atomic scientists. Harmondsworth: Penguin, 1960. 330p. (18cm.)
[B60]

JUNGMANN, Josef Andreas, 1889- .
The early liturgy, to the time of Gregory the Great.
Tr. Francis A. Brunner. Notre Dame, Ind.: U. of
Notre Dame Pr., 1959. 314p. 24cm. [LC62]

Same. L: Darton, 1960. 314p. 24cm. [LC62, IT13]

The Eucharistic prayer. (Das eucharistische Hochgebet.)
Tr. Robert L. Batley. L: Challoner, 1956. 55p.
(18.5cm.) [LC62, B56, IT9]

Same. Tr. Anon. Chicago: Fides, 1956. 55p. 19cm.
[LC62]

Handing on the faith. A manual of catechetics. (Kate-
chetik.) Tr. and rev. A. N. Fuerst. Freiburg: Herder;
L: Burns, 1959. 445p. 22cm. (22.5cm.) [LC62, B59,
IT12]

Same. NY: Herder, 1959. 445p. 23cm. [LC62, IT12]

The Mass of the Roman rite, its origins and development.
(Missarum Sollemnia.) Tr. Francis A. Brunner, rev.
Charles K. Riepe. L: Burns; NY: Benyiger, 1959.
26cm. (26.5cm.) [LC62, B59, IT12]

Public worship. (Der Gottesdienst der Kirche.) Tr.
Clifford Howell. L: Challoner, 1957. 249p. 22cm.
(22.5cm.) [LC62, B57, IT10]

Same. Subtitle, A survey. Tr. Clifford Howell. Collegeville, Minn.: Liturgical Pr., 1958. 249p. 24cm.
[LC62, IT12]

The sacrifice of the church. The meaning of the Mass.
(Vom Sinn der Messe als Opfer der Gemeinschaft.) Tr.
Clifford Howell. L: Challoner; Collegeville, Minn.:
Liturgical Pr., 1956. 71p. (18.5cm.) [LC62, B56,
IT9]

KADES, Hans, pseud. (i.e. Werlberger, Hans, 1906- .)
The doctor's secret. (First ed., without sanction.) Tr.
E. B. Ashton. NY: Dell, 1959. 255p. [IT12]

The great temptation. (Der Erfolgreiche.) Tr. E. E.
Ashton. L, Sydney: Angus, 1956. 317p. (20.5cm.)
[B56, IT9]

Same. L: Transworld, 1957. 317p. (318p.) (16.5cm.)
[B57, IT10]

KADES, Hans--
The house of crystal. (Monte Cristallo.) Tr. Paul
Selver. L: Angus, 1957. 254p. (20.5cm.) [B57,
IT10]

San Salvatore. (S--S--.) Tr. Anon. L: Angus, 1959.
3-256p. (20.5cm.) [B59]

KÄCH, Walter.
Rhythm and proportion in lettering. (Rhythmus und Pro-
portion in der Schrift.) Tr. Elizabeth Friedlander.
Olten: Walter-Verlag, 1956. 81p. 23 x 32cm. [LC62]

KÄHLER, Martin. See Braaten, Carl E., 1929- .
Christ, faith and history, an inquiry into the meaning of
Martin Kähler's distinction between the historical Jesus
and the Biblical Christ developed in its past and present.
(Der sogenannte historische Jesus und der geschichtliche,
biblische Christus, von M--K--.) Tr. Anon. n.p.,
1959. 2v. 28cm. [LC62]

KAESER, Hildegarde Johanna, 1904- .
Mimff-Robinson. Trs. Ruth Michaelis Jena and Arthur
Ratcliff. L: Oxford U. Pr., 1958. 184p. (22.5cm.)
23cm. [LC62, B58, IT11]

KÄSTNER, Erich, 1899- .
Baron Munchhausen, his wonderful travels and adventures.
Retold by E--K--. Trs. Richard and Clara Winston.
NY: Messner, 1957. 68p. 27cm. [LC62, IT10]

Don Quixote. Retold by E--K--. Trs. Richard and Clara
Winston. NY: Messner, 1957. 70p. 27cm. [LC62,
IT10]

Emil and the detectives. (Emil und die Detektive.) Tr.
Eileen Hall. Introd. Walter de la Mare. L: Cape,
1959. 190p. (20.5cm.) 21cm. [LC62, B59, IT12]

Same. Harmondsworth: Penguin, 1959. 127p. 18cm.
[LC62, B59, IT12]

Puss in boots. (Der gestiefelte Kater.) Retold by E--
K--. Trs. Richard and Clara Winston. NY: Messner,
1957. 66p. 27cm. [LC62, IT10]

A Salzburg comedy. (Der kleine Grenzverkehr.) Tr.

Cyrus Brooks. NY: Unger, 1957. 117p. 19cm. [LC 62, IT10]

The simpletons. (Die Schildbürger.) Retold by E--K--. Trs. Richard and Clarka Winston. NY: Messner, 1957. 69p. 27cm. [LC62, IT10]

Till Eulenspiegel, the clown. (T--E--.) Retold by E-- K--. Trs. Richard and Clara Winston. NY: Messner, 1957. 70p. 27cm. [LC62, IT10]

When I was a little boy. (Als ich ein kleiner Junge war.) Trs. Isabel and Florence McHugh. L: Cape, 1959. 187p. (20.5cm.) 21cm. [LC62, B59, IT12]

Same. NY: Watts, 1961, c1959. 187p. 22cm. [LC62]

KÄSTNER, Erich. See Munchhausen. English. Baron Munchhausen. NY, 1957. [LC62]

KAFKA, Franz, 1883-1924.
The castle. (Das Schloss.) Trs. W. and E. Muir. with add. material E. Williams and E. Kaiser. NY: Knopf, 1956. 481p. 20cm. [LC62]

Same. L: Penguin, 1957. 298p. 18cm. [LC62, B57]

Description of a struggle. Trs. Tania and James Stern. NY: Schocken, 1958. 240p. 21cm. [LC62, IT11]

Description of a struggle, and the great wall of China. Trs. Willa and Edwin Muir and Tania and James Stern. Definitive ed. L: Secker, 1960. 345p. (19cm.) [LC 62, B60]

The great wall of China. Stories and reflections. (Beim Bau der chinesischen Mauer.) Trs. Willa and Edwin Muir. NY: Schocken, 1960. 307p. 20cm. [LC62]

The trial. (Der Prozess.) Trs. Willa and Edwin Muir. Rev. materials. E. M. Butler. Definitive ed. L: Secker, 1956. 304p. 19cm. [LC62, B56]

Same. NY: Knopf, 1957. 340p. 20cm. [LC62, IT10]

KAHLE, Paul Ernst, 1875- .
The Cairo geniza. Tr. Anon. 2nd ed. Oxford, 1959.

KAHLE, Paul Ernst--
370p. 23cm. [LC62]

Same. NY, 1960. 370p. 23cm. [LC62]

KAISER, Georg, 1878-1945.
From morn to midnight. Tr. Ashley Dukes. In twenty
best European plays on the American stage. Ed. John
Gassner. NY: Hill, 1957. 655-679p. 106p. [LC62]

Gas 1. A play in 5 acts. Tr. Herman Scheffauer.
Introd. Victor Lange. NY: Ungar, 1957. 96p. 21cm.
[LC62, IT10]

KAISER, Rolf, 1909- . ed.
Medieval English. An Old English and Middle Englis anthology. (Alt- und Mittelenglische Anthologie.) Tr. Anon.
3rd ed., rev. and enl. Berlin, 1958. V. 22cm.
[LC62]

KALFUS, Radim.
Moravian church in pictures. (Unitas fratrum.) Tr.
Anon. Introd. J. B. Capek. Ed. Unitas Fratrum in
Czechoslovakia, Prague, 1957. 195p. 30cm. [LC62]

KALNEIN, Wend Graf.
Salem, past and present. Photos. Toni Schneiders and
Siegfried Lauterwasser. Tr. Anon. Lindau: Thorbecke,
L: Tiranti), 1958. 52p. (24cm.) [B60]

KAMPFFMEYER, Hans M., 1912- .
Housing enterprises for communal benefit in Germany.
Tr. Anon. Cologne: Gesamtverband Gemeinnütziger
Wohnungsunternehmen, 1956. 56p. [LC62]

KANDINSKY, Wassily, 1866-1944.
Kandinsky, 1866-1944. Tr. Anon. Introd. and notes
Herbert Read. L, 1959. 24p. 31cm. [LC62, B59]

Same. NY: Wittenborn, 1959. 24p. 31cm. [LC62]

Same. Text Will Grohmann. NY: Abrams, 1960. 36p.
37cm. [LC62]

Same. L: Beaverbrook Newspapers, c1960. V. (unp.)
[LC62]

KANT, Immanuel, 1724-1804.
The critique of judgement. Tr. James Creed Meredith.
Oxford: Clarendon, 1957. 246, 180p. 19cm. [LC62]

Critique of practical reason. (Kritik der reinen Vernunft.)
Tr. Lewis White Beck. NY: Liberal Arts, 1956. 168p.
21cm. [LC62, IT9]

Critique of practical reason and other works on the theory of ethics. Tr. Thomas Kingsmill Abbott. 6th ed.
L: Longmans, 1959. 368p. 22cm. [LC62]

Critique of pure reason. (Kritik der reinen Vernunft.)
Tr. J. M. D. Meiklejohn. Introd. A. D. Lindsay. L:
Dent; NY: Dutton, 1956. 483p. (19cm.) [B56]

Same. Tr. Norman Kemp Smith. L: Macmillan; NY:
St. Martin's., 1956. 681p. 23cm. [LC62]

Same. In commemoration of the centenary. Tr. F.
Max Müller. 2nd ed. rev. NY: Macmillan, 1957.
808p. 21cm. [LC62]

Same. Tr. Norman K. Smith. (abr.) NY: Modern
Lib., 1958. 335p. 19cm. [LC62, IT11]

Education. Tr. Annette Churton. Ann Arbor: U. of
Mich. Pr., 1960. 121p. 21cm. [LC62, IT13]

Foundations of the metaphysics of morals. What is en-
lightment. (Grundlegung zur Metaphysik der Sitten.)
Tr. Lewis W. Beck. NY: Liberal Arts, 1959. 92p.
21cm. [LC62, IT12, 13]

Fundamental principles of the metaphysic of ethics. Tr.
Thomas Kingsmill Abbott. 10th ed. L: Longmans,
1959. 102p. [LC62]

An Immanuel Kant reader. Tr. Anon. Editions with
commentary by Raymond B. Blakney. NY: Harper,
1960. 290p. 22cm. [LC62, IT13]

Kant's pre-critical esthetic, a study, together with a tr.
into Eng. of Kant's observations on the feeling of the
beautiful and sublime by John Turner Goldthwait. Ann
Arbor: Micro. of TW., 1957. 241l. [LC62]

KANT, Immanuel--
The moral law or Kant's groundwork of the metaphysic of morals. (Grundlegung zur Metaphysik der Sitten.) A new tr. with analysis and notes, H. J. Paton. 3rd ed. NY: Hutchinson, 1956. 151p. 24cm. [LC62]

Same. NY: Barnes, 1958. 151p. [LC62]

Observations on the feeling of the beautiful and sublime. (Beobachtungen über das Gefühl des Schönen und Erhabenen.) Tr. John T. Goldthwait. Berkeley: U. of California Pr., 1960. 125p. 19cm. [LC62, IT13]

Perpetual peace. (Zum ewigen Frieden.) Tr. Anon. Ed. and introd. Lewis White Beck. NY: Liberal Arts, 1957. 59p. 21cm. [LC62]

Religion within the limits of reason alone. (Die Religion innerhalb der Grenzen der blossen Vernunft.) Trs. Theodore M. Greene and Hoyt H. Hudson. With a new essay, John R. Silber. 2nd ed. La Salle, Ill.: Open Court, 1960. 190p. 21cm. [LC62]

Same: NY: Harper, 1960. 190p. 21cm. [LC62, IT13]

KANTOROWICZ, Ernst Hartwig, 1895- .
Frederick the Second, 1194-1250. Tr. E. D. Lorimer. L: Constable; NY: Ungar, 1957. 742p. (21.5cm.) 22cm. [LC62, B58, IT10]

KARFELD, Kurt Peter. See Dirks, Walter and Hausmann, Manfred, jt. authors.

KARGER (S.) A. G., Basel.
Rules for the preparation of manuscripts and bibliographies with a list of abbreviations of titles of current medical periodicals. Tr. Anon. Basel, 1958. 17p. [LC62]

KARLSRUHE. BADISCHE LANDESBIBLIOTHEK.
Miniatures of the Life of Our Lady, from the collection of medieval manuscripts in the Baden State Library, Karlsruhe, West Germany, with notes by Franz Schmitt. Tr. Anon. Westminster, Md.: Newman, 1960. 28p. 21cm.

[LC62]

KARPF, Nikolaus, ed.
Linhof practice, an introduction to Linhof cameras, their
accessories, and photographic technique. Eng. ver. E. F.
Linssen. Munich: Grossbild-Technik. L: Fountain,
1958. 216p. (29cm.) [B58]

KASEMEIER, Rolf.
Small Minox-big pictures. (Kleine Minox-grosse Bilder.)
Tr. Schuyler Jones. Seebruck/Chiemsee: Heering, 1959.
190p. 12 x 16cm. [LC62]

KASPAR, Karl.
New German architecture. Tr. H. J. Montague. Sel.
Gerd Hatje, Hubert Hoffman, and K--K--. Introd. H.
Hoffman. Texts and captions K--K--. L: Architectural,
1956. 219p. (220p.) (26.5cm.) [LC62, B57]

KATZ, Peter.
Justin's Old Testament quotations and the Greek Dodeka-
propheton scroll. Tr. Anon. Berlin: Akademie, 1957.
344-353p. 23cm. [LC62]

KATZ, Richard, 1888- .
Solitary life. (Einsames Leben.) Tr. Hetty Kohn. L:
Cape, 1958. 254p. (20.5cm.) 21cm. [LC62, B58,
IT11]

Same. NY: Reynald, 1959. 254p. 22cm. [LC62, IT12]

KAUFMANN, Herbert, 1920- .
Adventure in the desert. Tr. Stella Humphries. NY:
Obolenski, 1961. 1960. 218p. 22cm. [LC62, IT14]

The lost Sahara, a story of men, camels, thirst and sand.
(Der verlorene Karawanenweg.) Trs. I. and F. McHugh.
Illus. M. Richter. L: Harrap, 1960. 192p. (19.5cm.)
[B60]

The lost Sahara trail. (Die Himmelspiste.) Trs. I. and
J. McHugh. L: Harrap, 1960. 192p. (19.5cm.) [B60,
IT13]

The lost Sahara trail. A story of men, camels, thirst,
and sand. Tr. Isabel and Florence McHugh. NY, 1962.
1960. 192p. 22cm. [LC62]

204

KAUFMANN, Herbert--
Red moon and high summer. (Roter Mond und heisse
Zeit.) Tr. Stella Humphries. L: Methuen, 1960. 209p.
21cm. [LC62, B60]

KAUFMANN, Richard, 1914- .
The world is full of doors. (Die Welt ist voller Türen.)
Tr. Edward Fitzgerald. L: Hutchinson, 1957. 319p.
(20.5cm.) [LC62, B57, IT10]

KAUFMANN, Walter Arnold, ed. and tr. See Nietzsche,
Friedrich Wilhelm, 1844-1900.
The portable Nietzsche. NY: Viking, 1960. [LC62]

KAUTSKY, Karl, 1854-1938.
Communism in central Europe in the time of the Reformation. Trs. J. L. and E. G. Mulliken. NY: Russel,
1959. 293p. 22cm. [LC62, IT12]

Foundations of Christianity. Tr. Henry F. Mins. NY:
Russell, 1960. 401p. [IT13]

Thomas More and his Utopia. Tr. Anon. Fwd. Russell
Ames. NY, 1959. 250p. 21cm. [LC62, IT12]

KEETMAN, Peter, photog. See Kiesselbach, Dorothee.
Bavaria around the lakes. A picture book. (Bayerisches
Seenland.) Text Dorothee Kiesselbach. Tr. Christian
Mayer. Photog. P--K--. L: Tiranti, 1960. 96p. 24cm.
[B60]

KEETMAN, Peter, photog. See Göpel, Erhard.
Munich, a picture book. (München.) Eng. ver. L.W.
Sayers. Photos. P--K--. Text Erhard Göpel. Lindau,
Thorbecke, c1960. 95p. [LC62]

Same. L: Tiranti, 1960. 88p. (24cm.) [B60]

KELLER, Arnold, numismatist.
Paper money of the world. (Das Papiergeld des Zweiten
Weltkriegs und der Nachkriegszeit.) Tr. Jerome M.
Eisenberg. NY: Royal Coin Co., 1956. V. 22cm.
[LC62, IT9]

KELLER, Gottfried, 1819-1890.
The green Henry. (Der grüne Heinrich.) Tr. A. M.

Holt. L: Calder, 1960. 706p. (21cm.) [LC62, B60]

Same. NY: Grove, 1960. 706p. 21cm. [LC62, B60, IT13]

Little legend of the dance. Tr. William D. Hottinger. In Spender's Coll. 1960.

Selections in Loomis, C. G. 1960.

A village Romeo and Juliet. (Romeo und Julia auf dem Dorfe.) Tr. Paul Bernhard Thomas with B. Q. Morgan. NY: Ungar, 1960. 96p. 18cm. [LC62, IT13]

KELLER, Werner, 1909- .
The Bible as history. (Und die Bibel hat doch recht.) Tr. W. Neil. L: Hodder, 1956. (1957-LC) 429p. [LC62, B56, IT9]

Same. NY: Morrow, 1956. 452p. 22cm. [LC62, IT9]

KELLERMANN, Getulius, 1821-1900.
Memoirs of an engineer in the Confederate Army in Texas. Tr. Helen S. Sundstrom. Austin, Texas, 1957. 48p. 24cm. [LC62]

KELSEN, Hans, 1881- .
What is justice? Justice, law, and politics in the mirror of science. Collected essays. Tr. Anon. Berkeley: U. of California Pr., 1957. 397p. 24cm. [LC62]

KENYON, Max.
A Mozart letter book. Tr. Max Kenyon. L: Barker, 1956. 158p. 22cm. (22.5cm.) [LC57, B56]

Same. Westport, Conn.: Associated Booksellers, c1956. 158p. 22cm. [LC62]

KEPLER, Johann, 1571-1630.
The sidereal messenger of Galileo Galilei, and a part of the preface to Kepler's dioptics containing the original account of Galileo's astronomical discoveries. L: Dawsons, 1959. 111p. 21cm. [LC62]

KERENYI, Caroly, 1897- .
Archetypal images in Greek religion. Tr. Anon. NY: Pantheon, 195-. V. 27cm. [LC62]

KERENYI, Caroly--
Asklepios. Archetypal image of the physician's existence.
(Der göttliche Arzt.) Tr. Ralph Manheim. NY: Pantheon, 1959. 151p. 26cm. [LC62, IT12]

Same. L: Thames, 1960. 151p. 26cm. [LC62, B60]

The Gods of the Greeks. Tr. Norman Cameron. Harmondsworth: Penguin, 1958. 271p. 18cm. [LC62, B58]

Same. NY: Grove, 1960. 304p. 20cm. [LC62]

Greece in colour. (Griechenland.) Daphne Woodward extracts from poems by Goethe, Hölderlin, Rilke. Tr. Eric Peters. L: Thames, 1957. 33p. (34p.) 36cm. [LC62, B57]

Same. NY: McGraw, 1958. 33p. 36cm. [LC62]

The heroes of the Greeks. (Die Heroen der Griechen.) Tr. H. J. Rose. L: Thames, c1959. 439p. (22.5cm.) 23cm. [LC62, B59, IT12]

Same. NY: Grove, 1960. 439p. 23cm. [LC62, IT13]

KERKER, Gustave Adolph, 1857-1923. See Wilhelm, Julius and Willner, Alfred, jt. authors.

KERN, Fritz, 1884-1950.
The wildbooters. (Der Beginn der Weltgeschichte.) Tr. Anon. L: Oliver, 1960. 204p. (22cm.) [LC62, B60]

KERSTEN, Felix, 1898- .
The Kersten memoirs 1940-45. (Author, a Finn, was Himmler's personal physiotherapist and used his position to gain release of prisoners--German, Dutch, Jew, and Scand.) Trs. Constantine Fitzgibbon and James Oliver. Introd. H. R. Trevor-Roper. L: Hutchinson, 1956. 314p. 24cm. [LC62, B56, IT10]

Same. NY: Macmillan, 1957. 314p. 25cm. [LC62, IT10]

KETTIGER, Ernst and Vetter, Franz.
Furniture and interiors. (Möbel und Räume.) Tr. W. Kuske. Erlenbach-Zürich: Rentsch, 1957. 188p.

28cm. [LC62]

Same. Stuttgart: Rentsch, c1957. 188p. [LC62]

KEUSEN, Hans.
Picturesque India and the East. Tr. Anon. Bombay:
Taraporevala, c1958. 127p. 29cm. [LC62]

South Asia. 128 pictures in photogravure. 28 in colour.
Tr. Anon. L: Thames, 1958. 24p. (28.5cm.) 29cm.
[LC62, B58]

Same. NY: Praeger, 1958. (24p.) 28.5cm.) 29cm.
[LC62, B58]

KEYSERLING, Hermann Alexander, Graf von, 1880-1946.
Indian travel diary of a philosopher. Tr. J. Holroyd-
Reece. Bombay: Bharatiya Vidya Bhavan, 1959. 227p.
[LC62]

KIEPENHEUER, Karl Otto.
The sun. (Die Sonne.) Tr. A. J. Pomerans. L: Mayflower, 1959. 160p. (21.5cm.) [LC62, B59, IT12]

Same. Ann Arbor: U. of Michigan Pr., 1959. 160p.
22cm. [LC62, IT12]

Same. Ann Arbor edition, 1960. 160p. [IT13]

KIESSELBACH, Dorothee.
Bavaria around the lakes. A picture book. (Bayerisches
Seenland.) Tr. Christian Mayer. Text D--F---. Photog.
Peter Keetman. L: Tiranti, 1960. 96p. 24cm. [B60]

KIETZ, Gertraud.
New concepts in the theory of hearing. (Neue Vorstel-
lungen in der Theorie des Hörens.) Tr. Anon. Chicago:
1958. 21p. [LC62]

KIK, Richard, 1899- .
With Schweitzer in Lambarene. (Beim Organga am Lambarene. Geschichte aus dem Leben Albert Schweitzers.)
Tr. Carrie Bettelini. Philadelphia: Christian, 1959.
87p. 18cm. [LC62, IT12, 13]

KILLIAN, Hans, 1892- .
The show line. (Hinter uns steht nur der Herrgott.)

KILLIAN, Hans--
Tr. Stewart Thomson. L: Barrie, 1958. 205p.
(19cm.) [LC62, B58, IT11]

KING, Alexander, 1900- . Ed. See Altenberg, Peter,
1859-1919.
Alexander King presents Peter Altenberg's evocations of
love. Tr. Anon. NY, 1960. [LC62]

KIRSCHBAUM, Engelbert, 1902- .
The tombs of St. Peter and St. Paul. (Die Gräber der
Apostolfürsten.) Tr. John Murray. L: Secker; NY:
St. Martins, 1959. 247p. 24cm. [LC62, B59, IT12]

KIRSCHBAUM, Engelbert, 1902- . jt. author. See Hertling, Ludwig, Freiherr von, 1892- .

KIRST, Hans Hellmut, 1914- .
Forward, Gunner Asch. (Null-acht-fünfzehn, vol. 2.)
Tr. Robert Kee. Boston: Little, 1956. 368p. 22cm.
[LC62, IT9]

Gunner Asch goes to war. (Im Kreig. Null-acht-fünf-
zen, vol. 2.) Tr. Robert Kee. L: Weidenfeld, 1956.
335p. 19cm. [LC62, B56, IT9]

No one will escape, a novel. (Keiner kommt davon.)
Tr. Richard Graves. L: Weidenfeld, 1959. 412p.
(20.5cm.) 21cm. [LC62, B59, IT12]

Same. L: World, 1960. 446p. (17cm.) [B60]

The return of Gunner Asch. (Null-acht-fünfzehn (3), Der
gefährliche Endsieg des Soldaten Asch.) Tr. Robert Kee.
Boston: Little, 1957. 310p. 21cm. [LC62, IT10]

Same. L: Weidenfeld, 1957. 288p. (19cm.) [LC62,
B57, IT10]

The revolt of Gunner Asch. (Null-acht-fünfzehn (IV), In
der Kaserne.) Tr. Robert Kee. Toronto: Little, c1956.
311p. [LC62]

Same. Eng. title Zero . . . (1). Boston: Little, 1956.
311p. 21cm. [LC62]

The seventh day. (Keiner kommt davon.) Tr. Richard

Graves. Garden City, NY: Doubleday, 1959. 424p.
22cm. [LC62, IT12]

Zero eight fifteen, 2. Gunner Asch goes to war. Tr.
Robert Kee. L: Weidenfeld, 1956. 335p. (19cm.)
[B56]

Zero eight fifteen, 3. The return of Gunner Asch. A
novel. Tr. Robert Kee. L: Weidenfeld, 1957. 288p.
19cm. [LC62, B57]

Zero eight fifteen, a novel. Tr. Robert Kee. L:
Weidenfeld, 1955-1957. 3v. 19cm. [LC62]

KLAJ, Johann, 1616-1656.
Selections in Loomis, C. G. 1958.

KLEE, Paul, 1879-1940.
The inward vision. (Im Zwischenreich.) Tr. N. Guterman. L: Thames, c1958. 61p. 33cm. [LC62]

Same. NY: Abrams, 1958. 61p. 33cm. [LC62, IT12]

Same. 2nd ed. NY: Abrams, 1959. 61p. 33cm.
[LC62, IT12]

Paul Klee. Tr. Anon. Text Will Grohmann. NY:
Abrams, 1956. 24p. 23cm. [LC62]

Paul Klee drawings. Text Will Grohmann. Tr. Norbert
Guterman. L: Thames, 1960. (176p.) 19cm. [LC62,
B60]

Same. NY: Abrams, 1960. 447p. 30cm. [LC62,
IT13]

Pedagogical sketchbook. (Pädagogisches Skizzenbuch.)
Tr. and introd. Sibyl Moholy-Nagy. L: Faber, 1959.
60p. 24cm. [LC62]

Same. NY: Praeger, 1960. 60p. [LC62, IT13]

KLEE, Paul, 1897-1940, and Grohmann, Will.
Paul Klee, 1879-1940. Text Will Grohmann. Tr. Anon.
L: Collins, 1957. (34p.) 17cm. [LC62, B57]

KLEE, Paul, 1879-1940. See Grohmann, Will.

KLEE, Paul, 1879-1940. See Macke, August 1887-1914.
Diary of a trip to Tunisia. Tr. Anon. NY: Abrams,
1959. 60p. 24cm. [LC62]

KLEIN, Felix, 1849-1925.
Lectures on the icosahedron and the solution of equations
of the fifth degree. Tr. George Gavin Morrice. 2nd rev.
ed. NY: Dover, 1956. 289p. 21cm. [LC62]

Same. 305p. [IT9]

KLEIN, Melanie.
Envy and gratitude, a study of unconscious sources. Tr.
Anon. NY: Basic, 1957. 101p. 22cm. [LC62]

Same. L: Tavistock, 1957. 101p. (22.5cm.) 23cm.
[LC62, B57]

The psychoanalysis of children. (Die Psychoanalyse des
Kindes.) Authorized tr. Alix Strachey. L: Hogarth,
1959. 393p. (22.5cm.) [LC62, B59]

Same. NY: Grove, 1960. 399p. 21cm. [LC62, IT13]

KLEIN, Melanie, ed. with Paula Heinmann and R. E. Money-
Kyrle.
New directions in psycho-analysis. The significance of
infant conflict in the pattern of adult behavior. Tr. Anon.
NY: Basic, 1956. 534p. (22.5cm.) 23cm. [LC62,
B56]

Our adult world and its roots in infancy. Tr. Anon.
L: Tavistock, 1960. 15p. 24cm. [LC62]

KLEIST, Heinrich von, 1777-1811.
The broken pitcher. A comedy. (Der zerbrochene Krug.)
n.p., 1958. 80l. [LC62]

Earthquake in Chile. (Das Erdbeben in Chile.) Tr. M.
Hamburger. In Spender's Coll. 1960.

Katie of Heilbronn, 1808, or, Trial by fire. A great
historical drama of knighthood. (Das Kätchen von H--.)
Tr. Arthur H. Hughes. Hartford: Trinity College,
c1960. V. 22cm. [LC62]

The Marquise of O-, and other stories. Tr. Martin

Greenberg. Pref. Thomas Mann. NY: Criterion, 1960.
318p. 22cm. [LC62, IT13]

The Prince of Homburg. A play in 5 acts. (Prinz Friedrich von H--.) Tr. Charles E. Passage. NY: Liberal Arts, 1956. 83p. 21cm. [LC62, IT9]

KLEMM, Friedrich, 1902- .
A history of western technology. (Technik, eine Geschichte ihrer Probleme.) Tr. Dorothea Waley Singer. L: Allen, 401p. (3-402p.) (22.5cm.) 23cm. [LC62, B59, IT12]

Same. NY: Scribner, 1959. 401p. 23cm. [LC62, IT12]

KLEMPERER, Klemens von.
Germany's new conservatism. Its history and dilemma in the twentieth century. Fwd. Sigmund Neumann. Tr. Anon. Princeton, NJ: Princeton U. Pr., 1957. 250p. 22cm. [LC62]

KLENNER, Fritz.
The Austrian trade union movement. Tr. Edward Fitzgerald. Pref. Anton Proksch. Brussels: International Confederation of Free Trade Unions, 1956. 151p. 22cm. [LC62]

Same. Enl. ed. 1959. 156p. [LC62]

KLING, Karl, 1910- with Molter, G.
Pursuit of victory. The story of a racing driver. (Jagd nach dem Sieg.) Tr. Peter Myers. L: Bodley Head, (Lane), 1956. 192p. (21cm.) [LC62, B56, IT9]

KLIER, Henry. (also Heinrich.)
A summer gone. (Verlorener Sommer.) Tr. James Kirkup. L: Bles, 1959. 255p. [LC62, B59, IT12]

KNAUR, Kaethe, 1915- .
Dogs of character. (Schöne Hunde.) Tr. Kenneth Kettle. L: Macdonald, 1957. 111p. (25.5cm.) [LC62, B57]

KNIERIEM, August von, 1887- .
The Nuremberg trials. (Nürnberg, rechtliche und menschliche Probleme.) Tr. Elizabeth D. Schmitt. Chicago: Regnery; (L: Bailey), 1959. 561p. 24cm. (24.5cm.)

KNIERIEM, August von--
[LC62, B60, IT12]

KNOKE, Heinz, 1921- .
I flew for the Führer. (Die grosse Jagd. Bordbuch eines
deutschen Jagdfliegers.) Tr. John Ewing. L: Transworld,
1956. 11-192p. (16cm.) [B56, IT9]

Same. NY: Berkeley, 1959. 156p. [IT12]

KOBER, Adolf.
150 years of religious instruction. (Extract of two chaps.,
Aus 150 Jahren jüdischer Erziehung in Deutschland). Tr.
Anon. n. p., 1957. 98-118p. [LC62]

KOCH, Alexander, 1895- .
(Hotelbauten, Motels, Ferienhäuser.) Tr. Anon. (Ger.,
Fr., and Eng.) Stuttgart: Koch, 1958. 315p. 31cm.
[LC62]

Restaurants, cafes, bars. Tr. Anon. Stuttgart, 1959.
407p. 30cm. [LC62]

KOCSIS, Maria (Szirmai Foris)
History of folk cross stitch. With 278 coloured charts.
(Kreuzstich-Vorlagen.) Tr. and introd. Heinz Edgar
Kiewe. Ed. Andreas Foris. 3rd ed. Nuremberg: Se-
baldus, 1960. 85p. [LC62]

KOEHLER, John Philipp, 1859-1951.
The epistle of Paul to the Galatians. (Der Brief Pauli an
die Galater.) Tr. E. E. Sauer. Milwaukee: Northwestern, c 1957. 167p. 21cm. [LC62, IT13]

KÖHLER, Ludwig Hugo, 1880-1956.
Hebrew man. (Der hebräische Mensch.) Tr. Peter Run-
ham Ackroyd. L: SCM, 1956. 189p. 22cm. (22.5cm.)
[LC62, B56, IT9]

Same. Nashville: Abingdon, 1957. 160p. 21cm. [LC
62, IT9, 10]

Old Testament theology. (Theologie des Alten Testaments.
3rd rev. ed.) Tr. A. S. Todd. Philadelphia, Westminster,
1957. 257p. 24cm. [LC62]

Same. L: Lutterworth, 1957. 259p. 22cm. (22.5cm.)

[LC62, B57, IT10]

KÖHLER, Walter.
Lighting in architecture. (Lichtarchitektur.) Tr. Bertrand languages, Inc. NY: Reinholdt, (L: Chapman),
1959. 223p. (27.5cm.) 28cm. [LC62, B59, IT12]

KÖHLER, Wolfgang, 1887- .
The mentality of apes. Tr. Ella Winter (from 2nd rev.
ed.) L: Routledge, 1956. 336p. 22cm. [LC62]

Same. Harmondsworth: Penguin, 1957. 286p. (18.5cm.)
[B57]

Same. NY, 1959. 293p. 19cm. [LC62]

KOENIG, Lilli.
Nature stories of the Vienna woods. Tr. Anon.   NY:
Crowell, c1958. 158p. 24cm. [LC62, IT12]

Tales from the Vienna woods. (Die klaren Augen.) Tr.
Marjorie Latzke. L: Methuen, 1958. 158p. (159p.)
21cm. [LC62, B58, IT11]

KOENIGSWALD, Gustav Heinrich Ralph V., 1902- .
Meeting prehistoric man. (Begegnungen mit dem Vormen-
schen.) Tr. Michael Bullock. L: Thames, 1956. 216p.
(22.5cm.) 23cm. [LC62, B56, IT9]

Same. NY: Harper, c1956. 216p. 22cm. [LC62]

KOENIGSWALD, Harold von, 1906- .
The Soviet zone of Germany. Pictures of everyday life.
Tr. Anon. Esslingen: Bechtle, 1959. unp. 27cm.
[LC62]

KOEPPEN, Wolfgang, 1906- .
Death in Rome. (Der Tod in Rom.) Tr. Mervyn Savill.
L: Weidenfeld, 1956. 217p. (19.5cm.) 20cm. [LC62,
B56, IT9]

KOESTLER, Arthur, 1905- .
Darkness at noon. (Mittagsfinsternis.) Tr. Daphne
Hardy. NY: New American Lib., 1956. 188p. 18cm.
[LC62]

Same. L: Landsborough, 1959. 191p. (192p.) 18cm.

214

[B59, IT12]

Dialogue with death. Trs. Trevor and Phillis Blewitt.
NY: Macmillan. 1960. 214p. 21cm. [LC62, IT13]

KÖSTLER, Josef Nikolaus, 1902- .
Silviculture. (Waldbau.) Tr. Mark L. Anderson. Edinburgh, L: Oliver, 1956. 416p. 23cm. (23.5cm.)
[LC62, B56, IT9]

Same. L: Oliver, 1956. 416p. 24cm. [LC62]

KOFFKA, Kurt, 1886-1941.
The growth of the mind, an introduction to child psychology. (Die Grundlagen der psychischen Entwicklung.) Tr.
Robert Morris Ogden. Paterson, NJ: Littlefield, 1959.
426p. 21cm. [LC62, IT12]

KOGON, Eugen, 1903- .
The theory and practice of hell. The German concentration camps and the system behind them. (Der SS-Staat,
das System der deutschen Konzentrationslager.) Tr.
Heinz Norden. NY: Berkeley, 1958. 297p. [LC62,
IT11]

Same. 1960. 328p. [LC62]

KOHL, Johann Georg, 1808-1878.
Wanderings round Lake Superior. (Kitchi-Gami, oder
Erzählungen vom obern See.) Tr. Lascelles Wraxall
with omissions. New introd. Russell W. Friday. Minneapolis: Ross, 1956. 11p. 428p. 23cm. [LC62]

KOFLER, Oswald and others. Photo. See Sebass, Friedrich.

KOHLER, Ivo.
Orientation by aural clues. (From Die Pyramide, Naturwissenschaftliche Monatschrift, May 1957.) Tr. Anon.
Innsbruck, 1957. 15p. [LC62]

KOHLER, Marc.
The common market and investments. Tr. Josette L.
Hueni. NY: Vintage, 1960. 172p. 21cm. [LC62]

KOKOSCHKA, Oskar, 1886- .
Kokoschka. Tr. Anon. L: Faber, 1960. 24p.

(30.5cm.) 31cm. [LC62, B60]

KOLB, Fritz.
Himalaya adventure. (Einzelgänger im Himalaya.) Tr.
Lawrence Wilson. L: Lutterworth, 1959. 148p. (22
cm.) [LC62, B59, IT12]

KOLLWITZ, Käthe (Schmidt), 1867-1945.
Käthe Kollwitz, drawings. Tr. Anon. NY: Yoseloff,
1959. 35, 130p. 29cm. [LC62]

KOMMUNISTISCHE PARTEI DEUTSCHLANDS.
The Karlsruhe trial for banning the Communist Party of
Germany. Tr. C. P. Dutt. L: Lawrence, 1956. 127p.
19cm. [LC62]

KOMMUNISTISCHE PARTEI DEUTSCHLANDS, RESPOND-
ENT. KPD-Prozess. See Germany (Federal Republic,
1949- .)

KOPFERMANN, Hans, 1895- .
Nuclear moments. (Kernmomente.) Tr. E. E. Schneider. (From 2nd ed.) NY: Academic, 1958. 505p.
24cm. [LC62, IT11]

KOPP, Hans, 1910- .
Himalaya shuttlecock. (Sechsmal über den Himalaya.)
Tr. H. C. Stevens. L: Hutchinson, 1957. 191p. 22cm.
[LC62, B57, IT10]

KORSCHUNOW, Irina.
The piebald pup. (Der bunte Hund.) Adapt. Martha
Murphy. 1st ed. NY: McDowell, c1958. unp. 30cm.
[LC62]

KORTA, Helmut E., jt. author. See Rossberg, Ehrhard A.
Teleprinter switching. Princeton, NJ: Van Nostrand,
1960. [LC62, B60, IT13]

KOVARIK, Illa and Simanyu, Tibor.
The voice of fears. Ten poems. Tr. Sarah Gainham.
Vienna: ARS Hungarica, 1959. 26p. 30cm. [LC62]

KRAFFT-EBING, Richard, Freiherr von, 1840-1902.
Abberrations of sexual life. A medico-legal study for
doctors and lawyers brought up to date. (Psychopathia
sexualis, adpt.) Tr. Arthur V. Burbury. L: Staples;
Springfield, Ill.: Thomas, c1959. 345p. 23cm. [LC
62, IT13]

KRALIK, Heinrich, Ritter von Meyrswalden, 1887- . With
Wessely, O. and Kempf, B.
Austria, land of music. A brief survey of music and
musicians in Austria. Tr. Richard Rickett. Vienna:
Federal, 1959. V. 72p. 21cm. [LC62]

KRAMER, Franz.
Ski the new way. (So fährt man Ski in Österreich.) Tr.
Anon. NY: Sterling, 1960. 127p. 21cm. [LC62, IT13]

KRAMERS, Henrik Anthony, 1894-1952.
Collected scientific papers. Tr. Anon. Amsterdam:
North-Holland, 1956. 969p. 27cm. [LC62]

The foundations of quantum theory. (Theorien des Auf-
baues der Materie. Bd. 1, Abs. 1, die Grundlagen der
Quantentheorie.) Tr. D. ter Haar. Amsterdam:
North-Holland; NY: Interscience, 1957. 228p. (23.5
cm.) 24cm. [LC62, B57, IT10]

Same. 1958. 496p. 23cm. [LC62]

Quantum mechanics. (Die Grundlagen der Quantentheorie,
und Quantentheorie des Elektrons und der Strahlung.) Tr.
D. ter Haar. Amsterdam: North-Holland; NY: Interscience, 1957. 496p. 23cm. [LC62, IT10]

KRANCK, Klaus. See Reidy, A. E.

KRANCKE, Theodor and Brennecke, Hans Joachim.
The battleship Scheer. (RRR, das glückhafte Schiff.)
Tr. Edward Fitzgerald. L: Kimber, 1956. 200p.
(22.5cm.) 23cm. [LC62, B56, IT9]

Pocket battleship, the story of the Admiral Scheer. (RRR,
das glückhafte Schiff.) Tr. Anon. NY: Norton, 1958.
239p. 22cm. [LC62, IT11]

KRAUS, Hans Joachim.
The people of God in the Old Testament. Tr. Anon.
NY: Association, 1958. 92p. 20cm. [LC62]

KRAUSE, Aurel, 1848- .
The Tlingit Indians. Results of a trip. Tr. Erna Gunther. Seattle: U. of Washington Pr., 1956. 310p.
23cm. [LC62, IT9]

KRAUSE, Walter W.
Soroya, Queen of Persia. Tr. Marthe Taylor-Whitehead.
L: Macdonald, 1956. 9-208p. (22.5cm.) 23cm.
[LC62, B56, IT9]

KRAUSNICK, Helmut, jt. author. See Mau, Hermann.

KREIPE, Werner.
The battle of Britain. Tr. Anon. In Freidin, Seymour
Coll.

The fatal decisions. Tr. Constantine Fitzgibbon. Eds.
Seymor Freidin and W. Richardson. NY: Sloane, 1956.
202p. [LC62, IT9]

KREMLING, Ernsl, ed.
Munich and Southern Bavaria. (München und die bayeri-
schen Berge.) Tr. Anon. Munich: JRO, 1960. 76p.
115 x 20cm. [LC62]

KRETSCHMER, Ernst, 1888- .
Hysteria, reflex, and instinct. (Hysterie, Reflex und In-
stinkt.) Trs. Vlasta and Wade Baskin. NY: Philosophical Lib., 1960. 162p. 21cm. [LC62, IT13]

KREYSZIG, Erwin.
Differential geometry. Tr. Anon. Toronto: U. of
Toronto Pr., 1959. 352p. 24cm. [LC62]

KRICK, Mrs. Irvin L., ed.
See Womelsdorf, Pa. Zion Union Church. Tr. Anon.
Tr. of the Zion Union (Lutheran and Reformed) Church
records. Chicago, Ill., 1958. [LC62]

KRONER, Richard, 1884- .
Kant's Weltanschauung. (Kants W--.) Tr. John E. Smith.
Rev. R--K--. University of Chicago, L: Cambridge U.
Pr., 1956. 118p. (119p.) 20cm. [LC62, B56, IT9]

KROTT, Peter.
Demon of the north. Tr. of Ger. Tr. of Swed. Orig.
Tupu-Tupu-Tupu-. Tr. Edward Fitzgerald. NY: Knopf,
1959. 259p. [IT12]

Tupu-Tupu-Tupu. Tr. Edward Fitzgerald. L, 1958.
231p. (23p.) 22cm. [LC62, B58]

KRÜCK, Maria Josepha (von Fischer-Poturzyn), 1896- . ed.
Rudolf Steiner, recollections by some of his pupils. (Wir
erlebten R--S--.) Tr. Anon. Eds. Arnold Freeman and
Charles Waterman. L, 1957. 188p. 21cm. (21.5cm.)
[LC62, B58]

KRÜSS, James, 1926- .
Henrietta Chuffertrain. (Henriette Bimmelbahn.)
Verses by J--K--. Tr. Marion Koenig. Kingswood,
World's Work, 1960. 24p. (19.5 x 27.5cm.) 20 x 27
cm. [LC62, B60]

KRUG VON NIDDA, Roland, 1895- . See Anastasia Nikolaevna.
I, Anastasia. (Ich, Anastasia, erzähle.) Tr. Oliver Coburn. Notes by R--K-- von N--. L: Joseph, 1958.
282p. (22.5cm.) 23cm. [LC62, B58]

I am Anastasia. The autobiography of the Grand Duchess
of Russia. Tr. Oliver Coburn. NY: Harcourt, 1959.
282p. 23cm. [LC62, IT12]

KRUPP (FRIED.) AKTIENGESELLSCHAFT, ESSEN.
Krupp in the service of engineering progress. Essen,
1960. 42p. [LC62]

Krupp today. Essen, 1959. 1v. (unpaged) 21cm.
[LC62]

KRUPS, James. See Krüss, James.

KRUSE, Hans, 1921- .
The foundation of Islamic international jurisprudence.
Tr. Mohammad Aman Hobohm. Karachi: Pakistan His-
torical Society, 1956. 37p. 24cm. [LC62]

Same. Tr. Muhammad Shamtuddin. Karachi: Pakistan
Historical Society, 1956. 37p. [LC62]

Legal aspects of the peaceful utilization of atomic energy.
(Friedliche Verwendung der Atomenergie im Recht.) Tr.
Anon. Herne: Neue Wirtschafts-Briefe, 1960. 111p.
21cm. [LC62]

KRUSE, Willy, 1889-1945 and Dieckvoss, Wilhelm.
The stars. (Die Wissenschaft von den Sternen.) Tr.
Ralph Manheim. Ann Arbor: U. of Michigan Pr.; L:

Mayflower, 1957. 202p. (21.5cm.) 22cm. [LC62, B59, IT13]

KUBY, Erich, 1910- .
Rosemarie. (R--, des deutschen Wunders liebstes Kind.)
Tr. R. C. J. Muller. 1st American ed. NY: Knopf,
1960. 239p. 22cm. [LC62, IT13]

Same. L: Weidenfeld, 1960. 224p. (20.5cm.) [LC 62, B60, IT13]

KUČERA, M.
The face of Prague. Tr. Anon. Pref. and caps. Jiri Körber. Prague: Artia, 195-. 15p. [LC62]

KUCHLER, Kurt.
A summer spook, a light comedy in four acts. Tr. Anon. NY: Rosenfield, n.d. 1 vol. 28cm. [LC62]

KUDRNOFSKY, Wolfgang.
Greece. Tr. Dorothy Plummer. Introd. Ch. Kriekou-kis. n.p. Andermann, c1959. 60p. [LC62]

Salzburg and surroundings. Tr. G. A. Colville, Pano-rama, Andermann, c1958. 61p. [LC62]

Salzkammergut. Tr. Anon. Wien: Andermann, c1958. 61p. 18cm. [LC62]

Spain. (Spanien.) Tr. Anon. München: Andermann, 1957. [LC62]

KÜHN, Herbert, 1895- .
The rock pictures of Europe. (Die Felsbilder Europas.)
Tr. Alan Houghton Brodrick. L: Sidgwick, 1956. 230p. 22cm. (22.5cm.) [LC62, B57, IT9]

Same. Fair Lawn, NJ: Essential, 1956. i.e. 1957. 230p. 23cm. [LC62]

KÜHN, Johannes, 1887- .
The historical problem of tolerance. (From Autour de Michel Servet et de Sebastien Castellion, ed. B. Becter.)
Tr. Stuart Daggett, Jr. n.p., 1959. 35p. 29cm. [LC62]

KÜHNE, Paul, 1914- .
Home medical encyclopedia. (Lebe gesund, bleibe gesund.)

KÜHNE, Paul--
Medicine for the layman. A Guide to the intelligent use of your
doctor. (Lebe gesund, bleibe gesund.) Tr. Jean Cunningham.
L: Faber, 1957. 452p. (22.5cm.) 23cm. [LC62, B57]

KÜHNER, Hans.
Encyclopedia of the Papacy. (Lexikon der Päpste.) Tr.
Kenneth J. Northcott. NY: Philosophical Lib., 1958.
249p. 22cm. [LC62, IT11]

Same. L: Owen, 1959. 249p. (22cm.) [LC62, B59,
IT12]

KÜMMEL, Werner Georg, 1905- .
Promise and fulfilment. The eschatological message of
Jesus. (Verheissung und Erfüllung.) Tr. Dorothea M.
Burton. (From 3rd and compl. rev. ed.) L: SCM;
Naperville, Ill.: Allenson, 1957. 168p. 22cm. [LC62,
B57]

KÜMMEL, Werner Georg, 1905- . See Dibelius, Martin,
1883-1947.
Paul. (Paulus.) Tr. Frank Clarke. Philadelphia:
Westminster, 1957. 172p. 19cm. [LC62]

KÜMMERLY AND FREY, Bern.
All about Switzerland. (Kleines Schweizer Brevier.)
Bern, n.p., 1957. 24p. 13cm. [LC62]

KUENEN, D. J., Lorenz, Konrad, Tinbergen, Nicholas.
Schiller, Paul H., and Uexküell, Jakob von, contributors.
Instinctive behavior, the development of a modern con-
cept. Tr. and ed. Claire H. Schiller. Introd. Karl S.
Lashley. L: Methuen; NY: International U. Pr., 1957.
328p. (24cm.) [B59]

Same. NY: International U. Pr., 1957. 328p. 24cm.
[LC62]

KÜRENBERG,
Selections in Loomis, C. G. 1958.

KUHL, Curt.
The prophets of Israel. (Israels Propheten.) Trs.
Rudolf J. Ehrlich and J. O. Smith. Edinburgh, L:
Oliver; Richmond: Knox, 1960. 199p. (22.5cm.)
23cm. [LC62, B60, IT13]

KULTERMANN, Udo.
Architecture of today, a survey of new buildings through-
out the world. (Baukunst der Gegenwart.) Tr. Anon.
L: Zwemmer, 1958. 236p. (27.5cm.) 28cm. [LC62,
B59]

New Japanese architecture. (Neues Bauen in Japan.)
Tr. Anon. L: Architectural, 1960. 180p. 28cm.
[LC62]

KUNST AUS ÖSTERREICH. See Spitzmüller, Anna.

KUPPER, Walter.
Cacti. Ed. and tr. Vera Higgins. Illus. Pia Roshard.
Edinburgh, L: Nelson, 1960. 27p. (172p.) 30cm.
[LC62, B60]

KURTH, Alfred, 1916- .
The Swiss Forest Research Institute at Birmensdorf, near
Zurich. Tr. Anon. Zurich, 1959. 8p. [LC62]

KURTH, O. E. W. See Kurth, Rudolf.

KURTH, Rudolf, 1917- .
Introduction to the mechanics of stellar systems. Tr.
Anon. L, NY: Pergamon, 1957. 174p. 22cm. (22.5
cm.) [LC62, B57]

KURTHA, O. E. W. Rudolf.
Introduction to the mechanics of the solar system. Tr.
A. H. Batten. L, NY: Pergamon, 1959. 177p. [IT13]

KUSCH, Eugen, 1905- .
The immortal Nuremberg. (Nürnberg, Lebensbild einer
Stadt.) Tr. of 2nd ed. completely rev. text and illus.
Tr. Andrew L. White. Nuremberg: Carl, 1959. 25p.
27cm. [LC62]

India in pictures. (Indian im Bild.) Tr. Anon. Nuremberg: Carl, 1960. 31p. 30cm. [LC62]

Mexico in pictures. Tr. Anon. Nürnberg: Carl, 1957.
35p. 31cm. [LC62]

Same. NY: Architectural, 1958. 35p. 31cm. [LC62]

KUTTER, Markus. See Gerstner, Karl.

KWASNIK, Walter.
Aesthetic and playability requirements of electronic or-
gans. (From Frequenz, 1951.) Tr. D. A. Sinclair.
Ottawa, n.p., 1956. 28cm. [LC62]

LABOR COSTS IN THE EUROPEAN ECONOMIC COMMU-
NITY.
Tr. Anon. Patria translations. Eurosyndicat, Brussels,
1960. 30p. 30cm. [LC62]

LACH, Donald Frederick, 1917- . See Leibniz' Gottfried
Wilhelm Freiherr von, 1646-1716.
The preface to Leibniz' Novissima Sinica, commentary,
tr., text. Honolulu: U. of Hawaii Pr., 1957. [LC62]

LACHMANN, Ludwig Maurits.
Capital and its structure. Tr. Anon. L: London School
of Economics and Political Science, U. of London, Bell,
1956. 130p. (22.5cm.) 23cm. [LC62, B56]

LACHMUND, Margarethe.
Christians in a divided world. The attitude of Christians
in the tensions between East and West. (Die innere
Friede und die notwendige Unruhe.) Tr. Anon. L: The
East-West Relations Committee of the Society of Friends,
1959. 12p. 22cm. [LC62]

LAMADE, Erich, 1894- .
The craft of the artist. A workbook on fine arts paint-
ing and related crafts. Tr. Anon. Special editing W.
M. Nawrocki. NY, 1956. 210p. 28cm. [LC62]

LAND- UND HAUSWIRTSCHAFTLICHER AUSWERTUNGS-
UND INFORMATIONSDIENST, GODESBERG, GERMANY.
Agricultural organizations of the German Federal Republic. Tr. Anon. Bad Godesberg: Land- und Hauswirtschaftlicher Auswertungs- und Informationsdienst, 1958.
45p. [LC62]

Same. 4th ed. Bad Godesberg: Land- und Hauswirtschaftlicher Auswertungs- und Informationsdienst, 1960.
48p. [LC62]

Agriculture of the Federal Republic of Germany. (Die
Landwirtschaft der Bundesrepublik Deutschland.) Tr.

Anon. Bad Godesberg, 1956. 19p. [LC62]

Same. 4th ed. Bad Godesberg, 1958. 51p. [LC62]

Forestry in the Federal Republic of Germany. Tr. Anon. Bad Godesberg, 1958. 55p. [LC62]

Same. 3rd rev. ed. Bad Godesberg, 1960. 63p. [LC62]

LAND- UND HAUSWIRTSCHAFTLICHER AUSWERTUNGS-
UND INFORMATIONSDIENST, GODESBERG, GER. See
Germany (Federal Republic 1949- .)
Catalogue of technical schools, colleges and other educa-
tional institutes for agriculture, wine growing, horticul-
turc, and forcstry. Bundesministerium für Ernährung,
Landwirtschaft und Forsten. Tr. Anon. Bad Godesberg,
1959. [LC62]

LANDAU, Edmund Georg Hermann, 1877- .
Differential and integral calculus. (Einführung in die
Differentialrechnung und Integralrechnung.) Trs. Melvin
Hausner and Martin Davis. 2nd ed. NY: Chelsea, 1960.
367p. 24cm. [LC62]

Elementary number theory. Tr. Jacob E. Goodman.
NY: Chelsea, 1958. 256p. 24cm. [LC62, IT11]

Foundations of analysis. The arithmetic of whole, rational, irrational and complex numbers. Tr. F. Steinhardt. 2nd ed. NY: Chelsea, c1960. 136p. [LC62]

LANDESZENTRALBANK IN BERLIN.
Report on the economic and monetary development of
West Berlin. Tr. Anon. Berlin, n.d. (annual) v.
30cm. [LC62]

LANGE, Eitel, 1905- and Rolf.
Around the world with motorcycle and camera. Tr. Sus-
anne Perkins-Lutz. Los Angeles: Clymer, 1957. 232p.
22cm. [LC62]

LANGE, Friedrich Albert, 1828-1875.
The history of materialism and criticism of its present
importance. Authorized tr. Ernest Chester Thomas.
L: Routledge, 1957. 376p. 23cm. [LC62]

LANGE, Horst Heinz, 1924- . comp.
The fabulous fives. The six big fives of early white
New York jazz, a full discography of the original Dixie-
land jazz band, Earl Fuller's famous jazz band, Louisi-
ana Five, New Orleans Jazz Band, Original Memphis
Five, original Indiana Five. Tr. Anon. Lübbecke in
Westfallen: Uhle, c1959. 30p. [LC62]

LANGE, Johann Peter, 1802-1884.
The life of the Lord Jesus Christ, a complete critical
examination of the origin, contents and connection of the
Gospels. Tr. Anon. Grand Rapids: Zondervan, 1958.
3v. 22cm. [LC62]

LANGE, Kurt and Hirmer, Max, photog.
Egypt, architecture, sculpture, painting in three thousand
years. (Ägypten. Architektur, Plastik, Malerei in 3
Jahrtausenden.) Tr. Ronald H. Boothroyd. [BNB error-
Boothyard.] L, NY: Phaidon, 1956. 361p. (362p.)
31cm. (31.5cm.) [LC62, B56, IT9]

Same. 2nd rev. ed. , 1957. 363p. (39, 285-364p.)
32cm. [LC62, B57]

LANGE, Rolf, jt. author. See Lange, Eitel, 1905- .
Around the world with motorcycle and camera. Tr. Sus-
anne Perkins-Lutz. Los Angeles: Clymer, 1957. 232p.
22cm. [LC62]

LANIA, Leo, pseud. (i. e. Hermann, Lazar, 1896- .)
The foreign minister. (Der Aussenminister.) Tr. James
Stern (from ms.) NY, Boston: Houghton, 1956. 234p.
22cm. [LC62]

Same. L: Davies, 1957. 221p. (19.5cm.) [LC62,
B57, IT10]

LANKHEIT, Klaus.
Franz Marc. Watercolors, drawings, writings. (F--
M--, Zeichnungen und Aquarelle.) Tr. Norbert Guterman.
With text and notes Klaus Lankheit. NY: Abrams, 1960.
55p. 33cm. [LC62, IT13]

Same. L: Thames, 1960. 55p. 33cm. [LC62]

Same. (Unteilbares Sein.) Tr. Norbert Guterman. NY:
Abrams, 1960. 55p. [IT13]

LANKHEIT, Klaus. See Marc, Franz, 1880-1916.
Franz Marc. Tr. Norbert Guterman. L: Thames,
1960. 40p. 33cm. [LC62, B60]

Franz Marc. Watercolors, drawings, writings. NY:
Abrams, 1960. [LC62]

LANTSCHNER, Hellmut, 1909- .
Skiing for beginners. (Skischule.) Tr. Anon. Fwd.
Toni Sailer. L: Souvenir, 1959. (1960). 95p. (19cm.)
[LC62, B60, IT13]

LASKER, Edward, 1885- .
The adventure of chess. Tr. Anon. 2nd rev. ed. NY:
Dover, 1959. 296p. 21cm. [LC62]

Chess and checkers. The way to mastership. Complete
instructions for the beginner. Valuable suggestions for
the advanced player. Tr. Anon. 3rd rev. ed. NY:
Dover, 1960. 168p. 21cm. [LC62]

Chess strategy. (Schachstrategie.) Tr. J. Du Mont.
NY: Dover, 1959. 282p. 21cm. [LC62, IT12]

Go and Go-noku, the Oriental board games. Tr. Anon.
2nd rev. ed. NY: Dover, 1960. 215p. 21cm. [LC62]

LAST LETTERS FROM STALINGRAD.
(Letzte Briefe aus Stalingrad.) Tr. Anthony G. Powell.
L: Methuen, 1956. 70p. (9-70p.) (19.5cm.) 20cm.
[LC62, B56]

LATOUR, Anny.
Kings of fashion. (Magier der Mode.) Tr. Mervyn Sa-
vill. L: Weidenfeld, c1958. 270p. (271p.) (22.5cm.)
[LC62, B58, IT11]

Same. NY: Coward, 1958. 270p. 23cm. [LC62, IT11]

LAUTSCHNER, Hellmut. (IT13 error.) See Lantschner,
Hellmut, 1909- .

LEBER, Annedore, et al, eds.
Conscience in revolt. Sixty-four stories of resistance in
Germany, 1933-45. (Das Gewissen steht auf.) Tr. Rosemary O'Neill. Introd. Robert Birley. L: Vallentine,
1957. 270p. (22.5cm.) 23cm. [LC62, B57, IT10]

LEBER, Annedore--
Same. Westport, Conn. : Associated, 1957. 270p.
23cm. [LC62, IT10]

LECHENPERG, Harald, ed.
Olympic games, 1960. Squaw Valley and Rome. Tr.
Benjamin B. Lacy, Jr. NY: Barnes, 1960. 379p. 27cm.
[LC62]

LEDERER, Joe, 1907- .
Late spring. A novel. (Letzter Frühling.) Tr. David
Hardie. L: Cape, 1958. 253p. (19.5cm.) 20cm.
[LC62, B58]

LEDERMANN, Alfred and Trachsel, Alfred.
Creative playground and recreation centers. (Spielplatz
und Gemeinschaftszentrum.) Tr. Ernst Priefert. NY:
Praeger, 1959. 175p. 23 x 29cm. [LC62, IT12]

Playgrounds and recreation spaces. (Spielplatz und
Gemeinschaftszentrum.) Tr. Ernst Priefert. L: Architectural, 1959. 175p. (176p.) (22.5 x 28.5cm.) [LC
62, B59, IT12]

LEDIG, Gert, 1921- .
The brutal years. (Faustrecht.) Trs. Oliver Coburn and
Ursula Lehrburger. L: Weidenfeld, 1959. 192p. (19.5
cm.) 20cm. [LC62, B59, IT12]

The naked hill. A novel. (Die Stalinorgel.) Tr. Mervyn
Savill. L: Weidenfeld, 1956. 190p. (19cm.) [LC62,
B56, IT9]

Same. L: World Dist. , 1957. 190p. 17cm. [LC62,
B58, IT10, 11]

The tortured earth, a novel of the Russian front. (Die
Stalinorgel.) Tr. Mervyn Savill. Chicago: Regnery,
1956. 219p. 22cm. [LC62, IT9]

LEE, Peter H. , 1929- .
Studies in the Saenaennorae. Old Korean poetry. (Studien zum Saenaennorae: altkoreanische Dichtung; ein
Beitrag zur Wertung der japanischen Studien über altkoreanische Dichtung.) Tr. Anon. Roma: Instituto itali-
ano per il Medio ed Estremo Oriente, 1959. 212p. [LC62]

LE FORT, Gertrud Freiin von, 1876-   .
The wife of Pilate.   (Die Frau des Pilatus, Novelle.)
Tr. Marie C. Buehrle.   Milwaukee: Bruce, 1957.   63p.
18cm.   [LC62, IT10]

LEGIEN, Rudolf.
The four power agreements on Berlin.   Alternative solu-
tions to the status quo.   Tr. Trevor Davies.   Berlin:
Heymann, 1960 or 1961.   59p.   21cm.   [LC62]

LEHAR, Franz, 1870-1948.
The merry widow.   (Die lustige Witwe.)   New book and
lyrics Phil Park.   L: Glocken, 1958.   78p.   (19.5cm.)
20cm.   [LC62, B58]

Same.   71p.   25cm.   (Amateur operatic version).   [LC62]

LEHMANN, Arno.
It began at Tranquebar.   The story of the Tranquebar
mission and the beginnings of Protestant Christianity in
India.   Published to celebrate the 250th anniversary of
the landing of the first Protestant missionaries at Tranquebar in 1706.   Tr. M. J. Lutz.   Madras: Christian
Literature Soc., 1956.   185p.   22cm.   [LC62]

LEHMANN, Marcus, 1931-1890.
The family y Aguilar.   A story of Jewish heroism during
the Spanish Inquisition.   Adpt. Jacob Breuer.   NY: Reld-
heim, 1958.   284p.   20cm.   [LC62]

The story of Rabbi Akiba and his times.   (Akiba.)   Tr.
Joseph Leftwich.   L: Hatorah, 1956.   289p.   19cm.
[LC62]

Unpaid ransom.   Free rendition.   2nd ed.   NY: Merkos,
1956.   60p.   22cm.   [LC62]

LEHNERT, Martin.
Poetry and prose of the Anglo-Saxons.   2nd rev. ed.
Halle (Salle):   Niemeyer, 1956-60.   Vol. 1.   1960.
2v.   (173p.)   25cm.   [LC62, B57]

Poetry and prose of the Anglo-Saxons.   A textbook.
Berlin: VEB Deutscher Verlag der Wissenschaften,
1955-56.   173p.   2v.   24cm.   [LC62, IT9]

Poetry and prose of the Anglo-Saxons.   Dictionary.

LEHNERT, Martin--
Berlin, 1956. 247p. (24.5cm.) [LC62, B57, IT9]

LEHNHOFF, Joachim.
The homeward run. A story of German sailors, their
battles, and their loves under the shadow of defeat.
(Die Heimfahrt.) Tr. Lawrence Wilson. L: Weidenfeld,
1957. 224p. (19cm.) [B57]

Same. 244p. [IT10]

Same. L: Hamilton, 1958. 192p. (18cm.) [B58]

LEIBNIZ, Gottfried Wilhelm Freiherr von, 1646-1716.
A dialogue between a philosopher and a student of the
common laws of England. Tr. Anon. Milano: Giuffre,
1960. [LC62]

Philosophical papers and letters. Tr. and ed. with introd.
Leroy Loemker. Chicago: Chicago U. Pr.; L: Cam-
bridge U. Pr., 1956. 2v. 1228p. (591-1228p.) 22cm.
[LC62, B56]

Philosophical writings. Tr. Mary Morris. Introd. C. R.
Morris. L: Dent; NY: Dutton, 1956. 284p. (19cm.)
[LC62, B56]

The preface to Novissima Sinica. (N--S--.) Tr. Donald
F. Lach. Honolulu: U. of Hawaii Pr., 1957. 104p.
22cm. [LC62, IT10]

Same. 1958. 104p. [IT11]

LEIBNIZ, Gottfried Wilhelm Freiherr von, 1646-1716, and
Clarke, Samuel, 1675-1729.
The Leibniz-Clarke correspondence, together with extracts
from Newton's "Principia" and "Opticks." Ed. H. G. Alex-
ander. NY: Philosophical Lib., 1956. 200p. 19cm.
[LC62, B56]

LEIBRECHT, Walter, ed.
Religion and culture. Essays in honor of Paul Tillich.
1st ed. NY: Harper, 1959. 399p. 25cm. [LC62]

LEICHT, Hermann.
Pre-Inca art and culture. (Indianische Kunst und Kultur.)

Tr. Mervyn Savill. L: MacGibbon, n.d. 253p. (22.5 cm.) 23cm. [LC62, B60, IT13]

Same. NY: Orion, 1960. 253p. 23cm. [LC62, IT13]

LEICHTENTRITT, Hugo, 1874-1951.
Leichtentritt's history of the Motet, a study and tr. John Eugene Seaich (chaps. 7-15). Ann Arbor: Michigan, Microf. of TW. 1958. [LC62]

Music of the Western nations. Tr. Anon. Ed. and amplified Nicolas Slonimsky. Cambridge: Harvard U. Pr., 1956. 324p. 22cm. [LC62, B57]

LEIGH, Carolyn and Warnick, Clay, 1915- .
Heidi. A musical play based upon the novel by Johanna Spyri. (H--.) NY: French, 1959. 58p. 22cm. [LC62]

LEIP, Hans, 1893- .
The Gulf Stream story. (Der grosse Fluss im Meer.) Trs. H. A. Piehler and K. Kirkness. L: Jarrolds, 1957. 222p. (223p.) 22cm. [LC62, B57, IT11]

Portrait of a city. (Hamburg. Das Bild einer Stadt.) Tr. Anon. Hamburg: Hoffmann, 1959. 47p. 30cm. [LC62]

The river in the sea. (Der grosse Fluss im Meer.) Trs. H. A. Piehler and K. Kirkness. NY: Putnam, 1958. 222p. 22cm. [LC62, IT11]

LEIPZIGER MESSEAMT.
The Leipzig fair. A historical survey. Tr. Anon. Leipzig: Leipzig Fair Administration, 1959. 37p. [LC 62]

LEISINGER, Hermann.
Romanesque bronzes. (Romanische Bronzen.) Tr. Anon. L: Phoenix, 1958. 14p. (16p.) 22cm. (22.5cm.) [LC62, B58, IT9]

LEITHÄUSER, Joachim Gustave.
Inventors of our world. (Die zweite Schöpfung der Welt.) Tr. Michael Bullock. L: Weidenfeld, 1958. 257p. (22.5cm.) 23cm. [LC62, B58, IT11]

Inventors' progress. (Die zweite Schöpfung der Welt.)

LEITHÄUSER, Joachim Gustave--
Tr. Michael Bullock. 1st ed. Cleveland: World, 1959.
286p. 25cm. [LC62, IT12]

Worlds beyond the horizon. (Ufer hinter dem Horizont.)
Tr. Hugh Merrick. L: Allen, 1956. 372p. 24cm.
(24.5cm.) [LC62, B56, IT9]

LEITICH, Ann Tizia.
The Spanish riding school in Vienna. (Die spanische
Reitschule in Wien.) Tr. Stella von Musulin. Pref. A.
Pdhajsky. Munich: Nymphenburger Verlagshandlung;
L: Bailey, 1957. 55p. (20.5cm.) [B57]

LEMMER, Ernst, ed.
Berlin at the crossroads of Europe--at the crossroads of
the world. Trs. Michael S. Berenson and Edward Rutherford. Arranging and ed. Erich Böhl. Berlin: Verlag
Haupt and Puttkammer, 1958. 191p. 30cm. [LC62]

LENAU.
Selections in Loomis, E. G. 1960.

LENNARTZ, Annemarie.
Señora and the whales. (Señora darf nicht mit an Bord.)
Tr. Anne Scott. L: Lutterworth, 1959. 155p. (156p.)
(22.5cm.) 23cm. [LC62, B59, IT12]

LENZ, Johann Maria.
Christ in Dachau, or Christ victorious. Experiences in
a concentration camp. (Christus in Dachau. Ein re-
ligiöses Volksbuch und ein kirchengeschichtliches Zeugnis.)
Eng. text by Countess Barbara Waldstein. Vienna, 1960.
328p. 21cm. [LC62]

LEON, Victor, pseud. (i.e. Hirschfield, Victor, 1860-
1940.) and Stein, Leo, pseud. (i.e. Rosenstein, Leo,
1862- .)
The merry widow by Franz Lehar. (Die lustige Witwe.)
New Eng. ver. Christopher Hassall. L: Glocken, 1958.
78p. (19.5cm.) 20cm. [LC62, B58, IT11]

Same. New book and lyrics Phil Park. L: Glocken,
1958. (71p.) 20cm. [LC62]

LEONHARD, Wolfgang.
Child of the revolution. (Die Revolution entlässt ihre

Kinder.) Tr. C. M. Woodhouse. L: Collins, 1957.
447p. (22cm.) [LC62, B57, IT10]

Same. Chicago: Regnery, 1958. 447p. 22cm. [LC62,
IT11]

Same. 562p. [LC62]

LEPINSKI, Franz.
The German trade union movement. Tr. Anon. n.p.,
1959. 24p. [LC62]

LEPPICH, John.
Cries from the half-world. (Christus auf der Reeperbahn.)
Tr. Father Patrick. L: Blond, 1960. 252p. (21cm.)
22cm. [LC62, B60]

Same. O. S. P., Detroit: St. Paul, 1960. 181p. 19cm.
[LC62]

LERNET-HOLENIA, Alexander Maria, 1897- .
Count Luna, 2 tales of the real and the unreal. (1)
Baron Bagge, and (2) Count Luna. (Der Graf Luna, Ro-
man. Der Baron Bagge, Novelle.) Trs. (1) Richard and
Clara Winston, and (2) Jane B. Greene. Introd. Robert
Pick. NY: Criterion, 1956. 252p. 22cm. [LC62]

LESCHNITZER, Adolf, n.d.
The magic background of modern anti-semitism. An analysis of the German-Jewish relationship. (Saul und
David. Die Problematik der deutsch-jüdischen Gemeinschaft.) NY: International U. Pr.; (L: Bailey), 1956.
236p. (22.5cm.) 23cm. [LC62, B56, IT9]

LESIGANG, Hermann.
An essay on the liability for damages caused by use of
atomic power. Tr. Anon. n.p., 1958. 8p. 24cm.
[LC62]

LESSING, Gotthold Ephraim, 1729-1781.
Emilia Galotti, a tragedy in 5 acts. (E--G--.) Introd.
and tr. Anna Johanna Gode von Aesch. Great Neck, NY:
Barron's Educational, 1959. 104p. 19cm. [LC62, IT9]

Laocoon, an essay upon the limits of painting and poetry.
Tr. Ellen Frothingham. NY: Noonday, 1957. 245p.
19cm. [LC62, IT10]

LESSING, Gotthold Ephraim--
(1) Laocoon, (2) Nathan the wise, (3) Minna von
Barnhelm. (Laocoon, N-- der weise, and M-- von B---.)
Trs. (1), (2) William A Steel and (3) Anthony Dent. Ed.
William A. Steel. L: Dent; NY: Dutton, 1959. 294p.
(18.5cm.) 19cm. [LC62, B59]

Theological writings. Tr. and introd. Henry Chadwick.
L: Black, 1956. 110p. (22.5cm.) 23cm. [LC62,
B56]

Same. Stanford, California: Stanford U. Pr., 1957.
110p. 23cm. [LC62]

LETSCH, Heinz.
Captured stars. (Das Zeiss-Planetarium.) Tr. Harry
(i.e. Heinz) Spitzbardt. Ed. Roland Haupt. Jena:
Fischer; (L: Collet's), 1959. 183p. (24.5cm.) [LC
62, B60]

LETTOW-VORBECK, Paul Emil von, 1870- .
East African campaigns. (Meine Erinnerungen aus Ostafrika.) Tr. Anon. Fwd. John Gunther. NY: Speller,
1957. 303p. 22cm. [LC62]

LETTS, Malcolm Henry Ikin, 1882- . ed. and tr.
The travels of Leo of Rozmital through Germany, Flanders,
England, France, Spain, Portugal, and Italy, 1465-1467.
(Des böhmischen Herrn Leos von Rozmital Ritter-, Hof-
und Pilgerreise durch die Abendlande.) Cambridge, Eng.:
University Pr., 1957. 196p. 23cm. [LC62, B57, IT10]

LEUFKE, Aloys.
Ulm and its environ. (Ulm und seine Umgebung.) Tr.
Anon. Text Walter Rau. Ulm: Leufke, 195- . 24p.
26cm. [LC62]

LEUZINGER, Elsy.
Africa. The art of the Negro peoples. (Afrika, Kunst
der Negervölker.) Tr. Ann E. Keep. L: Methuen,
NY: Crown, 1960. 247p. (23.5cm.) 24cm. [LC62,
B60, IT13]

LEWIN, Kurt, 1890-1947.
A dynamic theory of personality. Trs. Donald K. Adams
and Karl E. Zener. NY: McGraw, 1959. 286p. 23cm.
[LC62, IT12]

Resolving social conflicts. Tr. Anon. Ed. Gertrud
Weiss Lewin. Fwd. Gordon W. Allport. NY: Harper,
c1958. 230p. [LC62]

LEWINSOHN, R., 1894- .
A history of sexual customs. (Eine Weltgeschichte der
Sexualität.) Tr. Alexander Mayce. L: Longmans, 1958.
424p. (22.5cm.) 23cm. [LC62, B58, IT11]

Same. NY: Harper, 1959. 424p. 22cm. [LC62, IT12]

LICHT, F. O.
Atlas of the world beet sugar industry. (Atlas der Welt-
rübenzuckerindustrie.) Tr. Anon. Ed. Hugo Ahlfeld.
(Fr., Ger. and Eng.) Ratzeburg, 1956. 68p. 30cm.
[LC62]

The sugar economies of India and the Far East. Tr.
Anon. Ratzburg, 1958. 38p. [LC62]

The sugar economies of the South American continent.
Tr. Anon. Ratzeburg, 1958. 30p. [LC62]

LICHT, Hans.
Sexual life in ancient Greece. (Sittengeschichte Griechen-
lands.) Tr. J. H. Freese. Ed. Lawrence H. Dawson.
L: Routledge, 1956. 556p. 23cm. [LC62]

LICHTENBERG, Georg Christoph, 1742-1799.
The Lichtenberg reader. Sel. writings. Ed. and introd.
by Trs. Franz H. Mautner and Henry Hatfield. Boston:
Beacon, 1959. 196p. 22cm. [LC62, IT12]

LICHTENBERG, Georg Christoph, 1742-1799. See Stern,
Joseph Peter.
Lichtenberg, a doctrine of scattered occasions. Tr.
Anon. Bloomington: Indiana U. Pr., 1959. [LC62]

LIDDELL HART, Basil Henry, 1895.
The German Generals talk. Tr. Anon. NY: Berkley,
1958. 5-252p. 17cm. [LC62]

LIEB, Norbert, 1907- , et al.
Augsburg, the town and our works. Augsburg: Maschin-
enfabrik. Augsburg-Nürnberg AG., 1959. 105p. [LC62]

LIEBERMANN, Rolf, 1910- .
School for wives. (Die Schule der Frauen.) Libretto nach
Molier, Heinrich Strobel. Ger. tr. Hans Weigel. Eng.
ver. Elizabeth Montagu. Vienna: Universal Edition,
1957. 24p. 20cm. [LC62]

LIEBKNECHT, Wilhelm Philipp Christian Martin Ludwig,
1826-1900.
On the political position of Social Democracy, particularly with respect to the Reichstag. No compromises, no
election deals. The spider and the fly. (Über die politische Stellung der Sozialdemokratie, and kein Kompromiss,
kein Wahlbündnis.) Tr. Anon. Moscow, FLP House,
1960. 126p. 20cm. [LC62]

LIEHL, Ekkehard and Feger, Robert.
Picturesque Black Forest. Eng. vers. Hansgeorge Raidl
and Linda Schein. Lindau: Thorbecke, 1957. 115p.
24cm. [LC62]

Picturesque Black Forest. (Schwarzwald.) Trs. Hans-
georg Raidl and Linda Schein. Photog. Toni Schneiders
and others. Text Robert Feger and Ekkehard Liehl.
Lindau: Thorbecke; L: Tiranti, 1960. 117p. (24cm.)
[B60]

LIEPMAN, Heinz, 1905- .
Rasputin, a new judgement. (R--, Heiliger oder Teufel.)
Tr. Edward Fitzgerald. L: Muller, 1959. 264p. (20.5
cm.) [LC62, B59, IT12]

Rasputin and the fall of Imperial Russia. (R--, Heiliger
oder Teufel.) Tr. Edward Fitzgerald. NY: Rolton, 1959.
264p. 21cm. [LC62]

Same. NY: McBride, 1959. 264p. 21cm. [LC62,
IT12]

LIESEL, Nikolaus.
The eastern Catholic liturgies. A study in words and
pictures. (Die Liturgien der Ostkirche.) Tr. Anon.
Fwd. Donald Atwater. Westminster, Md.: Newman,
1960. 168p. 26cm. [LC62]

LIETZMANN, Hans, 1875-1942.
The Bible. New Testament gospel. Tr. Anon. Greek:
Harmonies, 1957. Eng. ed. F. L. Cross. Oxford:

Blackwell, 1957. [LC62]

The era of the church fathers. A history of the early
church. Tr. Bertram Lee Woolf. 2nd ed. L: Lutterworth, 1958. 212p. 22cm. [LC62]

The founding of the Church Universal. Tr. Bertram Lee
Woolf. 3rd ed., rev. L: Lutterworth, 1958. 328p.
[LC62]

From Constantine to Julian. A history of the early
church. Tr. Bertram Lee Woolf. 2nd ed. L: Lutterworth, 1960. 340p. 23cm. [LC62]

History of the early church. Tr. Bertram Lee Woolf.
L: Lutterworth, 19--. v. 22cm. [LC62]

LILJE, Hans, 1899- .
The last book of the Bible. The meaning of the Revela-
tion of St. John. (Das letzte Buch der Bibel.) Tr. Olive
Wyon. Philadelphia: Muhlenberg, 1957. 286p. 22cm.
[LC62, IT10]

LINDENBERG, Vladimir, 1902- .
Meditation and mankind. Practices in prayer and medita-
tion throughout the world. (Die Menschheit betet.) Tr.
Betty Collins. L: Rider, 1959. 207p. (22cm.) [B59,
IT12]

LINDERMANN, Hannes, 1922- .
Alone at sea. (Allein über den Ozean.) Tr. Anon. Ed.
Jozefa Stuart. NY: Random, 1958. 180p. 21cm.
[LC62]

LINDNER, Gert.
The children's book of make and do. Tr. and adapt.
Oliver Coburn. L: Phoenix, 1959. 231p. (22cm.)
[B59, IT12]

LINFERT, Carl, 1900- . ed.
Hieronymus Bosch. The paintings. Tr. Joan Spencer.
Complete ed. L: Phaidon, 1959. 119p. (28cm.)
[LC62, B59, IT13]

LINGEMANN, Elfriede, ed.
Glossary of social work terms in Eng., Fr., and Ger.
2nd ed. imp. and enl. Tr. Anon. Köln: Heymann,

LINGEMANN, Elfriede--
1958. [LC62]

LINKE, Hans Joachim.
Upper wind radar. (From Radio und Fernsehen, 1957.)
n.p., 1957. 16l. 27cm. [LC62]

LION, Jindrich.
The old Prague Jewish cemetery. (Der alte jüdische
Friedhof in Prag.) Tr. Anon. Text J--L---. Photog.
Jan Lukas. Prague: Artia, 1960. 30p. 28cm. [LC
62]

LIPPERT, Marie.
The Matabeleland travel letters of Marie Lippert, 21
Sep.-23 Dec. 1891. Tr. Eric Rosenthal. Ed. D. H.
Varley. Cape Town: Friends of the South African Pub-
lic Lib., 1960. 56p. [LC62]

LIPPERT, Peter, 1879-1936.
The Jesuits, a self-portrait. (Zur Psychologie des
Jesuitenordens.) Tr. John Murray. Freiburg, NY:
Herder; Edinburgh, L: Nelson, 1958. 130p. (131p.)
19cm. [LC62, IT12]

Mary. (Maria.) Tr. Anon. Dublin: Clonmore; L:
Burns, 1958. 78p. (18.5cm.) 19cm. [LC62, B58,
IT11]

LIPPMANN-PAWLOWSKI, Mila, joint ed. See Breidenstein,
Hartwig, 1902- .
Salzburg and the Salzkammergut, a pictorial record . . .
descriptive text. Tr. Anon. Innsbruck: Pinguin, 1958.
[LC62]

LISSNER, Ivar, 1909- .
The Caesars, might and madness. (Die Cäsaren.) Tr.
J. Maxwell Brownjohn. NY: Putnam, 1958. 377p.
22cm. [LC62, IT11]

The living past. (So habt ihr gelebt.) Tr. J. Maxwell
Brownjohn. L: Cape, 1957. 462p. (23.5cm.) [LC62,
B57]

Same. NY: Putnam, 1957. 444p. 22cm. [LC62]

Power and folly, the story of the Caesars. (Die Cä-

saren.) Tr. J. Maxwell Brownjohn. L: Cape, 1958.
384p. (17-384p.) (23.5cm.) 24cm. [LC62, B58, IT11]

LITTMANN, Enno, 1875- .
The library of Enno Littmann, 1875-1958. Tr. Anon.
Introd. Maria Höfner. Leiden: Brill, 1959. 355p. 24
cm. [LC62]

LOBE, Mira.
The zoo breaks out. (Der Tiergarten reisst aus.) Tr.
and adpt. Norman Dale. L: Bodley, 1958. 128p.
[B58, IT11]

Same. L: Lane, 1958. 128p. 19cm. [B58]

Same. NY: Barnes, 1960. 128p. 21cm. [LC62, IT13]

LOCKEMANN, Georg, 1871- .
The story of chemistry. (Geschichte der Chemie.) Tr.
Anon. L: Owen, 1959. (1960.) 277p. (19cm.) [LC62,
B60, IT13]

Same. NY: Philosophical Lib., c1959. 277p. 20cm.
[LC62]

LÖBSACK, Theo, 1923- .
Earth's envelope. (Der Atem der Erde.) Trs. E. L. and
D. Rewald. L: Collins, 1959. 256p. (21.5cm.) 22
cm. [LC62, B59, IT12]

Our atmosphere. (Der Atem der Erde. Wunder und
Rätsel der Luft.) Trs. E. L. and D. Rewald. NY:
Pantheon, 1959. 256p. 23cm. [LC62, IT12]

LÖHNDORFF, Ernst Friedrich, 1899- .
The forest of fear. (Blumen Hölle am Jacinto.) Tr.
Mervyn Savill. L: Souvenir, 1956. 182p. (22.5cm.)
23cm. [LC62, B57]

Same. L: Transworld, 1957. 191p. (16.5cm.) [B57]

LÖHR, Aemiliana.
The great week. An explanation of the liturgy of Holy
Week. (Die heilige Woche.) Tr. D. T. H. Bridgehouse.
L: Longmans; Westminster, Md.: Newman, 1958. 211p.
19cm. [LC61, B58]

LÖHR, Aemiliana--
The Mass through the year. Vol. 1, Advent to Palm
Sunday. (Jahr des Herrn.) Tr. I. T. Hale. L: Long-
mans, 1958-59. 330p. (22.5cm.) 23cm. [LC62, B58]

The Mass throughout the year. Vol. 2, Holy Week to
the last Sunday after Pentecost. (Das herrenjahr.) Tr.
I. T. Hale. L: Longmans; Westminster, Md.: Newman, 1959. 304p. (22.5cm.) [B59, IT12]

LOEMKER, Leroy E., ed. and tr. See Leibniz, Gottfried
Wilhelm Freiherr von, 1646-1716.
Philosophical papers and letters. Chicago: U. of Chi-
cago Pr., 1956. [LC62]

LORIOT, pseud. (i.e. Vico von Buelow.)
Dong's best friend. (Auf den Hund gekommen.) Tr.
Anon. Introd. Wolfgang Hildesheimer. L: Hammond,
1958. 46p. (12 x 17cm.) [B58]

LÖSCH, Friedrich, 1903- , ed. See Jahnke, Eugen, 1863-
1921.
Tables of higher functions. Tr. Anon. 6th ed. rev.
NY: McGraw, 1960. [LC62]

LÖWE, Fritz, 1895- .
Exploration of "Inland Ice." Greenland and Antarctica.
(From Umschau, 1956.) Tr. Katherine Martinoff. Wil-
mette, Ill., 1959. 5p. 27cm. [LC62]

LOEWENICH, Walther von, 1903- .
Modern Catholicism. (Der moderne Katholizismus.) Tr.
Reginald H. Fuller. L: Macmillan; NY: St. Martin's,
1959. 378p. (379p.) 23cm. [LC62, D59, IT12]

Paul, his life and work. (Paulus, sein Leben und sein
Werk.) Tr. Gordon E. Harris. Edinburgh: Oliver,
1960. 160p. 22cm. (22.5cm.) [LC62, B60, IT13]

LOGAU.
Selections in Loomis, C. G. Sel. 1958.

LOHSE, Bernd, 1911- .
Australia and the South Seas. (Australien und Südsee
heute.) Tr. Kenneth S. Witton [IT12 error-Whutten.]
Edinburgh, L: Oliver, 1959. 119p. (24.5cm.) [LC62,
B59, IT12]

LOHSE, Bernd, joint ed. See Busch, Harald, 1904- . ed.
Art treasures of Germany.

LOHSE, Bernd, 1911- . See Busch, Harald, 1904- . ed.
Romanesque Europe.

LOOMIS, Chas. G.
Prose Selections from German 19th Century authors.
Berkeley, c1960. 821., 28cm. [LC67]

Selections from 12 German poets of the 19th Century.
Berkeley, 1960. 651., 28cm. [LC67]

Selections of German poetry from the beginning to 1720.
Berkeley, c1958. 521., 28cm. [LC67]

LORENZ, Konrad Z.
King Solomon's ring. New light on animal ways. Tr.
M. K. Wilson. Fwd. J. Huxley. L: Methuen, 1957.
202p. (208p.) (22cm.) [LC62, B57]

Man meets dog. (So kam der Mensch auf den Hund.)
Tr. Marjorie Kerr Wilson. L: Pan, 1959. (180p.)
189p. [B59, IT12]

LOWENFELD, Viktor.
The nature of creative activity. Experimental and comparative studies of visual and nonvisual sources of drawing, painting, and sculpture by means of the artistic
products of weak-sighted and blind subjects and of the art
of different epochs and cultures. (Vom Wesen schöpfer-
ischen Gestaltens.) Tr. O. A. Oeser. L: Routledge,
1959. 272p. [LC62]

LUCKEY, Hans, 1900- .
Free churches in Germany. Tr. Anon. Bad Nauheim:
Christian-Verlag, 1956. 16p. 21cm. [LC62]

LUCKHARDT, Wassili, ed. See Köhler, Walter.
Writer on electric lighting. Lighting in architecture. . .
Pictorial narrative... NY: Reinhold, 1959. [LC62]

LUCKNER, Felix Graf v., 1881- .
Out of an old sea chest. (Aus 70 Lebensjahren.) Tr.
Edward Fitzgerald. L: Methuen, 1958. 222p. (22.5
cm) [LC62, B58, IT11]

LUDWIG, Emil, 1881-1948.
Abraham Lincoln, and the times that tried his soul.
(Lincoln.) Trs. Eden and Cedar Paul. Greenwich,
Conn.: Fawcett, 1956. 284p. 18cm. [LC62, IT9]

Cleopatra, the story of a queen. Tr. Bernard Miall.
NY: Bantam, (L: Transworld), 1959. 245p. 18cm.
[LC62, B60, IT12]

The son of man. Tr. Anon. Fwd. Charles Francis
Potter. Greenwich, Conn.: Fawcett, 1957. 190p.
18cm. [LC62]

LÜBECK ARBEITET FÜR DIE WELT.
Hrsg. von der Verwaltung für Handel, Schiffahrt und
Gewerbe der Hansestadt Lübeck et al., (Ger. and Eng.)
Lübeck, 1956. 336p. [LC62]

LÜBKE, Anton, 1890- .
The world of caves. (Geheimnisse des Unterirdischen.)
Tr. Michael Bullock. L: Weidenfeld; NY: Coward-
McCann, 1958. 295p. (22.5cm.) 23cm. [LC62, B58,
IT11]

LUEG, Henry.
From St. Paul, Minnesota to Portland, Oregon in 1867.
Tr. Anon. Washington, 1956. 44p. [LC62]

LÜTGEN, Kurt.
Two against the Arctic. (Kein Winter für Wölfe.) Trs.
Isabel and Florence McHugh. NY: Pantheon. 1957.
239p. 22cm. [LC62, IT10]

LÜTH, Erich.
Israel. (I--.) Tr. Gladys Wheelhouse. Introd. Erich
Luth. [sic] Munich: Andermann, 1960. 61p. 30p. 12°
[LC62]

LÜTHI, Walter, 1901- .
St. John's Gospel, an exposition. (Johannes, das vierte
Evangelium, ausgelegt für die Gemeinde.) Tr. Kurt
Schoenenberger. Edinburgh, L: Oliver; Richmond, Va.:
Knox, 1960. 348p. (22.5cm.) 23cm. [LC62, B60,
IT13]

LÜTHI, Walter, 1901- , and Thurneyson, Eduard, 1888- .
Preaching, confession, the Lord's supper. (Predigt,

Beichte, Abendmahl.) Tr. Francis J. Brooke, III.
Richmond: Knox, 1960. 121p. 21cm. [LC62, IT13]

LÜTHY, Herbert, 1918- .
France against herself. (Frankreichs Uhren gehen anders.)
Tr. Eric Mosbacher. NY: Meridian, 1957. 476p. 21
cm. [LC62]

LÜTTGENS, Gustav.
(Deutschland. Städte und Landschaften nach farbigen
Originalen von G--L--.) Tr. Anon. (Ger., Russ., Eng.,
and Fr.) Berlin: Verlag der Nation, 1957. 11p. 41cm.
[LC62]

LUKAS, Jan.
The old Prague Jewish cemetery. (Der alte jüdische
Friedhof in Prag.) Tr. Anon. Text Jindrich Lion.
Prague: Artia, 1960. 30p. 28cm. [LC62]

LUKAS, Jan. See Lion, Jindrich.
The Prague ghetto. Tr. Anon. L: Spring, 1959.
[LC62]

LUKAS, Jan. photog.
Greece. (Hellas.) Tr. Anon. Text Edvard Valenta.
(Eng., Fr., Ger.) Prague: Artia, 195- . 21p. 28cm.
[LC62]

LULLIES, Reinhard, 1907- .
Greek sculpture. (Griechische Plastik, von den Anfängen
bis zum Ausgang des Hellenismus.) Tr. Michael Bullock.
Photos. Max Hirmer. L: Thames, 1957. 88p. 31cm.
(31.5cm.) [LC62, B56, IT10]

Same. Rev. ed. NY: Abrams, 1957. 88p. 31cm.
[LC62]

Same. L: Thames, 1957. 88p. [LC62]

Same. Rev. and enl. ed. Illus. Max Hirmer. L:
Thames, 1960. 115p. 31cm. [LC62]

Same. Rev. and enl. NY: Abrams, 1960. 115p. 31
cm. [LC62, IT13]

LUPOJANSKI, Jozef, compiler.
The Polish language in Opole Silesia in the years 1910-

LUPOJANSKI, Jozef--
1939. (Der Sprachgebrauch bei den Gottesdiensten in
Oberschlesien.) Tr. Anon. Warsaw: Western Pr.
Agency, 1957. 103, 49p. [LC62]

LUSAR, Rudolf.
German secret weapons of the 2nd World War. (Die
deutschen Waffen des II. Weltkrieges und ihre Weiterent-
wicklung.) Trs. R. P. Heller and M. Schindler. L:
Spearman, 1959. 264p. (27cm.) [LC62, B59, IT12]

Same. NY: Philosophical Lib., 1959. 264p. 23cm.
[LC62, IT12]

LUSTIG, Bruno.
New research in Soviet psychiatry. Tr. Anon. Berlin,
1957. v. 103p. 30cm. [LC62]

Soviet neurology. Tr. Anon. Berlin, 1956. 119p.
30cm. [LC62]

LUTHE, Wolfgang, jt. author. See Schultz, Johannes Heinrich, 1884- .
Autogenic training, a psychophysiologic approach in psychotherapy. By Johannes H. Schultz and Wolfgang Luthe.
NY: Grune, 1959. 289p. 24cm. [LC62]

LUTHER, Martin, 1483-1546.
Career of the reformer. I., writings, 1517-1520. Works.
v. 31. Ed. and tr. Harold J. Grimm et al. Philadelphia: Muhlenberg, 1957. 416p. 24cm. [LC62]

Career of the reformer. IV. works v. 34. Tr. Anon.
Ed. Lewis W. Spitz. Philadelphia: Muhlenberg, c1960.
387p. [LC62]

Same. 187p. [IT13]

Christian liberty. Tr. Anon. Philadelphia: Muhlenberg,
1957. 40p. 19cm. [LC62]

Church and ministry. Ed. and tr. Conrad Bergendorff,
et al. Philadelphia: Muhlenberg, 1958. v. 24cm.
[LC62, IT11]

Same. Works v. 40. 425p. [IT11]

Commentary on Genesis. (In primum librum mose enarrationes.) Tr. Theodore Mueller. Grand Rapids: Zondervan, 1958. 2v. 22cm. [LC62, IT11]

A commentary on St. Paul's epistle to the Galatians. Tr. Anon. L: Clarke, 1956. 567p. 23cm. [LC62]

Same. Tr. Theodore Graebner. 4th ed. Grand Rapids, Michigan: Zondervan, 1957. 251p. 20cm. [LC62]

Devotions and prayers. Sel. and tr. Andrew Kosten. Grand Rapids: Baker, 1956. 111p. 16cm. [LC62, IT9]

An explanation of Luther's small catechism, a handbook for catechetical instruction. (Der kleine Katechismus.) Tr. Joseph Stump. 2nd rev. ed. Philadelphia: Muhlenberg, 1960. 146p. 18cm. [LC62, IT13]

Large catechism. Tr. Robert H. Fischer. Philadelphia: Muhlenberg, 1959. 105p. 23cm. [LC62]

Lectures on Deuteronomy. Works. v. 9. Tr. Anon. Ed. J. Pelikan. Asst. ed. Daniel Poellot. St. Louis: Concordia, 1960. 334p. 24cm. [LC62, IT13]

Lectures on Genesis. Works. v. 1. Tr. George V. Schick. Ed. Jaroslav Pelikan. St. Louis: Concordia, 1958. v. 24cm. [LC62]

Luther's works. See under individual title.

The Martin Luther Christmas book. Tr. Roland H. Bainton. Philadelphia: Muhlenberg, 1959. 74p. 25cm. [LC62, IT12]

Martin Luther on the bondage of the will. (De servo arbitrio.) Trs. J. I. Packer and O. R. Johnston. L: Clarke, 1957. 323p. 22cm. [LC62, IT11]

Same. Westwood, NJ: Revell, 1957. 322p. 21cm. [LC62, IT11]

Reformation writings. v. 1, the spirit of the Protestant reformation. Tr. with introd. and notes Bertram Lee Woolf. (From definitive Weimar ed.) L: Lutterworth, 1956. 340p. (22.5cm.) [B56]

LUTHER, Martin--
Reformation writings, v. 2. The spirit of the Protestant
reformation. Tr. Anon. NY: Philosophical Lib., 1956.
340p. [IT9]

Selected psalms. Works. v. 12-14. Tr. L. W. Spitz,
Jr. et al. St. Louis: Concordia, 1955-1958. 3v. 24
cm. [LC62]

The sermon on the Mount (1) and the magnificant (2).
Works. v. 21. Ed. and tr. Jaroslav Pelikan (1) and
A. T. W. Steinhaeuser (2). St. Louis: Concordia, 1956.
383p. 24cm. [LC62]

Same. 463p. [IT9]

Sermons I. Works v. 51. Ed. and tr. John W. Doberstein. Philadelphia: Muhlenberg, 1959. 426p. 24cm.
[LC62, IT12]

Sermons on the Gospel of St. John. Works. v. 22. Tr.
Martin H. Bertram. Ed. Jaroslav Pelikan. St. Louis:
Concordia, 1957. v. 24cm. [LC62]

Same. 1959. 459p. [IT12]

Sermons on the Gospel of St. John, chaps. 6-8. Works.
v. 23. Tr. Martin H. Bertram. St. Louis: Concordia,
1959. 459p. [IT12]

Sermons on the passion of Christ. (Passion oder Historie
vom Leiden, Christi Jesu, unsers Heilands.) Trs. E.
Smid. 223p. 21cm. [LC62]

Small catechism with explanation. Tr. Anon. Rock Island, Ill.: Augustana, 1957. 98p. 22cm. [LC62]

Three treatises. Tr. Anon. Philadelphia: Muhlenberg,
1960. 316p. 18cm. [LC62]

What Luther says (anthology comp. Ewald M. Plass). Tr.
Anon. St. Louis: Concordia, c1959. 3v. 1667p. 25
cm. [LC62, IT12]

Word and sacrament II. Works v. 36. Tr. Abdel Ross
Wentz. Gen. ed. Helmut T. Lehmann. Philadelphia:
Muhlenberg, 1959. 401p. 24cm. [LC62, IT12]

Works. v. 1. Tr. Anon. Ed. Jaroslav Pelikan. St. Louis: Concordia, 1958. 24cm. [LC62]

Works. v. 1. Companion vol. Luther the expositor, introd. to the reformer's exegetical writings. Tr. Jaroslav Pelikan. St. Louis: Concordia, 1959. 286p. 24cm. [LC62]

Works. See under individual title.

LUTZ, Emil Hans Georg, 1904- .
Men with golden hands, a book of surgical miracles. (Die goldenen Hände.) Tr. W. H. Johnson. NY: Appleton, 1956. 269p. 21cm. [LC62, IT9]

LYSAKOWSKI, Karl von.
Marine phosphorescence and oceanic currents. (From Das Weltall, 1913.) Tr. L. G. Robbins. Washington Technical Services Branch, Division of Oceanography, U. S. Navy Hydrographic Office, 195-. 21. 27cm. [LC62]

MAAS, Paul, 1880- .
Textual criticism. (Textkritik. Pt. VII of Gercke Norden, Einleitung in die Altertumswissenschaft.) Tr. Barbara Flower. Oxford: Clarendon, 1958. 59p. 19cm. [LC 62, IT11]

Same. NY, Oxford: Clarendon, 1958. 70p. [IT11]

MAASS, Edgar, 1896- .
The magnificent enemies. Tr. Anon. L: Chatto, 1956. 330p. 21cm. [LC62, B56]

MAASS, Joachim, 1901- .
The Gouffé case. (Der Fall Gouffé.) Tr. Michael Bullock. L: Barrie, 1960. 581p. 21cm. [LC62]

Same. 481p. (21cm.) [B60]

Same. 1st American ed. NY: Harper, 1960. 434p. 22cm. [LC62]

MACH, Ernst, 1838-1916.
The analysis of sensations, and the relationship of the physical to the psychical. (Die Analyse der Empfindungen

MACH, Ernst--
und das Verhältnis des Physischen zum Psychischen.)
Tr. C. M. Williams. Rev. from 5th Ger. ed. Sydney
Waterlow. NY: Dover, 1959. 380p. 21cm. [LC62,
IT12]

The principles of physical optics. An historical and
philosophical treatment. Trs. John S. Anderson and A.
F. A. Young. NY: Dover, 195-. 324p. 21cm. [LC
62]

The science of mechanics. A critical and historical ac-
count of its development. Tr. Thomas J. McCormack.
New introd. Karl Menger. 6th ed. La Salle, Ill., L:
Open Court, 1960. 634p. (20.5cm.) 21cm. [LC62,
B60, IT13]

Space and geometry in the light of physiological, psycho-
logical, and physical inquiry. (Partly incorporated in
Erkenntnis und Irrthum, Skizzen zur Psychologie der
Forschung.) Tr. Thomas J. McCormack. La Salle, Ill.:
Open Court, 1960. 148p. 20cm. [LC62]

MACKE, August, 1887-1914. See also Paul Klee.
Tunisian watercolors and drawings, with writings by A--
M-- and others. (Die Tunisreise. Aquarelle und Zeichnungen.) Tr. N. Guterman. NY: Abrams; L: Thames,
1959. 55p. 33cm. (33 x 30.5cm.) [LC62, B60, IT12]

MACKE, Wolfgang. See Macke, August, 1887-1914.
Tunisian watercolors and drawings.

MACKU, Anton.
Vienna. (Wien.) Tr. Anon. L: Thames, 1957. 95p.
(96p.) (24.5cm.) [LC62, B57]

Same. NY: Studio, 1957. 95p. 25cm. [LC62]

MACLEOD, Sir George Fielden, bart., 1895- .
Bombs and bishops. With full text of Dr. Schweitzer's
appeal to humanity. Tr. Anon. Glasgow: Iona Community Publishing Dept., 1957. 23p. 22cm. [LC62]

MAEDER, Herbert. See Zuberbühler, Walter.
Alpstein; people and country. (A--; Land und Leute.)
Eng.: C. C. Palmer; Teufen: Niggli, 1956. [LC62]

MAGENER, Rolf, 1910- .
Prisoners bluff. (Die Chance war null.) Tr. Basil
Creighton. L: Hamilton, 1956. 192p. (18.5cm.)
[B56]

MAGNESIUM--A PLANT FOOD.
Essays on the problem of magnesium fertilizer by A.
Arland and others. Trs. G. and S. Lewin. Berlin:
Bergbauhandel, 1956. 239p. 21cm. [LC62]

MALLY, Leo Hans, 1901- . See Eckener, Lotte.
Oberammergau, scene of the passion play. Westminster,
Md.: Newman, 1960. [LC62]

MAN, Hermann. (IT12 error.) See Mau, Hermann.

MANET, Edouard, 1832-1883.
Edouard Manet, watercolors and pastels. (E--M--. Aquarelle und Pastelle.) Tr. Anon. Sel. and introd. Kurt Martin. NY: Abrams, 1959. 15p. 38cm. [LC62, IT13]

Same. Tr. Robert Allen. L: Faber, 1958. 70p. [LC62]

Same. 1959. 28p. (28cm.) [B59]

MANN, Erika, 1905- .
The last year. A memoir of my father. (Das letzte
Jahr. Bericht ueber meinen Vater.) Tr. Richard Graves.
L: Secker, 1958. 92p. 19cm. [LC62, B58, IT11]

The last year of Thomas Mann. Tr. Richard Graves.
NY: Farrar, 1958. 119p. 21cm. [LC62, IT11]

MANN, Heinrich, 1871-1950.
The blue angel. (Professor Unrat.) A modern rendition
and adpt. of Small town tyrant, Wirt Williams. NY:
New American Lib., 1959. 159p. [LC62]

Same. L: Hamilton, 1959. 160p. (18cm.) [B59]

MANN, Monika.
Past and present. (Vergangenes und Gegenwärtiges.)
Tr. Frances F. Reid and Ruth Hein. NY: St. Martin's,
1960. 175p. 22cm. [LC62, IT13]

MANN, Thomas, 1875-1955.
The beloved returns. (Lotte in Weimar.) Tr. H. T.

MANN, Thomas--
Lowe-Porter. NY: Knopf, 1957. 453p. 20cm. [LC62]

Buddenbrooks. (B---.) Tr. H. T. Lowe-Porter. L:
Penguin; NY: Vintage, 1957. 591p. 18cm. [LC62,
B57]

Same. 691p. [IT10]

Confessions of Felix Krull, confidence man. Memoirs,
pt. 1. (Bekenntnisse des Hochstaplers F--K--.) Tr.
Denver Lindley. NY: New American Lib., 1957. 319p.
18cm. [LC62, IT10]

Same. Harmondsworth: Penguin, 1958. 347p. (18.5
cm.) [B58]

Death in Venice and seven other stories. Tr. H. T. Lowe-
Porter. NY: Vintage, 1959. 404p. 18cm. [LC62]

Essays. Tr. H. T. Lowe-Porter. NY: Vintage, 1957.
369p. 19cm. [LC62]

Same. 2nd print. 1958. [IT 10]

Gladius dei. Tr. H. T. Lowe-Porter. In Spender's Coll.
1960.

Homage to Kafka in The Castle. Tr. Muirs. NY: Knopf,
1956. [LC62]

Joseph and his brothers. Tr. H. T. Lowe-Porter. L:
Secker, 1956. 1207p. 23cm. [LC62]

Last essays (On Schiller, Fantasy on Goethe, Nietzsche's
phil. in the light of recent history. Chekhov, a weary
hour.) Trs. Richard and Clara Winston and Tania and
James Stern. Also, H. T. Lowe-Porter i. e. A weary
hour. L: Secker, 1959. 217p. (22.5cm.) [LC62, B59,
IT12]

Same. NY: Knopf, 1959. 211p. 22cm. [LC62, IT12]

Letters to Paul Amann, 1915-1952. (Brief an P--A---.)
Tr. R. and C. Winston. Ed. Herbert Wegener. Middle-
ton, Conn.: Wesleyan U. Pr., 1960. 190p. 22cm.
[LC60, IT13]

The magic mountain. (Der Zauberberg.) Tr. H. T. Lowe-
Porter. Harmondsworth: Penguin, 1960. 716p. (18

cm.) [B60]

Preface to Kleist, Marquise von O. Tr. M. Greenberg.
NY: Criterion, 1960. [LC62]

A sketch of my life. (Lebensabriss.) Tr. H. T. Lowe-
Porter. NY: Knopf, 1960. 87p. 22cm. [LC62, IT13]

The transposed heads, a legend of India. Tr. H. T.
Lowe-Porter. NY: Vintage, 1959. 4p. l., 3-115, 2 l.
18.5cm. [IT12, PAS]

MANNHEIM, Karl.
Ideology and Utopia. An introduction to the sociology of
knowledge. Tr. and pref. Louis Wirth. L: Routledge,
1960. 318p. (21.5cm.) [B60]

MANSFELD, Michael.
I submit to no man. (Sei keinem untertan.) Trs. Robert
Cohen and Alan Earney. L: Angus, 1960. 234p. 20cm.
[LC62]

MANSTEIN, Fritz Erich von, 1887- .
Lost victories. (Verlorene Siege.) Ed. and tr. Anthony
G. Powell. Fwd. B. H. L. Hart. L: Methuen, 1958.
574p. (22.5cm.) 23cm. [LC62, B58, IT11]

Lost victories. Tr. Anthony Powell. Chicago: Regnery,
1958. 574p. 22cm. [LC62, IT11]

MANTHOS, Dimitri A.
The future of the tanker. An estimate of the world need
for oil tankers in 1965. (Weitschiffahrts-Archiv, hft. 3,
no. 3.) Tr. Anon. Bremen, 1957. 200p. [LC62]

MARBOE, Ernst, 1909- . ed.
The book of Austria. Trs. Gordon Shepherd and others.
Vienna: Österreichische Staatsdruckeri; (L: Allen), 1958.
542p. (20.5cm.) 21cm. [LC62, B59]

MARC, Franz, 1880-1916.
Franz Marc. Watercolors, drawings, writings. (F--M--,
Zeichnungen und Aquarelle.) Tr. Norbert Guterman. With
text and notes Klaus Lankheit. L: Thames, 1960. 55p.
33cm. [LC62]

Same. NY: Abrams, 1960. 55p. 33cm. [LC62]

MARC, Franz--
Same. (Unteilbares Sein.) Tr. Norbert Guterman. NY:
Abrams, 1960. 55p. [IT13]

MARCHESANI, Oswald.
Atlas of the occular fundus. (Atlas des Augenhinter-
grundes.) Tr. A. Philipp. NY: Hafner, 1959. 161p.
[LC62]

MAREK, Kurt W. See Ceram, C. W., pseud.

MARINATOS, Spyridon.
Crete and Mycenae. Tr. Anon. L: Thames, 1960.
[LC62]

Same. NY: Abrams, 1960. [LC62]

MARINGER, Johannes, 1902- .
The Gods of prehistoric man. (Vorgeschichtliche Re-
ligion.) Tr. Mary Ilford. 1st American ed. NY:
Knopf, 1960. 294p. 22cm. [LC62, IT13]

Same. L: Weidenfeld; NY: Knopf, c1960. 219p.
25cm. [LC62, B60]

MARLBOROUGH FINE ART, LTD., LONDON.
Art of revolt. Germany 1905-25. Tr. Anon. Pref.
and catalog ed. Will Grohmann. L, 1959. 183p. 19 x
22cm. [LC62]

Kandinsky, the road to abstraction exhibition, April/May
1960. L, 1960. 38p. 23cm. [LC62]

MARNAU, Alfred, 1918- .
The guest. (Das Verlangen nach der Hölle.) A novel.
L: Thames, 1957. 233p. (234p.) 19cm. [LC62, B57,
IT10]

Same. L: Thames, 1957. 242p. [IT10]

MARTIN, Gottfried, 1901- .
Kant's metaphysics and theory of science. (Immanuel
Kant, Ontologie und Wissenschaftstheorie.) Tr. P. G.
Lucas. NY: Barnes, 1956. 226p. [IT9]

MARTIN, Henno.
The sheltering desert. (Wenn es Krieg gibt, gehen wir

in die Wüste.) Tr. Edward Fitzgerald. L: Kimber, 1957. 234p. (24cm.) [LC62, B57, IT10]

Same. NY: Nelson, 1958. 236p. 25cm. [LC62, IT11]

MARTIN, Kurt, 1899- .
Edouard Manet, water-colours and pastels. (E--M--, Aquarelle und Pastelle.) Tr. Robert Allen. L: Faber, 1958. 20p. [LC62]

Same. 1959. 20p. [IT12]

Same. 1959. 28p. (28cm.) [B59]

Minnesänger. Tr. Anon. (Ger., Fr., and Eng.) Baden-Baden: Klein, 1960. v. 35cm. [LC62]

MARX, Karl, 1818-1883.
Capital. (Das Kapital.) Trs. E. and C. Paul. (From 4th Ger. ed.) L: Dent, 1957. 2v. [LC62]

Capital, a critical analysis of capitalist production. Trs. Samuel Moore and Edward Aveling. (From 3rd Ger. ed.) Moscow: FLP House, 1957. 2v. [LC62]

Capital, a critique of political economy. Vol. 3, Bk. 3. The process of capitalist production as a whole. (Das Kapital. Der Gesamtprozess der kapitalistischen Produktion.) Ed. F. Engels. Tr. Anon. Moscow: FLP House; L: Lawrence, 1960. 924p. (23cm.) [B60, IT13]

The class struggles in France, 1848-1850. Tr. Anon. Moscow: FLP House, 1960. 240p. 17cm. [LC62]

Economic and philosophic manuscripts of 1844. Tr. Martin Milligan. Moscow: FLP House; L: Lawrence, 1959. 208p. (212p.) 21cm. [LC62, B59]

Random thoughts. Aphorisms, reflections. (Deutsch--amerikanische Aphorismen. Betrachtungen, Sinnsprüche, Gereimtes, Ungereimtes.) Tr. Anon. NY: Drechsel, c1956. 47p. 19cm. [LC62]

Selected correspondence. Tr. Anon. Moscow: FLP House; L: Lawrence, 1956. 623p. (22.5cm.) [B56]

Selected writings in sociology and social philosophy.

MARX, Karl--
Tr. T. B. Bottomore. Eds. T. B. B-- and Maximilian
Rubel. L: Watts, 1956. 268p. (22.5cm.) 23cm.
[LC62, B56, IT9]

MARX, Karl, 1818-1883, and Engels, Fr., 1820-1895.
Basic writings on politics and philosophy. Tr. Anon.
Ed. Lewis S. Feuer. Garden City, NY: Doubleday,
1959. 497p. 19cm. [LC62, IT12]

Communist manifesto. Tr. Samuel Moore. Introd.
Stefan T. Possony. Chicago: Regnery, 1958. 83p. 17
cm. [LC62]

Communist manifesto, socialist landmark. Tr. Samuel
Moore. With a new appreciation Harold J. Laski. L:
Allen, 1959. 159p. [LC62]

Critique of the Gotha programme. Tr. Anon. Moscow:
FLP House, 1959. 73p. [LC62]

The German ideology, parts I and III. Tr. Anon. Ed.
and introd. R. Pascal. NY: International, 1960. 214p.
22cm. [LC62]

The Holy family, or critique of critical critique. Tr. R.
Dixon. Moscow: FLP House; L: Lawrence, 1956.
299p. (300p.) (20.5cm.) 21cm. [LC62, B57]

Karl Marx and Frederick Engels, selected works in two
volumes. Moscow: FLP House, 1958. 2v. 23cm.
[LC62]

Manifesto of the Communist Party by K--M-- and Frederick Engels. Tr. Samuel Moore. Moscow: FLP House,
1957. 111p. [LC62]

Marx and Engels on Malthus. Selections from the writ-
ings of Marx and Engels dealing with the theories of
Thomas Robert Malthus. Trs. Dorothea K. Meek and
Ronald L. Meek. Ed. Ronald L. Meek. New Delhi:
People's, 1956. 176p. [LC62]

On religion. Tr. Anon. Moscow: FLP House; L:
Lawrence, 1958. 379p. (20.5cm.) [B58, IT11]

MASCHINENBAU KIEL, A. G.
Diesel engines. Tr. Anon. Kiel, 1958. 1v. 21 x 30cm.
[LC62]

MASING, GEORG, 1885- .
The foundation of metallography. (Grundlagen der Metall-
kunde in anschaulicher Darstellung.) Tr. F. C. Thompson. L: Institute of Metals, 1956. 166p. 22cm.
[LC62]

MASS, Paul, 1880- .
Textual criticism. (Textkritik, pt. VII of Gerckenorden,
Einleitung in die Altertumswissenschaft, vol. 1, 3rd ed.)
Tr. Barbara Flower. Oxford: Clarendon, 1958. 59p.
[LC62]
Same. NY: Oxford, 1958. 70p. [LC62, IT11]

MASSMANN, Fr. Josef P. S. M.
Temperament, nerves & the soul. (From journal "Das innere Leben.") Tr. Norman C. Reeves. Cork: Mercier,
1956. 123p. [IT10]

MATHO, Karl.
Orchid growing for everyone, tropical and subtropical. (Or-
chideen der Tropen und Subtropen.) Tr. Anon. Illus Anne
Gallion-Krohn. L: Blandford, 1958. 170p. (21.5cm.)
22cm. [LC-from Dutch, BNB-from German] [LC62, B59,
IT12]

MATT, Leonard v.
Ancient Roman sculpture. (Römische Bildwerke.) Introd.
Bernard Andreae. L: Longmans, c1960. (29cm.)
[LC62, B60]

Architecture in ancient Rome. Tr. Bernard Andreae.
L: Longmans, 1960. 29cm. [LC62, B60]

MATT, Leonard v. See Hauser, Walter.
St. Francis of Assisi, a pictorial biography. (Franz von
Assisi.) Tr. Sebastian Bullough. L: Longmans; Chi-
cago: Regnery, 1956. 106p. 25cm. [LC62, IT9]

MATT, Leonard v. See Rahner, Hugo.

MATTHESON, Johann, 1681-1764.
Johann Mattheson's forty-eight thorough-bass test-pieces.
(Grosse General-Bass-Schule.) Tr. and commentary Harvey Phillips Reddick. Ann Arbor: Univ. Microfilms,
1957. [LC62]

MATTHIES, Hans Jürgen.
Medical student research work.   n. p. ,   1956.   91.   [LC 62]

MATTHIESSEN, Wilhelm, 1891-   .
Little Lottie.   (Lieselümpchen.)   Tr. Stella Humphries.
Illus. Irene Schreiber.   L: Burke, 1960.   3-124p.
(19. 5cm.)   [B60]

The Scarlet U.   (Das rote U.)   Tr. Stella Humphries.
L: Methuen, 1959.   128p.   (20. 5cm.)   [B59, IT12]

MATHIEU, Joseph, 1903-   . and Barlen, Sigrid.
Guiding principles for time and cost in documentation
work.   (From Forschungsbericht.)   Tr. Anon.   L: Ministry of Supply, 1959.   34p.   [LC62]

MATZENAUER, Hugh.   Illus.   See Molnar, E. G.
The voice of fear.   Ten poems.   Tr. Sarah Gainham.
Vienna: ARS Hungaria, 1959.   [LC62]

MAU, Hermann and Krausnick, Helmut.
German history, 1933-1945.   (Deutsche Geschichte der
Jüngsten Vergangenheit.)   Trs. Andrew and Eva Wilson.
L: Wolff, 1959.   157p.   19cm.   [LC62, B59, IT12]

MAY, Karl (Friedrich).
In the desert.   (Durch die Wüste.)   Tr. F. Billerbeck-
gentz.   Illus. J. Junghans.   Eng. eds. M. A. De Becker
and C. A. Willoughby.   Bamberg: Ustad-Verlag;   NY:
Willoughby;   (L: Pordes), 1955.   318p.   19cm.   [B59]

MAYER-KRAPOLL, Hermann.
The use of commercial fertilizers, particularly nitrogen,
in forestry.   Tr. and pub. Nitrogen Division, Allied
Chemical and Dye Corp. , NY, 1956.   111p.   24cm.
[LC62]

McSHANE, Rudolph, jt. author,   See Cutler, Ann.
The Trachtenberg speed system of basic mathematics.
Tr. and adapt. Garden City, NY: Doubleday, 1960.
[LC62]

MEEK, Ronald L. , ed.   See Marx, Karl, 1818-1883.

MEHRING, Franz, 1846-1919.   See   Corey, Lewis.
The social revolution in Germany.   Tr. Anon.   Boston:

The Revolutionary Age, n.d., [LC62]

MEICHSNER, Dieter.
Vain glory. (Weissi du, warum.) Trs. Charlotte and
A. L. Lloyd. L: Hamilton, 1960. 188p. (18cm.)
[B60]

MEINECKE, Friedrich, 1862-1954.
Machiavellism, the doctrine of raison d'état and its place
in modern history. (Die Idee der Staatsräson in der
neueren Geschichte.) Tr. Douglas Scott. Introd. W.
Star. L: Routledge, 1957. 438p. 22cm. (22.5cm.)
[LC62, B57, IT10]

Same. New Haven: Yale U. Pr., 1957. 438p. 23cm.
[LC62, IT10]

MEISSER-HROMATHA, Maria.
Austria. Art and works of art. (Österreich. Kunst und
Kunstschätze.) Trs. Oscar Konstandt and Gerald Morice.
Introd. Karl Oettinger. St. Johann, Tirol: Pinguin, 1956.
96p. 27cm. [LC62]

MEISSNER, Boris.
The Communist Party of the Soviet Union, party leader-
ship, organization and ideology. Tr. Fred Holling. Ed.
John S. Reshetar. With chapter on Twentieth Party
Congress. L: Atlantic, 1957. (6), 276p. (22cm.)
[B57]

MEISSNER, Carl B., 1830- .
Latin phrase-book. Tr. H. W. Auden. (From 6th ed.)
L: Macmillan; NY: St. Martin's, 1956. 338p. 18cm.
[LC62]

MEISSNER, Hans Otto.
The man with three faces. Tr. Anon. NY: Rinehart,
1956. 243p. 22cm. [LC62]

One-man safari. (Ich ging allein.) Tr. Robert Noble.
L: Jenkins, 1957. 188p. (22.5cm.) 23cm. [LC62,
B57]

MELCHERS, Ursula.
Bim in China. (B--.) Tr. James Cleugh. L: Muller,
1956. 166p. (19.5cm.) [B56]

MELLENTHIN, F. W. von, 1904- .
Panzer battles. A study of the employment of armor in
the 2nd World War, 1939-1945. Tr. H. Betzler. Ed.
L. C. F. Turner. L: Cassell, 1956. 378p. (22.5cm.)
[B55]

Same. U. of Oklahoma, 1956. 383p. 24cm. [LC62]

MEMMERS, Erwin Esser, 1916- .
Hobson and underconsumption. Tr. Anon. Amsterdam:
North-Holland, 1956. 152p. 22cm. [LC62]

A MEMORIAL GARLAND.
(O rare Hoffnung.) Tr. Anon. L: Putnam, 1960.
223p. (224p.) (23cm.) [LC62, B60]

MENDAX, Fritz, pseud.
Art fakes and forgeries. (Aus der Welt der Fälscher.)
Tr. H. S. Whitman. NY: Philosophical Lib., 1956.
222p. 23cm. [LC62, IT9]

MENNINGER, Karl, 1898- .
Mathematics in your world. (Mathematik in deiner Welt,
von ihrem Geist und ihrer Art zu denken.) Trs. P. S.
Morrell and J. E. Blamey. n.p., 291p. 22cm. [LC62]

MERCIER, Andre, ed.
Jubilee of relativity theory, Bern, 11-16 July, 1955.
(Fünfzig Jahre Relativitätstheorie. Verhandlungen.) Tr.
Anon. Eng., Fr., and Ger. ed. A--M-- and Michel
Kervaire. Basel: Birkhäuser, 1956. 286p. 23cm.
[LC62]

Thought and being. An inquiry into the nature of knowledge. Final text Alan Bloch. Basel: Verlag für Recht
und Gesellschaft, 1959. 156p. 23cm. [LC62]

MERCK, (E.) A. G.
Chromatography, with particular consideration of paper
chromatography. Tr. Anon. Darmstadt, 196-. 185p.
25cm. [LC62]

MERIAN. STÄDTE UND LANDSCHAFTEN.
Wolfsburg and the countryside between Harz and Heath.
Tr. Anon. Hamburg: Hoffmann und Campe, 1958. 64p.
28cm. [LC62]

MERSWIN, Rulmann, 1307-1382.
Mystical writings. The four beginning years /The book of
nine rocks. (Vier anfangende Jahre/Das Buch von den
neun Felsen.) Ed. and interpreted Thomas S. Kepler.
Philadelphia: Westminster, 1960. 143p. 21cm. [LC62]

MESMER, Franz Anton, 1734-1815.
Maxims on animal magnetism. Tr. Jerome Eden. Mt.
Vernon, NY: Eden, 1958. 78p. 23cm. [LC62, IT11]

A MESSAGE FROM BERLIN. THE SOVIET SEA AROUND US.
Berlin-Grunewald, Graphische Gesellschaft Grunewald,
1958. 24p. [LC62]

MESSNER, Johannes, 1891- .
Social ethics. Natural law in the modern world. Tr. J.
J. Doherty. St. Louis, Mo., L: Herder, 1957. 1018p.
24cm. [LC62]

METZ, Peter, 1901- .
The golden gospels of Echternach. (Das goldene Evangel-
ienbuch von Echternach im Germanischen Nationalmuseum
zu Nürnberg.) Trs. Ilse Schrier and Peter Gorge. L:
Thames, 1957. 96p. 32cm. (34cm.) [LC62, B57, IT
10]

Same. NY: Praeger, 1957. 96p. 34cm. [LC62, IT10]

MEYEN, Fritz.
The North European nations as presented in German University Publications, 1885-1957. A bibliography. (Die
nordeuropäischen Länder im Spiegel der deutschen Universitätsschriften, 1885-1957, eine bibliographie.) Tr.
Anon. Bonn, Bouvier; Charlottesville, Va.: Bibliographical Society of the U. of Virginia, 1959. 124p.
25cm. [LC62]

MEYER, Conrad Ferdinand.
Selections in Loomis, C. G. 1960.

MEYER, Franz Sales, 1849- .
Handbook of ornament. A grammar of art, industrial and
architectural designing in all its branches for practical
as well as theoretical use. Tr. Anon. NY: Dover, 1957.
548p. 21cm. [LC62]

MEYER, Franz. Writer on art. Ed.
Marc Chagall, his graphic work. Tr. Anon. NY:
Abrams, 1957. [LC62]

MEYER, Hanns.
(Am Wasser, 42 Bildtafeln.) Tr. Anon. (Ger., Eng.,
and Fr.) Bayreuth: Schwarz, 1960. v. 17cm. [LC
62]

(Schönes Bremen, ein Bildband.) Tr. Anon. Photo.
Hans Saebens. Introd. Rudolf Alexander Schröder, et al.
(Germ. and Eng.) Bremen: Schünemann, 1956. 31p.
71p. of illus. 28cm. [LC62]

MEYER, Hans Heinrich Joseph, 1858-1929.
The Barundi, an ethnological study of German East Africa.
(Die Barundi, eine völkerkundliche Studie aus Deutsch-
Ostafrika.) Tr. Helmut Hendzik. New Haven: Human
Relations Area Files, 1959. 293p. 20cm. [LC62]

MEYER, Jean Daniel.
Desert doctor. (Mit Kamel und Medizin.) Tr. Mervyn
Savill. L: Souvenir, 1960. 255p. 22cm. (22.5cm.)
[LC62, B60]

MEYER, Peter, 1894- . See Hürlimann, Martin, 1897- .
English cathedrals. L, NY: Thames, 1956. [LC62]

MEYER, Wendelin, 1882- .
Living the interior life. (Wahres innerliches Leben.)
Tr. Colman J. O. Donovan. Westminster, Md.: New-
man, 1958-1960. 2v. 22cm. [LC62]

To the least. A biography of Sister Mary Euthymia.
Tr. Herman J. Fister. Chicago: Franciscan, 1960.
85p. 18cm. [LC62, IT13]

MEYER-EPPLER, Werner.
Information theory. (Informationstheorie.) Tr. Anon.
Braunschweig: Vieweg, 1957. 118p. 30cm. [LC62]

The mathematic-acoustical fundamentals of electrical
sound composition. (From Tech. Hausmitt, 1954.) Tr.
H. A. G. Nathan. Ottawa, 1956. 321. 28cm. [LC62]

The terminology of electronic music. (From Tech.
Hausmitt, 1954.) Tr. D. A. Sinclair. Ottawa, 1956.

91. 28cm. [LC62]

MEYER-SCHWICKERATH, Gerd.
Light coagulation. (Lichtkoagulation.) Tr. Stephen M.
Drance. St. Louis: Mosby, 1960. 114p. 26cm. [LC62,
IT13]

MEYER-WAARDEN, Paul Friedrich, 1902- .
Electrical fishing. Tr. Anon. Rome, Food and Agriculture Organization of the United Nations, 1957. 77, 1p.
24cm. [LC62]

MICHAEL, Maurice (Albert) and Michael, Pamela (Kathleen).
German fairy tales, sel. from stories other than the
Brothers Grimm. Tr. and retold by M-- and P--M--.
Illus. Hazel Cook. L: Muller, 1958. 181p. (20.5cm.)
[B58]

MICHELS, Robert, 1876-1936.
Political parties. A sociological study of the oligarchical
tendencies of modern democracy. (From Italien ed. of
Zur Sociologie des Parteiwesens in der modernen Demo-
kratie.) Trs. Eden and Cedar Paul. Glencoe, Ill. :
Free Pr. , 1958. 434p. 22cm. [LC62]

Same. NY: Dover, 1959. 416p. 21cm. [LC62]

MIELKE, Otto, 1906- .
Disaster at sea. The story of the world's great mari-
time tragedies. (Katastrophen auf See.) Tr. M. Savill.
L: Souvenir, 1958. 235p. 22cm. [LC62, B58, IT10]

Same. NY: Fleet, 1958. 255p. 22cm. [LC62, IT10]

MIKSCHE, Ferdinand Otto, 1905- .
Atomic weapons and armies. Tr. Anon. NY: Praeger,
1958. 22p. [LC62]

The failure of atomic strategy and a new proposal for the
defense of the West. Tr. Anon. L: Faber; NY:
Praeger, 1959. 224p. (22.5cm.) 23cm. [LC62, B59]

MILICEVIC, Vladeta.
A king dies in Marseilles. The crime and its background.
(Der Königsmord von Marseille. Das Verbrechen und
seine Hintergründe.) Tr. Anon. Bad Godesberg: Hoh-
wacht, 1959. 134p. 21cm. [LC62]

MILLONIG, Egon.
Carinthia. Tr. Margaret D. Senft-Howie. Munich:
Andermann, c1960. 61p. 18cm. [LC62]

Romantic Germany. Tr. Dorothy Plummer. Introd.
Heinrich Zillich. Munich: Andermann, c1959. 60p.
18cm. [LC62]

MINDEN, GERMANY.
The battle of Minden. (Die Schlacht bei Minden.) Minden
in Westfalen: Bruns, 1959. 180p. 22cm. [LC62]

MINGOTTI, Antonio.
How to practice Sevcik's masterworks. (Wie übt man
Sevciks Meisterwerke für Violine.) Tr. Kitty Rokos. L:
Bosworth, 1957. 47p. (21.5cm.) [B57]

MISES, Ludwig von.
The anti-capitalistic mentality. Tr. Anon. Princeton,
NJ: Van Nostrand; L: Macmillan, 1956. 114p. (21.5
cm.) [B57]

Epistemological problems of economics. (Grundprobleme
der Nationalökonomie.) Tr. George Reisman. Princeton,
NJ, L: Van Nostrand, 1960. 239p. (23.5cm.) [B60]

MISES, Richard von, 1883-1953.
Positivism, a study in human understanding. (Kleines
Lehrbuch des Positivismus.) Trs. Jerry Bernstein and
Roger G. Newton. NY: Braziller, 1956. 404p. 22cm.
[LC57]

Same. 415p. [IT9]

Probability, statistics, and truth. (Wahrscheinlichkeit,
Statistik und Wahrheit.) 2nd rev. enl. ed. Hilda Geiringer. L: Allen; NY: Macmillan, 1957. 244p. 22
cm. (22.5cm.) [LC62, B57, IT10]

MITCHELL, John Wesley.
The nature of photographic sensitivity. (Die photograph-
ische Empfindlichkeit.) Tr. Anon. Darmstadt: Helwich,
1957. 35p. [LC62]

MITTELBERGER, Gottlieb.
Journey to Pennsylvania. (Reise nach Pennsylvanien im
Jahre 1750.) Eds. and trs. Oscar Handlin and John

Clive. Cambridge: Belknap, Harvard U. Pr., (L: Oxford U. Pr.), 1960. 102p. (21.5cm.) 22cm. [LC62, B60, IT13]

MOELLER, Philip, 1880- . See Schnitzler, Arthur, 1862-1931.
The lonely way. Play in five acts. Tr. Anon. NY: Rialto Service Bureau. n. d. [LC62]

MÖRIKE, Eduard Friedrich, 1804-1875.
Mozart's journey to Prague. (Mozart auf der Reise nach Prague.) Tr. Leopold von Loewenstein-Wertheim. L: Calder, 1957. 93p. (3-93p. 19cm. (19.5cm.) [LC62, B57, IT10]

Poems. (Gedichte.) Trs. Norah K. Cruickshank and Gilbert F. Cunningham. L: Methuen, 1959. 120p. 19cm. [LC62, B59, IT12]

Poems, selected and ed. Lionel Thomas. Tr. Anon. Oxford: Blackwell, c1960. 116p. [LC62]

Selections in Flores, Anthol. 1960.

Selections in Loomis, C. G. 1960.

MÖTTELI, Carlo.
10 years of free market economy in West Germany.
(From Neue Zürcher Zeitung, 8 Feb. 1959.) Tr. Anon.
Zürich, 1959. 15p. [LC62]

MOHR, Ulrich.
Atlantis. The story of a German surface raider. Tr. Anon. L: Hamilton, 1956. 224p. (18.5cm.) [LC62, B56]

Ship 16. The story of the secret German raider Atlantis, as told to A. V. Sellwood. Tr. Anon. NY: Day, 1956. 255p. 21cm. [LC62]

MOLL, Albert, 1862- .
The study of hypnosis. Historical, clinical, and experimental research in the techniques of hypnotic induction.
(Der Hypnotismus.) Tr. Anon. Introd. J. H. Conn.
NY: Institute for Research in Hypnosis, 1958. 410p.
21cm. [LC62]

MOLLIER, Hans. See List, Herbert.
Rome. Tr. Anon. NY: Hill, 1960. [LC62]

MOLNAR, E. G.
The voice of fears. Ten poems by Illa Kovarik and Tibor
Simanyi. Tr. Sarah Gainham. Vienna, ARS. Hungarica,
1959. 26p. 30cm. [LC62]

MOLTER, Günther.
Juan Manuel Fangio. Tr. Charles Meisl. L: Foulis,
1956. 184p. (22cm.) [B56, IT9]

MOLTER, Günther, jt. author. See Kling, Karl, 1910- .
Pursuit of victory. Tr. Peter Myers. L: Bodley
Head, c1956. [LC62]

MOMMSEN, Christian Matthias Theodor, 1817-1903.
History of Rome. (Römische Geschichte.) Tr. Anon.
Glencoe, Ill.: Free Pr., 1957. 5v. 20cm. [LC62,
IT10]

Same. New ed. Dero A. Sanders and John H. Collins.
NY: Meridian, 1958. 600p. 22cm. [LC62, IT11]

Same. Tr. Prof. Dickson. Abrg. C. Bryans and F. J.
R. Hendy. NY: Philosophical Lib., 1959. 542p. 20cm.
[LC62, IT13]

Same. L: Owen, 1960. 542p. (19cm.) [LC62, B60]

MORGENROTH, Otto.
The short-wave amateur's manual. (Taschenbuch für den
Kurzwellenamateur.) Pocket ed. Tr. E. G. Berends.
Berlin, Verlag Sport und Technik, 1958. 162p. 16cm.
[LC62]

MORGENSTERN, Christian, 1871-1914.
The moon sheep. (Das Mondschaf, eine Auswahl aus den
Galgenliedern.) Authorized Eng. ver. A. E. W. Eitzen.
Wiesbaden: Insel-Verlag, 1959. 63p. 18cm. [LC62]

Selections in Flores, Anthol. 1960.

MORTON, Friedrich, 1890- .
In the land of the Quetzal feather. (Xelahuh, Abenteuer
im Urwald v. Guatemala.) Tr. Otto Eisner. Illus. Fritz
Berger. NY: Devin-Adair, 1960. 208p. 21cm.

[LC62, IT13]

Xelahuh. (X--, Abenteuer im Urwald v. Guatemala.)
Tr. Otto Eisner. Illus. Fritz Berger. L: Hollis, c1959.
208p. (22cm.) [LC62, B59, IT12]

MORUNGEN, Heinrich v.
Selections in Loomis, C. G. 1958.

MORZFELD, Erwin.
He flew by my side. (Er flog an meiner Seite.) Tr.
Mervyn Savill. L: Macdonald, 1959. 336p. (20.5cm.)
[B59]

Same. 326p. [IT12]

MOSCHNER, Franz Maria, 1896- .
The kingdom of Heaven in parables. (Das Himmelreich
in Gleichnissen.) Tr. David Heimann. St. Louis: Herder, 1960. 326p. 21cm. [LC62, IT13]

MOSER, Hans Joachim, 1889- .
The German solo song and the ballad. Tr. Anon. Köln:
Arno Volk Verlag, c1958. 146p. 33cm. [LC62]

Heinrich Schütz, his life and work. Tr. Carl F. Pfat-
teicher. St. Louis: Concordia, c1959. 740p. 25cm.
[LC62]

MOSSE, Eric Peter, 1891- .
The conquest of loneliness. Tr. Anon. NY: Random,
1957. 241p. 22cm. [LC62]

MOYZISCH, Ludwig Carl.
Operation Cicero. (Der Fall Cicero.) Trs. Constantine
Fitzgibbon and Heinrich Fraenkel. L: Pantheon, 1956.
156p. [IT9]

Same. With postscript Franz von Papen. L: Hamilton,
1956. 156p. (18.5cm.) [B56]

Same. NY: Pyramid, 1958. 158p. [IT11]

MOZART, Johann Chrysostom Wolfgang Amadeus, 1756-1791.
Bastien and Bastienne, German singspiel in five scenes,
with sixteen musical numbers. (B-- und B---. Libretto.)
Eng. ver. Baird Hastings. Boston: Lily, 1959. 15p.

MOZART, Johann Chrysostom Wolfgang Amadeus--
21cm. [LC62]

Letters, selected from the letters of Mozart and his family. Tr. Emily Anderson. Ed. and introd. Eric Blom.
Harmondsworth, Middlesex: Penguin, 1956. 277p.
(278p.) 18cm. (18.5cm.) [LC62, B56]

The magic flute. (Die Zauberflöte.) Eng. ver. Edward
J. Dent. L: Oxford U. Pr., 1959. 48p. 19cm. [LC
62]

Same. Eng. ver. B. Hastings. Boston, 1958. 55p.
[LC62]

The magic flute. An opera in two acts. (Die Zauberflöte.) Trs. W. H. Auden and Chester Kallmann. NY:
Random, 1956. 108p. 24cm. [LC62, IT9]

Same. L: Faber, 1957. 120p. 23cm. [LC62]

A Mozart letter book. Tr. Max Kenyon. L: Barker,
1956. 158p. 22cm. (22.5cm.) [LC57, B56]

Same. Westport, Conn.: Associated Booksellers, c1956.
158p. 22cm. [LC62, IT9]

MOZART, Leopold, 1719-1787.
A treatise on the fundamental principles of violin playing.
Tr. Editha Knocker. Pref. Alfred Einstein. 2nd ed.
L, NY: Oxford U. Pr., 1959. 234p. 21cm. [LC62]

MRAZEK, Wilhelm.
Art treasures in Austria. Painted baroque ceilings.
(Kunst aus Österreich. Barocke Deckenmalerei.) Tr.
Anon. Bad Vöslau, Actiengesellschaft der Vöslauer
Kammgarnfabrik, 1960. 32p. 32cm. [LC62]

MUELLER, Gustav Emil, 1898- .
The interplay of opposites, a dialectical ontology. Tr.
Anon. NY: Bookman, 1956. 241p. 23cm. [LC62]

MÜLLER, Hans, 1882-1950.
The stars. A drama in four acts. Tr. Anon. n.p.,
n.d. 1v. 29cm. [LC62]

MÜLLER, Hans Richard, ed. See Egli, Emil.
Europe from the air. (Flugbild Europas.) Tr. E. Osers.
L: Harrap, 1959. 224p. (28.5cm.) [B59, IT12]

Same. NY: Funk, 1960. 223p. 29cm. [LC62]

MÜLLER, Heinz E.
Road slipperiness due to ice and snow, its formation, and
methods and obligations for its removal. (Eis-- und
Schneeglätte auf Strassen, ihre Bildung sowie Massnahmen
und Pflichten zu ihrer Beseitigung.) Tr. Anon. n.p.
1956. 17l. 26cm. [LC62]

MÜLLER, Jacobus Johannes, 1906- .
When Christ comes again. Tr. Anon. L, Edinburgh:
Marshall, 1956. 96p. [LC62]

MÜLLER, Margarethe, 1862- . and Wenckebach, Carla,
1853-1902, jt. authors.
Good luck. (Glück auf.) Tr. Helen Stoddard Reed. n.p.,
195-. 124l. 28cm. [LC57]

MUELLER, Marie Hinrichs.
Little Betta in the red heather country. Tr. Anon. NY:
Vantage, 1957. 118p. 21cm. [LC62]

MÜLLER, Rolf.
(Frankfurt am Main, Album der interessantesten und
schönsten Ansichten alter und neuer Zeit.) Tr. Anon.
Text in Ger., Fr., and Eng. Introd. R--M--. Hamburg,
Das Topographon, 1959. 18p. 23 x 30cm. [LC62]

MUELLER, Rudolf, 1904- and Steefel, Ernest.
Doing business in Germany. A legal manual. Tr. Anon.
Frankfurt-/Main: Knapp, 1960. 158p. 22p. [LC62]

...Monopolies and restrictive practices...Germany.
Tr. Anon. Essen: Hans-Soldan-Stiftung, 1958. 19,
1p. 24cm. [LC62]

MÜLLER, Theodor, 1904- . i.e. Müller-Alfeld, Theodor
et al, eds.
Portrait of a river. The Rhine from the Alps to the sea.
(Das Bildbuch vom Rhein.) Tr. Anon. Frankfurt/Main:
Umschau Verlag, c1956, 96p. 29cm. [LC62]

Same. L: Batsford, 1957. 86 i.e. 88p. (28.5cm.)

MÜLLER, Theodor--
29cm. [LC62, B57]

MÜLLER, Wolfgang Daniel, 1919- .
Man among the stars. (Du wirst die Erde sehen als
Stern.) Tr. Anon. NY: Criterion, 1957. 307p. 22cm.
[LC62]

MÜLLER-ALFELD, Theodor, 1904- .
The world is full of wonders. (Die Welt ist voller Wun-
der.) Tr. Anon. L: Thames, 1957. 224p. 27cm.
[B57]

Same. NY: Harper, 1957. 226p. 27cm. [LC62]

MUELLER-DIETZ, Heinz.
Medical education in the Soviet Union. Tr. Anon.
Berlin: Brandt, 1958. 132p. 21cm. [LC62]

MÜLLER-GUGGENBÜHL, Fritz.
Swiss-Alpine folk-tales. Tr. Katherine Potts. Illus.
Joan Kiddell-Monroe. L: Oxford U. Pr., 1958. 225p.
(22.5cm.) 23cm. [LC62, B58, IT11]

MÜNSTER, Ludwig.
Christ in his consecrated virgins. The marriage of the
lamb. (Hochzeit des Lammes.) Trs. Basil Stegmann
and Sister M. Margretta. Collegeville, Minn.: Liturgical Pr., St. John's, 1957. 140p. 19cm. [LC62, IT10]

MÜSELER, Wilhelm, 1887- .
Riding logic. (Reitlehre.) Tr. F. W. Schiller. L:
Methuen, 1957. 184p. 22cm. [LC62]

MUHLENBERG, Henry Melchior, 1711-1787. (Mühlenberg,
Heinrich Melchior.)
The journals of H--M--M--. Trs. Theodore G. Tappert
and John W. Doberstein. Philadelphia: Evangelical Lutheran Ministerium of Pennsylvania and Adjacent States,
1942-58. 3v. 27cm. [LC62]

The notebook of a colonial clergyman, condensed from the
journals of H--M--M--. Trs. and eds. Theodore G.
Tappert and John W. Doberstein. Philadelphia: Muhlenberg, 1959. 250p. 21cm. [LC62, IT12]

MUNCK, Johannes, 1904- .
Paul and the salvation of mankind. (Paulus in die Heils-
geschichte.) Tr. Frank Clarke. L: SCM, 1959. 351p.
24cm. [LC62, IT12]

Same. Richmond, Va.: Knox, 1959. 351p. 24cm.
[LC62, IT13]

MUNCHAUSEN, English.
Baron Munchhausen, his wonderful travels and adventures.
Retold by Erich Kästner. Trs. Richard and Clara Win-
ston. NY: Messner, 1957. 68p. 27cm. [LC62]

The real Münchhausen. Authentic tales of the fabulous
Baron of Bodenwerder. Retold by Angelita von Münchhausen. Tr. Anon. NY: Devin-Adair, 1960. 138p.
26cm. [LC62]

MÜNCHHAUSEN, Angelita von. See Munchausen, English.
The real Münchhausen. Authentic tales of the fabulous
Baron of Bodenwerder. Tr. Anon. NY: Devin-Adair,
1960. 138p. 26cm. [LC62]

MUNICH, Residenz. See The Age of Rococo.
4th exhibition, 15th July--15th September, 1958. Tr.
Anon. Munich: Rinn, 1958. [LC62]

MUNICH, INTERNATIONALE JUGENBIBLIOTHEK.
Children. Prize books, exhibition catalog, 1958. Tr.
Anon. Munich: International Youth Lib., 1959. 48p.
[LC62]

MUSIL, Robert, 1880-1942.
The man without qualities. (Der Mann ohne Eigenschaften.)
Trs. Eithne Wilkins and Ernst Kaiser. L: Secker, 1960.
445p. (22.5cm.) [B60]

Young Törless. (Die Verwirrungen des Zöglings Törless.)
Trs. Eithne Wilkins and Ernst Kaiser. NY: Noonday,
1958. 217p. (20.5cm.) [LC62]

Same. 226p. [IT11]

MUSPILLI. In Loomis, C. G.

NAGEL PUBLISHERS.
Germany. Tr. and adpt. Donald M. Christie. Pref.
Hugo Eckerer. Text C. Harald Karlinghausen und Hartmuth Merleker. Geneva: Nagel, (L: Muller), 1956,
672p. (16.5cm.) [B56]

Moscow and environs, (and) Leningrad and environs.
Tr. William H. Parker. Geneva: Nagel, (L: Clematis),
1958. 256p. (16.5cm.) [B58]

NAGLER, Alois Maria, 1907- .
Shakespeare's stage. Tr. Ralph Manheim. New Haven:
Yale U. Pr., 1958. 117p. 18cm. [LC62, IT11]

A source book in theatrical history. Tr. Anon. NY:
Dover, 1959. 611p. 21cm. [LC62]

NAWRATH, Alfred, 1890- .
Austria. 160 photographs by A--N-- and others. Tr.
Anon. Introd. H. E. Beran. NY: Studio, 1956. 24p.
(27p.) (30.5cm.) [LC62, B56]

Eternal India. The land, the people, the masterpieces of
architecture and sculpture of India, Pakistan, Burma, and
Ceylon. Tr. Anon. NY: Crown, c1956. 148p. 31cm.
[LC62]

Iceland, impressions of a heroic landscape. (Island,
Impressionen einer heroischen Landschaft.) By A--N--,
Sigurdur Thorarinsson and Halldor Laxness. Tr. B. M.
Charleston. Berne: Kümmerly; Chicago: Rand Mc
Nally, 1959. 57p. 31cm. [LC62]

Immortal India. 12 colour and 106 photographic reproductions of natural beauty spots, monuments of India's
past glory, beautiful temples, magnificent tombs and
mosques, scenic grandeur and picturesque cities, ancient
and modern. (Unsterbliches Indien.) Tr. Anon. Bombay: Taraporevala's Treasure House of Bks., 1956.
148p. 31cm. [LC62]

Land of the midnight sun. Tr. Dorothy Plummer.
Munich: Andermann, c1959. 61p. 18cm. [LC62]

NAWRATH, Alfred 1890- . Illus. See Schwarz, Heinrich M.
Sicily. 169 photographs. Tr. Anon. NY: Studio, 1956.

43p. 31cm. [LC62]

Same. L: Thames, 1956. 47p. (30.5cm.) [LC62, B56, IT9]

NEBESKY-WOJKOWITZ, René Mario de.
Oracles and demons of Tibet. The cult and iconography of the Tibetan protective deities. Tr. Anon. 's Graven-hage: Mouton, 1956. 666p. 25cm. [LC62, IT9]

Same. L: Oxford U. Pr., 1956. (66p.) 666p. 25cm. [LC62, B56]

Where the Gods are mountains. Three years among the people of the Himalayas. (Wo Berge Götter sind.) Tr. Michael Bullock. L: Weidenfeld, 1956. 256p. (22cm.) [LC62, B56, IT10]

Same. NY: Reynald, 1957. 256p. 23cm. [LC62, IT10]

NEHLERT, Gerhard, 1912- .
International judicial cooperation under German law. Tr. Anon. Essen: Hans-Soldan-Stiftung, 1958. 26p. 24cm. [LC62]

NEIDHART VON REUENTHAL.
Selections in Loomis, C. G. 1958.

The songs of Neidhart von Reuenthal, 17 summer and winter songs set to their original melodies with tr. and a musical and metrical canon. Trs. A. T. Hatto and R. J. Taylor. Manchester, Eng.: U. Pr., 1958. 112p. 22cm. (23cm.) [LC62, B58, IT11]

NELSON, Leonard, 1882-1927.
System of ethics. (System der philosophischen Ethik und Pädagogik, Teil 1.) Tr. Norbert Guterman. Fwd. H. J. Paton. Introd. Julius Kraft. New Haven: Yale U. Pr.; L: Oxford U. Pr., 1956. 285p. (24.5cm.) 25cm. [LC62, B57, IT9]

NERVI, Pier Luigi.
The works of Pier Luigi Nervi. (Bauten und Projekte.) Preface by P--L--N--. Tr. Ernst Priefert. L: Archi-tectural, 1957. 142p. (22.5 x 28.5cm.) [B58]

NESTROY, Johann Nepomuk, 1801-1862.
Liberty comes to Krähwinkel. (Tr. and freely adpt. from
Freiheit in Krähwinkel.) Trs. Sybil and Colin Welch.
NY: Columbia Microf. of TW., 1957. 641. [LC62]

NESTROY, Johann Nepomuk, 1801-1862. See Wilder,
Thornton Niven, 1897- .
The matchmaker. A farce in four acts. (Einen Jux will
er sich machen.) Tr. Anon. NY: French, 1957. [LC
62]

NETTL, Paul, 1889- .
Beethoven encyclopedia. Tr. Anon. NY: Philosophical
Lib., 1956. 325p. 24cm. [LC62, B57]

Same. L: Owen, 1957. 325p. 24cm. [LC62, B57]

Mozart and masonry. (Musik und Freimauerei, Mozart
und die königliche Kunst.) Tr. Anon. NY: Philosophical Lib., 1957. 150p. 23cm. [LC62]

NEUBAUER, Alfred.
Speed was my life. (Männer, Frauen und Motoren.) Trs.
Stewart Thompson and Charles Meisl. Fwd. Stirling
Moss. L: Barris, 1960. 207p. (22.5cm.) [LC62,
B60, IT13]

Same. NY: Potter, 1960. 207p. 23cm. [LC62]

NEUE ZÜRCHER ZEITUNG. See Steck, Fritz.
Visit to a people's commune in North China. Tr. Anon.
NY: U.S.J.P.R.S., 1959. [LC62]

NEUHÄUSLER, Engelbert.
The sacred way, biblical meditations on the passion of
Christ. (Der helige Weg.) Tr. Gregory J. Roettger.
Baltimore: Helicon, 1960. 128p. 21cm. [LC62, IT13]

NEUMANN, Erich.
The archetypal world of Henry Moore. (Henry Moore und
der Archetyp des Weiblichen.) Tr. R. F. C. Hull. L:
Routledge; NY: Pantheon, 1959. 138p. (26cm.) 27cm.
[LC62, B59, IT12]

Art and the creative unconscious, four essays. (Kunst
und schöpferisches Unbewusstes.) Tr. Ralph Manheim.
L: Routledge; NY: Pantheon, 1959. 232p. 21cm.

[LC62, B59, IT12]

NEUMANN, Erich. Commentary.
Amor and psyche. The physic development of the feminine. (Ein Beitrag zur seelischen Entwicklung des Weiblichen. Amor und Psyche.) A commentary on the tale by Apuleius, by Erich Neumann. Tr. Ralph Manheim. L: Routledge; NY: Pantheon, 1956. 181p. 21cm. [LC62, B56, IT9]

NEUMANN, Robert, 1897- .
The Plague House papers. Tr. Anon. L: Hutchinson, 1959. 207p. (208p.) 22cm. [LC62, B59]

NEUMAYER, Heinrich, 1905- .
Expressionism, with 24 illus. chosen by H--N--. Tr. Anon. L: Methuen, 1956. 62p. 18cm. [LC62]

Same. Prepared Edith Hoffmann. NY: Crown, 1958. 62p. 19cm. [LC62]

NEUPERT, Hanns.
Harpsichord manual, a historical and technical discussion. (Das Cembalo.) Tr. F. E. Kirby. Kassell, NY: Bärenreiter, 1960. 105p. 21cm. [LC62]

NEUSSER-HROMATKA, Maria.
Beautiful Vienna. (Das schöne Wien.) Text and notes. Tr. Anon. Innsbruck: Pinguin, c1959. 84p. (27cm.) [LC62, B59]

NEUWIRTH, Arnulf, 1912- . See Gore, Frederick.
Abstract art. (Abstraktion.) L: Methuen, 1956. 19p. 18cm. [LC62]

Same. NY: Crown, 1959. 19p. 19cm. [LC62]

NEVALINNA, Frithiof, 1894- and Nevalinna, Rolf Herman, 1895- .
Absolute analysis. (Die Grundlehcren der mathematischen Wissenschaften.) By F--N-- and R--H--N--. Tr. Anon. Berlin: Springer, 1959. 259p. 24cm. [LC62]

NEVANLINNA, Rolf Herman, 1895- jt. authors. See Nevanlinna, Frithiof, 1894- .

NEW GERMAN ARCHITECTURE.
Tr. H. J. Montague. Selected by Gerd Hatje, Hubert
Hoffmann and Karl Kaspar. Introd. Hubert Hoffmann.
Text and captions Karl Kaspar. (Ger. and Eng.) L:
Architectural; NY: Praeger, 1956. 219p. 27cm.
[LC62]

NEW YOUNG GERMAN POETS.
Ed. and tr. Jerome (Dennis) Rothenburg. San Francisco:
City Lights, 1959. 63p. 17cm. [LC62, IT12]

NIBELUNGENLIED. See Schönberner, Franz, 1892- .
The Nibelungenlied. Tr. Margaret Armour. Introd.
Franz Schönberner. Illus. Edy Legrand. NY: Printed
for Limited Ed. Club by J. Enschede en Zonen, Haarlem,
Holland, 1960. 250p. 30cm. [LC62]

NICOLAI, Johann Hermann Lorenz, 1766-1852.
The Nicolai notebook (or diary). Tr. Margaret Strasser.
New York, 1956. 14, 17p. 22cm. [LC62]

NIEBELSCHÜTZ, Wolf V.
Züblin-Bau. Tr. A. Laubenthal. Ed. A. G. Züblin.
Stuttgart: Cotta, 1958. 130p. 25cm. [LC62]

NIEDERMEYER, Albert, 1888- .
Compendium of pastoral medicine. (Compendium der
Pastoral-Hygiene.) Tr. Fulgence Buonanno. NY: Wagner,
1960. 492p. 22cm. [LC62]

NIELSEN, Thor.
The zeppelin story. Tr. Peter Chambers. L: Hamilton, 1957. 192p. (18.5cm.) [B57]

NIEMETSCHEK, Franz (Xaver).
Life of Mozart. (Leben des K. K. Kappelmeisters Wolfgang Gottlieb Mozart, 1798.) Tr. Helen Mautner. Introd. A. Hyatt King. L: Hyman, 1956. 87p. (22.5cm.)
[LC62, B57, IT9]

NIESE, Gerhard.
Physics is fun. Games and experiments not requiring
special apparatus. (Spiele und Experimente, physicalische
Beobachtungen und Versuche ohne Apparate.) Tr. Donald
I. Mitchell. Eds. Edgar Knowlton, Rudolph McShane and
Urban Schnaus. Washington: Astro, 1960. 150p. 22
cm. [LC62]

Same. 15p. [IT13]

NIESEL, Wilhelm.
The theology of Calvin. (Die Theologie Calvius.) Tr.
Harold Knight. Philadelphia: Westminster, 1956. 254p.
23cm. [LC62, IT9]

Same. L: Lutterworth, 1956. 254p. (22.5cm.) [B56]

NIETZSCHE, Friedrich Wilhelm, 1844-1900.
The birth of tragedy, the geneaology of morals. (Die
Geburt der Tragödie. Zur Genealogie der Moral.) Tr.
Francis Golffing. (1st ed.) NY: Doubleday, 1956.
299p. 18cm. [LC62, IT9]

Joyful wisdom. Tr. Thomas Common. Poetry ver. Paul
V. Cohn and Mande D. Petre. NY: Ungar, 1960. 370p.
(19cm.) [LC62, IT13]

My sister and I. Tr. and introd. Oscar Levy. (supposed author, F--W--N--.) NY: Bridghead, 1957.
254p. 21cm. [LC62]

The portable Nietzsche. Selected, tr., pref., and notes
Walter Kaufmann. NY: Viking, 1960. 687p. 18cm.
[LC62]

Thus spake Zarathustra. Tr. Marianne Cowen. Chicago: Regnery, 1956. unp. [IT9]

Thus spake Zarathustra, a book for all and no one. Tr.
Marianne Cowan. Los Angeles: Gateway, c1957. 394p.
18cm. [LC62]

Thus spake Zarathustra. Tr. A. Kille. Rev. M. M.
Bozman. Introd. Roy Pascal. L: Dent; NY: Dutton,
1958. 288p. (18.5cm.) [LC62, B58]

Unpublished letters. Tr. and ed. Kurt F. Leidecker.
NY: Philosophical Lib., 1959. 156p. 20cm. [LC62,
IT12]

Same. Tr. Karl (i.e. Kurt) F. Leidecker. L: Owen,
1960. 156p. 19cm. [LC62, B60, IT13]

The use and abuse of history. (Unzeitgemässe Betrachtungen, pt. 2.) Tr. Adrian Collins. Introd. Julius Kraft.

NIETZSCHE, Friedrich Wilhelm--
2nd rev. ed. NY: Liberal Arts, 1957. 73p. 21cm.
[LC62, IT10]

NIGG, Walter Georg, 1903- .
Warriors of God, the great religious orders and their
founders. (Vom Geheimnis der Mönche.) Ed. and tr.
Mary Ilford. L: Secker, 1959. (3-353p.) 353p.
(22.5cm.) 23cm. [LC62, B59, IT12]

Same. NY: Knopf, 1959. 353p. 25cm. [LC62, IT12]

NISSEN, Claus, 1901- . comp.
Herbals of five centuries. (Kräutterbücher aus fünf Jahrhunderten.) Trs. Werner Bodenheimer and Albert Rosenthal. 50 original leaves from Ger. , Fr. , Dutch, Eng. ,
It. , and Swiss herbals with an introd. and bibliography
by C--N--. Munich: Wolfe; Zurich: L'Art ancien,
1958. 86p. 30cm. [LC62]

NOGLY, Hans.
Anastasia, a novel. Tr. Stuart Hood. L: Methuen,
1957. 252p. (3-252p.) [LC62, B57, IT10]

Same. L: Landsborough, 1959. 192p. (18.5cm.)
[B59, IT12]

NOHL, Johannes, 1882- .
The black death, a chronical of the plague. (Der
schwarze Tod.) Tr. C. H. Clarke. Introd. Donovan
Fitzpatrick. NY: Ballantine, 1960. 160p. 18cm.
[LC62, IT13]

NOLDE, Emil, 1867-1956.
Emile Nolde. Tr. Norbert Guterman. Text Werner Haftmann. L: Thames; NY: Abrams, 1959. 44, 96p.
33cm. [LC62]

NOLDE, Emil. See Werner, Haftmann.

NOLDE, L.
Nolde memorial. Tr. Anon. Text in Eng. , Ger. or Fr.
Wien: Metten, 1958. 118p. 22cm. [LC62]

NORBU, Thubten Jigme, 1922- .
Tibet is my country. (Tibet verlorene Heimat.) By T--
J--N-- as told to Heinrich Harrer. Tr. Edward Fitz-

gerald. L: Hart-Davis, 1960. 264p. 22cm. [B60]

NORDDEUTSCHLAND.
87 Städte- und Landschaftsfotos. Tr. Anon. Ed. Hans
O. Lange. Ger. and Eng. (Caps. also Danish and
Swedish.) Stuttgart: Haus am Berg, 1959. 95p. 21cm.
[LC62]

NORK, Karl.
Hell in Siberia. Tr. Eleanor Brockett. L: Hale, 1957.
222p. (22.5cm.) 23cm. [LC62, B58, IT11]

Same. L: Spencer, 1959. 157p. (18cm.) [B60, IT13]

NOSHIRO, Kiyoshi, 1906- .
Cluster sets. (From Ergebnisse der Mathematik und
ihrer Grenzgebiete.) Tr. Anon. Berlin: Springer, 1960.
135p. 24cm. [LC62]

NOSSACK, Hans Erich, 1901- .
The meeting in the hallway. Tr. Chris. Middleton. In
Spender's Coll. 1960.

NOTH, Martin, 1902- .
The history of Israel. (Geschichte Israels.) Tr. Stanley
Godman. NY: Harper, 1958. 479p. 24cm. [LC62,
IT13]

Same. (From 2nd ed.) L: Black, 1958. 479p. 24cm.
[LC62, B58]

Same. Reprinted with corrections. L: Black, 1959.
479p. 24cm. [LC62]

Same. Tr. Rev. P. R. Ackroyd. L: Black, 1960.
487p. 24cm. [LC62, B60, IT13]

Same. 2nd ed. Tr. Anon. NY: Harper, 1960. 187p.
24cm. [LC62]

NOTRING DER WISSENSCHAFTLICHEN VERBÄNDE ÖSTER-
REICHS.
Austrian explorers of the world. (Österreicher als Erf-
orscher der Erde.) Tr. Anon. In Ger., Eng., and Fr.
Wien, 1956. 159p. 21cm. [LC62]

Austrian physicians in the service of mankind. (Öster-

NOTRING DER WISSENSCHAFTLICHEN VERBÄNDE ÖSTER-
REICHS--
reichische Ärzte als Helfer der Menschheit.) Tr. Anon.
In Eng. , Fr. , and Ger. Wien, 1957. 162p. [LC62]

Beauty and greatness found in a small country. (Unica
Austriaca, Schönes und Grosses aus kleinem Land.) Tr.
Anon. In Eng. , Fr. , and Ger. Wien, 1958. 167p.
21cm. [LC62]

NOVALIS, pseud. (i. e. Hardenberg, Friedrich Freiherr von
1772-1801.)
Hymns to the night, and other selected writings. Tr.
Charles E. Passage. NY: Liberal Arts, 1960. 72p.
21cm. [LC62, IT13]

Sacred songs of N--. (Geistliche Lieder.) Tr. Eileen
Hutchins. Aberdeen, Scotland: Selma, 1956. 57p. 21cm.
[LC62, B56, IT10]

Selections in Flores, Anthol. 1960.

Selections in Loomis, C. G. Prose. 1960.

NOVOTNY, Fritz, 1902- .
Painting and sculpture in Europe, 1780-1880. Tr. Anon.
Harmondsworth: Middlesex; Baltimore: Penguin, 1960.
288p. 27cm. [LC62]

NOWARRA, Heinz J.
Manual of German aircraft 1914 to 1918. Tr. Anon.
Berlin: 1957. 39p. [LC62]

NOWARRA, Heinz J. comp.
Von Richthofen and the Flying Circus. Comp. by H. J.
N-- and Kimbrough S. Brown. Ed. Bruce Rogertson.
Drawings William F. Hepworth. Letchworth, Herts, Eng. :
Harleyford, 1958. (207p.) 208p. 29cm. [LC62, B58]

NUNBERG, Herman.
Principles of psycho-analysis, their application to the
neuroses. (Allgemeine Neurosenlehre auf psychoanaly-
tischer Grundlage.) Trs. Madlyn Kahr and Sidney Kahr.
Fwd. Sigmund Freud. NY: International U. Pr. ; (L:
Bailey) 1955. 382p. (24cm.) [B56]

NUSSBAUMER, Johannes Evangelist, 1904- .
The rosary in pictures. A simple and easy manner in
which to say the rosary devoutly. Tr. D. Tuetey-Curran.
Switzerland: The Family Rosary, 1958. 103p. 15cm.
[LC62]

OBERAMMERGAU AND ITS PASSION PLAY, 1960. Official
Guide.
Publ. by Community of Oberammergau. Tr. Anon. L:
Benn, 1960. (122, 2-137p.) 156p. (18.5cm.) [LC62,
B60]

OBERAMMERGAU PASSION-PLAY.
The Passion Play at Oberammergau. A religious festival
play in three sections with 20 tableaus vivants. Written
in 1960 J. A. Daisenberger on basis of old texts. Music
Rochus Dedler, 1815. Official text 1960, rev. and newly
pub. by Community of Oberammergau. L: Benn, 1960.
137p. [LC62]

OBERBAYERN, LAND DER BERGE UND SEEN.
(Eng. and Ger.) Stuttgart: Haus am Berg, 1960? 95p.
[LC62]

OBERJOHANN, Heinrich.
My best friends are apes. Tr. Monica Brooksbank.
NY: Dutton, 1959. 191p. 21cm. [LC62, IT12]

My friend the chimpanzee. Tr. Monica Brooksbank.
(B58-from German ms.) LC62-parts originally Fr. L:
Hale, 1958. 191p. (22.5cm.) 23cm. [LC62, B58,
IT11]

OBERLÄNDER, Theodor, 1905- .
The world refugee problem, a lecture delivered to the
Rhein-Ruhr Club, 8th May, 1959. (Das Weltflüchtlings-
problem.) Tr. Anon. Düsseldorf, 1959. 24p. 21cm.
[LC62]

OBERMÜLLER, Rudolf.
Evangelism in Latin America, an ecumenical survey.
Tr. Anon. Publ. for the World Council of Churches by
United Society for Christian Literature. L: Lutterworth,
1957. 32p. (22.5cm.) 23cm. [LC62, B57]

OBERTH, Hermann, 1894- .
Man into space. New projects for rocket and space

OBERTH, Hermann--
travel. (Menschen im Weltraum, neue Projekte für Raketen und Raumfahrt.) Tr. G. P. H. de Freville. L:
Weidenfeld; NY: Harper, 1957. 232p. (20.5cm.) 22
cm. [LC62, B57, IT10]

The moon car. (Das Mondauto.) Tr. Willy Ley. (1st
American ed.) NY: Harper, 1959. 98p. 22cm. [LC
62, IT12]

OCONEE CO., SOUTH CAROLINA LIBRARY, WALHALLA.
See German Colonization Society, Charleston, South Caro-
lina.
German Colony protocol. Minute book of the German
Colonization Society. Tr. Anon. Walhalla, South Caro-
lina, 1960. [LC62]

ODA, Shigeru.
New trends in the regime of the seas. (Part 2 reprinted
from Zeitschrift für Ausländisches öffentliches Recht und
Völkerrecht, Bd. 18, Nr. 2. Dez, 1957) Stuttgart, 19--.
v. [LC62]

ODENWALD.
Introd. Friedrich Mössinger. Bayreuth: Schwarz, 195-.
Captions in Ger., Eng., and Fr. 46p. 17cm. [LC62]

OECHELHAEUSER, Adolf von, 1852-1923.
Heidelberg castle. Eng. text Louis de Branges de Bour-
cia, based on 7th Ger. ed. Rev. and enl. by Emil Hartmann and Aloys Wannemacher. Heidelberg: Hörning,
1956. 57p. 26cm. [LC62]

OESTERLE, Manfred and Hofner, Herbert H.
Spain in three days. (Die Entdeckung Spaniens durch
Amerika.) Tr. Anon. Mühlacker: Stieglitz, 1958.
72p. 19x29cm. [LC62]

ÖSTERREICHISCHER BERUFSSCHULLEHRERVERBAND.
The new official Austrian ski system. (Österreichischer
Schilehrplan.) Tr. Roland Palmedo. Ed. Austrian Assn.
of Professional Ski Teachers in collaboration with the
Federal Ministry of Education and others. L: Kaye;
NY: Barnes, 1958. 126p. 19cm. [LC62, B59, IT11,
12]

OGRIZEK, Dore, ed.
Germany. Tr. Paddy O'Hanlon. L: McGraw-Hill,
1956. 414p. (19.5cm.) [B56]

Japan. Tr. Paddy O'Hanlon. L: McGraw-Hill, 1957.
400p. (19.5cm.) [B57]

OHM, Thomas, 1892- .
Asia looks at Western Christianity. (Asiens Kritik am
abendländischen Christentum.) Tr. Irene Marinoff. 1st
ed. Freiburg: Herder; L: Nelson; NY: Herder, 1959.
251p. (252p.) (18.5cm.) 19cm. [LC62, B59, IT12]

OLD LAND, NEW PEOPLE.
Tr. Joan Becker. Berlin: Seven Seas, 1960. 214p.
19cm. [LC62]

OLIVIER, Stefan.
I swear and vow. Tr. Helen Sebba. (1st ed.) NY:
Doubleday, 1960. 358p. 22cm. [LC62, IT13]

OLLENHAUER, Erich.
German politics at a turning point. Bonn: Social Democratic Party of Germany, 1956. 33p. [LC62]

Security for all. Bonn: Social Democratic Party of Germany. Excerpts from his address delivered at Dortmund
June 16th, 1957. 16p. 15 x 21cm. [LC62]

OPITZ, Karlludwig.
The General. (Mein General.) Tr. Constantine Fitzgib-
bon. L: Muller, 1956. (2), 150p. 19cm. (19.5cm.)
[LC62, B56, IT9]

Same. NY: Day, 1957. 191p. 21cm. [LC62, IT10]

Same. NY: Ace, 1957. 144p. [IT10]

Same. L: Brown, 1958. 159p. (18cm.) [B58]

The Soldier. (Der Barras.) Tr. Constantine Fitzgibbon.
L: Viking, World Distributors, 1957. 191p. 17cm.
[B57, IT10]

OPITZ, Martin.
Selections in Loomis, C. G. 1958.

OPPENHEIM, David Ernst, 1881- . jt. author. See Freud, Sigmund, 1856-1939.
Dreams in folklore . . . Tr. Anon. NY: International U. Pr., 1958. [LC62]

OPPERMANN, Alfred.
Aeronautical English. Technical pocket-dictionary and manual of aviation. (Technisches Taschen-Wörter- und Handbuch der Luftfahrt.) Tr. Anon. München, n. p., 1957. v. 17cm. [LC62]

ORFF, Carl, 1895- .
Antigone. Libretto. Eng. tr. William Ashbrook. Music Carl Orff. Poem Friedrich Hölderlin. Terre Haute, Ind.: n. p., 1960. 341. [LC62]

ORYNSKI, Wanda, ed. See Hegel, George Wilhelm Friedrich, 1770- .
Hegel, highlights, an annotated selection. Trs. J. Sibres and J. B. Baillie. Philosophical Lib., 1960. 361p. 20cm. [LC62, IT13]

OSTROGORSKI, Georgije.
History of the Byzantine state. Tr. Joan Hussey. Oxford: Blackwell, 1956. 548p. (23.5cm.) 24cm. [LC 62, B56, IT9]

Same. New Brunswick, NJ: Rutgers U. Pr., 1957. 548p. 25cm. [LC62, IT10]

OSTROGROSKY George. See Ostrogorski, Georgije.

OSTROWSKA, Nina von.
Yellow communism. (From Politische Studien, v. 10, no. 106, 1959.) Tr. Anon. NY: U. S. J. P. R. S., 101. [LC62]

OSTROWSKI, Alexander M., 1893- .
Solution of equations and systems of equations. Tr. Anon. NY: Academic, 1960. 202p. 24cm. [LC62]

OSWARD, Maxim.
Asia Minor. Tr. Norma Deane. Introd. M--O---. L: Thames; NY: Morrow, 1957. 32p. (28.5cm.) 29cm. [LC62, B58, IT11]

OSWATITSCH, Klaus.
Gas dynamics. Eng. version, Gustav Kuerti. NY: Academic, 1956. 610p. 24cm. [LC62]

OTT, Ludwig, 1906- .
Fundamentals of Catholic dogma. (Grundriss der katholischen Dogmatik.) Tr. Patrick Lynch. Ed. in Eng. James Canon Bastible. Cork: Mercier; St. Louis, Mo.: Herder, 1957. 523p. 22cm. [LC62]

Same. 4th ed. St. Louis, 1960. Herder, 1960, 544p. 23cm. [LC62]

OTT, Wolfgang, 1923- .
Sharks and little fish. (Haie und kleine Fische.) Tr. Ralph Manheim. L: Hutchinson, 1957. 397p. (398p.) (20.5cm.) [LC62, B57, IT10]

Same. NY: Pantheon, 1957. 431p. 22cm. [LC62]

Same. 398p. [IT10]

Same. NY: Pantheon, 1958. 431p. 22cm. [LC62, IT11]

Same. NY: Dell, 1959. 416p. [IT12]

Same. Tr. Oliver Coburn. L: Arrow, 1960. 398p. 18cm. [B60]

OTTO, ARCHDUKE OF AUSTRIA, 1912- .
Monarchy in the atomic age. Text of two lectures given Jan. 26th and 27th 1960 in London and Cambridge at invitation of Cambridge University Royalists. L: Publ. for Cambridge University Royalists by Monarchist Pr. Assn., 1960. 16p. 22cm. [LC62]

The social order of tomorrow. State and society in the atomic age. (Soziale Ordnung von Morgen. Gesellschaft und Staat im Atomzeitalter.) Tr. Ivo Jarosy. Fwd. Christopher Hollis. L: Wolff, 1958. 158p. (19cm.) 20cm. [LC62, B59, IT12]

Same. Westminster, Md.: Newman, 1959. 158p. 19cm. [LC62]

OTTO, (Karl Ludwig) Rudolf, 1869-1937.
The idea of the holy, an inquiry into the non-rational
factor in the idea of the divine and its relation to the
rational. (Das Heilige.) Tr. John W. Harvey. 2nd ed.
L, NY: Oxford Univ. Pr., 1957. 232p. 22cm. [LC62]

Same. NY: Oxford U. Pr., 1958. 232p. 21cm.
[LC62, IT11]

Same. Harmondsworth: Penguin, 1959. 205p. (18.5cm.)
[B59, IT12]

The kingdom of God and the son of man. A study in the
history of religion. Trs. Floyd V. Filson and Bertram
Lee-Woolf. New and rev. ed. Boston: Starr King,
1957. 407p. 22cm. [LC62, IT10]

Mysticism East and West. A comparative analysis of the
nature of mysticism. Trs. Bertha L. Bracey and Rich-
enda C. Payne. NY: Meridian, 1957. 262p. 18cm.
[LC62, IT12]

OTTO-WASOW, Kurt.
The Bay of Naples. Tr. Anon. Introd. and commentaries William Sansom. Photos K--O--W--. 1st Eng.
ed. L: Batsford; NY: Viking, 1960. 19p. 25cm.
[LC62]

Florence. (Florenz.) Tr. Anon. Introd. and commentaries Sylvia Sprigge. Photos K--O--W--. 1st Eng. ed.
L: Batsford; NY: Studio in assn. with Viking, 1959.
19p. (20p.) 24.5cm.) 25cm. [LC62, B59]

Paris. Tr. Peter Gorge. Introd. and commentaries
Sven Stolpe. L: Batsford, 1958. 20p. (24.5cm.)
[LC62, B58]

Same. Studio in assn. with Viking, 1959. 19p. 25 x
23cm. [LC62]

Rome. Tr. Anon. Introd. Peter Quennell. Photos.
K--O--W--. L: Batsford, 1958. 19p. (24.5cm.)
[LC62, B58]

Same. NY: Studio, 1959. 19p. 25 x 23cm. [LC62]

Venice. Tr. Anon. Introd. and commentaries Anthony

Thorne. Photos K--O--W---. 1st Eng. ed. L: Batsford, 1960. 19p. [LC62]

Same. NY: Viking, 1960. 19p. 25cm. [LC62]

PABST, Helmut.
The outermost frontier, a German soldier in the Russian campaign. (Der Ruf der äussersten Grenze.) Trs. Andrew and Eva Wilson. L: Kimber, 1957. 204p. 22cm. (22.5cm.) [LC62, B57]

PAHLEN, Kurt, 1907- .
The magic world of music. (Ins Wunderland der Musik.) Tr. Oliver Coburn. L: Allen, 1959. 203p. (20.5cm.) 21cm. [LC02, B59, IT12]

PAHLKE, Jürgen.
Welfare economics. (Grundlage allgemeingültiger wirtschaftspolitischer Entscheidungen.) Tr. Anon. Berlin: Duncker, 1960. 83p. [LC62]

PAPPENHEIM, Fritz.
The alienation of modern man. An interpretation based on Marx and Tönnies. Tr. Anon. NY: Monthly Review, 1959. 189p. 22cm. [LC62]

PARACELSUS, 1493-1541.
Selected writings. (Lebendiges Erbe.) Ed. and introd. Jolande Jacobi. Tr. Norbert Guterman. NY: Pantheon, 1958. 289p. 24cm. [LC62, IT13]

PARS, Hans Helmuth, pseud. (i. e. Diebow, Hans and Schwarz van Berk, Hans.)
Pictures in peril. (Noch leuchten die Bilder.) Tr. Kathrine Talbot. L: Faber, 1957. 240p. (23cm.) [B57]

Same. NY: Oxford, 1957. 240p. 23cm. [LC62, IT10]

PARSCH, Pius, 1884- .
The church's year of grace. (Jahr des Heiles.) Tr. Wm. G. Heidt. Collegeville, Minn.: Liturgical Pr., 1959. 5v. 19cm. [LC62, IT13]

The liturgy of the Mass. 3rd ed. tr. and adpt. H. E. Winstone. Introd. Clifford Howell. L, St. Louis:

PARSCH, Pius--
  Herder, c1957. 334p. 23cm. [LC62, IT10]

PARTIKEL, Heinz Joachim.
  Koblenz. Tr. Anon. Introd. and caps. in Ger., Eng.,
  Dutch, and Fr. Osnabrück: Fromm, 1960. 57p. [LC
  62]

PASCAL, Roy, 1904- , ed. See Marx, Karl, 1818-1883.
  The German ideology, parts 1 and 3. Tr. Anon. NY:
  International, 1960. [LC62]

PASCAL, Roy, 1904- . Tr. See Goethe, Johann Wolfgang von, 1759-1832.
  Iphigenia in Tauris. A play. n.p. 1958. [LC62]

THE PASSION IN AFRICA.
  (Afrikanische Passion.) Tr. Anon. Introd. John Taylor.
  Photog. Hans Leuenberger. L: Mowbray, 1957. 62p.
  (28.5cm.) [B57]

PASTOR, Ludwig Freiherr von, 1854-1928.
  The history of the Popes from the close of the Middle
  Ages. Drawn from the secret archives of the Vatican
  and other original sources. (Geschichte der Päpste seit
  dem Ausgang des Mittelhalters.) Tr. Anon. L: Routledge; St. Louis: Herder, 1938-1961. 40v. 23cm.
  [LC62]

PATON, Herbert James, 1887- , ed. and tr. See Kant,
  Immanuel, 1724-1804.
  The moral law or Kant's groundwork of the metaphysics
  of morals. A new tr. with analysis and notes, H--J--
  P--. 3rd ed. L: Hutchinson, 1956. [LC62]

  Same. NY: Barnes, 1958. [LC62]

PATSCH, Joseph, 1881- .
  Our lady in the Gospels. (Maria, die Mutter des Herrn.)
  Tr. Basil Wrighton. L: Burns, 1958. 232p. (22.5cm.)
  [B58, IT11]

  Same. Westminster, Md.: Newman, 1958. 231p. 22
  cm. [LC62, IT11]

PAULI, Hertha Ernestine, 1909- .
  Bernadette and the lady. Tr. Anon. Illus. Georges

Vaux. NY: Vision, c1956. 1v. [LC62]

Bernadette, our Lady's little servant. Tr. Anon. Illus.
Georges Vaux. NY: Vision, 1956. 187p. 22cm.
[LC62]

Christmas and the saints. Tr. Anon. Illus. Rus Anderson. NY: Farrar, 1956. 190p. 22cm. [LC62]

Cry of the heart. The story of Bertha Suttner. Trs.
Richard and Clara Winston. NY: Washburn, 1957. 210p.
21cm. [LC62, IT10]

PAULI, Wolfgang, 1900- .
Theory of relativity. (From Relativitätstheorie in Ency-
clopädie der mathematischen Wissenschaften.) Tr. G.
Field with supplementary notes by author. L, NY: Per-
gamon, 1958. 241p. (25.5cm.) 26cm. [LC62, B58,
IT12]

PECHER, Eric.
Pope John XXIII, a pictorial biography. (Johannes
XXIII, eine Bildbiographie.) Tr. Margaret Shenfield. L:
Thames, 1959. 143p. (23.5cm.) [B59, IT12]

Same. NY: McGraw-Hill, 1959. 143p. 24cm. [LC62,
IT12]

PEIL, Rudolf, 1901- .
A handbook of the liturgy. (Based on completely rev. and
enl. version of first Ger. ed. of Handbuch der Liturgik
für Katecheten und Lehrer.) Tr. H. E. Winstone. NY:
Herder, 1960. n.p. [LC62, IT13]

Same. 1st ed. Freburg: Herder; Edinburgh, L:
Nelson, 1960. 316p. (317p.) (22.5cm.) 23cm. [LC62,
B60]

PEPJUNG, Carl H. P.
Conversion tables. (Umrechnungstabellen.) Text in Ger.
and Eng. Bremen, n.p. 1956. 234p. 15cm. [LC62]

PERRI.
From Walt Disney motion picture of Felix Salten's orig.
story. Adpt. Emily Broun. Illus. Dick Kelsey. L:
Adprint, 1958. (32.5cm.) [B58]

PERRY, Ben Edwin, 1892- .
The origin of the Book of Sinbad. (Sonderdruck aus
Fabula, Zeitschrift für Erzählforschung . . . Bd. 3, Heft 2,
1959.) Berlin: De Gruyter, 1960. 94p. 25cm. [LC
62]

PESTALOZZI, Johann Heinrich, 1746-1827.
My fate and experiences as director of my educational
institutes in Burgdorf and Iferten. Tr. and annot. J. C.
Osgood. n. p. (Harvard thesis), 1959. 1v. [LC62]

PETER, Hildemarie, 1921- .
The recorder, its traditions and its tasks. (Die Block-
flöte und ihre Spielweise in Vergangenheit und Gegenwart.)
Tr. Stanley Godman. Berlin: Lienau; L: Hinrichsen,
1958. 76p. 21cm. [LC62, B58, IT11]

Same. NY: Peters, 1958. 71p. 21cm. [LC62]

PETERS, Richard.
The story of the Turks, from empire to democracy. Trs.
Otto de Vuchetich and Salvator Attanasio. NY: Scribner,
1959. 235p. 22cm. [LC62, IT12]

PFANNENSTEIL, Wilhelm.
The healing power of West German natural medicinal
waters for export. (Über den Heilwert der westdeutschen
natürlichen Versand-Heilwässer.) Tr. Anon. (Issued by
the Deutscher Bäderverband.) Kölner Universitätsver-
lag, 1960. 23p. [LC62]

PFEIFFER, Gerd, 1919- , ed. See Germany, Federal
Republic, 1949- .
Action against the Communist Party of Germany. Reprint of documents for hearings initiated by petition of the
federal government to establish the unconstitutionality of
the Communist Party of Germany before the First Senate
of the Federal Constitutional Court. Washington, D. C. ,
1957. [LC62]

PFEIFER, Otto, landscape photog.
Switzerland, country and mountains. Tr. Dorothy Plummer. Introd. Hans Rolf Schmid. Munich: Andermann,
1958. 61p. 18cm. [LC62]

PFIEGLER, Michael, 1891- .
Priestly existence. Tr. Francis P. Dinneen. West-

minster, Md.: Newman, 1957. 425p. 22cm. [LC62]

PHODE, Gotthold, ed.
The genesis of the Oder-Neisse line in the diplomatic negotiations during World War II, sources and documents. (Quellen zur Entstehung der Oder-Neisse-Linie in den diplomatischen Verhandlungen während des Zweiten Weltkrieges.) Tr. Anon. Compiled and ed. G--P-- and Wolfgang Wagner. Stuttgart: Brentano, 1959. 287p. 24cm. [LC62]

PICARD, Barbara Leonie.
German hero-sagas and folk tales. Retold by B--L--P--. Illus. Joan Kiddell-Monroe. 1st ed. NY: Walck, 1958. 196p. 23cm. [LC62]

Same. L: Oxford U. Pr., 1958. 196p. (197p.) (22.5cm.) [LC62, B58]

PICARD, Jacob.
The marked one, and twelve other stories. (Der Gezeichnete.) Tr. with introd. Ludwig Lewisohn. Philadelphia: J. P. S. A. 1956. 267p. 19cm. [LC62, IT9]

PICARD, Max, 1888- .
The atomization of modern art. (Die Atomisierung in der modernen Kunst.) Tr. S. Godman. L: Vision, 1958. 38p. (19cm.) [LC62, B58, IT11]

PICASSO, Pablo, 1881- .
Picasso, introd. Gernanda Wittgens. Tr. Eric Mosbacher. Milan, Silvana Editoriale D'Arte, 1957. 11p. [LC62]

PICASSO, Pablo. See Bolliger, Hans.

PICKARD, Max. See Picard, Max.

THE PICTURE ENCYCLOPEDIA OF ART. See The Praeger Picture . . .
A comprehensive survey of painting, sculpture, architecture and crafts, their methods, styles and technical terms, from the earliest time to the present day. Tr. Anon. L: Thames, 1958. 584p. (30cm.) [B58]

PIDOLL, Carl, 1888- .
Eroica, a novel. Nikolaus Zmeskall von Domanovetz's

PIDOLL, Carl--
reminiscences of Beethoven. Tr. Anthony Powell. L:
Methuen, 1956. 218p. 19cm. [LC62, B56, IT9]

Same. NY: Vanguard, 1957. 218p. 21cm. [LC62,
IT10]

PIEPER, Josef, 1904- .
Happiness and contemplation. (Glück und Kontemplation.)
Trs. Richard and Clara Winston. NY: Pantheon, 1958.
124p. 21cm. [LC62, IT11]

Same. L: Faber, 1958, (1959). 128p. (19.5cm.)
20cm. [LC62, B59, IT12]

Justice. (Über die Gerechtigkeit.) Tr. Lawrence E.
Lynch. L: Faber, 1957. 3-125p. (19.5cm.) [B57]

Leisure, the basis of culture. Tr. Alexander Dru.
Introd. T. S. Eliot. NY: Pantheon, 1958. 168p. 19cm.
[LC62]

Prudence. (Traktat über die Klugheit.) Trs. Richard and
Clara Winston. NY: Pantheon, 1959. 96p. 21cm.
[LC62, IT12]

Same. L: Faber, 1960. 79p. 19cm. (19.5cm.)
[LC62, B60, IT13]

Scholasticism, personalities and problems of medieval
philosophy. (Scholastik. Gestalten und Probleme der
mittelalterlichen Philosophie.) Trs. R. and C. Winston.
NY: Pantheon, 1960. 192p. 21cm. [LC62, IT13]

The silence of St. Thomas, three essays. (Über Thomas
von Aquin and philosophia negativa.) Trs. John Murray
and Daniel O'Connor. L: Faber, 1957. (122p.) 125p.
(19.5cm.) 20cm. [LC62, B57]

Same. NY: Pantheon, 1957. 122p. 22cm. [LC62,
IT10]

PIERHAL, Jean.
Albert Schweitzer. The life of a great man. (A--S--.)
Tr. Anon. L: Lutterworth, 1956. 160p. (22.5cm.)
23cm. [LC62, B56]

Same. NY: Philosophical Lib. , c1957. 160p. 23cm.
[LC62]

PIES, Otto.
The victory of Father Karl. (Stephanus heute. Karl
Keisner, Priester und Opfer.) Tr. Salvator Attansio.
L: Gollancz, 1957. 210p. (22.5cm.) [B57]

Same. NY: Farrar, 1957. 210p. 22cm. [LC62, IT10]

PINTSCH ELECTRO GMBH, Constance.
Telecommunication development report, 1956. Konstanz,
1956. 36p. [LC62]

PIONTEK, Heinz, 1925- .
Selections in Rothenberg, 1959.

PISCHEL, Emy.
Bouquets. Eighteen coloured engravings which faithfully
reproduce the orig. watercolours flowers and fruit by
Jean Louis Prevost. Introd. E--P--. L: Macdonald,
1960. 44p. (41cm.) [B60]

PIT, Ludwig.
(Darmstadt. Eine Liebeserklärung.) Ein Fotobuch von
Ludwig Pit, Idee und Texte von Klaus Schmidt. Caps in
Ger., Fr., and Eng. Darmstadt: Roether, 1960. 126p.
26cm. [LC62]

PIUS FRANCISKUS, Father.
Mother love, a manual for Christian mothers with instructions for the archconfraternity of Christian mothers.
(Mutterliebe.) Eng. rev. Bertin Roll. NY: Pustet,
1960. 691p. 15cm. [LC62, IT13]

PLANCK, Max Karl Ernst Ludwig, 1858-1947.
A survey of physical theory. Formerly titled, A survey
of physics. (Physikalische Rundblicke.) Trs. R. Jones
and D. H. Williams. NY: Dover, 1960. 117p. 21cm.
[LC62, IT13]

General mechanics. (Einführung in die allgemeine Mechanik.) Tr. Henry L. Brose. NY: Macmillan, 1957.
272p. 21cm. [LC62]

The mechanics of deformable bodies. (Einfuehrung in die
Mechanik deformierbarer Körper.) Tr. Henry L. Brose.
NY: Macmillan, 1957. 234p. 21cm. [LC62]

PLANCK, Max Karl Ernst Ludwig--
The new science. Three complete works: Where is science going. The universe in the light of modern physics. The philosophy of physics. Tr. Anon. L: Meridian, 1959. 328p. 22cm. [LC62, IT12]

Same. Trs. James Murphy and W. H. Johnston. NY: Meridian, 1959. 328p. 21cm. [LC62, IT12]

Theory of electricity and magnetism. (Einführung in die Theorie der Elektrizität und des Magnetismus.) Tr. Henry L. Brose. NY: Macmillan, 1957. 247p. 21cm. [LC62]

The theory of heat radiation. (Vorlesungen über die Theorie der Wärmestrahlung.) Tr. Martin Masius. NY: Dover, 1959. 224p. 21cm. [LC62, IT12]

Theory of light. (Einführung in die theoretische Optik.) Tr. Henry L. Brose. NY: Macmillan, 1957. vi. 216p. 21cm. [LC62]

PLATEN, A. G. v.
Selections in Flores. Anthol. 1960.

Selections in Loomis, C. G. 1960.

PLASS, Ewald Martin, 1898- . See Luther, Martin, 1483-1546.
What Luther says, an anthology. St. Louis: Concordia: c1959. [LC62]

PLATTNER, Felix Alfred, 1936- .
Christian India. (Christliches Indien.) Tr. Mollie Seton-Karr. Introd. Trevor Huddleston. Photos. B. Moosebrugger. L: Thames; NY: Vanguard, 1957. 147p. (29.5cm) 30cm. [LC62, B57, IT10]

Same. L, NY: Thames, 1957. 1470. [LC62]

PLIVIER, Theodor, 1892-1955.
Berlin. (B--.) Trs. Louis Hagen and Vivian Milroy. L: Hammond, 1956. 446p. 21cm. [LC62, B56, IT9]

Same. Abrig. NY: Ace, c1956. 383p. 18cm. [LC62]

Same. Garden City, NY: Doubleday, 1957. 446p. 22cm.

[LC62, IT10]

Moscow. (M--.) Tr. Stuart Hood. L: Hamilton, 1956. 319p. (18.5cm.) [B56]

Stalingrad, the death of an army. (S--.) Tr. H. Langmead Robinson. L: Hamilton, 1956. 351p. (18cm.) [B56]

Same. 356p. [IT9]

Same. NY: Berkley, 1958. 349p. [IT11]

POBE, Marcel, 1907- . See Gantner, Joseph, 1896- . The glory of Romanesque art. Tr. Anon. NY: Vanguard, 1956. [LC62]

POGE, Marcel, 1907- . See Gantner, Joseph, 1896- . Romanesque art in France. L: Thames, 1956. [LC62]

PODHAJSKY, Alois. The Spanish Riding School of Vienna. Tr. Anon. Vienna: Bruder Rosenbaum, 1956. 47p. [LC62]

POEL, William, 1852-1934. W--P--. Prompt-book of fratricide punished. (Der bestrafte Brudermord.) Tr. Anon. Supposed author Johannes Velten. L, Pr. for the Society, 1956. 35p. 23cm. [LC62, B58]

PÖTZL, Otto. Preconscious stimulation in dreams, associations and images. Tr. Anon. Classical studies by O--P--, Rudolf Allers and Jakob Teler. Introd. Charles Fisher. NY: International U. Pr., c1960. 156p. 23cm. [LC62]

POLLOCK, Frederick, 1894- . Automation, a study of its economic and social consequences. (Automation, Materialien zur Beurteilung der ökonomischen und sozialen Folgen.) Trs. W. O. Henderson and W. H. Chaloner. NY: Praeger, 1957. 276p. 23cm. [LC62]

Same. 254p. [IT10]

POOTMANN, Franz Joseph. Secrets of the animal world. (Wie im Paradies.) Tr.

POOTMANN, Franz Joseph--
Mervyn Savill. L: Souvenir, 1959. 176p. (22cm.)
[LC62, B59, IT12]

POPIOLEK, Kazimierz.
The last attempt to germanize Opole Silesia. Ed. K--
P--. and Waclaw Sobanski. Poznan-Warszawa: Western
Pr. Agency, 1959. 35p. 21cm. [LC62]

POPPER, Karl Raimund, 1902- .
The high tide of prophecy. Hegel, Marx, and the after-
math. Tr. Anon. 3rd ed. rev. L: Routledge, 1957.
391p. [LC62]

The logic of scientific discovery. (Logic der Forschung.)
Tr. Anon. L: Hutchinson, 1959. 479p. (480p.)
(23.5cm.) 24cm. [LC62, B59, IT12]

Same. NY: Basic, 1959. 479p. 25cm. [LC62, IT12]

PORCUPINE, Peter, pseud. See Cobbett, William.
Description of an old book.

PORTMANN, Adolf. (i. e. Charles Adolphe Portmann-De-
villers, 1897- .)
Animal camouflage. (Tarnung im Tierreich.) Tr. A. J.
Pomerans. Ann Arbor: Michigan U. Pr.; L: Mayflow-
er, 1959. 111p. (112p.) 21cm. (22cm.) [LC62, B59,
IT12]

PORTMANN, Heinrich.
Cardinal von Galen. (Kardinal v. G--.) Tr. and adpt.
with introd. R. L. Sedgwick. L: Jarrolds, 1957. 255p.
(22cm.) [LC62, B57, IT10]

PORTZELLANFABRIK LORENZ HUTSCHENREUTHER A. G.
Hundred years of porcelain. Tr. Anon. Title and text
in Eng. and Spanish. Selb: Bavaria, 1957. 69p. 22 x
22cm. [LC62]

THE PRAEGER PICTURE ENCYCLOPEDIA OF ART.
A comprehensive survey of painting, sculpture, architecture and crafts, their methods, styles and technical terms,
from the earliest times to the present day. Prep. with assist. of James Cleugh. L: Thames; NY: Praeger,
1958. 584p. 30cm. [LC62, B58]

PREUSS, Walter, 1895- .
Cooperation in Israel and the world. Tr. Shlomo Barer.
Jerusalem: Mass, 1960. 279p. 22cm. [LC62]

PREVOST, Jean Louis. See Pischel, Emy.

PRIEN, Günther.
I sank the Royal Oak. Tr. Comte de la Vatine. L:
Spencer, 1957. 158p. (18.5cm.) [B57]

PRITZKE, Herbert.
Bedouin doctor. The adventures of a German in the
Middle East. (Nach Hause kommst du nie.) Tr. Richard
Graves. L: Weidenfeld, 1957. 257p. 22cm. (22.5cm.)
[LC62, B57, IT10]

Same. 1st Am. ed. NY: Dutton, 1957. 255p. 21cm.
[LC62, IT10]

PROBST, Brunhilde.
The burning seal. Biography of Mother Mary Clara
Pfaender, foundress of the Franciscan Sisters of Salzkot-
ten. Tr. Anon. Chicago: Franciscan Herald Pr.,
1960. 129p. 22cm. [LC62]

PRÜFFER, Olaf H.
Early man east of the Mississippi. (Steinzeitfragen der
alten and neuen Welt.) Tr. Anon. Cleveland: Cleveland
Museum of Natural History, 1960. 421-455p. 30cm.
[LC62]

PTAK, Heinz Peter.
Venezuela, today. (V--, heute.) Tr. Anon. Photos
Carlos Enrique Humke-Fritzsche. Bad Boll, Deutschland:
Klemmerberg, 1956. 123p. 33cm. [LC62]

PÜCHLER-MUSKAN, Hermann von. See Pückler-Muskau,
Hermann von.

PÜCKLER-MUSKAU, Prince Herman Ludwig Heinrich von.
A regency visitor, the English tour of Prince Pückler-
Muskau described in his letters, 1826-1828. Tr. Sarah
Austin. Ed. with introd. E. M. Butler. L: Collins,
1957. 384p. (21.5cm.) 22cm. [LC62, B57, IT10]

Same. (Brief eines Verstorbenen.) NY: Dutton, 1958.
[LC62]

PUMP, Hans Wilhelm, 1915-1957.
Before the big snow. (Vor dem grossen Schnee.) Tr.
Robert Kee. L: World Distributors, 1960. 220p.
17cm. [B60]

Before the great snow. (Vor dem grossen Schnee.) Tr.
Robert Kee. NY: Harcourt, 1958. 239p. 21cm.
[LC62, IT11]

Same. L: Deutsch, 1959. 239p. (204p.) (19cm.)
[B59, IT12]

PURSCHKE, Hans Richard.
The puppet theatre in Germany. (Puppenspiel in Deutsch-
land.) Tr. Walter Moss. Darmstadt: Neue Darmstädter
Verlagsanstalt, c1957. 18p. [LC62]

PUSS IN BOOTS.
Puss in boots. Tr. Anon. Illus. Pauline Hodder. L:
Blackie, 1957. 28p. 19cm. [LC62]

PUTLITZ, Wolfgang Gans, Edler Herr zu 1899- .
The Putlitz dossier. (Unterwegs nach Deutschland. Erin-
nerungen eines ehemaligen Diplomaten.) Tr. Anon. L:
Wingate, 1957. 252p. (22.5cm.) 23cm. [LC62, B57]

QUADFLIEG, Josef, 1924- .
The saints and your name. (Das Buch von den heiligen
Namenspatronen.) Tr. Margaret Goldsmith. Illus. Johan-
nes Grueger. NY: Pantheon, 1958. 159p. 21cm. [LC62]

QUENNELL, Peter.
Rome. Introd. Peter Quennell. Photo. Kurt Otto-Wasow.
L: Batsford, 1958. 19p. (24.5cm.) [LC62, B58]

Same. NY: Studio, 1959. 19p. 25 x 23cm. [LC62]

RAD, Gerhard von, 1901- .
Moses. Tr. Anon. Ed. Stephen Neill. L: United Society for Christian Literature, Lutterworth, 1960. 80p.
(18.5cm.) 19cm. [LC62, B60]

Same. NY: Association, 1960. 80p. 19cm. [LC62]

RADEMACHER, Hans, 1892- , and Toeplitz, Otto, jt.
authors.
The enjoyment of mathematics. Selections from mathe-
matics for the amateur, by H--R-- and Otto Toeplitz.
(Von Zahlen und Figuren.) Tr. Herbert Zukerman.
Princeton, N. J: Princeton U. Pr., 1957. (L: Oxford
U. Pr.), 1957. 204p. (24.5cm.) 25cm. [B57, IT10]

RADNANYI, Netty (Reiling), 1900- .
Two novelettes, revolt of the fishermen of Santa Barbara.
Trs. J. and R. Mitchell. A price on his head. Tr. E.
Wulff. Tr. ed. V. Stone. Berlin: Seven Seas, 1960.
295p. [LC62]

RAEDER, Erich, 1876- .
My life. (Mein Leben.) Tr. Henry W. Drexel. Annap-
olis, U. S. Naval Inst., 1960. 430p. 24cm. [LC62,
IT13]

Struggle for the sea. (Mein Leben.) Tr. Edward Fitzgerald. L: Kimber, 1959. 270p. (22.5cm.) [LC62,
B59, IT12]

RAHNER, Hugo, 1900- . ed.
Notes on the spiritual exercises. Tr. Anon. Maryland:
Woodstock College Pr., 1956. 336p. [LC62]

The parish, from theology to practice. (Die Pfarre,
von der Theologie zur Praxis.) Tr. Robert Kress. Westminster, Md.: Newman, 1958. 142p. 23cm. [LC62,
IT11]

St. Ignatius of Loyola, a pictorial biography. Tr. John
Murray. L: Longmans; Chicago: Regnery, 1956.
106p. 25cm. [LC62, B56, IT9]

RAHNER, Karl, 1904- .
Encounters with silence. (Worte ins Schweigen.) Tr.
James M. Dernske. Westminster, Md.: Newman, 1960.
87p. 21cm. [LC62, IT13]

Free speech in the church. (Das freie Wort in der Kirche,
zwei Essays.) Tr. G. R. Lamb. L, NY: Sheed, 1959.
82p. 18cm. [LC62, IT12]

Same. NY: Sheed, n. d. 112p. 20cm. [LC62]

RAHNER, Karl--
Happiness through prayer. Tr. Anon. L: Burns; Dublin: Clonmore; Westminister [sic], Md.: Newman, 1958. 109p. 19cm. [LC62, B58, IT11]

RAMON, Frans. See Boschvogel, F. R., pseud.

RANDOW, Heinz.
Zoo search in Ceylon, capturing rare creatures in Ceylon's jungles and swamps. (Auf Tierfang in Ceylons Dschungeln und Gewässern.) Tr. Charles Johnson. Illus. Heiner Rothfuchs. L: Harrap, 1958. 208p. (22cm.) [B58]

Same. NY: Doubleday, 1958. 234p. 22cm. [LC62]

RASP-NURI, Grace, 1899- .
Yusuf. (Yusuf der Türkenjunge.) Tr. J. Maxwell Brown-John. L: Cape, 1957. 224p. (20.5cm.) [B57, IT10]

Same. NY: Criterion, 1958. 222p. 22cm. [LC62, IT11]

RATHJENS, Carl, 1887- .
Jewish domestic architecture in San'a Yemen. With an introd. and an appendix on seventeenth century documents relating to Jewish houses in San'a by S. D. Goitein. Tr. Anon. Jerusalem: The Israel Oriental Society, 1957. 80, 11p. [LC62]

RAU, Heinrich.
Address presented by the acting prime minister at the celebration on the occasion of the 400th anniversary of the founding of the Friedrich Schiller University, Jena, on Sept. 2, 1958. (Rede des Stellvertreters des Vorsitzenden des Ministerrates Heinrich Rau auf dem Staatsakt anlässlich der 400-Jahr-Feier der Friedrich-Schiller-Universität Jena.) Tr. Anon. Jena, n.p., 1958. 50p. [LC62]

RAUCH, Georg von.
A history of Soviet Russia. Trs. Peter and Annette Jacobsohn. L: Thames, 1957. 493p. 24cm. [LC62, B57, IT10]

Same. NY: Praeger, 1957. 493p. 25cm. [LC62, IT10]

Same. Rev. ed. NY: Praeger, 1958. 530p. 24cm.
[LC62]

Same. NY: Praeger, 1958. 512p. 21cm. [LC62]

Same. L: Stevens, 1958. 520p. 24cm. [LC62]

RAVENSBRÜCK.
(Ger., Russian, Fr., and Eng.) Berlin: Kongressver-
lag, 1960. 151p. 34cm. [LC62]

Same. L: Lockwood, 1958. 202p. (24cm.) [B58]

REAUTSCHNIG, Joseph, ed.
(Graz, die Stadt im Grünen. Ein Bildband.) Text Paul
Anton Keller und Walter V. Semetkowski. Tr. Anon.
(Ger., Eng., and Fr.) Graz: P. Cieslar Nachfolger,
1959. 48p. 22cm. [LC62]

(Steiermark. Ein Bildband.) Tr. Anon. Text Theo
Herbst. Introd. Elek Vajda. (Pref. in Ger., remaining
text in Ger., Eng. and Fr.) Graz: Verlag Styria, 1960.
67p. 24cm. [LC62]

REDDICK, Harvey Phillips, 1920- .
Johann Mattheson's forty-eight thorough-bass test-pieces.
Tr. Anon. Ann Arbor: U. Microf., Michigan Lib.
Photoduplication service, 1957. unp. [LC62]

REDLICH, Fritz, 1892- .
Academic education for business. Its development and
the contribution of Ignaz Jastrow (1856-1937) in commemoration of the hundredth anniversary of Jastrow's birth.
Tr. Anon. n. p., 1957. 35-91p. [LC62]

Looting and booty, 1500-1815. (De praeda militari.)
Tr. Anon. Wiesbaden: Steiner, 1956. 79p. 23cm.
[LC62]

REDLICH, Hans Ferdinand, 1903- .
Alban Berg, the man and his music. (Alban Berg.
Versuch einer Würdigung.) Tr. Anon. L: Calder;
NY: Abelard-Schumann, 1957. 316p. 22cm. [LC62]

REDLICH, Josef, 1869-1936.
The history of local government in England. (Englische
Lokalverwaltung.) Reissue of book 1 of Local government

REDLICH, Josef--
in England by J-- R-- and Francis W. Hirst. Ed., introd. and epilogue Bryan Keith-Lucas. Tr. Anon. L:
Macmillan; NY: St. Martin's, 1958. 261p. (22.5cm.)
23cm. [LC62, B58]

REGLER, Gustav, 1898- .
The owl of Minerva. The autobiography of G--R--.
(Das Ohr des Malchus.) Tr. Norman Denny. L: Hart-
Davies, 1959. 375p. [LC62, IT12]

Same. NY: Farrar, 1960. [IT12]

REICH, Hanns.
Children of many lands. (Kinder aus aller Welt.) Tr.
Anon. NY: Hill, c1958. 119p. 29cm. [LC62]

Same. L: Cassell, 1959. (8)p. 29cm. [B59]

Portrait of Southern Africa. (Südafrika.) Tr. Anon.
L: Collins, 1956. 95p. (28.5cm.) 29cm. [LC62,
B56, IT9]

Yugoslavia. Tr. Anon. Photos by H--R-- et al. Captions Alois Schmaus. Historical notes Alois Schmaus
and Oton Grosdic. Introd. Lord St. Oswald. L: Cassel, 1960. 11, 6p. 29cm. [LC62]

REICH, Hanns. See Eldjarn, Kristjan, 1916- .
Ancient Icelandic art. Tr. Anon. München, c1957.
[LC62]

REICH, Wilhelm, 1897-1957.
Character analysis. (Charakteranalyse, psychischer Kontakt und vegetative Strömung.) Tr. Theodore P. Wolfe.
3rd enl. ed. L: Vision, 1958. 516p. 22cm. [LC62]

Character-analysis, principles and technique for psychoan-
alysts in practice and in training. (Charackteranalyse, technik und grundlagen für studierende und praktizierende analy-
tiker and Psychischer kontakt und vegetative strömung...)
Tr. Theodore P. Wolfe. 2nd ed. L: Vision, 1958. 328p.
24cm. [LC62]

Selected writings. An introduction to orgonomy. Tr.
Anon. NY: Farrar, 1960. 557p. 23cm. [LC62]

REICHENBACH, Hans, 1891-1953.
Atom and cosmos. The world of modern physics. Tr.
Edward S. Allen. NY: Braziller, 1957. 300p. 21cm.
[LC62, IT10]

The direction of time. Tr. Anon. Ed. Maris Reichenbach. Berkeley: U. of California Pr., 1956. 280p.
(24.5cm.) 25cm. [LC62, B57]

From Copernicus to Einstein. Tr. Ralph B. Winn. NY:
Philosophical Lib., 1957. 93p. 19cm. [LC62]

Modern philosophy of science, selected essays. Tr. and
Ed. Maria Reichenbach. NY: Humanities Pr., 1959.
219p. [IT12, 13]

Same. Fwd. Rudolf Carnap. L: Routledge, 1959.
214p. 22cm. [B59]

The philosophy of space and time. (Philosophie der Raum-
Zeit-Lehre.) Trs. Maria Reichenbach and John Freund.
Introd. Rudolf Carnap. NY: Dover; L: Constable,
1957. 295p. (20.5cm.) [B58]

Same. NY: Dover, 1958. 295p. 21cm. [LC62, IT10]

The rise of scientific philosophy. Tr. Anon. 1st paper-
bound ed. Berkeley: U. of California Pr., 1958. 333p.
(18.5cm.) 19cm. [LC62, B57]

REICHGAUER, Edward.
Union in God through the body of Christ, Corpus Christi
mysticum, the church. Tr. Jerome Coller. Collegeville, Minn.: Liturgical Pr., 1959. 38p. 22cm. [LC
62]

REIDEL, Marlene. See Stearns, Monroe.
Eric's journey. Tr. Anon. Philadelphia: Lippincott,
1960. [LC62]

Kassimir's journey. Tr. Anon. Philadelphia: Lippincott, 1959. unp. [LC62]

REIDY, Affonso, 1909- .
(Affonso Eduardo Reidy. Bauten und Projekte.) Tr.
Anon. Introd. S. Giedion. Text Klaus Franck. (Eng.
and Ger.) Teufen AR, Switz.: Niggli, 1960. 143p.

REIDY, Affonso--
[LC62]

Same. Tr. D. Q. Stephenson. Stuttgart: Hatje, 1960.
143p. 23 x 27cm. [LC62]

The works of Affonso Eduardo Reidy. (A--E--R--.
Bauten und Projekte.) Introd. S. Giedion. Text Klaus
Franck. Introd. tr. Mary Hottinger. Text tr. D. Q.
Stephenson. Eng. and Ger. NY: Praeger, 1960. 143p.
23 x 27cm. [LC62, IT13]

REIK, Theodor, 1888- .
The compulsion to confess. (Geständniszwang und Straf-
bedürfnis.) Tr. Anon. NY: Farrar, 1959. 439p.
22cm. [LC62]

The creation of woman. Tr. Anon. NY: Braziller,
1960. 159p. 22cm. [LC62]

The haunting melody, psychoanalytic experiences in life
and music. Tr. Anon. 1st Evergreen ed. NY: Grove,
1960. 376p. 21cm. [LC62]

Listening with the third ear. The inner experience of a
psychoanalyst. Tr. Anon. NY: Grove, 1956. 514p.
21cm. [LC62]

Masochism in modern man. (Aus Leiden Freuden.) Trs.
Margaret H. Beigel and Gertrud M. Kurth. L: Calder;
NY: Grove, 1957. 439p. 21cm. [LC62, B57, IT10]

Mystery on the mountain. The drama of the Sinai revelation. Tr. Anon. NY: Harper, 1959. 210p. 23cm.
[LC62]

Myth and guilt, the crime and punishment of mankind.
Tr. Anon. L: Hutchinson, 1958. 335p. 22cm. [LC62,
B58]

Same. NY: Braziller, 1957. 336p. 22cm. [LC62]

Of love and lusts, on the psychoanalysis of romantic and
sexual emotions. Tr. Anon. NY: Farrar, 1957. 623p.
22cm. [LC62]

Same. NY: Grove, 1958. 623p. [LC62]

Ritual. Four psychoanalytic studies. (Probleme der Religionspsychologie.) Pref. Sigmund Freud. Tr. Douglas Bryan. NY: Grove, 1962. 1958. 367p. 22cm. (22.5cm.) [LC62, B58]

Ritual. Psycho-analytic studies. Tr. Douglas Bryan. Pref. Sigmund Freud. L: Bailey; NY: International U. Pr., 1958. 367p. (22.5cm.) [LC62, B58]

The search within. The inner experiences of a psychoanalyst. Tr. Anon. NY: Farrar, 1956. 657p. 22cm. [LC62]

Same. NY: Grove, 1958. 657p. [LC62]

The secret self. Psychoanalytic experiences in life and literature. Tr. Anon. NY: Grove, 1960. 320p. 21 cm. [LC62]

Sex in man and woman, its emotional variations. Tr. Anon. NY: Noonday, 1960. 249p. 22cm. [LC62]

REIMANN, Hans, 1889- . See Max Brod.
Hush the gallant soldier. Tr. Anon.

REINERS, Ludwig, 1896- .
Frederick the Great. An informal biography. (Friedrich.) Tr. Lawrence P. R. Wilson. L: Wolff, 1960. 304p. (22.5cm.) 23cm. [LC62, B60, IT13]

REINHARDT, Fritz.
Brighteyes, the story of a golden hamster. (Hansel Knopfauges Abenteuer.) Tr. Rosemary Davidson. Illus. Benedek. L: Constable, 1958. (4), 98p. (24.5cm.) [B58]

REINMAR von Zweter.
Selections in Loomis, C. G. 1958.

REIST, Werner, 1895- , ed.
Switzerland, life and activity. A bird's-eye view in the middle of the twentieth century. Tr. Anon. 5th ed. Zürich, Mensch und Arbeit, c1960. [LC62, IT13]

RELOUGE, i.e. See Relouge, Joseph Egon.

RELOUGE, Joseph Egon, ed.
Masterpieces of figure painting. (Gemalte Schönheit.)
Tr. Mervyn Savill. NY: Viking, Bonanza, c1959. 262p.
29cm. [LC62, IT13]

The nude in art. (Gemalte Schönheit.) Tr. Mervyn Savill. L: Batsford, 1959. 262p. (264p.-BNB, IT.)
29cm. [LC62, B60, IT12]

REMARQUE, Erich Maria, 1898- .
All quiet on the Western front. (Im Westen nichts Neues.)
Tr. A. W. Wheen. Boston: Little, c1958. 291p. 20cm.
[LC62]

The black obelisk. (Der schwarze Obelisk.) Tr. Denver
Lindley. L: Hutchinson, 1957. 368p. (20.5cm.)
[B57, IT10]

Same. NY: Harcourt, 1957. 434p. 21cm. [LC62,
IT10]

A time to love and a time to die. (Zeit zu lieben und
Zeit zu sterben.) Tr. Denver Lindley. NY: Popular,
1958. 287p. [IT11]

REMBRANDT, Hermanszoon van Rijn, 1606-1669.
Drawings, a critical and chronological catalogue by Otto
Benesch. Tr. Anon. 1st complete ed. L: Phaidon,
1954-57. 469p. 6v. 34cm. [LC62]

Paintings, drawings, and etchings. The three early bi-
ographies. Catalogue and notes Ludwig Goldscheider.
Introd. Henri Focillon. Tr. Anon. L: Garden City,
NY: Phaidon, c1960. 207p. 32cm. (32.5cm.) [LC62,
B60]

Same. L: Phaidon, 1960. 207p. 32cm. [LC62, B60]

Rembrandt. By H. Heun. Tr. Anon. Captions in Ger.,
Eng., and Fr. Bayreuth: Schwarz, 1957. 4p. [LC62]

REMY, Heinrich, 1890- .
Treatise on inorganic chemistry. (Lehrbuch der anorgan-
ischen Chemi.) Tr. J. S. Anderson. Ed. J. Kleinberg.
Amsterdam, NY: Elsevier, 1956. 800p. 2v. 26cm.
[LC62, B56, IT9]

RENDTORFF, Heinrich, 1888- .
The pastor's personal life. (Das persönliche Leben des
evangelischen Botschafters.) Tr. Walter G. Tillmanns.
Minnesota: Augsburg, 1959. 68p. 20cm. [LC62, IT12]

RENSCH, Bernhard, 1900- .
Evolution above the species level. (Neuere Probleme der
Abstammungslehre.) Tr. Anon. L: Methuen, 1959.
419p. 24cm. [LC62]

Same. Tr. Dr. Altvogt. NY: Columbia U. Pr., 1960.
419p. 25cm. [LC62, IT13]

RETI, Richard, 1889-1929.
Masters of the chessboard. Tr. M. A. Schwendemann.
L: Bell, 1958. 211p. 23cm. [LC62]

Modern ideas in chess. Tr. John Hart. NY: Dover,
1960. 181p. [LC62]

REU, Johann Michael, 1869-1943.
Thomasius Old Testament selections. (Die alttestament-
lichen Perikopen nach der Auswahl von Prof. Dr. Thomasius.) Tr. Max L. Steuer. Columbus, Ohio: Wartburg,
1959. 704p. 23cm. [LC62, IT12]

REUTER, Albert. Writer on air pollution.
Untersuchung von Kraftfahrzeug-Auspuff-Gasen auf gesund-
heitsschädliche Substanzen und deren Beseitigung durch
Filter.) Tr. Anon. From (Deutsches Kraftfahrtforschung
und Strassenverkehrstechnik. Heft 126.) Düsseldorf:
VDI-Verlag, 1959. 25p. [LC62]

REVESZ, Geza, 1878-1955.
The origins and prehistory of language. (Ursprung und
Vorgeschichte der Sprache.) Tr. J. Butler. L: Longmans; NY: Philosophical Lib., 1956. 240p. (22.5cm.)
23cm. [LC62, B56, IT9]

REYNA, Guglielmo, 1852-1931.
Eucharistic reflections. Devout considerations on the
Holy Eucharist and heart to heart talks with Jesus in the
Blessed Sacrament. Adpt. Winfried Herbst from the Ger-
man tr. by Ottilie Boediker. L: Sands; Westminster,
Md.: Newman, 1957. 404p. 21cm. (21.5cm.) [LC62,
B59, IT12]

REYNARD THE FOX.
The history of Reynard the fox. Tr. and printed William
Caxton in 1481. Ed. Donald B. Sands. Cambridge:
Harvard U. Pr., 1960. 224p. 22cm. [LC62]

REZZORI, Gregor v.
First meeting with the Hussar. Tr. Catherine Hutter.
1st ed. (Private printing.) NY: Harcourt, 1959. 31p.
20cm. [LC62]

The Hussar. (Ein Hermelin in Tschernopol.) Tr. Cath-
erine Hutter. NY: Harcourt, 1960. 343p. 21cm. [LC62,
IT13]
Same. L: Deutsch, 1960. 343p. (21cm.) [B60]

RICE, David Talbot, 1903- .
The art of Byzantium, text and notes. Tr. Anon. L:
Thames, 1959. 348p. 31cm. [LC62]

Same. NY: Abrams, 1959. 348p. 32cm. [LC62]

THE RHINE, HEART OF EUROPE.
Introd. Max Geisenheyner. Tr. W. Friedrich. Text
Ger. and Eng. Munich: Andermann, c1959. 62p. [LC
62]

RICHARDSON, William (Holt) and Freidin, Seymour, eds.
The fatal decisions. Tr. Constantine Fitzgibbon. Com-
mentary Siegfried Westphal. Introd. Cyril Falls. L:
Joseph, 1956. 261p. (23.5cm.) [B56]

RICHEY, Margaret Fitzgerald, tr.
Medieval German lyrics. Edinburg, L: Oliver, 1958.
90p. (19cm.) [LC62, B58, IT11]

RICHTER, Friedrich.
Martin Luther and Ignatius of Loyola, spokesmen for two
worlds of belief. (Martin Luther und Ignatius von Loyola.) Tr. Leonard F. Zwinger. Westminster, Md.:
Newman, 1960. 248p. 21cm. [LC62, IT13]

RICHTER, Hans Werner, 1908- .
Beyond defeat. (Die Geschlagenen.) Tr. Anon. L:
Hamilton, 1960. 191p. 18cm. [B60]

They fell from God's hands. (Sie fielen aus Gottes Hand.)
Tr. Geoffrey Sainsbury. NY: Dutton, 1956. 349p.
21cm. [LC62, IT9]

Same.   L: Harrap, 1956.   335p.   (20.5cm.) [B56, IT9]

Same.   L: World Distributors, 1957.   320p.   (17cm.)
[IT10]

RICHTER, Lore.
  Islands of the Sahara through the oases of Libya.   (Inseln
  der Sahara durch die Oasen Libyens.)   Tr. Hermann
  Ehlert.   Leipzig: Edition Leipzig, 1960.   128p.   31cm.
  [LC62]

RICHTER, Nikolaus Benjamin, 1910- and Richter, Lore,
  jt. authors.
  Libya. (Libyen.) By N-- and Lore R--, Tr. Anon.
  (Ger. and Eng.) Heidelberg: Keyser, 1960.   32p.   32cm.
  [LC62]

RIEDMANN, Alois.
  The truths of Christianity.   Vol. 1.   The truth about God
  and his works.   Tr. Anon.   Cork, Ireland: Mercier,
  1959.   287p.   [IT13]

  The truths of Christianity.   Tr. Anon.   NY: Herder,
  1960.   22cm.   [LC62]

RIEHL, Matthias.
  Orchids.   (Grosse Liebe zu Orchideen.)   Tr. Anon.   L:
  Deutsch, 1958.   59p.   (61p.)   (27.5cm.)   28cm.   [LC62,
  B58]

RIEKER, Hans Ulrich, 1920- .
  Beggar among the dead.   (Bettler unter Toten, als buddhis-
  tischer Bettelmönch in Indien.)   Tr. Edward Fitzgerald.
  L: Rider, 1960.   224p.   22cm.   [LC62, B60]

  The secret of meditation.   Tr. A. J. Pomerans.   NY:
  Philosophical Lib., 1957.   176p.   22cm.   [LC62, B56]

RILKE, Rainer Maria, 1875-1926.
  Angel songs.   (Engellieder.)   Tr. Rhoda Coghill.   Dublin:
  Dolman, 1958.   1p. 1, 7, (1)p.   300 copies printed.   25cm.
  (24.5cm.)   [B59, IT11]

  The cornet.   The manner of loving and dying of the cornet Christoph Rilke, (Weise von Liebe und Tod des Cornets
  Christoph Rilke.)   Tr. Constantine Fitzgibbon.   L: Wingate, 1958.   32p.   (20.5cm.)   [LC62, B58, IT11]

RILKE, Rainer Maria--
Duino elegies. (Duineser Elegien.) Ger. text with Eng.
trs. introd. and commentary, J. B. Leishman and Stephen
Spender. 3rd ed. L: Hogarth, 1957. 160p. 22cm.
[LC62]

The duino elegies. (Duineser Elegien.) Tr. and illus.
Harry Behn. Mt. Vernon, NY: Peter Pauper, 1957.
unp. 19cm. [LC62, IT10]

Ewald Tragy. (E--T--) Tr. Lola Gruenthal. (Eng. and
Ger.) L: Vision, 1958. 104p. 19cm. [LC62, B58]

Same. NY: Twayne, 1958. 104p. 19cm. [LC62, IT13]

Same. (IT error) 1959. [IT12]

Gym period. Tr. Carl Niemeyer. In Spender's Coll.
1960.

The lay of the love and death of Cornet Chrstopher
Rilke. Tr. M. D. Herter Norton. (Ger. and Eng.) Rev.
ed. NY: Norton, 1959. 69p. 22cm. [LC62, IT12]

The letters. Tr. N. Wydenbruck. L: Hogarth, 1958.
294p. 23cm. [LC62, B58, IT11]

The letters of Rainer Maria Rilke and Princess Marie
von Thurn and Taxis. (Briefwechsel zwischen Rainer
Maria Rilke und Marie von Thurn und Taxis.) Tr. and
introd. Nora Wydenbruck. Ed. Ernst Zinn. Norfolk,
Conn.: New Directions, 1958. 294p. 23cm. [LC62]

The notebooks of Malte Laurids Brigge. (Aufzeichnungen
des Malte Laurids Brigge.) Tr. M. D. Herter Norton.
NY: Capricorn, 1958. 237p. 19cm. [LC62, IT12]

Poems, 1906-1926. (Gedichte 1906-1926.) Tr. and introd.
James Blain Leishman. L: Hogarth, 1957. 402p.
(22.5cm.) [LC62, B57, IT10]

Same. Conn.: New Directions, c1957. 402p. 23cm.
[LC62, IT10]

Requiem and other poems. Tr., introd. and notes J. B.

Leishman. 2nd ed. rev. and enl. L: Hogarth, 1957.
157p. 23cm. [LC62]

Rilke and the Arabian Nights, with two unpublished tr. by
Walter Grossmann. Cambridge, Mass., 1960. 461-468p.
26cm. (27cm.) [LC62]

Selected letters. Tr. Anon. Ed. Harry T. Moore.
Garden City, NY: Doubleday, 1960. 404p. 18cm.
[LC62]

Selected poems. Tr. C. F. MacIntyre. 2nd ed. Berkeley: U. of California Pr.; L: Cambridge U., 1956.
147p. (149p.) (18.5cm.) 19cm. [LC62, B57, IT9]

Same. 3rd ed. Berkeley: U. of California Pr., 1958.
147p. 19cm.

Selected works. Vol. 1, prose, tr. G. C. Houston.
Introd. J. B. Leishman. Vol. 2, poetry, tr. J. B.
Leishman. NY: New Directions, 1960. 2 vol. 23cm.
[LC62, IT13]

Selected works. Vol. 2, poetry. Tr. J. B. Leishman.
L: Hogarth, 1960. 384p. (22.5cm.) [B60]

Selection in Chase, G. H. Tr. poems from the German.

Selection in Hoegler, R. G.

Selections in Flores, Anthol. 1960.

Selections in Kerenyi, C. Greece in colour, 1957.

Selections in Willoughby, L. A.

Sonnets of Orpheus, written as monument for Wera Ouc-
kama Knoop. (German text with Eng. trs.) Tr. J. B.
Leishman. 2nd rev. ed. L: Hogarth, 1957. 173p.
no cm. [LC62]

Sonnets to Orpheus. Tr. C. F. MacIntyre. Berkeley:
U. of California Pr., 1960. 142p. 19cm. [LC62, IT13]

RIMLI, Eugen Theodor.
Switzerland for travellers and tourists. Tr. Anon. L:
Galley, c1960. 388p. (18.5cm.) [LC62, B60]

RINSER, Luise, 1911- .
Nina, a novel. (Mitte des Lebens.) Trs. Richard and
Clara Winston. Chicago: Regnery, 1956. 284p. 22cm.
[LC62, IT9]

Rings of glass. Trs. Richard and Clara Winston. Chicago: Regnery, 1958. 176p. 21cm. [LC62, IT11]

RITSCHL, Dietrich.
Christ, our life. (Vom Leben in der Kirche. Der tages-
lauf der evang. Gemeinde.) Tr. J. Colin Campbell.
Edinburgh, L: Oliver, 1960. 114p. (22.5cm.) 23cm.
[LC62, IT13]

A theology of proclamation. Tr. Anon. Richmond:
Knox, 1960. 190p. 21cm. [LC62]

RITTER, Christiane.
Woman in the polar night. Tr. Jane Degras. L: Hamilton, 1956. 159p. (18.5cm.) [B56]

RITTER, Gerhard, 1888- .
The German resistance. Carl Goerdeler's struggle a-
gainst tyranny. (Carl Goerdeler und die Widerstands-
bewegung.) Tr. R. T. Clark. L: Allen, 1958. 330p.
(3-331p.) (22.5cm.) 23cm. [LC62, B58, IT11]

Same. NY: Praeger, 1959. 330p. 23cm. [LC62, IT12]

The Schlieffen plan, a critique of a myth. (Der Schlief-
fenplan.) Trs. Andrew and Eva Wilson. Fwd. B. H.
Liddell Hart. L: Wolff, 1958. 195p. (22.5cm.)
[LC62, B58]

Same. NY: Praeger, 1958. 195p. 22cm. [LC62]

RITTLINGER, Herbert, 1909- .
Ethiopian adventure, from the Red Sea to the blue Nile.
(Schwarzes Abenteuer.) Tr. Eva Wilson. L: Odhams,
1959. 224p. 23cm. [LC62, B59, IT12]

THE RIVIERA FROM PORTOFINO TO MARSEILLES.
(Die Riviera von Portofino bis Marseille.) Tr. Anon.
L: Thames, 1957. 20p. (24.5cm.) [B57]

ROADS TO ROME, FROM PISA, BOLOGNA AND RAVENNA
TO THE ETERNAL CITY.
(Wege nach Rom.) Tr. Anon. L: Thames, 1958. 20p.
(24.5cm.) [B58]

ROBACK, Abraham Aaron, 1890- .
Freudiana, including unpublished letters from Freud,
Havelock Ellis, Pavlov, Bernard Shaw, Romain Holland,
et al. , presented by A--A--R--. Tr. Anon. Cambridge,
Mass.: Sci-Art, 1957. 240p. 24cm. [LC62]

ROBERTSON, Edwin Hanton, ed. and tr.
Paul Schneider, the pastor of Buchenwald. A free tr.
of story told by his widow, with quotations from diary
and letters. Tr. E--H--R--. L: SCM, 1956. 128p.
(19cm.) [B56]

ROCKER, Rudolf, 1873- .
The London years. An abridgement from the memoirs.
Tr. Joseph Leftwich. L: Anscombe, 1956. 3-360p.
22cm. (22.5cm.) [LC62, B57, IT10]

Milly Witkop-Rocker. Tr. Anon. Berkeley Heights, NJ:
Oriole, 1956. (Private edition printed for the author.)
18p. 21cm. [LC62]

ROEDELBERGER, Franz Adam.
Holidays in Switzerland. (Das Schweizerbuch von Wandern,
reisen, Fliegen.) Tr. Anon. Bern: Buchverlag Verbandsdruckerei, 1956. 264p. 25cm. [LC62]

Southern Switzerland. (Das Sonnenbuch vom Bündnerland,
vom Wallis und Tessin.) Tr. Anon. Bern: Buchverlag
Verbandsdruckerei, c1957. 284p. 25cm. [LC62]

ROEDER, Bernhard.
Kartorga, an aspect of modern slavery. (Der Katorgan.)
Tr. Lionel Kochan. L: Heinemann, 1958. 271p. 22cm.
(22.5cm.) [LC62, B58, IT10]

ROEDER, Franz, 1774-1840.
The ordeal of Captain Roeder, from the diary of an offi-
cer in the First Battalion of Hessian Lifeguards during the
Moscow campaign of 1812-13. Tr. and ed. Helen Roeder.
L: Methuen, 1960. 248p. (22.5cm.) 23cm. [LC62,
B60]

ROEHLER, Klaus.
The dignity of night. (Die Würde der Nacht.) Trs. John
and Necke Mander. L: Barrie, 1960. 143p. (20.5cm.)
21cm. [LC62, B60]

RÖPKE, Wilhelm, 1899- .
A humane economy. The social framework of the free
market. (Jenseits von Angebot und Nachfrage.) Tr.
Elisabeth Henderson. Chicago: Regnery, 1960. 312p.
22cm. [LC62, IT13]

International order and economic integration. (Internationale Ordnung.) Trs. Gwen E. Trinks, Joyce Taylor
and Cicely Käufer. Dordrecht: Reidel, c1959. 276p.
23cm. [LC62]

Welfare, freedom, and inflation. Tr. Anon. L: Pall
Mall, 1957. 70p. 22cm. [LC62]

RÖSLER, Jo Hanns, 1899- .
God's second door. (Mitleid verbeten. IT¹² error: Mitleid verboten.) Trs. Leonore Sierigk and Eduard Galla-
gher. Cork, Ireland: Mercier, 1958. 90p. 23cm.
[LC62, IT12]

Same. L: Painted Postcards, 1958-59. 90p. (22.5cm.)
[LC62, IT12]

RÖTHEL, Hans Conrad, 1909- .
Modern German painting. (Moderne deutsche Malerei.)
Trs. Desmond and Louise Clayton. L: Eyre, 1958.
103p. 33cm. [LC62, IT11]

Same. NY: Reynald, 1957. 103p. 33cm. [LC62,
IT10]

ROGGE, Bernhard, 1901- .
The German raider Atlantis. By Wolfgang Frank and B--
R---. Captain Rogge's own story of his two year's voyage on the Atlantis. Tr. R. O. B. Long. NY: Ballantine, 1956. 154p. 21cm. [LC62, IT9]

Under ten flags. The story of the German commerce
raider Atlantis. (Schiff 16.) Tr. R. O. B. Long. L:
Weidenfeld, 1957. 185p. (186p.) 22cm. (22.5cm.)
[LC62, B57]

Same. L: Landsborough, 1960. 160p. (18cm.) [B60, IT13]

ROGISTER, Maximilian von.
Momella, an African game paradise. (M--.) Tr. Diana
Pyke. L: Odhams, 1957. 208p. (21.5cm.) [B57]

ROGOSINSKI, Werner, 1894- .
Fourier series. (Fouriersche Reihen.) Trs. Harvey
Cohn and F. Steinhardt. 2nd ed. NY: Chelsea, c1959.
176p. 17cm. [LC62]

ROHRBACH, Paul, 1869-1956.
FL. a century and a quarter of Reederei F. Laeisz.
owners of the Flying P nitrate clippers. (FL. die Geschichte einer Reederei.) Tr. from Hans Dulk Ger. ed. by
Antoinette G. Smith. U. S. ed. J. Ferrell Colton. Flag-
staff, Ariz.: Cotton, 1957. 244p. 27cm. [LC62]

ROLL, Christian.
Peiping and the national minorities. Tr. Anon. NY:
U. S. J. P. R. S., 1959. 111. 27cm. [LC62]

ROLLENHAGEN, George, 1542-1609, supposed author.
Alte newe Zeutung. A sixteenth-century collection of
fables with English summaries. Ed. Eli Sobel. Berkeley: U. of California Pr., 1958. 64p. 26cm. [LC62]

THE ROMAN CATHOLIC CHURCH IN BERLIN IN THE
SOVIET ZONE OF GERMANY.
Tr. Anon. Berlin: Morus Verlag, 1959. 64p. 21cm.
[LC62]

Same. Berlin: Morus Verlag, 1959. 63p. 21cm.
[LC62]

ROMMEN, Heinrich Albert, 1897- .
The natural law. Study in legal and social history and
philosophy. (Die ewige Wiederkehr des Naturrechts,
1936.) Tr. Thomas R. Hanley. Rev. and enl. St.
Louis: Herder, 1959. 290p. 24cm. [LC62]

ROPKE, Wilhelm.
A humane economy, the social framework of the free
market. Tr. Elizabeth Henderson. L: Wolff, 1960.
312p. 22cm. [B60]

ROSEMAN, Ernst, 1901- .
The big race. (Das grosse Rennen.) Tr. E. Evand.
Cambridge, Mass.: Bentley, 1956. 88p. 19 x 28cm.
[LC62, IT9]

ROSENBERG, Arthur, 1889-1943.
Austria. Travel guide. Tr. F. J. G. Merley. Paris,
NY: Nagel, 1958. 342p. 16cm. [LC62]

ROSENBERGER, Erwin.
Herzl as I remember him. Tr. and abr. Louis J. Herman. NY: Herzl, 1959. 251p. 22cm. [LC62, IT12]

ROSMER, Ernst, pseud. (i.e. Bernstein, Elsa Porges,
1866- .)
King's children, a German fairy tale in 3 acts. By
Ernst Rosner (i.e. Rosmer pseud.) (Königskinder.)
NY: Rosenfield, n.d. 3 pts. TW. 27cm. [LC62]

ROSSBERG, Ehrhard A., jt. author. See Korta, Helmut E.
Teleprinter switching. By E--A--R-- and Helmut E.
Korta. (Fernschreib-Vermittlungstechnik.) Trs. Johannes
Thieme and Hans M. Seyringer. Princeton, NJ: Van
Nostrand, 1960. 351p. 24cm. [LC62, B60, IT13]

ROSSENFELD, Friedrich, 1902- . See Feld, Friedrich,
pseud.

ROSSMANITH, Gebhard.
(Salzburg, Stadt und Land. Ein Bildwerk.) Tr. Anon.
Fwd. Josef Klaus and Stanislaus Pacher. (Ger., Eng.,
Fr., and Italian.) Neuauflage. Innsbruck: Verlag der
Tiroler Graphik, 1956. 76p. 27cm. [LC62]

ROTH, Alfred, 1903- .
The new school. (Das neue Schulhaus.) Tr. Anon.
NY: Praeger, 1958. 279p. 26cm. [LC62]

Same. Zürich: Girsberger, 1957. 279p. 25cm.
[LC62]

ROTHAMMEL, Karl, jt. author. See Morgenroth, Otto.
The short-wave amateur's manual. Tr. Anon. Pocket
ed. Berlin: Verlag Sport und Technik, 1958. [LC62]

ROTHENBURG, Jerome Dennis, 1931- . Ed. and tr.
New young German poets. San Francisco: City Lights,

1959. 63p. 17cm. [LC62]

ROTHENBURG OVER THE TAUBER, WITH 40 COLOUR
PICTURES AND TOWN MAP.
(Rothenburg ob der Tauber.) Tr. Mary Ann Long.
Holstein, 1960. 18, 38p. 20cm. [LC62]

ROUBIER, Jean, 1896- .
Benelux: Holland, Belgium, Luxembourg. (Holland,
Belgien, Luxembourg.) Tr. Anon. 100 photos J--R--.
Text Joseph Delmelle. L: Thames, 1958. 96p. (24.5
cm.) [LC62, B58, IT11]

ROYCE, Hans. See Zimmerman, Erich, ed.
Germans against Hitler. July 20, 1944. Bonn: Berto-
Verlag, c1960. [LC62]

RUBEN, Walter.
Kalidasa. The human meaning of his works. (Kalidasa.
Die menschliche Bedeutung seiner Werke.) Tr. Joan
Becker. Berlin: Akademie-Verlag, 1957. 105p. [LC62,
IT10]

RUBINSTEIN, Akiba.
Chess masterpieces, 100 sel. games. Tr. Barnie F.
Winkelmann. NY: Dover, 1960. 192p. 21cm. [LC62,
IT13]

RUCK-PAUQUET, Gina.
Little Hedgehog. (Der kleine Igel.) Tr. Anon. Illus.
Marianne Richer. L: Constable; NY: Hastings House,
1959. 32p. 26cm. [LC62, B59, IT12]

RUDEL, Hans Ulrich.
Stuka pilot. (Trotzdem.) Tr. Lynton Hudson. Fwd.
Group Captain Douglas Bader. L: Transworld, 1957.
319p. (16.5cm.) [B57]

Same. NY: Ballantine, 1958. 239p. 18cm. [LC62,
IT11]

RÜBER, Johannes, 1928- .
Bach and the heavenly choir. (Die Heiligsprechung des
Johann Sebastian Bach.) Tr. Maurice Michael. Cleve-
land: World, 1956. 150p. 21cm. [LC62, IT10]

Same. L, NY: Daves, (Stamped Lon. ed.), 1956. 176p.

314

RÜBER, Johannes--
19cm. [LC62, B56, IT9]

RÜCHARDT, Eduard, 1888- .
Light, visible and invisible. Tr. Frank Gaynor. Wood-
thorpe, Nottingham: Hall; Ann Arbor: U. of Michigan
Pr., 1958. 201p. (3-201p.) (21.5cm.) 22cm. [LC62,
B58, IT11]

RÜSCHLIKON SWITZERLAND.
Baptist theological seminary. Introduction to theological-
study. Tr. Anon. Rüschlikon, 1960. 2v. in 1. [LC62]

RÜTTNER, Jacques Rudolf.
Silicosis in Switzerland, 1945-1960. (Die Silikose in der
Schweiz.) Tr. Anon. (Eng. and Ger.) Basel: Karger,
1960. 150p. [LC62]

RUGE, Friedrich.
The German navy story, 1939-1945. (Der Seekrieg 1939-
1945.) Tr. M. G. Saunders. Annapolis: U.S. Naval
Institute, 1957. 440p. 24cm. [LC62, IT10]

Sea warfare 1939-1945. A German viewpoint. (Der
Seekrieg 1939-1945.) Tr. M. G. Saunders. L: Cassell,
1957. 337p. 22cm. [LC62, B57]

RUGE, Gerd.
Pasternak, a pictorial biography. (Pasternak, eine Bild-
biographie.) Trs. Beryl and Joseph Avrach. L: Thames;
NY: McGraw, 1959. 143p. 24cm. [LC62, B59, IT12]

RUHMER, Eberhard.
Tura, paintings and drawings. Tr. Anon. L, NY:
Phaidon, dist. by Garden City Bks, 1958. 184p. 31cm.
[LC62, B58]

RULAND, Wilhelm, 1869-1927.
Legend of the Rhine, with illus. by celebrated artists.
Tr. Anon. Köln/Rhein: Hoursch, 195-. 289p. 20cm.
[LC62]

RUPERTI, Marga, 1918- . See Knaur, Käthe, 1915- .
Dogs of character. (Schöne Hunde.) Tr. Kenneth Kettle.
L: Macdonald, 1957. 111p. (25.5cm.) [LC62, B57]

RUTENBORN, Guenter, 1912- .
The sign of Jonah, a play in 9 scenes. Tr. George
White. NY: Nelson, 1960. 91p. 21cm. [LC62, IT13]

The word was God, book by book through the Book of
Books. Tr. Elmer E. Foelber. NY: Nelson, 1959.
228p. 22cm. [LC62, IT12]

RUTHERFORD, Mrs. Dorothea, 1890- .
Threshold. (Vor Tag.) Trs. Marie Budberg and Tania
Alexander. Little: Toronto, 1956. 313p. [LC56]

RYTZ, W. See Hans Schwarzenbach.

SAAZ, Johannes von (Jan Zatecky, supposed author) c1380-
c1414.
Death and the plowman or The Bohemian plowman, a dis-
putatious and consolatory dialogue about death from the
year 1400. (Der Ackermann aus Böhmen.) Tr. Ernest
N. Kirrmann. (From the modern Ger. ver. of Alois
Bernt.) Chapel Hill: U. of North Carolina Pr., 1958.
40p. 24cm. [LC62, IT11]

SAEBENS, Hans. Photo. See Meyer, Hanns.

SAILLANT, Louis.
Workers and unions in the fight against capitalist monopo-
lies, the responsibilities of the unions and the workers
towards the plan for total disarmament, the organisation
of peace and the development of economic and social progress, speech to the all-German workers conference,
Berlin, November, 1959. L: W. F. T. U., 1960. 40p.
(21. 5cm.) [B60]

SALTEN, Felix, pseud. (i. e. Saltzmann, Sigmund, 1869-
1945.)
Bambi. Tr. Anon. Illus. Girard Goodenow. Garden
City, NY: Junior Delux Ed., 1956. 190p. 22cm.
[LC62]

Bambi. Based on orig. story. Tr. Anon. L: Publicity;
(Great Golden Story Bks.), 1956. 44p. (27.5cm.) [B56]

Perri. (P---.) From the Walt Disney Motion Picture.
Text Roy E. Disney. Adpt. from Screen play W. Hibler
and R. Wright. NY: Simon, 1958. 78p. 26cm. [LC62]

SALTEN, Felix--
Same. L: Harrap, 1958. 80p. (25.5cm.) [B58]

Walt Disney's Perri and her friends, based on "Perri."
(Die jugend des Eichhörnchens Perri.) Adpt. Annie N.
Bedford. NY: Simon, 1956. unp. 27cm. [LC62]

Same. Adpt. Emily Brown. L: Adprint, 1958. 26p.
(32.5cm.) [B58]

SALTZMANN, Sigmund, 1869-1945. See Salten, Felix,
pseud.

SANDEN, Walter von, 1888- .
Ingo. The story of my otter. (Ingo. Die Geschichte
meines Fischotters.) Tr. D. I. Vesey. L: Museum,
1956. 109p. [LC62, IT9]

Same. NY: Longmans, 1959. 109p. 22cm. [LC62,
IT12]

SANDS, Donald B., ed. See Reynard the Fox.
The history of Reynard the Fox. Tr. and printed William
Caxton in 1481. Cambridge: Harvard U. Pr., 1960.
[LC62]

SANNWALD, Rolf, and Stohlers, Jacques.
Economic integration, theoretical assumptions and conse-
quences of European unification. (Wirtschaftliche Integra-
tion.) Tr. Herman F. Karreman. L: Oxford U. Pr.,
Princeton, NJ: U. Pr., 1959. 260p. (22.5cm.) 23cm.
[LC62, B60]

Same. Princeton, NJ: U. Pr., 1959. 276p. [IT12]

SARTORI and BERGER, Kiel.
With sail, steam, and diesel, from the hundred years of
S-- and B--, Kiel, shipowners and shipmates. Compiled
Studio Kraft Sachisthal. Tr. Anon. Kiel, 1958. 171p.
19 x 27cm. [LC62, IT10]

SARTRE, Jean-Paul. See Streller, Justus, 1892- .

SAUER, Erich.
The triumph of the crucified, a survey of historical revelation in the New Testament. (Der Triumph des Gek-
reuzigten.) Tr. G. H. Lang. Fwd. A. Rendle Short.

Grand Rapids, Mich.: Eerdmans, 1957. 207p. 23cm.
[LC62]

SAUER, Friedrich.
The "Vierka" wine book. Eng. ver. Humphrey Wake-
field. Liverpool: Leigh-Williams, 1960. 2, 32p.
(18cm.) [B60]

SAUERBRUCH, Ferdinand.
A surgeon's life. Trs. Fernand G. Renier and Anne
Cliff. L: Hamilton, 1957. 248p. (18cm.) [B57]

SCHACHNOWITZ, Selig.
The light from the west. (Orig. pub. in Der Israelit.)
Tr. Joseph Leftwich. L: Keren Hatorah Committee,
1958. 270p. (18.5cm.) 19cm. [LC62, B58, IT11]

SCHACHT, Hjalmar Horace Greeley, 1844- .
Confessions of the old wizard. (76 Jahre meines Lebens.)
Tr. Diana Pyke. Boston: Houghton, 1956. 484p. 22
cm. [LC62, IT9]

SCHÄDLER, Alfred, 1927- .
(Allgäu.) Tr. Anon. Introd. Alfred Weitnauer. Photo.
L. Aufsberg. (Ger., Eng., and Fr.) Bayreuth:
Schwarz, 195-. 4-42p. 17cm. [LC62]

SCHAEFER, Willfried.
The unions and productivity, practical experience and
training in Western Germany. Paris: organization of
European Economic Cooperation, European Productivity
Agency Trade Union Research and Information Service,
1956. 38p. [LC62]

SCHAFFRAN, Emerich, 1883- .
Dictionary of European art. (Taschen-Lexikon der Kunst.)
Tr. Kenneth J. Northcott. NY: Philosophical Lib., 1958.
283p. 19cm. [LC62]

Same. L: Owen, 1959. 283p. 19cm. [LC62, B59,
IT12]

SCHAPER, Edzard Hellmuth, 1908- .
The dancing bear. (Das Tier.) Tr. Norman Denny. L:
Bodley Head, 1960. 244p. (19cm.) 20cm. [LC62,
B60]

SCHAPER, Edzard Hellmuth--
Star over the frontier. (Stern über der Grenze.) Trs.
Isabel and Florence McHugh. Illus. Richard Seewald.
Baltimore, Helicon, 1960. 64p. 21cm. [LC62, IT13]

SCHARP, Heinrich, 1899- .
How the Catholic Church is governed. (Wie die Kirche
regiert wird.) From 4th ed. Tr. Anneliese Derrick.
NY, Freiburg: Herder, 1960. 167p. 19cm. [LC62,
IT13]

Same. Freiburg: Herder; Edinburgh, L: Nelson,
1960. 168p. (19cm.) [B60]

SCHAUB, Franz.
The great peace of Krassnikowa, a novel. (Der grosse
Friede von Krassnikowa.) Tr. Kenneth T. Duffield. L:
Holburn, 1958. 3-177p. 19cm. [LC62]

Same. 1960. [B60]

SCHEIBERT, Justus, 1831-1903.
Seven months in the rebel states during the North American War, 1863. (Sieben Monate in den Rebellenstaaten
während des nordamerikanischen Krieges, 1863.) Tr.
Joseph C. Hayes. Tuscaloosa, Alabama: Confederate,
1958. 166p. 22cm. [LC62, IT11]

SCHELER, Max Ferdinand, 1874-1928.
On the eternal in man. (Vom Ewigen in Menschen.) Tr.
Bernard Noble. Eds. John McIntyre and Ian T. Ramsey.
L: SCM, 1960. 480p. 23cm. [LC62, B60]

Philosophical perspectives. (Philosophische Weltanschauung.) Tr. Oscar A. Haac. Boston: Beacon, 1958.
144p. 22cm. [LC62, IT11]

SCHELLENBERG, Walter, 1910-1952.
Hitler's secret service. (1st ed. abr. from the Labyrinth,
Memoiren.) Ed. and tr. Louis Hagen. NY: Pyramid,
1958. 222p. 20cm. [LC62, IT9]

The Labyrinth, memoirs. Tr. L. Hagen. NY: Harper,
1956. 423p. 22cm. [LC62]

The Schellenberg memoirs. Tr. (from ms.) Louis
Hagen. Introd. Alan Bullock. L: Deutsch, 1956. 479p.

(22cm.) [LC62, B56, IT9]

SCHELLING, Friedrich Wilhelm Joseph von, 1775-1854.
The ages of the world. Tr., introd. and notes Freder-
ich de Wolfe Bolman, Jr. Ann Arbor, Mich., 1960.
251p. 22cm. [LC62]

SCHENK, Erich, 1902- .
Mozart and his times. (W. A. Mozart, eine Biographie.)
Trs. Richard and Clara Winston. NY: Knopf, 1959.
492p. 25cm. [LC62, IT12]

Same. L: Secker, 1960. 452p. (25.5cm.) [LC62,
B60, IT12]

SCHENK, Gustav, 1905 .
The book of poisons. (Das Buch der Gifte.) Tr. Michael
Bullock. L: Weidenfeld, 1956. 235p. (22.5cm.)
[LC62, B56, IT9]

SCHENK, Robert, jt. ed. See Schmidt, George, 1896- .
ed.
Form in art and nature. (Kunst und Naturform.) Basel,
Basilius, 1960. 129p. 20cm. [LC62]

SCHENKENDORF, Werner.
The charm of Lake Constance. Tr. Edith A. Gorty.
Lindau: Thorbecke; L: Tiranti, 1960. 123p. (24cm.)
[B60]

SCHERCHEN, Hermann, 1891- .
Handbook of conducting. Tr. M. D. Calvocoressi. L:
Oxford U. Pr., 1956. 243p. 22 x 17cm. [LC62]

Same. L, NY: Oxford U. Pr., 1956. c1933. 342p.
20cm. [LC62]

SCHIDER, Fritz, 1846-1907
An atlas of anatomy for artists. Tr. Bernard Wolf.
Rev. M. Auerbach. Bibliography Adolf Placzek. NY:
Dover, 1957. v. 29cm. [LC62]

SCHIEDER, Theodor, ed. See documents on the expulsion
of the Germans from Eastern-Central-Europe.

SCHIEL, Jacob Heinrich Wilhelm, 1813- .
Journey through the Rocky Mountains and the Humboldt

SCHIEL, Jacob Heinrich Wilhelm--
Mountains to the Pacific Ocean. (Reise durch die Felsengebirge und die Humboldtgebirge nach dem Stillen Ozean.)
Tr. Thomas N. Bonner. Norman: U. of Oklahoma Pr.,
1959. 114p. 24cm. [LC62, IT12]

The land between. Dr. James Schiel's account of the
Gunnison-Beckwith Expedition into the West, 1853-1854.
(Reise durch die Felsengebirge und die Humboldtgebirge
nach dem Stillen Ocean.) Eds., annot., and trs. Frederick W. Bachmann and William Swilling Wallace. Los
Angeles: Westernlore (Great West and Indian series, 9.)
1957. 162p. 21cm. [LC62]

SCHIELE, Egon, 1890-1918. See Benesch, Otto.
Egon Schiele as a draughtsman by Otto Benesch. Tr.
Anon. Vienna: State Printing Office of Austria, 195-.
13p. 34cm. [LC62]

SCHIFFERS, Heinrich, 1901- .
The quest for Africa, 2000 years of exploration. (Wilder
Erdteil Afrika.) Tr. Diana Pyke. L: Odhams, 1957.
352p. 23cm. [LC62, B57, IT10]

Same. NY: Putnam, 1958. 352p. 22cm. [LC62, IT
10]

SCHIKANEDER, Emanuel and GIESECKE, Carl Ludwig.
The magic flute. (Die Zauberflöte.) Eng. ver. Auden
and Chester Kallman. NY: Random House, 1956. 108p.
24cm. [LC62, IT9]

Same. L: Faber, 1957. 120p. (22.5cm.) 23cm.
[LC62, B57]

Libretto for the magic flute. Trs. Ruth and Thomas
Martin. NY: Metropolitan, 1958. 228p. [LC62]

SCHILDBERGER, Friedrich. See Diesel, Eugen, 1889- .
jt. authors.

SCHILDBÜRGER. See The Simpletons.

SCHILDER, Paul, 1886-1940. And Kauders, Otto.
The nature of hypnosis. (Über das Wesen der Hypnose.)
Tr. Gerda Corvin. L: Bailey, 1956. 204p. (22.5cm.)
[B56]

Same. NY: International U. Pr., 1956. 204p. 23cm. [LC62, IT9]

SCHILLER, Johann Christoph Friedrich von, 1759-1805.
Don Carlos, infante of Spain, a drama in 5 acts. (D--
C--.) Tr. Charles E. Passage. NY: Ungar, 1959.
216p. 21cm. [LC62, IT12]

Friedrich Schiller, an anthology for our time. In new
Eng. tr. and orig. Ger. by Jane Bannard Greene,
Charles E. Passage, and Alexander Gode von Aesch.
Account of his life and work, Frederick Ungar. NY:
Unger, c1959. 450p. 22cm. [LC62, IT13]

The maiden from Orleans. A romantic tragedy. (Die
Jungfrau von Orleans.) Tr. John T. Krumpelmann.
Chapel Hill: U. of North Carolina Pr., 1959. 130p.
23cm. [LC62, IT12]

Mary Stuart. (Maria Stuart.) Tr. Guenther Reinhart.
i.e. Reinhardt., Brooklyn: Barron's, 1958. 116p.
21cm. [LC62]

Mary Stuart. (Derived from Schiller's Maria Stuart) A
play in 6 scenes. Authors Jean Stock Goldstone and
John Reich. NY: Dramatists Play Service, Inc., 1958.
86p. 20cm. [LC62]

Mary Stuart. Freely tr. and adpt. Stephen Spender.
Pref. Peter Wood. L: Faber, 1959. 3-101p. 22cm.
(22.5cm.) [LC62, B59, IT12]

Mary Stuart. A tragedy. A new unabr. tr. with introd.
Sophie Wilkins, Great Neck, NY: Barron's ed. series.
1959. 166p. 19cm. [LC62, IT13]

Wallenstein. A historical drama in 3 pts. (W--.) Tr.
Charles E. Passage. L: Owen, 1958. 275p. (21.5
cm.) 23cm. [LC62, B59, IT11]

Same. NY: Ungar, 1958. 275p. 21cm. [LC62, IT11]

Wallenstein. (W--.) Rev. ed. Tr. Charles E. Passage. NY: Ungar, 1960. 275p. 21cm. [LC62]

SCHILLING, Rosy.
Astronomical medical calendar. Tr. Anon. Lexington:

SCHILLING, Rosy--
U. of Kentucky, 1958. 6p. 28cm. [LC62]

Astronomical medical calendar, studio of Diebolt Lauber
at Hagenau, 15th century, c1430-50. Containing consid-
erable folklore material. Tr. Anon. Chillicothe, Ohio,
Ohio Valley Folk Research Project, The Ross County
Historical Society, 1958. 61. [LC62]

SCHILLING, Wilfred.
The fear makers. Tr. Oliver Coburn. (1st American
ed.) Garden City, NY: Doubleday, 1960. 312p. 22cm.
[LC62, IT13]

The fear makers, an anonymous novel. Tr. Oliver Coburn. L: Joseph, 1959. 296p. 21cm. [LC62]

SCHILPP, Paul Arthur, 1897- , ed.
Albert Einstein, philosopher-scientist. Tr. Anon. 1st
Harper Torchbooks Ed. NY: Harper, 1959. 2v. 781p.
21cm. [LC62]

Same. 2nd ed. L: Hamilton, 1959. 2v. (20.5cm.)
[B60]

Kant's pre-critical ethics. Fwd. H. J. Paton. Tr. Anon.
2nd ed. Evanston, Ill.: Northwestern U. Pr., 1960.
199p. 24cm. [LC62]

The philosophy of Ernst Cassirer. Contains Spirit and
life in contemporary philosophy. (Geist und leben in der
philosophy der gegenwart.) Trs. Robert Walter Bretall
and P--A--S--. Ed. P--A--S--. NY: Tudor, 1958.
936p. 25cm. [LC62]

The philosophy of Karl Jaspers. Tr. Anon. NY: Tudor;
L: Cambridge U. Pr., 1957. 918p. (24.5cm.) 25cm.
[LC62, B58, IT10]

SCHIMPER, Andreas Fran Wilhelm, 1856-1901.
Plant-geography upon a physiological basis. (Historiae
naturalis classica.) Tr. William R. Fisher. Rev. and
Ed. Percy Groom and Isaac Bayley Balfour. Oxford:
Clarendon; Weinheim/Bergstr.: Englemann; Codicote/
Herts.: Wheldon, 1960. 839p. 25cm. [LC62]

SCHINDLER, Manfred.
(Freude. Frohsinn, glückliche menschen.) Tr. Anon.
Berlin, Verlag Tribüne, 1957. unp. 29cm. (Ger.,
Russ., Eng., and Fr.) [LC62]

SCHINDLER, Otto, 1906- .
Freshwater fishes. (Unsere süsswasserfische.) Tr. and
Ed. P. A. Orkin. L, NY: Thames, 1957. 243p. 20cm.
(25.5cm.) [LC62, B57, IT10]

SCHINDLMAYR, Adalbert, 1912- .
Useful plants. (Welche nutzpflanze ist das.) Tr. and
Ed. Allan A. Jackson and Jean P. Jackson. L, NY:
Thames, 1957. 127p. (20.5cm.) 21cm. [LC62, B57,
IT10]

SCHIRACH, Henriette von.
The price of glory. Tr. and adpt. Willi Frischauer. L:
Muller, 1960. 9-222p. 22cm. (22.5cm.) [LC62, B60,
IT14]

SCHIRMBECK, Heinrich.
Blinding light. (Ärgert dich dein rechtes auge.) Tr.
Norman Denny. L: Collins, 1960. 447p. 22cm. [LC
62, B60]

SCHLAMM, William Siegmund.
Germany and the East-West crisis. The decisive chal-
lenge to American policy. (Deutschland.) Tr. Anon. NY:
McKay, 1959. 237p. [LC62, IT12]

SCHLATTER, Adolf, 1852-1938.
The church in the New Testament period. (Die geschichte
der ersten Christenheit.) Tr. Paul P. Levertoff. NY:
Macmillan, 1956. 347p. [IT9]

SCHLEGEL, A. W.
Selections in Loomis, C. G. Prose. 1960.

SCHLEGEL, (Carl Wilhelm) Friedrich (von).
Literary notebooks, 1797-1801. Tr. Anon. Ed., introd.
and commentary Hans Eichner. L: Athlone, 1957. 7,
342p. (22.5cm.) [B57]

Selections in Loomis, C. G. Prose. 1960.

SCHLEIERMACHER, F. E. D.
On religion, speeches to its cultured despisers. Tr. J.
Oman. NY: Harper, 1958. 287p. 21cm. [LC62, IT11]

SCHLINK, Edmund, 1903.
The victor speaks. (Der erhöhte spricht.) Tr. Paul F.
Koehneke. St. Louis: Concordia, 1958. 126p. 20cm.
[LC62]

SCHMALENBACH, Eugen, 1873-1955.
Dynamic accounting. (Dynamische bilanz.) Trs. G. W.
Murphy and Kenneth S. Most. L: Gee, 1959. 222p.
(22.5cm.) [LC62, B59]

Same. 212p. [IT12]

SCHMALENBACH, Werner, 1917- .
African art. Tr. Glyn T. Hughes. NY: T. Yoseloff,
1960. 175p. 32cm. [LC62]

SCHMELLER, Alfred.
Cubism. (Kubismus.) Tr. Hilde Spiel. L: Methuen,
1956. 62p. (63p.) (18.5cm.) 19cm. [LC57, B56, IT9]

Same. NY: Crown, 1957. 62p. 19cm. [LC62]

Same. 1959. [IT12]

Surrealism. Tr. Hilde Spiel. L: Methuen, 1956.
(62p.) 63p. (18.5cm.) [LC62, B56, IT9]

Same. NY: Crown, 1957. 62p. 19cm. [LC62]

SCHMELTZER, Kurt.
The axe of bronze, a story of Stonehenge. Tr. Anon.
Illus. M. A. Charlton. L: Constable, 1958. 143p.
(21cm.) [LC62, B58, IT11]

Same. NY: Sterling, 1958. 142p. 21cm. [LC62]

The raft. Tr. Katya Sheppard. Illus. Adam Turyn. L:
Constable, 1960. 160p. (20.5cm.) [B60]

SCHMID, Carlo, co-author. See Brandt, Leo.

SCHMID, (Johann) Christoph von.
The basket of flowers. (Das blumenkörbchen.) Tr.

Anon. L: Blackie, 1959. 192p. (19cm.) [B59]

SCHMID, Karl, 1896- .
The place of the intellectual in the community. Address
delivered on the eve of the Hamburg state elections,
Nov., 1957. Bonn: Social Democratic Party of Germany,
1957. 16p. 21cm. [LC62, IT10]

SCHMID, Karl, 1896- . See the second industrial revolution. Bonn, 1956.

SCHMID, Martin, 1889- .
The Grisons. (Graubünden.) Tr. Anon. (Ger., Eng.,
and Dutch.) Zürich: Rentsch, 1960. 22p. 29cm.
[LC62, IT13]

SCHMID, Peter, 1916- .
Beggars on golden stools. Report on Latin America.
(Nachbarn des Himmels.) Tr. Mervyn Savill. NY:
Praeger, 1956. 327p. 23cm. [LC62, IT9]

Same. . . . A journey through Latin America. L:
Weidenfeld, 1956. 327p. (22.5cm.) [LC62, B56]

In the shadow of the dragon. (Paradies im Drachen-
schlund.) Tr. Mervyn Savill. L: Weidenfeld, 1957.
288p. (22.5cm.) 23cm. [LC62, B57]

The new face of China. (China, Reich der neuen Mitte.)
Tr. Ewald Osers. L: Harrap, 1958. 167p. (21.5cm.)
22cm. [LC62, B58]

Same. NY: Pitman, 1959. 167p. 22cm. [LC62, IT12,
13]

SCHMIDT, Dietmar.
Pastor Niemöller. (Martin Niemöller.) Tr. Lawrence
Wilson. NY: Doubleday, 1959. 224p. 22cm. [LC62,
IT12]

Same. L: Odhams. 224p. 23cm. [LC62, IT12]

SCHMIDT, Georg, 1896- .
15 drawings by German and Swiss masters of the 15th
and 16th centuries. Tr. Philip O. Troutman. Published
by Ciba on the 75th anniversary of their foundation and
in memory of their gift to the print room of the Öffent-

SCHMIDT, Georg--
liche Kunstsammlung, Basle. Basle: Ciba, 1959. 54p.
38cm. [LC62, IT13]

Form in art and nature. (Kunst und Naturform.) Tr.
Anon. Introd. Adolf Portmann. (Ger., Eng., and Fr.)
Basel: Basilius, 1960. 129p. 20cm. [LC62]

Franz Marc. Tr. John Turnbull. Milan: Uffici, 1960.
30p. 35cm. [LC62]

SCHMIDT, George, 1896- . Ed. See Schenk, Robert,
jt. ed.

SCHMIDT, Helmut, 1918- .
Military disengagement in Central Europe, a speech.
Nov. 5, 1959. Tr. E. W. Schnitzer. Santa Monica, Calif.
Rand Corp. 1960. 15p. 29cm. [LC62]

SCHMIDT, Karl Ludwig, et al.
Basileia. By K--L--S--, H. Kleinknecht, K. G. Kuhn,
and Gerhard von Rad. (At head of title--Bible key words
from Gerhard Kittel's Theologisches Wörterbuch zum
Neuen Testament.) Tr. H. P. Kingdon. L: Black, 1957.
61p. (20.5cm.) 21cm. [LC62, B58]

SCHMIDT, Martin.
The young Wesley. Tr. L. A. Fletcher. L: Epworth,
1958. 48p. (18.5cm.) [LC62, B58, IT11]

SCHMIDT-GLASSNER, Helga. See Baum, Julius, 1882- .
German Cathedrals.

SCHMIEDER, Ludwig, 1884- .
(Fuehrer durch Heidelberg und Umgebung.) Rev. ed. Tr.
Anon. (Ger., Eng., and Fr.) Heidelberg, J. Hörning,
1958. 128p. 17cm. [LC62]

SCHMIRGER, Gertrud, 1900- . See Ellert, Gerhart, pseud.

SCHMULLER, Aaron.
Crossing the borderland. Poems, prose poems, and poetical translations. Tr. Anon. Pref. Marjorie Dippel
Sharp. Introd. Alfred Dorn. L: Villiers, 1959. 88p.
22cm. [LC62]

SCHNABEL, Ernst, 1913- .
Anne Frank, a portrait in courage. (Anne Frank, Spur eines Kindes.) Trs. Richard and Clara Winston. NY: Harcourt, 1958. 192p. 22cm. [LC62, IT11]

The footsteps of Anne Frank. (Anne Frank, Spur eines Kindes.) Trs. Richard and Clara Winston. L, NY: Longmans, 1959. 160p. (20.5cm.) 21cm. [LC62, B59, IT12]

The voyage home. (Der sechste Gesang.) Tr. Denver Lindley. 1st ed. NY: Harcourt, 1958. 184p. 21cm. [LC62, IT11]

Same. L: Gollancz, 1958. 184p. (20.5cm.) [B58, IT11]

SCHNEIDER, Bruno F.
John Rood's sculpture. Trs. Desmond and Louise Clayton. Minneapolis: U. of Minn. Pr., 1958. 112p. 28 cm. [LC62, IT11]

Renoir. Trs. Desmond and Camille Clayton. NY: Crown, 1958. 95p. 29cm. [LC62, IT11]

SCHNEIDER, Johannes, 1895- .
Baptism and church in the New Testament. Tr. Ernest A. Payne. L: Carey, 1957. 53p. (18.5cm.) 19cm. [LC62, B57]

The letter to the Hebrews. Tr. William A. Mueller. Grand Rapids: Eerdmans, 1957. 139p. 23cm. [LC62]

SCHNEIDER, Kurt, 1887- .
Clinical psychopathology. (Beiträge zur Psychiatrie.) Tr. M. W. Hamilton. NY: Grune, 1959. 173p. 23cm. [LC62, IT13]

Psychopathic personalities. (Die psychopathischen Persönlichkeiten.) Tr. M. W. Hamilton. Fwd. E. W. Anderson. L: Cassell, 1958. 163p. (18.5cm.) 19cm. [LC62, B58, IT11]

Same. Springfield, Ill.: Thomas, 1958. 163p. 19cm. [LC62]

SCHNEIDER, Paul, 1867-1939.
The pastor of Buchenwald. A free tr. of the story told
by his widow, with many quotations from his diary and
letters. (Der Prediger von Buchenwald. Das Martyrium
Paul Schneiders.) Tr. Edwin Hauton Robertson. NY:
Macmillan, 1956. 128p. [IT9]

Same. L: SCM, 1956. 128p. 19cm. [LC62, B56,
IT9]

SCHNEIDER, Reinhold, 1903- .
Holy women. (Der Bilderkreis.) Adpt. Annelise Derrick.
Freiburg im Breisgau: Herder, 1958. 19p. 19cm.
[LC62]

Saint John. Adpt. Annelise Derrick. Freiburg: Herder,
1957. 17p. 19cm. [LC62]

Same. L: Interbook, 1957. 19p. [B57]

SCHNEIDERFRANKEN, Joseph Anton, 1876-1943.
The book of happiness by Bo Yin Ra (pseud.) Tr. Anon.
NY: William-Frederick, 1960. 47p. 23cm. [LC62]

SCHNEIDERS, Toni and others. Photog. See Liehl, Ekkehard.
Picturesque Black forest. (Schwarzwald.) Trs. Hans-
georg Reidl and Linda Schein. Photog. Toni Schneiders
and others. Text Robert Feger and Ekkehard Liehl.
Lindau: Thorbecke; L: Tiranti, 1960. 117p. (24cm.)
[B60]

SCHNITZLER, Arthur, 1862-1931.
Casanova's homecoming. (Casanovas Heimfahrt.) Trs.
Maurice Eden and Cedar Paul. L: World Distributors,
1959. 128p. (17cm.) [B59, IT12]

La ronde. (Reigen.) Trs. Frank and Jaqueline Marcus.
Illus. Philip Gough. L: Harborough, 1959. 124p.
(18cm.) [B59, IT12]

The lonely way. Play in five acts. Tr. Julian Leigh.
NY: Rialto, n.d. 1v. TW. 29cm. [LC62]

The lonely way. Play in five acts. Acting version
Philip Moeller. NY: Rialto, n.d. 34, 44, 281. TW.
29cm. [LC62]

SCHNITZLER, Theodor.
The mass in meditation. Tr. Rudolph Kraus. St. Louis:
Herder, 1959. 1v. 21cm. [LC62, IT12]

Same. V2. 137p. [IT 13]

Same. Vol. 2. (Die Messe in der Betrachtung.) St.
Louis, L: Herder, 1960. 317p. (21cm.) [B60]

SCHÖNBERGER, Arno, 1915- . and Soehner, Haldor.
The age of Rococo. (Die Welt der Rokoko.) Trs. Margaret D. Senft-Howie and Brian Sewell. Munich: Rinn,
1958. 322p. 22cm. [LC62]

Same. Tr. Daphne Woodward. L: Thames, 1960.
(392p.) 393p. 35cm. (45cm.) [LC62, B60, IT13]

The Rococo age. Art and civilization of the 18th c.
(Die Welt der Rokoko.) Tr. Daphne Woodward. Collab-
orator Theodor Mueller. NY: McGraw, 1960. 393p.
35cm. [LC62, IT13]

SCHOENBERNER, Franz, 1892- . See Nibelungenlied.
The Nibelungenlied. Tr. Margaret Armour. NY: J. E.
Zonen; Haarlem: Holland, 1960. [LC62]

SCHOENEN, Paul.
Belgium. (Belgien.) Tr. Salvator Altanasio. Baltimore:
Helicon, 1959. 115p. 18cm. [LC62, IT12]

SCHÖNFELDT, Christl, ed.
The Vienna philharmonic orchestra. Documents from the
archives of the Vienna philharmonic orchestra. Tr.
Anon. Wien: Bergland, 1957. 112p. 18cm. [LC62]

SCHOLZ, Arno, 1904- . With Meysel, Theodor F.
Israel, land of hope. A report in pictures. Tr. Patrick Lynch. Berlin-Grunewald: Arani; NY: Heinman,
1959. 54p. 22 x 23cm. [LC62]

SCHOLZ, Arno, 1904- .
Outpost Berlin. (Insel Berlin.) Designed Paul Fischer.
Tr. Patrick Lynch. Berlin-Grunewald: Arani, 1960.
101p. [LC62]

SCHOLZ, Hans.
Through the night. (Am grünen Strand der Spree.) Tr.

SCHOLZ, Hans--
Elisabeth Abbot. NY: Crowell, 1959. 350p. 22cm.
[LC62, IT12]

SCHOPENHAUER, Arthur, 1788-1860.
The art of literature. Tr. T. Bailey Saunders. Ann
Arbor: U. of Mich. Pr., 1960. 114p. 21cm. [LC62]

Essay on the freedom of the will. (Über die Freiheit des
menschlichen Willens.) Tr. Konstantin Kolenda. NY:
Liberal Arts, 1960. 103p. 21cm. [LC62, IT13]

On human nature. Essays partly posthumous, in ethics
and politics. Sel. and Tr. Thomas Bailey Saunders. L:
Allen; NY: Barnes, 1957. 132p. 19cm. [LC62]

The philosophy of Schopenhauer. Tr. I. Edman. NY:
Modern Libr., 1956. 376p. [LC62]

Selections. Tr. Anon. Ed. D. H. Parker. NY: Scribner, 1956. 447p. [LC62]

Same. NY: Scribner, 1960. 447p. [IT13]

The world as will and idea. Trs. R. B. Haldane and J.
Kemp. 2nd ed. L: Routledge, 1957. 3v. 21cm.
[LC62]

The world as will and representation. (Die Welt als Wille
und Vorstellung.) Tr. E. F. J. Payne. Indian Hills,
Colo.: Falcon's Wing, 1958. 2v. 22cm. [LC62, IT11]

SCHOTT, Rudolf, 1891- .
Florentine painting. (Meisterwerke der florentinischen
Malerei.) Tr. M. Heron. L: Thames, 1959. 103p.
(23.5cm.) 24cm. [LC62, B59, IT12]

SCHOTT, Rolf. See Schott, Rudolf.

SCHOTT, Siegfried, 1897- .
Wall scenes from the mortuary chapel of the Mayor
Paser at Medinet Habu. Tr. Elizabeth B. Hauser. Chi-
cago: U. of Chicago Pr., 1957. 21p. 30cm. [LC62]

Same. L: Cambridge U. Pr.; Chicago: Chicago U.
Pr., 1957. 21p. (30cm.) [B58]

SCHRAMM, Friedrich Karl.
The Bundeshaus. The work of the German Bundestag and
Bundesrat. Tr. Anon. Fwd. Eugen Gerstenmaier. 4th
ed. Bonn: Beinhauer, 1958. 32p. 20cm. [LC62]

SCHRAMM, Wilbur (Lang), compiler.
One day in the world's press, fourteen great newspapers
on a day of crisis, Nov. 2, 1956. Tr. Anon. Facsimile
Reproductions. Ed., introd. and commentary Wilbur
Schramm. Stanford, Calif.: Stanford U. Pr.; L: Ox-
ford U. Pr., 1959. 138p. (45cm.) [B60]

SCHRAMM, Wilhelm, Ritter von, 1898- .
Conspiracy among Generals. (Der 20. Juli in Paris.)
Tr. R. T. Clark. L: Allen, 1956. 215p. (216p.)
(22.5cm.) 23cm. [LC62, B56, IT9]

Same. NY: Scribner, 1957. c1956. 215p. 23cm.
[LC62, IT9, 10]

Same. L: Spencer, 1959. 157p. (18cm.) [B60, IT13]

SCHREIBER, Hermann, 1920- , and SCHREIBER, Georg,
1922- .
Vanished cities. (Versunkene Städte.) Trs. Richard and
Clara Winston. NY: Knopf, 1957. 344p. 22cm. [LC
62, IT10]

Same. L: Weidenfeld, 1958. 344p. (22.5cm.) [B58,
IT11]

SCHREIER, Otto, 1901-1929. and Sperner, Emanuel 1905- .
Introduction to modern algebra and matrix theory. (Einführung in die analytische Geometrie und Algebra.) Trs.
Martin Davis and Melvin Hausner. NY: Chelsea, 1959.
378p. 24cm. [LC62, IT13]

SCHRENCK VON NOTZING, Albert Philibert Franz Freiherr
von, 1862- .
The use of hypnosis in psychopathia sexualis. (Die Sug-
gestionstherapie bei krankhaften Erscheinungen des Ge-
schlechtssinnes.) Tr. Charles Gilbert Chaddock. NY:
Institute for Research in Hypnosis, 1956. 320p. 25cm.
[LC62, IT9]

SCHRÖDINGER, Erwin, 1887- .
Science theory and man. Originally published as Science

SCHRÖDINGER, Erwin--
and the human temperament. Trs. James Murphy and
W.H. Johnston. NY: Dover, 1957. 223p. 21cm. [LC
62]

Same. L: Allen, 1958. 27-223p. 20cm. (20.5cm.)
[LC62, B58, IT11]

SCHRÖTER, C. See Schröter, Ludwig.

SCHRÖTER, Heinz.
Stalingrad. (Stalingrad . . . bis zur letzten Patrone.)
Tr. C. Fitzgerald. L: Joseph, 1958. 263p. (22.5cm.)
23cm. [LC62, B58, IT11]

Same. NY: Dutton, 1958. 263p. 21cm. [LC62, IT12]

Same. L: Pan, 1960. 316p. (317p.) (18cm.) [LC62,
B60]

SCHRÖTER, Ludwig.
Alpen-Flora. (Taschenflora des Alpenwanderers.) Text
C. Schröter. Photo. L. Schröter. (Ger., Fr., and
Eng.) Zürich: Raustein, 1956. 52p. 21cm. [LC62]

SCHUBERT, Kurt, 1923- .
The Dead sea community, its origin and teachings. (Die
Geminde vom Toten Meer.) Tr. John W. Doberstein.
NY: Harper, 1959. 178p. 22cm. [LC62, IT12]

Same. L: Block, 1959. (20.5cm.) 21cm. [LC62,
B59, IT12]

Israel, state of hope. Tr. Heinz Messinger. Photos.
Rolf Vogel. Stuttgart: Schwabenverlag, 1960. c1957.
87p. 29cm. [LC62]

SCHÜCKING, Levin Ludwig, 1878- .
Character problems in Shakespeare's plays. A guide to
the better understanding of the dramatist. Tr. Anon.
Gloucester, Mass.: Smith, 1959. 269p. 21cm. [LC62]

SCHÜLLER, Sepp.
Forgers, dealers, experts, adventures in the twilight of
art forgers. (Fälscher, Händler, und Experten. Das
zwielichtige Abenteuer der Kunstfälschungen.) Tr. James
Cleugh. L: Barker, 1960. 200p. (22.5cm.) 23cm.

[LC62, B60]

Forgers, dealers, experts, strange chapters in the history of art. (Fälscher, Händler und Experten. Das zwielichtige Abenteuer der Kunstfälschungen.) Tr. James Cleugh. NY: Putnam, 1960. 200p. 23cm. [LC62, IT13]

Rome. Tr. Lawrence Atkinson. Baltimore: Helicon, 1958. 128p. 17cm. [LC62, IT11]

SCHULENBURG, Ernst von, 1849-1907.
Sandusky then and now. (Sandusky einst und jetzt.) Trs. Marion Cleaveland Lange and Norbert A. Lange. Cleveland: Western Reserve Hist. Soc., 1959. 325p. 22cm. [LC62, IT13]

SCHULER, Josef Egon, ed. See Franz Bauer.
Interiors for contemporary living. An international survey in color. (Das schöne Zuhause.) Tr. Anon. Introd. Cathrin Seifert. Text Franz Bauer. NY: Architectural, 1960. 204p. 27cm. [LC62, IT14]

SCHULLER, Victor.
The sky ablaze. (Mit Eichenlaub und Schwertern ging eine welt Zugrunde.) Tr. Mervyn Savill. L: Kimber, 1958. 256p. (20.5cm.) [B58, IT11]

SCHULTHESS, Emil.
Africa. (Afrika.) Tr. Anon. NY: Simon, 1959. 54p. 33cm. [LC62]

Same. L: Collins, 1960. 1v. 33cm. [LC62]

SCHULTHESS, Emil, et al.
Antarctica. A photographic survey. Tr. Peter Gorge. NY: Simon, 1960. 1v. 22 x 36cm. [LC62, IT13]

SCHULTZ, Johannes Heinrich, 1884- . and Luthe, Wolfgang.
Autogenic training, a psychophysiologic approach in psychotherapy. By Johannes H. Schultz and Wolfgang Luthe. NY: Grune, 1959. 289p. 24cm. [LC62]

SCHULZ, Adolf John, 1883-1956.
Studies in philosophy. Tr. Anon. (Ger. and Eng.) Adelaide, Australia: Griffin, 1960. 310p. 22cm. [LC62]

334

SCHULZ, Guenther, Torsten, 1909- .
Sailing round Cape Horn. (Unter Segeln rund um Kap
Horn.) Tr. Anon. (Ger., Dan., and Eng.) Hamburg:
Dulk, 1956. 225p. [IT9]

SCHUMANN, Robert Alexander, 1810-1856.
On music and musicians. (Gesammelte Schriften über
Musik und Musiker.) Tr. Paul Rosenfeld. Ed. Konrad
Wolff. L: Dobson, 1956. 274p. 24cm. [LC62]

SCHUSTER, Alfred B.
The art of two worlds, studies in pre-Columbian and
European cultures. Tr. Anon. Berlin: Gebr. Mann,
1958. 188p. 26cm. [LC62]

Same. NY: Praeger, 1959. 188p. 26cm. [LC62]

SCHWAB, Hermann.
Jewish rural communities in Germany. Tr. Anon. L:
Cooper, 1957. 93p. (22.5cm.) 23cm. [LC62, B57]

SCHWABACHER, Joseph.
The popular Alsatian. Tr. Anon. 5th ed. reprinted and
rev. L: Popular Dogs, 1958. 245p. 22cm. [LC62]

SCHWABEDISSEN, Walter.
The Russian air force in the eyes of German commanders.
Trs. Helmut Heitmann and George E. Blau. n.p. USAF
Historical Division, Research Studies Institute, Air U.,
1960. 434p. 27cm. [LC62]

SCHWAHN, Christian.
Workshop methods for gold- and silversmiths. (Rezept
und Werkstattbuch für den Gold- und Silverschmied.)
Tr. W. Jacobsohn. NY: Chemical, 1960. 144p. 19cm.
[LC62, IT13]

Same. L: Heywood, 1960. 144p. (18.5cm.) [LC62,
B60, IT13]

SCHWANKL, Alfred, 1897- .
Bark. (Die Rinde. Das Gesicht des Baumes.) Tr.
Herbert L. Edlin. NY: Thames, 1956. 100p. [IT9]

Same. L: Thames, 1956. 100p. (20.5cm.) [B56,
IT9]

What wood is that? (Welches Holz ist das.) Tr. H. L.
Edlin. NY: Studio, 1956. 163p. 21cm. [LC62, IT9]

Same. L: Thames, 1956. 163p. 21cm. [LC62, B56,
IT9]

SCHWANTES, Gustav, 1881- .
Flowering stones and mid-day flowers. Tr. Vera Higgins.
L: Benn, 1957. 420p. 25cm. [LC62, B57, IT10]

Same. NY: De Graff, 1958. 439p. [IT11]

SCHWARZ, Ernst, 1886-1958.
The conditions of workers employed in the world sugar
industry, a survey. (Die Arbeiter in der Zuckerindustrie
der Welt.) Geneva, 1959. 88p. 29cm. [LC62]

SCHWARZ, Heinrich M.
Sicily. (Sizilien.) Tr. Anon. NY: Studio, 1956. 43p.
31cm. [LC62]

Same. L: Thames, 1956. 43p. 31cm. [IT9]

SCHWARZ, Rudolf, 1897- .
The church incarnate, the sacred function of Christian
architecture. (Vom Bau der Kirche.) Tr. Cynthia Harris. Chicago: Regnery, 1958. 231p. 26cm. [LC62]

SCHWARZ VAN BERK, Hans and Diebow, Hans. See Pars,
Hans Helmuth, pseud.

SCHWARZENBACH, Hans, 1911- .
Decorative trees and shrubs. (Unsere Gartenpflanzen.)
Tr. Herbert L. Edlin. (Text Hans Zaugg and Hans
Coaz.) NY: Viking, 1960. 1v. 32cm. [LC62, IT13]

Same. L: Thames, 1960. 1v. 32cm. [LC62]

SCHWARZSCHILD, Leopold, 1891-1950.
Karl Marx, the red Prussian. Tr. Margaret Wing. NY:
Grosse, 1958. 422p. [LC62]

Same. 431p. [IT11]

SCHWEBELL, Gertrude C.
Where magic reigns. German fairy tales since Grimm.
Tr. Anon. Illus. Max Barsis. NY: Day, 1957. 318p.

SCHWEBELL, Gertrude C. --
24cm. [LC62]

SCHWEINITZ, Hellmut von.
Brothers to all men. Tr. Anon. Bromdon, Eng.:
Woodcrest; Rifton, NY: 1959. 19p. 21cm. [LC62]

SCHWEITZER, Albert, 1875-1965.
African notebook. (Afrikanische Geschichten.) Tr. Mrs.
C. E. B. Russell. Bloomington, Ind.: Indiana U. Pr.,
1958. 144p. 20cm. [LC62, IT10]

Albert Schweitzer. An anthology. Tr. Anon. Ed. Chas.
R. Joy. Enl. ed. Boston: Beacon, 1956. 355p. 20cm.
[LC62]

Same. Boston: Beacon, 1960. c1947. 355p. [LC62]

The animal world. Tr. C. R. Joy. Boston: Beacon,
1958. 209p. 21cm. [LC62, IT10]

Goethe. Tr. Anon. L: Adam, 1959. [LC62]

Goethe, his personality and his work. Address to the
Goethe Bicentennial Convocation, Aspen, Colorado, July
6-8, 1949. Tr. Anon. Chicago: Albert Schweitzer Education Foundation, 1959. 7p. 28cm. [LC62]

Indian thought and its development. (Die Weltanschauung
der indianischen Denker.) Tr. Mrs. C. E. B. Russell.
Boston: Beacon, 1957. 272p. 21cm. [LC62]

The light within us. (Von Licht in uns.) Tr. Anon. NY:
Philosophical Lib., 1959. 58p. 20cm. [LC62, IT12]

Same. Sel. Richard Kik. L: Calder, 1959. 58p.
(18.5cm.) [B59]

Memoirs of childhood and youth. (Aus meiner Kindheit
und Jugendzeit.) Tr. C. T. Campion. 1st American ed.
NY: Macmillan, 1958. 78p. 21cm. [LC62]

More from the primeval forest. (Mitteilungen aus lambarene. -it, or das Urwaldspital zu Lambarene. -L. C.)
Tr. C.T., (C. S. in IT.) Campion. (LC note -NY ed.
title The Forest Hospital at Lambarene.) L: Black,
1956. 128p. 19cm. [LC62, B56, IT9]

Same. Tr. Anon. L: Collins, 1958. (New ed.) 127p.
(18cm.) [B58, IT11]

Music in the life of Albert Schweitzer, with selections
from his writings by Charles R. Joy. Pref. Charles
Munch. Tr. Anon. Boston: Beacon, 1959. 300p. 21
cm. [LC62]

My childhood and youth. (Aus meiner Kindheit und Jugendzeit.) Tr. C. T. Campion. L: Allen, 1960. 3-96p.
(18.5cm.) [B60]

An obligation to tomorrow. Tr. Anon. NY: n.p. 1958.
8p. 28cm. [LC62]

On the edge of the primeval forest. (Zwischen Wasser
und Urwald.) Tr. C. T. Campion. L: Collins, 1956.
126p. 18cm. [LC62, B56]

Peace or atomic war. (Broadcasts from Norway, 1958.)
Tr. Anon. L: Black, 1958. 28p. (21.5cm.) 22cm.
[LC62, B58]

Same. NY: Holt, 1958. 47p. 21cm. [LC62]

The philosophy of civilization. Tr. C. T. Campion.
NY: Macmillan, 1960. 347p. [LC62, IT13]

The psychiatric study of Jesus, exposition and criticism.
(Die psychiatrische Beurteilung Jesu.) Tr. and introd.
Charles R. Joy. Fwd. Winifred Overholser. Boston:
Beacon, 1956. 79p. 24cm. [LC62]

Same. Boston: Beacon, c1958. 79p. [LC62]

The quest of the historical Jesus. A critical study of
its progress from Reimarus to Wrede. (Von Reimarus
zu Wrede.) Tr. W. Montgomery. Pref. P. C. Burkitt.
NY: Macmillan, 1956. 413p. 22cm. [LC62]

Same. Tr. Anon. L: Adams, 1956. 410p. 23cm.
[LC62]

The rights of the unborn and the peril today. Tr. Anon.
Chicago: Albert Schweitzer Education Foundation, 1958.
11p. 28cm. [LC62]

SCHWEITZER, Albert--
A selection of writings of and about Albert Schweitzer.
Tr. Anon. Boston, Massachusetts, 1958. 83p. 26cm.
[LC62]

SCHWEITZER, Albert. See Pierhal, Jean.

SCHWEIZER, Eduard, 1913- .
Lordship and discipleship. (Erniedrigung und Erhöhung
bei Jesus und seinen Nachfolgern.) Tr. with revisions
by author. L: SCM, 1960. 136p. 22cm. [LC62, B60,
IT13]

Same. Naperville, Ill.: Allenson, 1960. [LC62, IT13]

SCHWEIZER, Eduard, 1913- , et al.
Spirit of God. Tr. A. E. Harvey. L: Black, 1960.
119p. 21cm. [LC62, B61]

SCHWEIZERISCHER WERKBUND, ZÜRICH.
The home today. Swiss catalogue of goods. Tr. Anon.
(Eng., Fr., and Ger.) Ed. Alfred Altherr. Teufen,
Switz.: Niggli; L: Tiranti, 1960. 167p. (21cm.)
[B60]

SCHWIDEFSKY, Kurt, 1905- .
An outline of photogrammetry. (Grundriss der Photo-
grammetrie. Orig. title, Einführung in die Luft und
Erdbildmessung.) Tr. John Fosberry. L: Pitman,
1959. 326p. (23.5cm.) 24cm. [LC62, B59, IT12]

Same. NY: Pitman, 1959. 326p. 24cm. [LC62, IT12]

SEAICH, John Eugene. See Leichtentritt, Hugo, 1874-1951.

SECKEL, Dietrich, 1910- .
Emakimono, the art of the Japanese painted hand-scroll.
(Emaki.) Tr. J. Maxwell Brownjohn. Fwd. and photos
Akihisa Hase. L: Cape, 1959. 238p. 30cm. (30.5
cm.) [LC62, B59]

Same. NY: Pantheon, 1959. 238p. 30cm. [LC62]

THE SECOND INDUSTRIAL REVOLUTION.
Speeches by Leo Brandt and Carlo Schmid at the Social
Democratic Party Congress, held from July 10-14, 1956,
in Munich. Bonn, 1956. 59p. [LC62]

SEDLMAYR, Hans, 1896- .
Art in crisis, the lost center. (Verlust der Mitte.) Tr.
Brian Battershaw. L: Hollis, 1957. 266p. 22cm.
(22.5cm.) [LC62, B58, IT9]

Same. Chicago: Regnery, 1958. 266p. 23cm. [LC62,
IT11]

SEEBASS, Friedrich, 1901- .
South Tyrol. (Südtirol, alte Adige.) Tr. Anon. Photo.
Oswald Kofler and others. Königstein im Taunus:
Köster, 1960. 120p. 27cm. [LC62]

SEEBERG, Reinhold, 1859-1935.
Text book of the history of doctrines. Tr. Charles E.
Hay. Grand Rapids: Baker, 1956. 2v. in 1. unp.
23cm. [LC62]

SEELIG, Carl, 1894- .
Albert Einstein, a documentary biography. (A--E-- und
die Schweiz. Later publ. as, A--E---. Eine dokumentar-
ische Biographie.) Tr. Mervyn Savill. L: Staples,
1956. 240p. 20cm. [LC62, B56, IT9]

SEEMANN, Margarete, 1893-1949.
The Hummel-book by Berta Hummel. Poems and pref.
Margarete Seemann. Tr. Lola Ch. Eytel. 7th ed.
Stuttgart: Fink, (Label. NY: Heinman.) 1960. 64p.
[LC62]

SEGHERS, Anna, pseud. [i.e. Radnanyi, Netty (Reiling).]
1900- .
Revolt of the fishermen of Santa Barbara. A price on
his head. Tr. Eva Wulff. Eds. Jack and Renate Mitchell, Valerie Stone. Berlin: Seven Seas; L: Collet's,
1960. 295p. (19cm.) [B61]

SEIDLER, Herbert, 1905- .
The study of German literature. Inaugural lecture delivered 22 Oct. 1958. Tr. Anon. Johannesburg: Wit-
watersrand U. Pr., 1959. 18p. [LC62]

SEIDLMAYER, Michael, 1902- .
Currents of mediaeval thought, with special reference to
Germany. (Weltbild und Kultur Deutschlands im Mittel-
alter. Band 1, abschnitt 6.) Tr. D. Barker. Ed.
Geoffrey Barraclough. Oxford: Blackwell, 1960. 175p.

SEIDLMAYER, Michael--
(22.5cm.) 23cm. [LC62, B60]

SEKLER, Eduard Franz.
Wren and his place in European architecture. Trs. Mr.
and Mrs. Peter Murray. L: Faber, 1956. 3-217p.
26cm. [LC62, B56]

Same. NY: Macmillan, 1956. 217p. 26cm. [LC62]

SELINKO, Annemarie.
Desiree. (D--.) Trs. A. Bender and E. W. Dickes.
L: Pan, 1959. 538p. (17.5cm.) [B59]

Same. 537p. [IT12]

SELLWOOD, Arthur V. See Mohr, Ulrich.
Ship. 16. Atlantis. The story of a German surface
raider. Tr. Anon. L: Hamilton, 1956. 224p. (18.5cm.)
[B56]

Ship 16. The story of the secret German raider Atlantis, as told to A. V. Sellwood. Tr. Anon. NY: Day,
1956. [LC62]

SELVI, Arthur Mark, 1912- , et al.
Folklore of other lands. Folk tales, proverbs, songs,
rhymes, and games of Italy, France, the Hispanic world
and Germany. By Arthur M. Selvi, Lothar Kahn, and
Robert C. Soule. Illus. Tullio Crali. NY: Vanni, 1956.
279p. 24cm. [LC62]

SENDEN, Marius von.
Space and sight, the perception of space and shape in
the congenitally blind before and after operation. (Raum-
und Gestaltauffassung bei operierten Blindgeborenen.) Tr.
Peter Heath. Appendixes A. H. Riesen, G. J. Warnock
and J. Z. Young. L: Methuen, 1960. 348p. (22.5cm.)
23cm. [LC62, B60]

Same. Glenco, Ill.: Free Pr., 1960. 348p. 23cm.
[LC62]

SENTJURC, Igor.
Prayer for an assassin. (Gebet für den Mörder.) Tr.
Cornelia Schaffer. NY: Doubleday, 1959. 240p. 22cm.
[LC62, IT12]

Same. L: Longmans, Green, 1960. 240p. (20.5cm.)
21cm. [LC62, B60, IT13]

SERLIO, Sebastiano, 1475-1552.
   The Renaissance stage. Documents of Serlio, Sabbattini,
   and Furtenbach. Trs. Allardyce Nicoll, John H. Mc
   Dowell and George R. Kernodle. (Italian and Ger.)
   Coral Gables, Fla.: U. of Miami Pr., 1958. 256p.
   25cm. [LC62, IT12]

SETHE, Paul, 1901- .
   A short history of Russia. (Kleine russische Geschichte.)
   Trs. Richard and Clara Winston. Chicago: Regnery,
   1956. 192p. 18cm. [LC62, IT9]

SEUNIG, Waldemar.
   Horsemanship. (Von der Koppel bis zur Kapriole.) Tr.
   Leonard Mins. NY: Doubleday, 1956. 390p. 24cm.
   [LC62, IT9]

   Same. L: Hale, 1958. 352p. (23.5cm.) [B58,
   IT10]

   Same. NY: Doubleday, 1960. 352p. 24cm. [LC62,
   IT13]

SEYDEWITZ, Max, jt. author. See Seydewitz, Ruth.

SEYDEWITZ, Ruth, and Seydewitz, Max, jt. authors.
   Anti-Semitism in West Germany. (Der Antisemitismus
   in der Bundesrepublik.) Tr. Anon. Berlin: Committee
   for German Unity, 1956. 80p. 24cm. [LC62]

SHALL, Sybil.
   Berlin today. Sightseeing, shopping, restaurants, night
   life, useful tips, history, music, theatre. A complete
   guide. Tr. Anon. Berlin: Frick, 1958. 129p. [LC
   62]

SHETTLES, Landrum Brewer.
   Ovum humanum. Growth, maturation, nourishment, fer-
   tilization and early development. Tr. Anon. (Ger.,
   Fr., and Eng.) Munich: Urban; L, NY: Hafner, 1960.
   79p. (24.5cm.) [B60]

342

SHILLING, Ton, 1919- .
Tiger men of Anai. Tr. E. W. Dickes. L: Allen,
n. d. 1v. [LC62]

SICK, Helmut, 1910- .
Tukani. (Tukani, unter Tieren und Indianern Zentral-
Brasiliens bei der ersten Durchquerung von S. nach NW.)
Tr. R. H. Stevens. L: Burke, 1959. 240p. (22.5cm.)
23cm. [LC62, B59, IT12]

Same. NY: Eriksson-Taplinger, 1960. 240p. 23cm.
[LC62, IT13]

SICKERT, Adolf.
(Tiroler Bilderbuch. Das Land im Gebirge.) Tr. Anon.
Photo. Adolf Sickert. (Ger., Eng. and Fr.) Innsbruck:
Rauch, 1960. 19, 79p. 25cm. [LC62, IT14]

SIEGFRIED, Ruth.
Missionary diary. Tr. (ms.) Elisabeth Balshaitis.
Illus. James Moss. L: Salvationist, 1956. 208p.
(22.5cm.) 23cm. [LC62, B57]

SIEGLER, Heinrich Freiherr von, 1899- .
The reunification and security of Germany. A documentary basis for discussion. Tr. Anon. Bonn: Siegler,
1957. 184p. 24cm. [LC62]

SIEGNER, Otto.
Spain, an art-book. Photo. Otto Siegner. Tr. Anon.
Munich-Pallach: Simon, n. d. 239p. 27cm. [LC62]

This is Scandinavia. Denmark, Sweden, Norway. An
art-book. Text Hans Obergerthmann. Munich-Pallach:
Simon, 195-. 239p. [LC62]

Yugoslavia, an art-book. Text Arnold Schulz. Munich-
Pallach; Simon, 195-. 239p. [LC62]

SIEGRIST, Henry, See Sigerist, Henry.

SIELMANN, Heinz.
My year with the woodpeckers. (Das Jahr mit den Spechten.) Tr. Sidney Lightman. L: Barrie, 1959. 139p.
(23.5cm.) 24cm. [LC62, B59, IT12]

Windows in the woods. (Das Jahr mit den Spechten.)

Tr. S. Lightman. NY: Harper, 1959. 139p. 24cm.
[LC62, IT13]

SIEMENS, Georg, 1882-   .
  History of the House of Siemens. Trs. A. F. Rodger and
  Lawrence N. Hole. Freiburg, Alber, 195- . 1v. 29cm.
  [LC62, IT10, 11]

SIENKIEWICZ, Henryk.
  Portrait of America. Letters of H--S--. Ed. and Tr.
  Charles Morley. NY: Columbia U. Pr.; L: Oxford U.
  Pr., 1959. 300p. (22cm.) [B59]

SIGERIST, Henry Ernest 1891-   .
  The great doctors. A biographical history of medicine.
  (Grosse Ärzte, eine Geschichte der Heilkunde in Lebens-
  bildern.) Trs. Eden and Cedar Paul. 3rd ed. Garden
  City, NY: Doubleday, 1958. 422p. [LC62, IT13]

SILBER, Käte.
  Pestalozzi, the man and his work. (P--, der Mensch und
  sein Werk.) Tr. Anon. L: Routledge, 1960. 335p.
  (22.5cm.) 23cm. [LC62, B60]

SILESUS, Angelus.
  Selections in Loomis, C. G. 1958.

SILLMANN, Karl.
  Marzipan--quickly modelled, easily sold. (Marzipan--
  rasch geformt, leicht verkauft. Ein Lehrbuch des ra-
  tionellen Arbeitens mit Marzipan.) Tr. Anon. Basel:
  Coba, 1956. 96p. 21 x 20cm. [LC62]

SILVESTER, Roman.
  Life in Germany plus tourist and buyers guide to Vienna
  and Austria. Tr. Anon. Vienna: European Pub., 1959.
  137, 40p. 20cm. [LC62]

SIMANYI, Tibor. See Kovarik, Illa.

SIMMEL, Georg, 1858-1918.
  Sociology of religion. (Die Religion.) Tr. Curt Rosen-
  thal. NY: Philosophical Lib., 1959. 76p. [LC62,
  IT13]

SIMMEL, Georg. See Wolff, Kurt H.

SIMON, Karl Guenter.
(Pantomime, Ursprung, Wesen, Möglichkeiten.) Tr. Anon.
(Ger. Fr. or Eng.) München, Nymphenburger, 1960. 95p.
25cm. [LC62]

THE SIMPLETONS.
(Die Schildbürger.) Retold Erich Kastner. [sic] Trs.
Richard and Clara Winston. Illus. Horst Lenke. NY:
Messner, 1957. 69p. 27cm. [LC62]

SINDEN, Margaret J., 1915- .
Gerhart Hauptmann, the prose plays. Tr. Anon. Toronto: U. of Toronto Pr.; L: Oxford U. Pr., 1957.
238p. 22cm. [LC62, B58]

SINGER, Eric, 1896- .
Personality in handwriting, the guiding image in graphol-
ogy. Tr. Anon. Illus. Gertrude Elias. Westport,
Conn.: Associated Booksellers, 1956. 120p. 23cm.
[LC62, IT10]

THE SLEEPING BEAUTY.
Tr. Anon. L: Nelson, 1959. 58p. (19.5cm.) [B59]

SMITH, Irving Norman, 1909- . (not by)
Letters from Germany and Poland. Tr. Anon. Ottawa:
Ottawa Journal, 1960. 38p. 23cm. [LC62]

SMITH, Ronald Gregor.
Johann George Hamann, 1730-1788, a study in Christian
existence, with selections from his writings. Tr. Anon.
L: Collins, 1960. 270p. 22cm. [LC62, B60]

Same. NY: Harper, 1960. 270p. 22cm. [LC62]

SNELL, Bruno, 1896- .
The discovery of mind, Greek origins of European
thought. (Die Entdeckung des Geistes.) 2nd ed. Tr. T.
G. Rosenmeyer. NY: Harper, 1960. 323p. 21cm.
[LC62, IT13]

SNYDER, Louis Leo, 1907- .
Documents of German history. Tr. L--L--S--, et al.
New Brunswick, NJ: Rutgers U. Pr.; L: Paterson,
1958. 619p. 24cm. (24.5cm.) [LC62, B59, IT11]

SOBOTTA, Johannes, 1869-1945.
Atlas of descriptive human anatomy. (A-- der deskriptiven Anatomie des Menschen.) Ed. and tr. Eduard Uhlenhuth. 7th Eng. ed. NY: Hafner, 1957. 3v. 26cm.
[LC62]

SOHM, Rudolf, 1841-1917.
Outlines of church history. Tr. May Sinclair. Pref.
H. M. Gwatkin. Introd. James Luther Adams. Boston:
Beacon, 1958. 260p. 21cm. [LC62]

SOKOLOW, Helena.
Bible rhapsodies. Tr. E. W. Shanahan. (From ms.)
Tel-Aviv: Massada, 1956. 104p. [IT10]

SOLTIKOW, Michael Alexander, Graf.
The cat, a true story of espionage. (Die Katze.) Tr.
Mervyn Savill. L: MacGibbon, 1957. 227p. (22.5cm.)
23cm. [LC62, B57]

SOMMER, Fedor, 1864-1930.
The iron collar. A novel of the counter reformation.
(Die Schwenckfelder.) Tr. Andrew S. Berky. Pennsburg,
Pa.: Schwenkfelder Library, 1956. 261p. 22cm.
[LC62, IT10]

SOMMER, Louise, Ed. and Tr.
Essays in European economic thought. Princeton, NJ;
L: Van Nostrand, 1960. 229p. 24cm. [LC62, B60,
IT13, 14]

SONNLEITHNER, Joseph and Georg Friedrich Treitschke.
Fidelio . . . Music by Ludwig van Beethoven, Eng. version Joseph Machlis. NY: Ballantine, 1959. 42p.
23cm. [LC62]

Same. NY: Oceana, 1959. 296p. 23cm. [LC62, IT
13]

SPANDEY, Will. (Willy Spande)
Death face. (Das Totengesicht.) Tr. Anon. Balve I.
Westfalen: Hoenne verlag, 1957. 254p. [IT10]

SPANGENBERG, August Gottlieb, 1704-1792.
Exposition of Christian doctrine as taught in Protestant
Church of the United Brethren or Unitas Fratrum. (1st
Ger. ed. 1779, Latin title idea, Fidel fratrum.) Tr.

SPANGENBERG, August Gottlieb--
Anon. Pref. Benjamin La Trobe. Fwd. J. Kenneth
Pfohl and Edmund Schwarze. 3rd Eng. ed. Winston-
Salem, North Carolina, distributed by Board of Christian
Education of the Southern Province of Moravian Church,
1959. 551p. [LC62]

SPANUTH, Juergen.
Atlantis, the mystery unravelled. (Das enträtselte At-
lantis.) Tr. Anon. NY: Citadel, 1956. 207p. 22cm.
[LC62, IT9]

Same. L: Arco, 1956. 207p. 22cm. (22.5cm.)
[LC62, B56]

SPEE, F. von.
Selection in Loomis, C. G. 1958.

SPEISER, Werner.
China, spirit and society. Tr. George Laurence. L:
Methuen, 1960. 256p. 24cm. [LC62]

SPELTZ, Alexander.
The styles of ornament. (Der Ornamentstil.) Tr. David
O'Connor. (From 2nd Ger. ed.) NY: Dover, 1959.
64p. 22cm. [LC62, IT13]

SPENDER, Stephen, 1909- .
Great German short stories. Tr. Anon. Ed. and introd.
Stephen Spender. NY: Dell, 1960. 264p. 17cm.
[LC62, IT13]

SPERBER, Manes.
The lost bay. (Sequel to The wind and the flame.)
B-56-The lost boy. (Die verlorene Bucht. LC-La
baie perdue.) Tr. Constantine Fitzgibbon. L: Deutsch,
1956. 304p. (20.5cm.) [LC62, B56, IT9]

SPERVOGEL.
Selections in Loomis, C. G. 1958.

SPEYR, Adrienne von.
The handmaid of the Lord. Tr. Alexander Dru. L:
Harvill, 1956. 174p. (22.5cm.) [B56]

Meditations on the Gospel of St. John. (Die Streitreden
Johannes, 2, Betrachtungen über sein Evangelium.) Tr.

Alexander Dru (Don in It). L: Collins, 1959. 191p.
22cm. [LC62, B59, IT12]

The word, a meditation on the prologue to St. John's
Gospel. (Das Wort wird Fleisch.) Tr. Alexander Dru.
L: Collins, 1953-59. 2v. 23cm. [LC62, IT12]

SPITZMUELLER, Anna.
Art treasures in Austria, Goldsmith's works. (Kunst aus
Österreich, Goldschmiedearbeiten.) Tr. Anon. Bad
Vöslau, Actien-Gellschaft der Vöslauer Kammgarn-Fabrik,
1957. 27p. [LC62]

Art treasures in Austria. Gothic sculpture. (Kunst aus
Österreich. Gotische Plastik.) Tr. Anon. Bad Vöslau,
Wiener Kleiderstoff- und Tuchfabrik Gesellschaft, 1960.
30p. [LC62]

Art treasures in Austria, masterpieces of European paint-
ing. (Kunst aus Österreich, Meisterwerke europäischer
Malerei.) Tr. Anon. Bad Vöslau, 1955 or 1956. 30p.
[LC62]

Art treasures in Austira, tapestries. (Kunst aus Österreich, Tapisserien.) Tr. Anon. Bad Vöslau, Actien-
Gesellschaft der Vöslauer Kammgarn-Fabrik, 1956 or 1957.
23p. [LC62]

SPOERL, Alexander.
Living with a car. (Mit dem Auto auf du.) Tr. and adpt.
Otto Gregory. L: Muller, (Dist. by NY, Sportshelf).
1960. 249p. (250p.) (20.5cm.) 21cm. [LC62, B60,
IT13]

SPRINGORUM, Friedrich.
Majorea, sunlight on a sea-girt Isle. Tr. Britta M.
Charleston. Berne: Kümmerly; Chicago: Rand Mc
Nally, 1960. 152p. 31cm. [LC62, IT13]

SPULER, Bertold, 1911- .
The Muslim world, a historical survey. (Geschichte der
islamischen Länder.) Tr. F. R. C. Bagley. Leiden:
Brill, 1960. 1v. 25cm. [LC62, IT13, 14]

SPYRI, Johanna (Heusser), 1827-1901.
All alone in the world. "The story of Rico." and
"Wiseli's way." Tr. M. E. Calthrop. Illus. Michael

SPYRI, Johanna (Heusser)--
Ross. L: Dent, 1958. 172p. (20.5cm.) [LC62, B58]

Same. NY: Dutton, 1959. 172p. 21cm. [LC62, IT12]

The children's Christmas carol. Adpt. Darlene Geis.
Tr. Anon. NJ: Prentice-Hall; L: Bailey, 1957. 89p.
24cm. [LC62, B58]

Heidi. Ed. and abr. Deborah Hill. Illus. Grace Dalles
Clarke. NY: Simon, 1956. 96p. 27cm. [LC62]

Heidi. Tr. Eileen Hall. (Puffin Story Bks., ed. Eleanor Graham, no. 97.) Harmondsworth: Penguin, 1956.
18cm. (18.5cm.) [LC62, B56]

Heidi. Tr. Marian Edwards. L: Blackie, 1956. 357p.
(19.5cm.) [B56]

Heidi. Tr. Anon. Intro. Adeline B. Zachert. Philadelphia: Winston, 1957. 278p. 22cm. (The Children's
classics) [LC62]

Heidi. Tr. Anon. L: Murrays Book Sales, 1957. 3-
284p. (19cm.) (Abbey classics) [B57]

Heidi. Tr. Anon. L: Dean, 1957. 214p. (19.5cm.)
[B57]

Heidi. Tr. Anon. Illus. Janet Smalley. L: Peveril.
1957. 248p. (19.5cm.) [B57]

Heidi. Tr. Anon. NY: Scribner, 1958. 380p. [LC62,
IT12]

Heidi. A new translation. Tr. Joy Law. Pictures
Chas. Mozley. NY: Watts; L: Mayflower, 1959.
256p. (22.5cm.) 23cm. [LC62, B59, IT12]

Heidi. Tr. Louise Brooks. (Shirley Temple ed.) NY:
Random, 1959. 252p. 20cm. [LC62, IT12]

Heidi. Tr. Helen B. Dole. L: Macdonald, 1960.
326p. (21.5cm.) [B60]

Heidi. Tr. M. Rosenbaum. L: Collins, 1960. 224p.
(19cm.) [B60, IT14]

The pet lamb and other Swiss stories. (Beim Weiden-
Joseph.) Trs. M. E. Calthrop and E. M. Popper. L:
Dent, 1956. 245p. (20cm.) [B56]

Same. NY: Dutton, 1956. 244p. 20cm. [LC62]

STACHELSCHEID, Carl August.
Born of fire, steel, a color picture book. Eng. version
Barrows Mussey. Pref. and picture captions Heinz
Todtmann. Stuttgart: Strache, 1956. 104p. 20cm.
[LC62]

STADLER, Wolfgang, 1924- .
European art, a traveller's guide. (Führer durch die
europäische Kunst.) NY: Herder, 1960. 298p. 25cm.
[LC62, IT13]

Same. L: Nelson, 1960. 300p. (24.5cm.) [B60]

STAUB, Christian, 1918- .
Circus. A book of photographs by C--S--. Tr. Anon.
Sketches Hanny Fries. Introd. Grock. L: Lane, c1957.
(1956.) 104p. (115p.) (27.5cm.) [LC62, B58]

STAUDINGER, Josef.
Holiness of the priesthood. Meditations and readings for
priests. (Heiliges Priestertum.) Tr. John J. Coyne.
Westminster, Md.: Newman, 1957. 546p. 17cm.
[LC62, IT11]

Same. Dublin: Clonmore; L: Burns, 1958. 546p.
(17.5cm.) [B58, IT11]

STAUFFER, Ethelbert, 1902- .
Jesus and his story. (Jesus, Gestalt und Geschichte.)
Tr. Dorothea M. Barton. L: SCM, 1960. 192p.
(19.5cm.) [LC62, B60, IT13]

Same. Trs. Richard and Clara Winston. NY: Knopf,
1960. 243p. 22cm. [LC62, IT13]

New Testament theology. (Die Theologie des Neuen Testaments.) Tr. J. Marsh. NY: Macmillan, 1956.
573p. 24cm. [LC62, IT 9]

STECHOW, Wolfgang, 1896- . See Bruegel, Pieter the
elder.

STECKERL, Fritz, Ed. and Tr.
The fragments of Praxagoras of Cos and his school.
Leiden: Brill, 1958. 132p. 25cm. [LC62]

STEFFEN, Albert, 1884- .
Burning problems, to those who bear the responsibility.
Tr. Rex Raab. Dornach, Switz.: Verlag für Schöne
Wissenschaften, 1957. 72p. 21cm. [LC62]

STEIN, Edith, 1891-1942.
The science of the cross, a study of St. John of the
cross. (Kreuzeswissenschaft.) Tr. Hilda Graef. Chicago: Regnery, 1960. 243p. 22cm. [LC62, IT13]

Same. L: Burns, 1960. 243p. (22.5cm.) 23cm.
[LC62, B60, IT13]

Writings. Sel. Tr. and Introd. Hilda Graef. Westminster, Md.: Newman, 1956. 206p. 22cm. [LC62,
IT9]

Same. L: Owen, 1956. 7-206p. 22cm. [LC62, B56]

STEINBACHER, Georg.
Cage and garden birds. (Knauers Vogelbuch.) Tr. P.
Gorge. L: Batsford, 1959. 272p. (20cm.) [LC62,
B59, IT12]

Same. NY: Viking, 1959. 272p. 20cm. [LC62, IT13]

STEINER, Alexis.
Kriki, the wild duck. (Kriki und ihre Kinder.) Tr. E.
Hurd. L: Harrap, 1959. 64p. (24cm.) [B59, IT12]

Same. NY: Watts, 1960. 62p. 24cm. [LC62, IT13]

Kriki and the fox. (Kriki, das tapfere Entlein.) Tr.
Renata Symonds. Vienna, L: Harrap, 1960. 64p.
(24cm.) [B60]

STEINER, Rudolf, 1861-1925.
The apocalypse of St. John. Tr. Anon. Ed. rev. 1958,
M. Cotterell. L: Anthroposophical, 1958. 222p.
(22.5cm.) 23cm. [LC62, B59]

The apocalypse of St. John. Twelve lectures with an
introductory lecture given in Nuremberg, June 1908.

Tr. Anon. (From shorthand reports unrev.) Ed. rev. M. Cotterell. L: Anthroposophical, 1959. 222p. (22.5cm.) [B59]

Ascension and pentecost. Six lectures. Tr. George Adams, J. Davy and D. S. Osmond. Rev. and ed. Arthur Pearce Shepherd. L: Anthroposophical, 1958. 87p. (22.5cm.) 23cm. [LC62, B58]

The change in the path to supersensible knowledge. Tr. Anon. L: Anthroposophical, 1959. 22p. 17cm. [LC 62, B59]

Christ and the human soul. Four lectures by R--S--, given at Norrkoeping, July 12-16, 1914. Tr. Anon. Rev. ed. M. Cotterell. L: Steiner, 1956. 55p. 22cm. [B56]

Cosmic memory, prehistory of earth and men. (Aus der Akasha-Chronik.) Tr. Karl E. Zimmer. Englewood, NJ: Steiner, 1959. 273p. 22cm. [LC62, IT12, 13]

The cycle of the year as breathing-process of the earth. The four great festival seasons of the year. Five lectures given in Dornach 31 March to 8 April, 1923. Tr. Rev. M. Cotterell. L: Anthroposophical, 1956. 76p. 23cm. [B56]

Deeper secrets of human history in the light of the Gospel of St. Matthew. Three lectures given in Berlin 1, 9, and 23 November 1909. Trs. D. S. Osmond and A. P. Shepherd. From shorthand reports unrev. by R--S--. Rev. ed. L: Anthroposophical, 1957. 80p. 19cm. [LC62, B57, IT11]

Easter. Eight lectures given between the years 1908 and 1921. Tr. from shorthand reports unrev. R--S--. Ed. and rev. D. S. Osmond, A. P. Shepherd and C. Dubrovik. L: Anthroposophical, 1956. 124p. (125p.) 22cm. [LC62, B56]

Eurythmy as visible speech. Fifteen lectures given at Dornach, Switz., 24th June to 12th July, 1924. Tr. and rev. V. and J. Compton-Burnett and S. and C. Dubrovik from shorthand reports unrev. by R--S--. (Rev. ed. from 2nd Ger. ed.) Ed. I. De Jaager. L: Anthroposophical, 1956. 287p. (22.5cm.) [B56]

STEINER, Rudolf--

F. Nietzsche, fighter for freedom. (F. Nietzsche, ein Kämpfer gegen seine Zeit.) Tr. Margaret Ingram de Ris. Englewood, NJ: Steiner, 1960. 222p. 22cm. [LC62, IT13]

The foundation stone. Dornach, Switzerland, 24 Dec. 1923 to 1 Jan. 1924. Tr. with introd. George Adams. L: Anthroposophical, 1957. 59p. (22.5cm.) 23cm. [LC62, B57]

From Jesus to Christ. Ten lectures given at Karlsruhe, 5th to 14th October, 1911. Tr. from shorthand report unrev. by R--S--. L: Steiner, 1956. 142p. 22cm. [LC62]

Genesis, secrets of the Bible story of creation. (Die Geheimnisse der Biblischen Schöpfungsgeschichte.) Trs. Dorothy Lenn with Owen Barfield. From rev. 3d ed. L: Anthroposophical, 1959. 139p. (22cm.) 23cm. [LC62, B59, IT12]

Good fortune, its reality and its semblance. Tr. from Ms. R. H. Bruce. L: Anthroposophical, 1956. 31p. (32p.) (18.5cm.) 19cm. [LC62, B57, IT9]

Human questions and cosmic answers. Man and his relation to the planets. Four lectures given at Dornach, Switz., 25th June to 2nd July, 1922. Tr. from shorthand reports unrev. by R--S--. Trs. V. Compton-Burnett, et al. L: Anthroposophical, 1960. 69p. (71p.) (22.5cm.) [LC62, B60]

The inner nature of man and the life between death and a new birth. (Inneres Wesen des Menschen und Leben zwischen Tod und neuer Geburt.) Trs. D. S. Osmond and C. Davey. L: Anthroposophical, 1959. 111p. (22.5 cm.) [B60, IT13, 14]

Karmic relationships, esoteric studies. Tr. G. Adams. L: Anthroposophical, 1955-6. Vol. 1. (205p.) 22cm. Vol. 2 (258p.) 22cm. [LC62, B57]

Same. Vol. 3. 1957. 179p. (22cm.) [B58, IT11]

Same. Vol. 4. 1957. 156p. (22cm.) [B57]

Knowledge of the higher worlds and its attainment. (Wie erlangt man Erkenntnisse des höheren Lebens.) Tr. G. Metaxa. 3rd ed. rev. M. Cotterell. L: Anthroposoph- ical, 1958. 248p. (16.5cm.) 17cm. [LC62, B58, IT11]

Links between the living and the dead, (and), transforma- tion of earthly forces into clairvoyance. Two lectures given to members of the Anthroposophical Society in Ber- gen, 10th and 11th October, 1913. (Die lebendige Wech- selwirkung zwischen Lebenden und Toten, (and), die Um- wandlung menschlicher Kräfte zu Kräften der hellseher- ischen Forschung.) Trs. D. S. Osmond and C. Davy. Tr. from shorthand reports unrev. by R--S--. L: Anthroposophical, 1960. 40p. (21.5cm.) [B60, IT14]

The Lord's prayer. (Das Vaterunser.) Tr. Anon. L: Anthroposophical, 1958. 30p. (18.5cm.) [B58, IT11]

Love and its meaning in the world. (Die Liebe und ihre Bedeutung in der Welt.) A lecture given to members of The Anthroposophical Society at Zürich, 17th December, 1912. Trs. D. S. Osmond with S. and E. F. Derry from shorthand report unrev. by R--S--. L: Anthropo- sophical, 1960. 20p. 22cm. [B60, IT14]

Major writing. Tr. Anon. Englewood, NJ: Steiner, 19--. [LC62]

The Michael mystery. (Vol. 2 of the letters . . .) Tr. E. Bowen-Wedgewood. 2nd ed. rev. George Adams. L: Anthroposophical, 1956. 186p. (22.5cm.) [LC62, B56, IT9]

Michaelmas. The significance of the impulse of Michael. Lectures given between the years 1913 and 1924. Tr. from shorthand reports unrev. by R--S--. Ed. and rev. M. Cotterell. L: Anthroposophical, 1957. 81p. (82p.) (22.5cm.) 23cm. [LC62, B57]

Mysticism at the dawn of the modern age. (Die Mystik im Aufgang des neuzeitlichen Geisteslebens und ihr Ver- hältnis zur modernen Weltanschauung.) Tr. Karl E. Zim- mer. Englewood, NJ: Steiner, 1960. 253p. 22cm. [LC62, IT13, 14]

Occult history . . . 6 lectures. 1910-1911. (Okkulte

354

STEINER, Rudolf--
Geschichte.) Trs. D. S. Osmond and C. Davy. L:
Anthropos., 1957. 123p. (124p.) (22.5cm.) 23cm.
[LC62, B57]

The redemption of thinking, a study in the philosophy of
Thomas Aquinas. (Die Philosophie des Thomas von
Aquino.) Tr. and ed. with introd. and epilogue A. P.
Shepherd and Mildred Robertson Nicoll. L: Hodder,
1956. 191p. 20cm. [LC62, B56, IT9]

Reincarnation and karma. Their significance in modern
culture. (Wiederverkörperung und Karma und ihre Bedeutung für die Kultur der Gegenwart.) Five lectures
given to members of the Anthroposophical Society during
January to March 1912 in Berlin and Stuttgart. Trs.
D. S. Osmond et al. From shorthand reports unrev. by
R--S--. L: Anthroposophical, 1960. 95p. (22.5cm.)
23cm. [LC62, B60, IT14]

A road to self-knowledge. Tr. Anon. Rev. ed. M. Cotterell. L: Anthroposophical, 1956. 86p. (19cm.)
[B56]

Speech and drama. (Sprachgestaltung und dramatische
Kunst.) Tr. Mary Adams. L: Anthroposophical, 1960.
419p. 22cm. (22.5cm.) [LC62, IT13]

Supersensible influences in the history of mankind. Tr.
(ms.) Dorothy S. Osmond. L: Steiner, 1956. 83p.
(22.5cm.) 23cm. [LC62, B56, IT9]

The tasks and aims of spiritual science. (Die Geistes-
wissenschaft, ihre Aufgaben und Ziele.) Lectures given
(at) Stuttgart, 13th November, 1909. Tr. D. S. Osmond
from shorthand report unrev. by R--S---. L: Anthroposophical, 1960. 35p. 17cm. [B60, IT14]

The threshold of the spiritual world. Tr. Anon. Rev.
ed. M. Cotterell. L: Anthroposophical, 1956. 99p.
19cm. [LC62, B56]

STEINERT, Harald.
The atom rush. (Goldsucher unseres Jahrhunderts.) Tr.
and adpt. Nicholas Wharton. L: Thames, 1958. 183p.
(22.5cm.) 23cm. [LC62, B58, IT11]

STEINGRAEBER, Erich.
Antique jewelry. (Alter Schmuck. Die Kunst des europäischen schmuckes.) Tr. Anon. NY: Praeger, 1957. 191p. 29cm. [LC62, IT10]

Antique jewelry, its history in Europe from 800 to 1900. (Alter Schmuck. Die Kunst des europäischen Schmuckes.) Tr. Peter Gorge. L: Thames, 1957. 191p. (192p.) (28.5cm.) [LC62, B57]

STEINMANN-BRUNNER, Elsa, 1901- .
Lia and the red carnations. (Lia und die roten Nelken.) Trs. Richard and Clara Winston. NY: Pantheon, 1960. 221p. 21cm. [LC62, IT13]

The son of the gondolier. Trs. Richard and Clara Winston. NY: Pantheon, 1958. 191p. 22cm. [LC62, IT11]

STEKEL, Wilhelm, 1868-1940.
Impotence in the male, the psychic disorders of sexual function in the male. Authorized Eng. version Oswald H. Boltz. Introd. Emil A. Gutheil. NY: Liveright, 1959. 2v. unp. 23cm. [LC62]

The interpretation of dreams, new developments and technique. Authorized tr. Eden and Cedar Paul. L: Vision, 1960. 2v. V1. 308p. V2. 309-618p. (22.5cm.) [B60]

The meaning and psychology of dreams. Trs. Eden and Cedar Paul. Introd. William J. Fielding. NY: Avon, 1956. 305p. 17cm. [LC62]

Patterns of psychosexual infantilism, disorders of the instincts and the emotions, the parapathiac disorders. Tr. Anon. Ed. and introd. Emil A. Gutheil. NY: Grove, 1959. 412p. 21cm. [LC62]

STENGER, Erich.
The march of photography. (Siegeszug der Photographie in Kultur.) Tr. Edward Epstean. Additional material tr. H. W. Greenwood. L, NY: Focal, 1958. (302p.) 304p. (22.5cm.) 23cm. [LC62, B58, IT11]

STEPANEK, Otakar.
Birds of field and forest. Tr. G. Theiner. Illus. E.
Demartini. Text O--S--. L: Spring, 1959. 162, 6p.
(26.5cm.) [B59]

STERBA, Editha and Sterba, Richard.
Beethoven and his nephew. A psychoanalytic study of
their relationship. Tr. Willard R. Trask. L: Dobson,
1957. 351p. (22.5cm.) [LC62, B57, IT10]

STERBA, Richard, jt. author. See Sterba, Editha.
Beethoven and his nephew. L: Dobson, 1957.

STERN, Joseph Peter.
Lichtenberg, a doctrine of scattered occasions, recon-
structed from his aphorisms and reflections. Tr. Anon.
(Ger. and Eng.) Bloomington: Indiana U. Pr., 1959.
381p. 25cm. [LC62]

STERNBERG, Fritz, 1895- .
The military and industrial revolution of our time. (Die
militaerische und die industrielle revolution.) Tr.
Edward Fitzgerald. L: Stevens, 1958. 359p. 22cm.
[LC62, B59]

Same. NY: Praeger, 1959. 359p. 22cm. [LC62,
IT12]

STERNHEIM, Carl, 1878-1943.
The underpants. Eng. version Eric Bentley. n.p.
c1957. Microf. of TW. [LC62]

Same. In Bentley, the modern theatre Vol. 6, 1960.

STEUBEN, Fritz.
The stable in Bethlehem. (Im Stall von Bethlehem.)
Tr. John Beer. Illus. Willy Kretzer. L: Joseph, 1960.
48p. (20.5cm.) [B60]

The way to Bethlehem. (Der Weg nach Bethlehem) Tr.
John Beer. Illus. Willy Kretzer. L: Joseph, 1960.
45p. (20.5cm.) [B60]

STICKELBERGER, Emanuel, 1884- .
Calvin. (C--.) L: Clarke, 1959. 174p. 23cm.
(21.5cm.) [LC62, B59, IT12]

STIELER, Kaspar.
Selections in Loomis, C. G. 1958.

STIERLI, Josef, ed.
Heart of the saviour. A symposium on the Sacred
Heart. (Cor salvatoris.) Tr. Paul Andrews. (From
2nd Ger. ed.) NY: Herder; Edinburgh, L: Nelson
1957. 268p. (22.5cm.) [B59]

STIFTER, Adalbert, 1805-1888.
Brigitta. Tr. Edward Fitzgerald. L: Rodale, 1957.
81p. 23cm. (23.5cm.) [LC62, B57, IT10]

Brigitta. Tr. Ilsa Borea. In Spender's Coll., 1960.

Selections in Loomis, C. G. Prose. 1960.

STIFTERVERBAND FÜR DIE DEUTSCHE WISSENSCHAFT.
Industry and science. (Wirtschaft und Wissenschaft.)
Papers read by leading personalities on problems of science. n. p. Discussion Committee Science and Industry,
1958. 31p. [LC62]

Scientific and academic life in Western Germany. A
handbook. Tr. Anon. Ed. in cooperation with Inter-
nationes. Ed. F. E. Nord, drawings R. Spermann.
Essen: Bredeney, 1957. 183p. 22cm. [LC62]

STOCKHAUSEN, Karlheinz.
Electronic musical composition. No. 2, 1953. Tr. D. A.
Sinclair. Ottawa, 1956. 20l. 28cm. [LC62]

STÖCKLER, Heinrich.
The Leica in professional practice. (Die Leica in Beruf
und Wissenschaft.) By Heinrich Stöckler in collaboration
with leading professional and scientific photographers and
specialists. Tr. W. Edward Roscher for Leica Foto-
grafie. L: Fountain, 1956. 540p. 22cm. [B56]

STOIBER, Rudolf Maria, 1925- .
Mystery on the floating hotel. Tr. Anon. Illus. Romu-
lus Candea. Boston: Houghton, 1958. 216p. 22cm.
[LC62]

STORM, Theodor, 1817-1888.
Viola tricolor (1), and Curator Carsten (2). Trs. (1)
B. Q. Morgan and (2) Frieda M. Voigt. L: Calder,

STORM, Theodor--
1956. (9), 117p. 19cm. [LC62, B56, IT9]

Viola tricolor, the little stepmother (1), and Curator
Carsten (2). Trs. (1) B. Q. Morgan and (2) Frieda M.
Voigt. NY: Ungar, 1956. 117p. 19cm. [LC62, IT9]

Selections in Loomis, C. G. 1960.

STOUDT, John Joseph, 1911- , Ed. and Tr.
Private devotions for home and church. Tr. and compiled J--J--S---. Philadelphia: Christian Education,
1956. 173p. 23cm. [LC62]

STRACHE, Wolf, 1910- .
Forms and patterns in nature. Tr. Felix Kaufmann.
NY: Pantheon, 1956. 22p. 32cm. [LC62, IT9]

Same. L: Owen, 1959. 3-23p. (31.5cm.) [B59, IT12]

STRACHE, Wolf, 1910- , Ed.
Principality of Liechtenstein. (Fürstentum L---.) Eds.
W--S-- and Dr. Gantner. Photos Baron von Falz-Fein,
et al. Introd. Alexander Frick. Stuttgart: Verlag "Die
Schönen Bücher," 1958. 64p. 27cm. [LC62]

STRACHEY, James, Ed. See Freud, Sigmund 1856-1939.
The standard edition . . .

STRACK, Hermann Leberecht, 1848-1922.
Introduction to the Talmud and Midrash. (Einletung in
Talmud und Midras.) Tr. Anon. NY: Meridian, J. P.
S.A., 1959. 372p. 20cm. [LC62]

Same. 389p. [IT12]

STRAKOSCH, Elizabeth, Ed. and Tr. See Tauler, Johannes
c1300-1361.
Signpost to perfection. (Predigten.) Selected, Ed., and
tr. Elizabeth Strakosch. L: Blackfriars, 1958. 140p.
(19.5cm.) [LC62, B58]

STRASSER, Stephan, 1905- .
The soul in metaphysical and empirical psychology. Tr.
Henry J. Koren. Pittsburgh: Duquesne U., 1957. 275p.
27cm. [LC62]

STRATER, Paul.
The heart of Mary, sacrificial altar of Christ's love.
Tr. Mother Mary Aloysi Kiener. NY: Pustet, 1957.
170p. 22cm. [LC62]

STRATIL-SAUER, Lotte.
The children of the Hollatal. (Die Kinder vom Hollatal.)
Trs. I. and F. McHugh. Illus. Grete von Wille-Burck-
hardt. L: U. of London Pr., 1959. 176p. 22cm.
[LC62, B59, IT12]

STRATMANN, Franziskus Maria, 1883- .
War and Christianity today. Tr. J. Doebele. L: Black-
friars, 1956. 134p. (22.5cm.) 23cm. [LC62, B56,
IT9]

Same. Westminster, Md.: Newman, n.d. 134p. 22cm.
[LC62]

STRAUSS, Johann, 1825-1899.
The gipsy baron, a new version of Johann Strauss's
famous operetta. (Der Zigeunerbaron.) Orig. libretto
Ignatius Schnitzer. Book by Phil Park and Conrad Car-
ter. Lyrics Phil Park. Music arr. and adpt. Ronald
Hanmer. L: Weinberger, 1956. 93p. 25cm. [LC62,
B56]

The gipsy baron. (Der Zigeunerbaron.) Eng. libretto by
Maurice Valency. NY: Schirmer; L: Chappel, c1959.
1960. 72p. [LC62]

Same. L: Chappel, 1960. (5), 72p. (25.5cm.) [B60]

STRAUSS, William Sigfrid, 1910- .
Summary of the report of the Ministry of Justice on the
Federal Republic of Germany Draft Copyright Law.
(Based on Entwürfe des Bundesjustisministeriums zur
Urheberrechtsreform.) Tr. Anon. Washington, U.S.
Copyright Office, 1960. 7l. 28cm. [LC62]

STRECKER, Karl, 1861- .
Introduction to medieval Latin. Tr. and rev. Robert B.
Palmer. Berlin: Weidmann, 1957. 159p. 20cm.
[LC62]

STRELLER, Justus, 1892- .
Jean-Paul Sartre. To freedom condemned, a guide to

STRELLER, Justus--
his philosophy. (Zur Freiheit verurteilt.) Tr. and introd.
Wade Baskin. NY: Philosophical Lib., 1960. 163p.
19cm. [LC62]

STROOP, Juergen, 1895- .
The report of J--S-- concerning the uprising in the
ghetto of Warsaw and the liquidation of Jewish residential
area. Tr. D. Dabrowska with material from Nazi conspiracy and aggression. Introd. and notes B. Mark.
Washington, 1946. V. III. Warsaw: Jewish Historical
Institute, 1958. 123p. 20cm. [LC62, IT11]

STRUTZ, Herbert.
Beautiful Carinthia, a pictorial record. (Schönes Karn-
ten.) Tr. Oscar Konstandt. Introd. Herbert Strutz.
Innsbruck: Pinguin, 1960. 72p. 27cm. [LC62]

STUCKENSCHMIDT, Hans Heinz, 1901- .
Arnold Schoenberg. Trs. Edith T. Roberts and Humph-
rey Searle. NY: Grove, 1960. 168p. 23cm. [LC62,
IT13]

Same. L: Calder, 1960. 168p. 20cm. (22.5cm.)
[LC62, B60]

STÜBEL, Hans, 1885- .
The Mewu Fantzu, a Tibetan tribe of Kansu. Tr. Fried
Schutze. New Haven: Human Relations Area Files, 1958.
66p. 23cm. [LC62, IT11]

STUMPFF, Karl, 1895- .
Planet earth. (Die Erde als Planet.) Tr. Philip Wayne.
Ann Arbor: U. of Mich. Pr., 1959. 191p. 21cm.
[LC62, IT12]

Same. L: Mayflower, 1959. 192p. 22cm. [B59]

Same. Trs. Egon Larsen and Frank Pickering. Ann
Arbor: U. of Mich. Pr., 1959. 191p. 20cm. [LC62]

Same. 1960. [IT13]

SUCHENWIRTH, Richard, 1896- .
Historical turning points in the German Air Force war
effort. Tr. Patricia Klamerth. Maxwell AFB, Ala.,
ASAF, Hist. Div. Research Studies Institutes, Air U.,

1959. 143p. 27cm. [LC62, IT12]

SWIRIDOFF, Paul.
(Rotenburg ob der Tauber.) Tr. Anon. Text Eduard
Krueger. Schwäbish Hall: Schwend, 1957. 1v. (Ger.,
Eng., and Fr.) [LC62]

THE SWISS ALPS.
(Schweizer Alpenstrassen.) Tr. Anon. L: Thames,
1958. 20p. (24.5cm.) [B59]

SZEMERENYI, Oswald, 1913- .
Studies in the Indo-European system of numerals. (Indo-
germanische Bibliothek.) Tr. Anon. Heidelberg: Winter,
1960. 190p. [LC62]

TABAK, Israel, 1904- .
Heine and his heritage. A study of Judaic lore in his
work. Tr. Anon. NY: Twayne, 1956. 338p. 24cm.
[LC62]

TAGGER, Theodore, 1891- . See Bruckner, Ferdinand.
(pseud.)

T'AI I CHIN HUA TSUNG CHIH.
The secret of the golden flower, a Chinese book of life.
Tr. Richard Wilhelm. Tr. (into English) Cary F.
Baynes. European commentary C. G. Jung. L: Rout-
ledge, 1957. 151p. 25cm. [LC62]

TAMMELO, Ilmar, 1917- .
Justice and doubt. An essay on the fundamentals of
justice. (From Osterreichische Zeitschrift für öffentliches Recht.) Tr. Anon. Wien: Springer, 1959. 307-
417p. 23cm. [LC62]

Same. Philadelphia: Lippincott, 1960. 81p. 26cm.
[LC62, IT13]

TAPPERT, Theodore Gerhardt, 1904- , Ed. and Tr.
The book of Concord. The confessions of the Evangelical
Lutheran Church. Philadelphia: Muhlenberg, 1959.
717p. 23cm. [LC62]

TARRASCH, Siegbert, 1862-1934.
Best games of chess. Sel. and ann. Tr. Fred Rein-

TARRASCH, Siegbert--
feld. NY: Dover, 1960. 385p. 22cm. [LC62]

Three hundred chess games. Trs. Robin Ault and John
Kirwan. n. p. , 1959-1961. 2v. 28cm. [LC62]

TAULER, Johannes ca. 1300-1361.
Signposts to perfection. (Die Predigten.) Ed. and tr.
Elizabeth Strakosch. L: Blackfriars; St. Louis:
Herder, 1958. 140p. 19cm. (19.5cm.) [LC62, B58,
IT11, 12]

TAUT, Bruno, 1880- .
Houses and people of Japan. 2d ed. Tr. Mrs. Balk,
improved by Mr. Redman and Prof. Herai. Tokoyo:
Sanseido, 1958. 326p. 27cm. [LC62]

TAYLOR, Ronald Jack and Hatto, Arthur Thomas. Trs.
See Neidhardt von Reuental.

TELLENBACH, Gerd, 1903- .
Church, state and Christian Society at the time of the
investiture contest. Tr. R. F. Bennett. Oxford: Blackwell, 1959. 196p. 22cm. [LC62]

TERRA, Helmut de.
Man and mammoth in Mexico. (Urmensch und Mammut.)
Tr. Alan Houghton Brodrick. L: Hutchinson, 1957.
191p. (24cm.) [B57]

TESSIN, Brigitte von.
The bastard. (Der Bastard.) Tr. Mervyn Savill. L:
Barrie, 1958. 724p. (20.5cm.) 21cm. [LC62, B58,
IT11]

Same. NY: McKay, 1959. 724p. 22cm. [LC62, IT11]

TESSIN, Marion von.
The long-haired elephant child. (Die Geschichte vom
haarigen Elefantenkind.) Tr. Anon. NY: Pantheon,
1958. 48p. 27cm. [LC62, IT12]

TESSMANN, Günter, 1884- .
The fang people, an ethnographic monograph on a West
African Negro group. (Die Pangwe, völkerkundliche
Monographie eines westafrikanischen Negerstammes.)
Tr. Richard Neuse. New Haven: Human Relations Area

Files, 1959-1960. 2v. 20cm. [LC62]

TETENS, Alfred Friedrich, 1835-1909.
Among the savages of the South Seas. (Von Schiffsjungen zum Wasserschout.) Tr. Florence M. Spoehr. Stanford: U. Pr., Oxford U. Pr., 1958. 107p. (22.5cm.) 23cm. [LC62, B58, IT11]

TETZEL, Gabriel. See the travels.

TETZNER, Lisa, 1894- .
The girl in the glass coach. (Das Mädchen in der Glaskutsche.) Tr. F. Miller (Muller in B58). L: Frederick, Blackie, 1958. 116p. (20cm.) [B58, IT11]

THEILER, Carl Richard.
Men and molecules. What chemistry is and what it does. (Männer und Moleküle.) Tr. E. Osers. L: Harrap, 1960. 214p. (215p.) (24cm.) [LC62, B60]

THEIMER, Walter.
Encyclopedia of world politics. Ed. rev. and enl. Peter Campbell. L: Faber, 1958. 471p. [LC62]

THIEL, Erich.
The Soviet Far East. A survey of its physical and economic geography. (Sowjet-Fernost.) Trs. Annelie and Ralph M. Rookwood. L: Methuen, 1957. 388p. (22.5cm.) 23cm. [LC62, B57]

Same. NY: Praeger, 1957. 388p. 23cm. [LC62]

THIEL, Rudolf, 1899- .
And there was light, the discovery of the universe. (Und es ward Licht.) Trs. Richard and Clara Winston. NY: Knopf, 1957. 415p. 25cm. [LC62]

Same. L: Deutsch, 1958. 396p. (23cm.) [LC62, B58, IT11]

Same. NY: New American Library; L: Müller, 1960. 384p. (18cm.) [LC62, B60, IT13]

THIELICKE, Helmut, 1908- .
Between God and satan. (Zwischen Gott und Satan.) Tr. C. C. Barber. Edinburgh: Oliver, 1958. 84p. 22cm. (22.5cm.) [LC62, B58, IT11]

Same. Grand Rapids: Eerdmans, 1958. 84p. 23cm.

THIELICKE, Helmut--
[LC62, IT12]

Our Heavenly Father.   Sermons on the Lord's prayer.
(Das Gebet, das die Welt umspannt.)   Tr. and introd.
John W. Doberstein.   NY: Harper, 1960.   157p.   22cm.
[LC62, IT13]

Same.   L: Clarke, 1960.   192p.   (22cm.)   [B60]

The waiting father.   Sermons on the parables of Jesus.
(Das Bilderbuch Gottes.   Reden über die Gleichnisse
Jesu.)   Tr. and introd.   John W. Doberstein.   NY:
Harper, 1959.   192p.   22cm.   [LC62, IT12]

THOMAS, M. Z., pseud.   (i. e. Zottmann, Thomas Michael
1915- .)
Alexander von Humboldt, scientist, explorer, adventurer.
(Draussen wartet das Abenteuer, Alexander von Humboldt
und Sein Freund Aime auf kühner Fahrt ins Unbekannte.)
Tr. Elizabeth Brommer.   NY: Pantheon, 1960.   192p.
22cm.   [LC62, IT13]

THOMPSON, Stith, 1885- , Ed.
Our heritage of world literature.   Rev. ed. S--T-- and
John Gassner.   NY: Dryden, 1956.   1432p.   [LC62]

Same.   NY: Holt, 1958.   1432p.   [LC62]

THORNE, Anthony.
Venice.   Introd. and commentaries Anthony Thorne.
Photos. Kurt Otto-Wasow.   1st Eng. ed. NY: Viking,
1960.   19p.   25cm.   [LC62]

Same.   L: Balsford, 1960.   19p.   [LC62]

THORNWALD, Jürgen.
The century of the surgeon.   (Das Jahrhundert der Chir-
urgen, nach den Papieren meines Grossvaters.)   Tr.
Anon.   L: Thames, 1957.   416p.   22cm.   (22.5cm.)
[LC62, B57]

Same.   NY: Pantheon, 1957.   432p.   24cm.   [LC62]

Defeat in the East.   Russia conquers-Jan/May 1945.
Former title, Flight in the winter.   (Es begann an der
Weichsel.   Das Ende an der Elbe.)   Tr. Fred Wieck.

NY: Ballantine, 1959. 256p. [LC62, IT12]

The triumph of surgery. (Das Weltreich der Chirurgen.) Trs. Richard and Clara Winston. L: Thames, 1960. 483p. (22.5cm.) 23cm. [LC62, B60, IT13]

Same. NY: Pantheon, 1960. 454p. 24cm. [LC62, IT13]

THUN, Roderich.
The magic jewel. (Das indische Zauberkästchen.) Tr. Anon. NY: Viking, 1960. 46p. 27cm. [LC62, IT13]

THURN UND TAXIS, Marie, Prinzessin v., 1855-1934.
Memoirs of a Princess. (ms.) Tr. Nora Wydenbruck. L: Hogarth, 1959. 224p. (20.5cm.) 21cm. [LC62, B59, IT12]

THURN UND TAXIS, Marie, Prinzessin v., 1855-1934.
See Rilke, Rainer Maria. The letters . . .

THURNEYSON, Eduard, 1882- . See Lüthi, Walter, jt. author.

TICHY, Herbert, 1912- .
Cho Oyu, by favor of the Gods. (Cho Oyu, Gnade der Götter.) Tr. Basil Crieghton. Fwd. Sir John Hunt. L: Methuen, 1957. 196p. (22.5cm.) 23cm. [LC62, B57, IT10]

TIDINGS OUT OF BRAZIL.
(Copia der newen Zeytung aus Presillg Landt.) A publ. from the James Ford Bell Collection in the U. of Minnesota Library. Tr. Mark Graubard. Commentary and notes John Parker. Minneapolis: U. of Minnesota Pr., 1957. 48p. 20cm. [LC62]

Same. L: Oxford U. Pr., 1958. 48p. 20cm. [B58]

TIECK, Ludwig.
Selections in Loomis, C. G. Prose. 1960.

TIETZE-CONRAT, Erika, 1883- .
Dwarfs and jesters in art. Tr. Elizabeth Osborn. L, NY: Phaidon, 1957. 110p. (111p.) (27.5cm.) 28cm. [LC62, B57, IT10, 11]

TIETZE-CONRAT, Erika--
Georg Ehrlich. Fwd. Eric Newton. L: Batsford, 1956.
24p. 26cm. [LC62]

TILLICH, Paul, 1886- .
Biblical religion and the search for ultimate reality. L:
Nisbet, 1956. 85p. (20.5cm.) [B56]

The new being. L: SCM, 1956. 179p. (19cm.)
[B56]

The Protestant era. Tr. James Luther Adams. Abr.
ed. Chicago: U. of Chicago Pr., 1957. 242p. 21cm.
[LC62]

The religious situation. (Die religöse Lage der Gegenwart.) Tr. Helmut Richard Niebuhr. L: Thames;
NY: Meridian, 1956. 21p. 19cm. [LC62, B56, IT10]

TIROL.
Official festive publication presented on the occasion of
the Tiroler Landesfeier 1809-1959. (Offizielle Festschrift
der Tiroler Landesfeier 1809-1959.) Tr. Anon. Schrift-
leitung und Gestaltung Josef Schroeder. Innsbruck, 1959.
104p. 28cm. [LC62]

TISCHER, Werner.
And so we bombed Moscow alone. The exciting personal
story of one man's experiences in the German Luftwaffe.
NY: Greenwich, 1960. 94p. 22cm. [LC62]

TODTMANN, Heinz, 1908- . See Stachelscheid, Carl
August.
Born of fire, steel. A color picture book. Pref. and
captions H--T--. Stuttgart: Strache, 1956. [LC62]

TÖNNIES, Ferdinand, 1855-1936.
Community and society. (Gemeinschaft und Gesellschaft.)
Tr. and ed. Charles P. Loomis. Michigan State U. Pr.,
1957. 298p. 24cm. [LC62]

TOEPFFER, Joachim, jt. author. See Boehle, Bernd,
1906- .
Where to stay in Germany. A guide to 300 of her finest
hotels and restaurants. (Rast auf Reisen.) Trs. Moira
Lane and Heribert Rück. New, enl. and rev. ed. L:
Stanford, 1958. 320p. 25cm. [LC62, B58]

TOEPLITZ, Otto, 1881-1940. See Rademacher, Hans, 1892- .
The enjoyment of mathematics. Selections from mathematics for the amateur. (Von Zahlen und Figuren.) Tr. Herbert Zuckerman. Princeton, NJ: Princeton U. Pr., (L: Oxford U. Pr.), 1957. 204p. (24.5cm.) 25cm. [LC62, B57, IT10]

TOMAN, Walter.
A kindly contagion. Stories. Tr. Harry Zohn. Indianapolis: Bobbs-Merrill, 1959. 218p. 21cm. [LC62, IT12]

TOURIST TRAVEL SERVICE, Basel.
Travel guide, the key to Switzerland. (Der Schlüssel zur Schweiz.) 1958. 304p. 21cm [LC62]

TOUSSAINT, Mathias Maria Friedrich, 1899- .
From ore to steel. The pictorial story of iron and its conversion to steel. (Der Weg des Eisens.) Tr. F. A. Rudolph. 4th ed. Düsseldorf: Verlag Stahleisen, 1958. 144p. 24cm. [LC62]

TRACHSEL, Alfred. See Ledermann, Alfred.
Creative playgrounds and recreation centers. (Spielplatz Gemeinschaftszentrum.) Tr. F. A. Praeger, 1959. [LC62]

TRAKL.
Selections in Flores, Anthol. 1960.

TRALBAUT, Mark Edo.
Van Gogh. (Van Gogh. Eine Bildbiographie.) Tr. Margaret Shenfield. L: Thames, c1959. 143p. (144p.) [LC62, B59, IT12]

Same. Van Gogh. A pictorial biography. Tr. M--S--. NY: Viking, 1959. 143p. 24cm. [LC62, IT13]

TRAUTWEIN, Friedrich.
The electronic monochord. Tr. H. A. G. Nathan. Ottawa, 1956. 121. 28cm. [LC62]

THE TRAVELS.
Of Leo of Rozmital through Germany, Flanders, England, France, Spain, Portugal and Italy, 1465-1467. Tr. Malcolm Letts. The Hakluyt Soc. at the Univ.

THE TRAVELS--
   Cambridge: U. Pr., 1957. 196p. 23cm. [LC62, B57,
   IT10]

TRAVEN, Bruno, pseud.
   The cotton pickers. (Die Baumwollpflücker.) Tr. Eleanor
   Brockett. L: Hale, 1956. 190p. (19.5cm.) 20cm.
   [LC62, B56, IT9]

   The death ship. The story of an American sailor. (Das
   Tottenschiff.) Tr. Eric Sutton. L: Cape, 1959. 388p.
   (20cm.) [LC62, B59, IT12]

   The treasure of the Sierra Madre. (Der Schatz der Si-
   erra Madre.) Tr. Basil Creighton. Harmondsworth:
   Middlesex, Penguin, 1956. 255p. 18cm. (18.5cm.)
   [LC62, B56, IT9]

   Same. L: Hutchinson Educational, 1960. 199p. [IT13]

TREUE, Wilhelm, 1909- .
   Art plunder. The fate of works of art in war, revolution,
   and peace. (Kunstraub.) Tr. Basil Creighton. L:
   Methuen, 1960. 264p. (22.5cm.) 23cm. [LC62, B60]

   Doctor at court. (Mit den Augen ihrer Leibärzte.) Tr.
   Frances Fawcett. L: Weidenfeld, 1958. 205p. (206p.)
   (22.5cm.) 23cm. [LC62, B58]

   Same. NY: Roy, 1958. 209p. 23cm. [LC62, IT13]

TRIEBOLD, Karl, ed.
   Healthy school--happy children. (Gesunde Schule--frohe
   Kinder.) (Ecole Saine-enfants joyeux.) Tr. Anon. Hrsg.
   Deutsche Gesellschaft für Freilufterziehung und Schul-
   gesundheitspflege, 1959. unp. 22 x 23cm. [LC62]

TROELTSCH, Ernst, 1865-1923.
   Christian thought, its history and application. Tr. Anon.
   Ed. Baron F. v. Hügel. NY: Meridian, 1957. 191p.
   19cm. [LC62]

   Lectures on the ideas of natural law and humanity. Tr.
   Ernst Barker. In Gierke, Otto F. v. Natural law and
   the theory of society. Boston: Beacon, 1957. [LC62]

   Same. Cambridge: U. Pr., 1958. [LC62]

Protestantism and progress. Tr. W. Montgomery.
Boston: Beacon, 1958. 210p. 21cm. [LC62, IT11]

The social teaching of the Christian churches. (Die
Soziallehren der christlichen Kirchen und Gruppen.) Tr.
Olive Wyon. L: Allen; NY: Macmillan, 1956. 2v.
1019p. 24cm. [LC62]

Same. NY: Harper, 1960. 2v. 21cm. [LC62, IT13]

TSCHICHOLD, Jan, 1902- .
The ampersand, its origin and development. (Formen-
wandlungen der Et-Zeichen.) Tr. Frederick Plaat. L:
Woudhuysen, 1957. 24p. (20.5cm.) 21cm. [LC62,
B58, IT10]

TUCHOLSKY, Kurt, 1890-1935.
The world is a comedy. A Tucholsky anthology. Tr. and
Ed. with critical essay Harry Zohn. Cambridge, Mass.:
Science-Art, 1957. 240p. 21cm. [LC62]

TÜRPITZ, Erika.
Oberammergau's first Christ. (Der erste Christus von
Oberammergau.) Frankfurt/Main: Main-Verlag; L:
Bailey, 1959. 128p. 21cm. [LC62, B60]

TYLINEK, Erich and Stepanek, Otakar.
The animal world. Tr. Helen Watney. L: Spring, 1959.
13p. 29cm. [B60]

TYLINEK, Erich, photog.
Introducing Chi Chi. The lovable giant panda. Text
Heidi Ute Demmer. L: Spring, 1960. 82p. (28cm.)
[B60]

UHLAND.
Selections in Loomis, C. G. 1960.

ULBRICHT, Walter, 1893- .
Disarmament, peaceful coexistence and friendship with all
peoples. Address given before diplomatic corps of German Democratic Republic Sept. 26, 1960. Berlin, 1960.
14p. 20cm. [LC62]

Government declaration on the development of agricultural production co-operatives. Delivered in the People's

ULBRICHT, Walter--
Chamber, by Walter Ulbricht. Berlin, 1960. 30p. 21cm.
[LC62]

ULMER, Eugen, 1903- .
Collected papers. v. p. n. d. 24cm. [LC62]

The protection of performing artists, producers of sound
recording, and broadcasting organizations, a study in international and comparative law. (Der Rechtsschutz der
ausübenden Künstler, der Hersteller von Tontragern und
der Sendegesellschaften in internationaler und rechtsver-
gleichender Sicht.) Trs. Hubert Secretan and Evelyn
Dunne. Washington, 1957. 77p. 27cm. [LC62]

ULRICH, Heinrich Hermann.
. . . Evangelism in Germany, an ecumenical survey.
(Die Kirche und ihre missionarische Aufgabe. Tatschen
und Probleme der Evangelisation in Deutschland.) Eng.
ver. Frank H. De Jonge and Robert L. Bilheimer. Ed.
D. T. Niles. L: Lutterworth, 1958. 30p. 22cm.
[LC62, B58]

ULRICH, Rolf, 1920- .
Coffee and caffeine. (Der Kaffee und das Coffein.) Tr.
Janet Ellingham. Bristol: Wright, 1958. 52p. (21.5
cm.) [LC62, B58, IT11]

UNGAR, Frederick. See Schiller, John Christoph Friedrich
von, 1759-1835.
Friedrich Schiller, an anthology for our time. NY:
Ungar, c1959. [LC62]

UNGEWITTER, Georg Gottlob, 1820-1864.
Details for stone and brick architecture in Romanesque
and Gothic style. (Vorlegeblätter für Ziegel- und Steinar-
beiten.) Tr. Anon. 3rd ed. NY: Hessling, 19--.
21. 44cm. [LC62]

UNION DER LEITENDEN ANGESTELLTEN.
(Leitende Angestellte in Wirtschaft und Gesselschaft.) Tr.
Anon. Essen: n. p., 1957. (Ger., Eng., Fr., and Italian.)
107p. 21cm. [LC62]

UNTERSUCHUNGSAUSSCHUSS FREIHEITLICHER JURISTEN.
Catalogue of injustice. (Dokumente des Unrechts. Das
SED-Regime in der Praxis.) Tr. Anon. Berlin-Zehlendorf-

West, 1959. 180p. 17cm. [LC62]

Ex-Nazis in the services of the German Democratic Republic. (Ehemalige Nationalsozialisten in Pankows Diensten.) Berlin-Zehlendorf-West, 1959. 64p. 21cm. [LC62]

The investigating committee of free jurists as seen by the German and foreign press. Tr. Anon. Berlin-Zehlendorf-West, 195-. 32p. 21cm. [LC62]

VACANO, Otto Wilhelm von, 1910- .
The Etruscans in the ancient world. (Die Etrusker in der Welt der Antike.) Tr. Sheila Ann Ogilvie. L: Arnold, 1960. 195p. (22.5cm.) 23cm. [LC62, B60]

VAHLEFELD, Rolf and Jacques, Friedrich, jt. authors.
Garages and service stations. (Garagen- und Tankstellenbau.) Tr. E. M. Schenk. L: Hill, adpt. I. Innes Elliott and C. R. Fowkes, 1960. 263p. 29cm. [LC62, B60]

VAJTA, Vilmos.
Luther on worship, an interpretation. (Die Theologie des Gottesdienstes bei Luther.) Tr. U. S. Leupold. Philadelphia: Muhlenberg, 1958. 200p. 21cm. [LC62]

VALENTIN, Erich, 1906- .
Beethoven, a pictorial biography. (Beethoven, eine Bildbiographie.) Tr. Norma Deane. L: Thames, 1958. 147p. (148p.) (24cm.) [LC62, B58, IT11]

Same. NY: Studio, 1958. 147p. 24cm. [LC62]

Mozart. A pictorial biography. (Mozart, Eine Bildbiographie.) Tr. M. Shenfield. München: Kindler; L: Thames, 1959. 143p. (144p.) (24cm.) [LC62, B59, IT12, 13]

Same. NY: Viking, 1960. 143p. 24cm. [LC62, IT13]

VALENTIN, Erich, 1906- , jt. author. See Dent, Edward Joseph, 1876- .
The earliest compositions of Wolfgang Amadeus Mozart. München: H. Rinn, 1956. [LC62]

VANGEROW, Oskar.
Scraping techniques, an introduction for would-be graphic artists. (Die Schabetechnik, eine Arbeitsanleitung für den werdenden Grafiker.) Tr. Anon. Munich: Vangerow, c1959. 85p. [LC62]

Same. Vienna, 1959. 85p. 25cm. [LC62]

VEGA, Georg Freiherr von, 1754-1802.
Logarithmic tables of numbers and trigonometrical functions. Tr. W. L. F. Fischer. Princeton, NJ: Van Nostrand, 1957. 575p. 24cm. [LC62]

Seven place logarithmic tables of numbers and trigonometrical functions. Tr. Anon. NY: Hafner, 1957. 575p. 23cm. [LC62]

10 place logarithms including Wolfram's tables of natural logarithms. Reprint 1794 ed. (Vollständige Sammlung grösserer logarithmisch-trigonometrischer Tafeln, nach Adrian Vlack's [sic] arithmetica logarithmical und trigonometria artificialis, verb., neu geordnet und vermehrt.) Tr. Anon. NY: Hafner, 1958. 684p. [LC62]

VEIT, Otto, 1898- , et al.
Changes in monetary policy and their consequences. (Die veränderte Währungspolitik und ihre Folgen.) Tr. Anon. Frankfurt/Main: Knapp, c1957. 215p. 21cm. [LC62]

VELDEKE, Heinrich von. See Heinrich von Veldeke.

VELTEN, Johannes, 1640-1692. Supposed author.
William Poel. Prompt-book of fratricide punished. (Der bestrafte Brudermord.) Tr. Anon. Supposed author Johannes Velten. L: Printed for the Society, 1956. 35p. 23cm. [LC62, B58]

VERKEHRSVEREIN DER HANSESTADT BREMEN.
Bremen, the city and the harbour. (Bremen, die Stadt und der Hafen.) Tr. Anon. Bremen, 19--. 74p. [LC62]

VERMEER, Johannes, 1632-1675.
Jan Vermeer, the paintings. Tr. and introd. R. H. Booth-Royd. L: Phaidon; NY: Garden City Bks., 1958. 155p. (156p.) 31cm. (31.5cm.) [LC62, B58]

VIENNA. Kunsthistorisches Museum, Schatzkammer.
Catalogue of the crown jewels and the ecclesiastical
treasure chamber, by H. Fillitz. (Kunsthistorisches Museum, Schatzkammer.) Tr. G. Holmes. Vienna, 1956.
64p. [LC62]

VIETTA, Egon, pseud. (i. e. Fritz, Egon.)
Stage-dancing in Germany, a pictorial survey of the bal-
let. Tr. Anon. Darmstadt: Neue Darmstädter Verlagsanstalt, 1956. 79p. 21cm. [LC62]

VIRCHOW, Rudolf (Ludwig Carl).
Disease, life, and men. Selected essays. Tr. and introd.
Lelland J. Rather. Stanford U. Pr., 1958. 273p.
23cm. [LC62, IT11]

Same. Stanford (Calif.): U. Pr.; L: Oxford U. Pr.,
1959. 273p. (22.5cm.) [B59]

VOEGLI, Max.
Prince of Hindustan. (Prinz von Hindustan.) Trs. Ruth
Michaelis-Jena and Arthur Ratcliff. L: Oxford U. Pr.,
1960. 224p. (22.5cm.) [B60]

VOGEL, Alfred.
The nature doctor. A kaleidoscopic collection of helpful
hints from the Swiss folklore of healing. (Der kleine
Doktor.) Tr. Anon. 7th ed. Teufen (AR), Switzerland,
Bioforee-Verlag, 1959. 391p. 21cm. [LC62]

VOGEL, Rolf, photog. See Schubert, Kurt, 1923- .
Israel, state of hope. Tr. Heinz Messinger. Text and
captions Kurt Schubert. Photos Rolf Vogel. Stuttgart:
Schwabenverlag, 1960. 87p. 29cm. [LC62]

VOIGTS, Heinrich, 1895- .
Meteorology in the German secondary schools. (From
Meteorologische Rundschau.) Vol. 9. no. 5 /6. Tr.
Anon. Berlin, n.p., 1956. 141. 36cm. [LC62]

VOLKMANN, Hans, 1900- .
Cleopatra. A study in politics and propaganda. (Kleo-
patra. Politik und Propaganda.) Tr. T. J. Cadoux.
L: Elek; NY: Sagamore, 1958. 244p. 22cm. (22.5
cm.) [LC62, B58, IT11]

VOLKMANN, Kurt.
The oldest deception. Cups, and balls in the 15th and
16th centuries. Tr. Barrows Mussey. Minneapolis:
Jones, 1956. 48p. 21cm. [LC62]

VOLZ, Wilhelm Theodor August Hermann, 1870- .
Eastern Germany colonial reservation. (Die Ostdeutsche
Wirtschaft.) Tr. Anon. 2nd ed. Warsaw: Western Pr.
Agency, 1957. 38p. 17p. 21cm. [LC62]

VON BEKESY, Georg. See Bekesy, Georg von.

VON BORSIG, Arnold, 1899- . See Borsig, Arnold von.

VON MISES, Ludwig. See Mises, Ludwig von.

VON SCHULENBURG, Ernst. See Schulenburg, Ernst von.

VOSSLER, Karl, 1872-1949.
Mediaeval culture. An introd. to Dante and his times.
(Die göttliche Komödie.) Tr. William Cranston Lawton.
NY: Ungar, 1958. 24cm. [LC62, IT11]

WACHSMUTH, Günther.
Reincarnation as a phenomenon of metamorphosis. (Die
Reinkarnation des Menschen als Phänomen der Matamor-
phose.) 2nd ed. Tr. Olin D. Wannamacher. Dornach:
Switzerland; Philadelphia: Anthroposophic, 1960. 236p.
[IT13]

WAERDEN, Bartel Leendert van der, 1903- and Nieuergelt,
E. Wätjen, Richard Lacey, 1891- .
Dressage riding. A guide for the training of horse and
rider. (Das Dressurreiten.) Tr. V. Saloschin. Fwd.
V. D. S. Williams. L: Allen, 1958. 113p. (25.5cm.)
26cm. [LC62, B58]

WAGGERL, Karl Heinrich.
The most beautiful Alpine flowers. Water-colours by
Mila Lippmann-Palowski. Tr. Oscar Konstandt. St.
Johann/Tyrol: Pinguin; L: Thorsons, 1957. 48p.
(15.5cm.) [B57]

WAGNER, Richard, 1813-1883.
The flying Dutchman. (Der fliegende Holländer.) Tr.
Publicity Dept., Decca Record Co., 1956. 47p.

(22cm.) [B56]

WAGNER, Wilhelm Richard.
The ring of the Nibelung. (Der Ring des Nibelungen.)
Tr. with fwd. Stewart Robb. NY: Dutton, 1960. 340p.
19cm. [LC62, IT13]

WAGNER, Wolfgang.
The genesis of the Oder-Neisse line. A study in the
diplomatic negotiation during World War II. (Die Ents-
tehung der Oder-Neisse linie in den diplomatischen
Verhandlungen während des Zweiten Weltkrieges.) Tr.
Anon. Stuttgart: Brentano-Verlag, 1957. 168p. 24cm.
[LC62]

The partitioning of Europe. A history of the Soviet ex-
pansion up to the cleavage of Germany, 1918-1945. (Die
Teilung Europas. Geschichte der sowejetischen Expansion
bis zur Spaltung Deutschlands, 1918-1945.) Tr. Anon.
Stuttgart: Deutsche Verlags-Anstalt, 1959. 239p. 21cm.
[LC62]

WAISMANN, Friedrich.
Introd. to mathematical thinking. Tr. Theodore J. Ben-
ac. NY: Harper, 1959. 260p. 21cm. [LC62, IT12]

WALDEMAR, Charles.
The mystery of sex. (Magie der Geschlechter.) Trs.
Lara and Andrew Tilburg. L: Elek, 1960. 284p.
[LC62]

WALDER, Hans, 1920.
Drive structure and criminality. (Triebstruktur in Krimi-
nalität.) Tr. Marvin W. Webb. Springfield, Ill.:
Thomas; Oxford: Blackwell Scientific Publications, 1959.
174p. (23.5cm.) 24cm. [LC62, B59, IT12]

WALESKA, Mathilde. See Walewska, pseud.

WALEWSKA, pseud. (i.e. Waleska, Mathilde.)
Dearest mama. The life story of a bad girl. (Meine
schöne Mama.) Tr. Constantine Fitzgibbon. L: Barrie,
1956. 159p. (19cm.) [LC62, B56, IT9]

Same. L: Brown, 1960. 159p. (18.5cm.) [B60]

My lovely mama. (Meine schöne Mama.) Tr. Anon.

WALEWSKA, pseud--
Indianapolis: Bobbs-Merrill, 1956. 179p. 21cm.
[LC62]

WALLNER, Albert.
My U. S. notebook. (Mein Amerikabuch.) Tr. Anon.
Wien: Omnis-Selbstverlag, c1960. 287p. [LC62]

WALSER, Martin, (1927- .)
The Gadarene Club. (Ehen in Philipsburg.) Tr. Eva
Figes. L: Longmans, 1960. 273p. 19cm. [LC62,
B60, IT13]

WALSER, Robert, 1878-1956.
A village tale. Tr. Christopher Middleton. In Spender's
Coll. 1960.

The walk and other stories. (Der Spaziergang.) Tr.
Christopher Middleton. L: Calder, 1957. 104p.
(19.5cm.) [LC62, B57, IT10]

WALTER, Bruno, 1876- .
(Gustav Mahler.) Trs. Lotte Walter Lindt, et al. L:
Hamilton, 1958. 133p. (20.5cm.) 21cm. [LC62, B58,
IT11]

Same. NY: Knopf, 1958. 175p. 20cm. [LC62, IT11]

WALZ, Heinz, 1907- , and Graves, Rosemary, jt. authors.
Britain past and present. (Ein kulturkundliches Lese-
buch.) Tr. Anon. München: Huber, 1957. 147p. 21
cm. [LC62]

WALZ, Karlheinz.
Spring problems. (Walz's Federfragen by Bernhard
Sterne.) Tr. Anon. NY: Society of Automotive Engi-
neers, 1958? 91p. 28cm. [LC62]

WARNS, Johannes.
Baptism. Studies in the original Christian baptism, its
history and conflicts. (Die Taufe.) 2nd ed. Tr. G. H.
Lang. L: Paternoster, 1957. 352p. (22cm.) 23cm.
[LC62, B58]

Same. Grand Rapids, Mich.: Kregel, 1958. 352p.
23cm. [LC62]

WASSERMANN, Felix M.
Alexander von Humboldt as an international figure.
(Auf Urwaldflüssen, aus Humboldt: Reise in die Aequin-
octial-Gegenden.) Tr. Helmut de Terra. n. p., Philadelphia, 1959. 18-26p. 25cm. [LC62]

WASSERMANN, Jacob, 1873-1934.
The Maurizius case. (Der Fall Maurizius.) Tr. C.
Newton. NY: Liveright, 1959. 546p. [LC62]

WE ARE NOW CATHOLICS. See Goethe, Rudolf.

WEBER, Alfred, 1868- .
Theory of the location of industries. Tr. Carl J. Fried-
rich. L: Cambridge U. Pr.; Chicago: U. of Chicago
Pr., 1957. 256p. 21cm. [LC62, B57]

WEBER, Eduard.
Cut-out model of the human brain. An aid to the story
of the cerebrum, ready punched cut-outs. Tr. Anon.
From 3rd ed. NY: Hafner, 1957. 4p. [LC62]

WEBER, Hans Ruedi.
The communication of the Gospel to illiterates. Based
on a missionary experience in Indonesia. Tr. Olga
Pilpel. Eds. Erik W. Nelsen and E. J. Binger. L:
SCM, 1957. 127p. (21.5cm.) 22cm. [LC62, B57]

WEBER, Karl, 1880- .
The Swiss press, an outline. (Profil der Schweizer
Presse.) Tr. Max Nef. Berne: Lang, 1960. 46p.
18cm. [LC62]

WEBER, Max, 1864-1920.
Ancient Judaism. Trs. and ed. Hans H. Gerth and
Don Martindale. Glencoe, Ill.: Free Pr., 1960.
484p. 21cm. [LC62]

The city. (Die Stadt.) Trs. Don Martindale and Gertrude [sic] Neuwirth. L: Heinemann, 1960. 242p.
(22.5cm.) 23cm. [LC62, B60]

WEBER, Max--
Same. Trs. Don Martindale and Gertrud Neuwirth.
Glencoe, Ill.: Free Pr., 1958. 242p. 22cm. [LC62,
IT11]

From Max Weber. Essays in sociology. Trs. and Ed.
with introd. H. H. Gerth and C. Wright Mills. L:
Routledge, 1957. 490p. 25cm. [LC62]

Same. NY: Oxford, 1958. 501p. [LC62, IT11]

General economic history. Tr. Frank H. Knight. Glencoe, Ill.: Free Pr., 1958. 401p. 8° [LC62]

The Protestant ethic and the spirit of capitalism. Tr.
Talcott Parsons. Fwd. R. T. Tawney. NY: Scribner,
1956. 2-292p. 23cm. [LC62]

Same. Students ed. NY: Scribner, 1958. 292p. 22cm.
[LC62, IT11]

The rational and social foundations of music. (Die
rationalen und soziologischen Grundlagen der Musik.)
Trs. and Ed. Don Martindale, Johannes Riedel and Gertrude Neuwirth. Carbondale, South Ill.: Ill. U. Pr.,
1958. 148p. 22cm. [LC62, IT11]

The religions of India, the sociology of Hinduism and
Buddhism. (Hinduismus und Buddhismus.) Trs. Hans
N. Gerth and Don Martindale. Glencoe, Ill.: Free Pr.;
L: Allen, 1958. 392p. (21cm.) [LC62, B59, IT11]

The theory of social and economic organization. (Wirtschaft und Gesellschaft.) Trs. A. M. Henderson and
Talcott Parsons. Glencoe, Ill.: Free Pr., 1957. 436p.
24cm. [LC62, IT11]

WEBER, Otto Heinrich, 1902- .
Ground plan of the Bible. (Grundriss der Bibelkunde.)
Tr. Harold Knight. From 4th Ger. ed. L: Lutterworth;
Philadelphia: Westminster, 1956. 221p. (22.5cm.)
23cm. [LC62, IT12, 13]

WECKHERLIN.
Selection in Loomis, C. G. 1958.

WEDEKIND, Frank, 1864-1918.
The solar spectrum. Those who buy the Gods of love.
An idyll from modern life. (Das Sonnenspektrum.) Trs.
Dietrich Faehl and Eric Vaughn. n. p. 1958. 571.
30cm. [LC62, IT12]

Spring's awakening. (Frühlingserwachen.) In Bentley,
The modern theatre Vol. 6. 1960.

WEEREN, Friedrich August 1907- . See Deich, Friedrich,
pseud.

WEIDEL, Wolfhard.
Virus. (Virus. Die Geschichte vom geborgten Leben.)
Tr. Lotte Streisinger. L: Mayflower, 1959. 159p.
(21.5cm.) [D50, IT13]

Same. Ann Arbor: U. of Michigan Pr., 1959. 159p.
22cm. [LC62, IT12]

WEIGER, Josef.
Mary, mother of the faith. (Maria, die Mutter des
Glaubens.) Tr. Ruth M. Bethell. Chicago: Regnery,
1959. 259p. 25cm. [LC62, IT12]

Same. Introd. Romano Guardini. L: Burns, 1959.
263p. (24.5cm.) [B60, IT13]

WEIGERT, Hans, 1896- .
The dance. Tr. Anon. Milan: Uffici, 1959. 31p.
35cm. [LC62]

Dutch painting, 17th century. Trs. Desmond and Camille
Clayton. Milan: Uffici, 1960. 31p. 35cm. [LC62]

The nativity. Text Hans Weigert. Milan: Uffici, 1958.
31p. 35cm. [LC62]

WEIKL, Ludwig.
Stir up the fire. Considerations on the priesthood.
(Entfache die Glut.) Trs. I. and F. McHugh. Milwaukee:
Bruce 1959. 233p. 21cm. [LC62, IT12]

WEILER, Clemens, 1909- .
Jawlensky. Tr. John Garrett. Milan: Uffici, 1959.
27p. [LC62]

WEINGARTNER BLESSING FOR A JOURNEY.
In Loomis, C. G.

WEINSTOCK, M. D.
Light in the darkness. Selected stories. Tr. K. Szasz.
L: n.p., 1957-59. 89p. 19cm. [LC62]

WEISENBORN, Günther, 1902- .
The fury. (Die Furie.) Trs. Richard and Clarissa
Graves. L: Hutchinson, 1956. 264p. 19cm. (19.5
cm.) [LC62, B56, IT9]

WEISKERN, Franz Wilhelm.
Bastien and Bastienne, German singspiel in five scenes,
with sixteen musical numbers. (B-- und B--. Libretto.) Eng. ver. Baird Hastings. Boston: Lily, 1959.
15p. 21cm. [LC62]

The magic flute. (Die Zauberflöte.) Eng. ver. Edward
J. Dent. L: Oxford U. Pr., 1959. 48p. 19cm.
[LC62]

WEISS, Albert Maria, 1844-1925.
The Christian life. (Apologie des Christentums.) Tr.
Sister M. Fulgence. L: Herder, 1956. 166p. 21cm.
[LC62]

WEISS, Johannes, 1863-1914.
Earliest Christianity, a history of the period A.D. 30-
150. Ed. and tr. with introd. Frederick C. Grant.
NY: Harper, 1959. (21cm.) [LC62, B59, IT11]

The secret of individuality reflected in a hundred historical lives. Tr. Hector Wilshire. (pp. 1-233, vol.
1, and last chap. of vol. 2 with author from ms.)
Sydney, L: Angus, 1957. (22cm.) [LC62, B58]

World without frontiers. Trs. Kathryn Linden and Wini-
fred Richardson in collaboration with author. 2nd ed.
Sydney, L: Angus, 1958. 221p. (22.5cm.) 23cm.
[LC62, B59, IT11]

WEISSBERG, Alexander Cybulski.
Advocate for the dead. The story of Joel Brand. (Die geschichte von Joel Brand.) Trs. Constantine Fitzgibbon and Andrew Foster-Melliar. L: Deutsch, 1958. 255p. 22cm. [LC62, B58, IT11]

Same. L: Landsborough, 1959. 190p. (18.5cm.) [B59]

Desperate mission. Joel Brandt's story. (Geschichte von Joel Brand.) Trs. Constantine Fitzgibbon and Andrew Foster-Melliar. NY: Criterion, 1958. 310p. 22cm. [LC62]

WEISS-SONNENBURG, Hedwig.
Plum-blossom and Kai Lin. (Pflaumenblüte und Kai Lin.) Tr. Joyce Emerson. L: U. of London Pr., 1958. 127p. (128p.) (22cm.) [B58, IT11]

Same. NY: Watts, 1960. 127p. 21cm. [LC62, IT13]

WEIZSÄCKER, Carl Friedrich Freiherr von, 1912- .
The history of nature. (Die Geschichte der Natur.) Tr. Fred D. Wieck. Chicago: U. of Chicago Pr., 1959. 191p. 21cm. [LC62, IT12]

Same. Tr. Fred D. Wieck. Chicago: U. of Chicago Pr., 1959. 197p. [IT12]

The rise of modern physics. (Physik der Gegenwart.) Tr. Arnold J. Pomerans. NY: Braziller, 1957. 150p. 22cm. [LC62]

WEIZSÄCKER, Carl Friedrich Freiherr von, 1912- , and Jiufs, J., jt. authors.
Contemporary physics. (Physik der Gegenwart.) Tr. Arnold J. Pomerans. L: Hutchinsons Scientific and Technical Publications, 1957. 150p. (22cm.) [LC62, B57]

WELTY, Eberhard, 1902- .
A handbook of Christian social ethics (V.1) Man in society. (Herders Sozialkatechismus.) Tr. Gregor Kirstein. Rev. and adpt. John Fitzsimons. NY: Herder, n.d. v. 22cm. [LC62, IT13]

WENCKEBACH, Carla, 1853-1902.   See Müller, Margarethe,
1862- , jt. authors.

WENDELBERGER, Elfrune.
The Alps in bloom.   (Die Alpen blühen.)   Trs. Oscar
Konstandt and Jean Thow.   Innsbruck: Pinguin,   c1958.
55p. 16cm.   [LC62, IT12]

Same.   L: Thorsons, 1958.   56p.   (15.5cm.)   [B58,
IT11]

WENDT, Herbert, 1914- .
In search of Adam.   Man's quest for his earliest ances-
tors.   (Ich suchte Adam.)   Tr. James Cleugh.   Boston:
Houghton, 1956.   540p.   22cm.   [LC62, IT9]

Out of Noah's ark, the story of man's discovery of the
animal kingdom.   (Auf Noahs Spuren.)   Tr. M. Bullock.
L: Weidenfeld,   469p.   (22.5cm.)   23cm.   [LC62, B59,
IT12]

Same.   Boston: Houghton, 1959.   464p.   22cm.   [LC62,
IT13]

The road to man.   (Wir und die Tiere.)   Tr. Helen Sebba.
Garden City, NY: Doubleday, 1959.   431p.   24cm.   (LC
62, IT12]

Same.   L: Lutterworth, 1960.   252p.   (253p.)   (23cm.)
[LC62, B60, IT13]

WERFEL, Franz V., 1890-1945.
Embezzled heaven.   Tr. Moray Firth.   NY: Dell, 1959.
384p.   [IT12]

God's kingdom of Bohemia.   The tragedy of a leader.
Tr. Ruth Langner.   n.p., 19--.   116l.   39cm.   [LC62]

Jacobowsky and the Colonel.   Adapt. S. N. Behrman.
In Twenty best European plays on the American stage.
Tr. Anon.   Ed. John Gassner.   NY, n.p.,   1957.   300-
479p.

Juarez and Maximilian.   Includes light and property
plots.   Tr. Anon.   n.p., n.d.   1 Vol.   28cm.   [LC62]

Mirror man.   A magic trilogy.   Eng. ver. Ruth Lang-

ner.   NY: Rialto Service Bureau, 19--.   30cm.   1 Vol.
v. p.   30cm.   [LC62]

Paul among the Jews.   Tr. Ruth Langner.   NY: Rialto
Service Bureau.   n. d.   1 Vol.   v. p.   28cm.   [LC62]

The song of Bernadette.   (Das Lied der Bernadette.)
Tr. Ludwig Lewisohn.   NY: Viking, 1956.   575p.   [IT9]

Same.   L: Collins, 1958.   445p.   (18cm.)   [B58, IT11]

Spiegelmensch, a magic trilogy.   (S--.)   Tr. Ruth Langner.   n. p. , 19--.   33, 98, 671.   28cm.   [LC62]

WERLBERGER, Hans, 1906- .   See Kades, Hans, pseud.

WERNER, Bruno Erich, 1896- .
Modern architecture in Germany.   (Neues Bauen in
Deutschland.)   Tr. Anon.   2nd ed.   Munich: Bruckmann,
1956.   79, 1p.   [LC62]

WERNER, Heinz, 1890- .
Comparative psychology of mental development.   (Einführung in die Entwicklungspsychologie.)   Tr. E. B. Garside.   Fwd.   Gordon W. Allport.   Rev. ed.   NY: International U. Pr. , 1957.   564p.   22cm.   [LC62]

WERNER, Helmut, 1905- .
From the Aratus globe to the Zeiss planetarium.   Tr.
A. H. Degenhardt.   Fwd. Harold Spencer Jones.   Stutt-
gart: Fischer, 1957.   204p.   22cm.   [LC62]

WERNER, Martin, 1887- .
The formation of Christian dogma.   An historical study
of its problems.   (Die Entstehung des christlichen Dog-
mas.)   Tr. and introd.   S. G. F. Brandon.   L: Black,
1957.   352p.   (23. 5cm.)   24cm.   [LC62, B57]

Same.   NY: Harper, 1957.   352p.   23cm   [LC62]

THE WESSOBRUNNER PRAYER.   (Wessobrunner Gebet.)
In Loomis, C. G.

WETHEKAM, Cili.
Dudu.   An adventure story from Germany.   (Dudu.)
Tr. Anon.   Stuttgart: Herold Verlag, 1956.   Leicester:
Brockhampton, 1959.   120p.   (20cm.)   [B59, IT12]

WETTACH, Charles Adrien. See Grock, pseud.

WETTER, Gustav Andreas.
Dialectical materialism, a historical and systematic sur-
vey of philosophy in the Soviet Union. (Der dialektische
Materialismus.) Tr. Peter Heath. Rev. ed. with au-
thor's additions. L: Routledge, 1958. 609p. (22.5cm.)
[B58]

WEYMAR, Paul.
Adenauer, his authorized biography. Tr. Peter de
Mendelssohn. 1st ed. NY: Dutton, 1957. 509p. 22cm.
[LC62]

Konrad Adenauer. The authorized biography. (Konrad
Adenauer.) Adpt. and tr. Peter de Mendelssohn. L:
Deutsch, 1957. 543p. (21.5cm.) [LC62, B57]

WICKENBURG, Eric Graf von, 1903- .
Treasures of painting in Vienna. Tr. Anne Clulow.
Wien: Kunstverlag Wolfrum, 1960. 15p. 20cm.
[LC62]

WIDMANN, Walter and Schütte, Karl
Stars. (Welcher stern ist das.) Tr. and ed. Arthur
Beer. L: Thames, 1957. 224p. (20.5cm.) [LC62,
B57]

WIDMOSER, Eduard.
South Tyrol and the Dolomites. (Südtirol und Dolomiten.)
Trs. Oscar Konstandt and Ralph D. Oppenheimer. Introd. Erich Kofler. Photos. Heinz Müller-Brunke, R.
Löble, A. Sichert et al. Innsbruck: Pinguin; Frank-
furt/Main: Umschau; L: Thorsons, 1959. 96p.
(24.5cm.) [LC62, B59]

South Tirol, a problem of justice. Tr. Anon. Innsbruck: Bergisel, 1957. 19p. 30cm. [LC62]

WIECHERT, Ernst Emil, 1887-1950.
Tidings. (Missa sine nomine.) Trs. Marie Heynemann
and Margery B. Ledward. NY: Macmillan, 1959. 302p.
22cm. [LC62, IT12]

WIESER, Friedrich Freiherr von, 1851-1926.
Natural value. Tr. Christian A. Malloch. Ed. with a
pref. and analysis William Smart. NY: Kelley, 1956.

243p. 22cm. [LC62]

WIESINGER, Alois, 1885- .
Occult phenomenon in the light of theology. (Okkulte
Phänomene im Lichte der Theologie.) Tr. Brian Batter-
shaw. L: Burns, 1957. 294p. 22cm. (22.5cm.)
[LC62]

Same. Westminster, Md.: Newman, 1957. 294p.
22cm. [LC57, IT10]

WIGHTON, Charles and Peis, Günther.
Hitler's spies and saboteurs. Based on the German
secret service war diary of General Lahousen. Tr.
Anon. 1st ed. NY: Holt, 1958. 285p. 22cm. [LC62]

They spied on England. Based on the German secret
war diary of General Lahousen. Tr. Anon. L: Odhams, 1958. 320p. (21.5cm.) [B58]

WIGNER, Eugene Paul.
Group theory and its application to the quantum mechanics
of atomic spectra. (Gruppentheorie und ihre Anwendung
auf die Quantemmechanik der Atomspektren.) Tr. J. J.
Griffin. NY: Academic, 1959. 372p. (23.5cm.) 24
cm. [LC62, B59]

WIGNER, Eugene Paul. See Eisenbud, Leonard.
Nuclear structure. Tr. Anon. Princeton, NJ: Princeton U. Pr., 1958. [LC62]

WIGNER, Eugene Paul. See Weinberg, Alvin Martin,
1915- .
The physical theory of neutron chain reactors. Tr.
Anon. Chicago: U. of Chicago Pr.; L: Cambridge U.
Pr., 1958. 801p. 24cm. [LC62]

WIKENHAUSER, Alfred, 1883- .
New Testament introduction. (Einleitung in das Neue
Testament.) Tr. Joseph Cunningham. 1st ed. Freiburg:
Herder, 1958. 579p. 23cm. [LC62]

Same. NY: Herder, 1958. 579p. (22.5cm.) [LC62]

Same. Edinburgh; L: Nelson, 1958. 580p. (22.5
cm.) [B59, IT12]

WIKENHAUSER, Alfred--
Pauline mysticism. Christ in the mystical teaching of
St. Paul. (Die Christusmystik des Apostels Paulus.)
1st ed. Tr. J. Cunningham. Freiburg: Herder, 1960.
255p. 22cm. [LC62]

Same. Edinburgh, L: Nelson, 1960. 3-256p. 22cm.
[B60]

Same. NY: Herder, 1960. 255p. 23cm. [LC62,
IT13]

WILDER, Thornton Niven, 1897- . See Nestroy, Johann
Nepomuk, 1801-1862.
The matchmaker. A farce in four acts. (Einen Jux will
er sich machen.) Tr. Anon. NY: French, 1957.
[LC62]

WILHELM, Hellmut, 1905- .
Change. 8 lectures on the I ching. (Die Wandlung, acht
Essays zum I-Ging.) Tr. Gary F. Baynes. NY: Pan-
theon, 1960. 111p. 23cm. [LC62, IT13]

WILHELM, Julius. See Kerker, Gustave Adolph, 1923-
1957.
Two little brides. In three acts. Book by James T.
Powers and Harold Atteridge. Lyrics Arthur Anderson.
L: Haymarket, n.d. 52, 53, 361. 27cm. [LC62]

WILLEMSEN, Carl Arnold, 1902- . and Odenthal, Dagmar.
Apulia, imperial splendor in southern Italy. (Apulien,
Land der Normannen, Land der Staufer.) Tr. Daphne
Woodward. L: Thames, 1959. 257p. (28cm.) 29cm.
[LC62, B59, IT12]

Same. NY: Praeger, 1959. 257p. 29cm. [LC62,
IT13]

WILLI, Heinrich. See Heinrich, Willi.

WILLNER, Alfred. See Kerker, Gustave Adolph, 1857-1923.
Two little brides. In three acts. Book by James T.
Powers and Harold Atteridge. Lyrics Arthur Anderson.
L, Haymarket, n.d. 52, 53, 361. 27cm. [LC62]

WILMS, Hieronymus, 1878- .
Divine friendship according to St. Thomas. (Die Gottes-

freundschaft nach dem heiligen Thomas.) Tr. Sister
Mary Fulgence. L: Blackfriars, 1958. 132p. 19cm.
(19.5cm.) [LC62, B58, IT12]

Same. Dubuque, Iowa: Priory, c1958. 132p.

As the morning star. The life of St. Dominic. Tr. A.
Dominican Sister of the Perpetual Rosary. Milwaukee:
Bruce, 1956. 134p. 21cm. [LC62]

WILMS, Jerome. See Wilms, Hieronymus, 1878- .

WILMS, Jerome.
Lay Brother, artist and saint. (Der selige Jakob Grie-
singer aus Ulm.) Tr. Sister M. Fulgence. L: Blackfriars, 1957. 153p. (19.5cm.) [B57]

WILSON, Barbara Ker, 1929- .
Fairy tales of Germany. Tr. Anon. L: Cassell; NY:
Dutton, 1959. 44p. (21cm.) [LC62, B59]

WINDELBAND, Wilhelm, 1848-1915.
History of ancient philosophy. Tr. Herbert Ernst Cush-
man. NY: Dover, 1956. 393p. 21cm. [LC62, IT11]

A history of philosophy. Tr. James H. Tufts. NY:
Harper, 1958. 2v. 21cm. [LC62]

Same. 2nd ed. NY: Macmillan, 1956. 726p. 21cm.
[LC62]

WINDISCH, Hans, 1891- .
The manual of modern photography. (Die neue Foto-
schule. Die Technik.) Tr. Frank Willy Frerk. Vaduz:
Liechtenstein, Heering; L: Fountain, 1956. (292p.)
(22cm.) [B57]

Same. Fred. Willy Frerk. Philadelphia: Rayelle,
1956. 291p. 22cm. [LC62]

WINGLER, Hans Maria.
Introduction to Kokoschka. (Kokoschka-Fibel.) Tr.
Peter Gorge. L: Thames, 1958. 142p. (143p.)
(17.5cm.) 18cm. [LC62, B58, IT11]

Oskar Kokoschka. The work of the painter. (O--K--.)
Trs. Frank S. C. Budgen, J. P. Hodin and Ilse Schrier

WINGLER, Hans Maria--
with Mrs. D. P. Hodin. Salzburg: Galerie Welz; L:
Faber, 1958. 401p. 30cm. (30.5cm.) [LC62, B58,
IT11]

WINNER, Gerhard. See Eheim, Fritz.

WINTERFELD, Henry.
Castaways in Lilliput. (Telegramm aus Liliput.) Tr.
Kyrill Schabert. NY: Harcourt, 1960. 188p. 21cm.
[LC62, IT13]

Detectives in togas. (Caius ist ein Dummkopf.) Trs.
Richard and Clara Winston. NY: Harcourt, 1956. 205p.
22cm. [LC62, IT9]

Same. Tr. Katya Sheppard. L: Constable, 1957. 199p.
(20.5cm.) 21cm. [LC62, B57, IT10]

Star girl. (Kommt ein Mädchen geflogen.) Tr. Kyrill
Schabert. NY: Harcourt, 1957. 191p. 21cm. [LC62,
IT10]

WINTERNITZ, Moriz, 1863-1937.
A history of Indian literature. (Geschichte der indischen
Litteratur. [sic] Tr. S. Ketkar. U. of Calcutta, 1959.
184p. [LC62, IT13]

WINTERSWYL, Ludwig Athanasius.
The resurrection. Eng. adapt. Annelise Derrick. Freiburg: Herder; L: Interbook, 1957. 9p. (11p.)
(19cm.) [LC62, B57]

WIRTH, David, 1885- .
Veterinary clinical diagnosis. (Einführung in die klinische
Diagnostik der inneren Erkrankungen und Hautkrankheiten
der Haustiere.) Tr. Annie I. Littlejohn. L: Bailliere,
1956. 232p. (23.5cm.) 24cm. [LC62, B56, IT9]

WITTELS, Fritz, 1880-1950.
Freud and his time, the influence of the master psycholo-
gist on the emotional problems in our lives. Tr. Louise
Brink. L: Owen, 1956. 451p. (22.5cm.) [LC62, B56,
IT9]

Same. NY: Grosset, 195-. 451p. 21cm. [LC62]

WITTENWEILER, Heinrich, 15th cen.
Wittenweiler's ring, and the anonymous Scots poem
Colkelbie sow. Tr. George Fenwick Jones. Chapel
Hill: U. of North Carolina Pr., 1956. 246p. 23cm.
[LC62, IT9]

WITTGENSTEIN, Ludwig, 1889-1951.
Philosophical investigations. (Philosophische Untersuchungen.) Tr. G. E. M. Anscombe. Oxford: Blackwell,
1958. 232p. (246p.) (22.5cm.) 23cm. [LC62, B58,
IT11]

Preliminary studies for the philosophical investigations.
Tr. Anon. Oxford: Blackwell, 1958. 185p. (22.5cm.)
23cm. [LC62, B58]

Same. NY: Harper, 1958. 185p. 22cm. [LC62]

Remarks on the foundations of mathematics. Eds. G. H.
von Wright, R. Rhees and G. E. M. Anscombe. Tr.
G. E. M. Anscombe. Oxford: Blackwell, 1956. 196,
196e, 197-204p. (434p.) (22.5cm.) 25cm. [LC62]

Same. NY: Macmillan; Oxford: Blackwell, 1956.

Tractatus logico-philosophicus. Tr. Anon. Introd.
Bertrand Russell. L: Routledge, 1958. 207p. 23cm.
[LC62]

WÖLFFLIN, Heinrich, 1864-1945.
Classic art, an introduction to the Italian Renaissance.
(Die klassische Kunst. Eine Einführung in die italienische
Renaissance.) Trs. Peter and Linda Murray. L, NY:
Phaidon, 1959. 296p. 26cm. [LC62]

Principles of art history. The problem of development
of style in later art. Tr. M. D. Hottinger. NY: Dover,
1956. 237p. [LC62, IT9]

WOLF, Siegfried Helmut.
The magic of the Alps. (Photos.) Tr. Oskar Konstandt.
L: Thorsons; St. Johann/Tirol: Pinguin, 1957. 80p.
(15.5cm.) 16cm. [LC62, B57]

WOLFF, Kurt H., 1912- . and Georg Simmel, 1858-1918.
A coll. of essays, with tr. and a bibliography. Columbus:
Ohio State U. Pr., 1959. 396p. 22cm. [LC62, IT13]

WOLFRAM VON ESCHENBACH.
Schionatulander and Sigune, an episode from the story of
Parzival and the Grail.   Tr. with explanatory frame-
work Margaret Fitzgerald Richey.   2nd ed.   Edinburgh,
L: Oliver, 1960.   61p.   19cm.   [LC62, B60]

Studies of Wolfram von Eschenbach.   Tr. Margaret Fitzgerald Richey.   With Eng. verse of passages from his
poetry.   (Parzival, Willehalm and Titurel.)   Edinburgh,
L: Oliver, 1957.   226p.   (22.5cm.)   [B57]

WOLLHEIM, Gerth.
The Shakespeare picture book.   Berlin: Wam Osterhof
Kommanditgesellschaft, 1959.   66p.   21cm.   [LC62]

WOLTERECK, Heinz, 1901- .
A new life in old age.   (Das Alter ist das zweite Leben.)
Tr. Charlotte Holdane.   L: Reinhardt, 1958.   194p.
(20.5cm.)   [LC62, B58, IT11]

A new life in your later years.   (Das Alter ist das
zweite Leben.)   Tr. Charlotte Holdane.   Fwd. Lord Amul-
ree.   Introd. Edward J. Lorenze.   NY: Dial, 1959.
194p.   22cm.   [LC62]

WOMELSDORF, Penn.   Zion Union Church.
Translation of the Zion Union (Lutheran and Reformed)
Church records of Womelsdorf, Berks County, Penn.,
begun Nov. 16, 1794.   (Half title, Gemeinschaftliches
hochdeutsches Kirchenprotokol zur Zionskirche in Womelsdorf.)   Tr. Anon.   Ed. Mrs. Irvin L. Krick.   Chicago,
Ill. , 1958.   95, 391.   28cm.   [LC62]

A WORLD WITHOUT JEWS.
(Zur Judenfrage.)   Tr. Dagobert D. Runes.   NY: Philosophical Lib. , (L: Calder), 1959.   51p.   (18.5cm.)
20cm.   [LC62, B59, IT12]

THE WORKS OF PIER LUIGI NERVI.   See Nervi, Pier
Luigi.

WORRINGER Wilhelm, 1881- .
Form in Gothic.   (Formprobleme der Gotik.)   Tr. and
ed. with introd. Sir Herbert Read.   L: Tiranti, 1957.
181p.   (23cm.)   [LC62, B57]

WÜRTHWEIN, Ernst, 1909- .
The text of the Old Testament, an introduction to Kittel-
kahle's "Biblia Hebraica." (Der Text des Alten Testaments.) Tr. Peter R. Ackroyd. NY: Macmillan; L:
Blackwell, 1957. 173p. (24cm.) [LC62, B57]

WUESTHOFF, Freda d. 1956.
There is no time to be lost, man in the atomic age.
(Es ist keine Zeit mehr zu verlieren. Der Mensch im
Atomzeitalter.) Tr. Anon. Ravensburg: Maier, (Ger.,
Fr., Eng., Russian, Swedish, Dutch, Span., and Ital.)
1957. 132p. 22cm. [LC62]

WUHRMANN, Ferdinand and Wunderly, Charlie, jt. authors.
The human blood proteins, methods of examination and
their clinical and practical significance. (Die Bluteiweis-
skörper des Menschen.) Tr. Harvey T. Adelson. NY:
Grune, 1960. 491p. 25cm. [LC62]

WULF, Trolli Neutzsky.
The gypsy girl. Tr. Theodore Mueller. L: Oliphants,
1960. 3-122p. (20cm.) [B60]

WURST, Werner.
Exakta manual. The complete guide to miniature photog-
raphy with the Exakta camera. Tr. F. Bradley. L:
Fountain, 1960. 419p. (22.5cm.) [B60]

WUNDERLY, Charlie, jt. auth. See Wuhrmann, Ferdinand.

WYSS, Johannes David.
The Swiss family Robinson. Tr. Anon. L: Dent,
1956. 454p. 21cm. [LC62]

The Swiss family Robinson. Tr. Anon. Ed. Roger
Manvell. L: Collins, 1957. 349p. (21.5cm.) [B57]

The Swiss family Robinson. Adpt. and abr. Felix
Sutton. NY: Grosset, 1960. 61p. 29cm. [LC62]

The Swiss family Robinson (Der schweizerische Robinson.) Tr. and abr. Audrey Clark. (After the version
by H. Frith.) NY: Dutton, (1957.) 1958. 341p.
(20.5cm.) 21cm. [LC62, B57, IT11]

The Swiss family Robinson. Tr. Anon. Ed. Wm. H.
G. Kingston. L: Macdonald, 1960. 377p. (21.5cm.)

WYSS, Johannes David--
[B60, IT13]

YESUDIAN, Selvarajan and Haich, Elisabeth.
Yoga uniting East and West. (Yoga in den zwei Welten.)
Tr. J. P. Robertson. NY: Harper, 1956. 160p. 22
cm. [LC62, IT9]

Same. Fwd. T. Huzella. L: Allen, 1956. 160p.
(161p.) (22.5cm.) 23cm [LC62, B56, IT9]

YOSHIDA, Tetsuro, 1894-1956.
Gardens of Japan. (Der japanische Garten.) Tr. Marcus
G. Sims. L: Architectural; NY: Praeger, 1957.
187p. (28cm.) [LC62, B58]

YOSELOFF, Thomas, 1913- . See Eulenspiegel.
The further adventures of Till Eulenspiegel. By T--Y--.
Based on a tr. by Lillian Stuckey. NY: Yoseloff, 1957.
122p. 24cm. [LC62]

ZADE, Hans Peter, 1907- .
Heatsealing and high-frequency welding of plastics.
(Thermisches und Hochfrequenzschweissen von Kunst-
stoffen.) Tr. Anon. Fwd. Henri L. Leduc. NY:
Interscience. L: Temple, 1959. 211p. (22.5cm.)
23cm. [LC62, B59]

ZAND, Herbert, 1923- .
The well of hope. (Der Weg nach Hassi el Emel.) Tr.
Norman Denny. L: Collins, 1957. 158p. (159p.)
(20cm.) [LC62, B57, IT10]

ZAPF, Hermann.
About alphabets. Some marginal notes on type design.
(Über Alphabete.) Tr. Paul Standard. NY: Typophiles,
1960. 117p. 18cm. [LC62]

Autobiography in type. From Hermann Zapf's Manuale
typographicum. Tr. Anon. n.p., 1959. 33-471.
31cm. [LC62]

ZASSENHAUS, Hans.
Lie-rings and lie-algebras. Tr. Anon. Canadian mathematical congress, U. of Alberta, 1957. 1v. 28cm.

[LC62]

The theory of groups. (Lehrbuch der Gruppentheorie.)
Tr. Anon. 2nd ed. NY: Chelsea, 1958. 265p. 24cm.
[LC62]

The theory of groups. Tr. Anon. Göttingen: Vanden-
hoeck, c1958. 265p. 24cm. [LC62]

ZAUGG, Hans, and Coaz, Hans. See Schwarzenbach,
Hans, 1911- .
Decorative trees and shrubs. (Unsere Gartenpflanzen.)
Tr. and adpt. Herbert L. Edlin. L: Thames; NY:
Viking, 1960. 133p. 32cm. (32.5cm.) [LC62, B60,
IT13]

ZAUNMUELLER, Wolfram.
A critical bibliography of language dictionaries. (Bib-
liographisches Handbuch der Sprachwörterbücher.) Tr.
Anon. NY, L: Hafner; Stuttgart: Hiersemann, 1958.
2-495p. (COL.-LC) (28cm.) [LC62, B59]

ZECHLIN, Ruth, 1899- .
The complete book of handcrafts. (Werkbuch für Mädchen.) Trs. Peter Gorge and F. Sylvia Weston. Boston: Bradford, 1959. 328p. 25cm. [LC62]

The girl's book of crafts. (Werkbuch für Mädchen.)
Trs. Peter Gorge, F. Sylvia Weston and James Norbury.
L: Batsford, 1959. 328p. (24.5cm.) [LC62, B59,
IT12]

ZEISER, Bruno. See Zieser, Benno.

ZEISBERGER, David, 1721-1808.
David Zeisberger's official diary. Tr. Paul Eugene
Mueller. NY: Columbia U. Pr., c1956. 263l. 29cm.
[LC62]

From Fairfield to Schönbrun, 1798. Tr. Anon. Ed.
Leslie R. Gray. n.p., 1957. 35p. [LC62]

Official diary, Fairfield, 1791-1795. Tr. and ed. Paul
Eugene Mueller. Ann Arbor: University Microf. of TW,
1956. Publ. no. 17,070. [LC62]

ZELLER, Eduard, 1814-1908.
Outlines of the history of Greek philosophy. Tr. L. R.
Palmer. NY: Meridian, 1960. 349p. 18cm. [LC62]

ZIESER, Benno, 1922- .
In their shallow graves. (Rote Leuchtkugeln.) Tr. Alec
Brown. L: Elek, 1956. 208p. (22.5cm.) 23cm.
[LC62, B56, IT9]

Same. L: World Distributors, 1957. 255p. (17cm.)
[B57]

The road to Stalingrad. (Rote Leuchtkugeln.) Tr. Alec
Brown. NY: Ballantine, 1956. 152p. 21cm. [LC62,
IT9]

ZIMMERLI, Walther, 1907- . and Jeremias, Joachim.
The servant of God. (Theologisches Wörterbuch zum
Neuen Testament.) Tr. Anon. L: SCM, 1957. 9-120p.
(21.5cm.) 22cm. [LC62, B57]

Same. Naperville, Ill.: Allenson, 1957. 120p. 22cm.
[LC62]

ZIMMERMANN, Erich, ed.
Germans against Hitler, July 21, 1944. (Zwanzigster
Juli 1944.) Trs. Allan and Lieselotte Yahraes. Comp.
Hans Royce. Pub. by Press and Information Office of the
Federal German Government, Bonn: Berto, c1960.
328p. [LC62]

ZIMNIK, Reiner.
Drummers of dreams. (Die Trommler für eine bessere
Zeit.) Tr. E. M. Hatt. L: Faber, 1960. 61p.
(25.5cm.) [B60, IT14]

Jonah, the fisherman. (Jonas der Angler.) Trs. and
ed. Richard and Clara Winston. NY: Pantheon, 1956.
(unp.) 31cm. [LC62, IT9]

Same. L: Faber, 1957. 61p. (63p.) (30.5cm.)
[B57, IT10]

The proud white circus horse. (Der stolze Schimmel.)
Tr. E. M. Hatt. NY: Pantheon, 1957. unp. 30cm.
[LC62]

Same.   L: Faber, 1958.   45p.   (25.5cm.) [B58, IT11]

ZINNER, Ernst, 1886- .
The stars above us or the conquest of supersitition.
(Sternglaube und Sternforschung.) Tr. W. H. Johnston.
L: Allen, 1957.   141p.   (142p.) (22.5cm.) 23cm.
[LC62, B57]

Same.   NY: Scribner, 1957.   141p.   23cm.   [LC62]

ZIRKEL, Wilhelm.
A thousand years of Erlaheim.   Tr. Lisbeth Sass.   NY:
Johnson, 1960.   59p.   31cm.   [LC62]

ZOTTMANN, Thomas Michael, 1915- .   See Thomas, M.
Z., pseud.

ZSCHIETZSCHMANN, Willy, 1900- .
Hellas and Rome.   The classical world in picture.
(Hellas und Rom.) Tr. Hedi Schnabl.   L: Zwemmer,
1959.   (1960.) 304p.   (23.5cm.) 24cm.   [LC62, B60]

Same.   NY: Universe, 1960.   304p.   24cm.   [LC62, IT
13]

ZUBERBÜHLER, Walter.
Alpstein, people and country.   (Land und Leute.) Eng.
version C. C. Palmer.   Photos. Herbert Maeder.
Teufen: Niggli, 1956.   104p.   23cm.   [LC62]

ZUCKERKANDL, Victor.
The sense of music.   Tr. Anon.   Princeton, NJ: Princeton U. Pr., 1959.   246p.   25cm.   [LC62]

Sound and symbol, music and the external world.   Tr.
Willard R. Trask.   L: Routledge, 1956.   399p.   (23.5
cm.) 24cm.   [LC62, B56]

Same.   NY: Pantheon, 1956.   399p.   24cm.   [LC62,
IT9]

ZUCKMAYER, Carl, 1896- .
The Captain of Koepenick.   (Der Hauptmann von K--.)
Tr. Elizabeth Montagu.   Microf. of TW.   Columbia U.,
1958.   105l.   [LC62]

The cold light, a drama in three acts.   (Das kalte Licht.)

ZUCKMAYER, Carl--
Tr. Elizabeth Montagu. Microf. of TW. Columbia U.,
1958. 145l. [LC62]

ZÜBLIN, A. G. ed. See Niebelschütz, Wolf v.

ZULLINGER, Hans, 1893- .
The Behn-Rorschach test. (Der Behn-Rorschach-Test.)
Tr. Cardon Klinger. Bern: Huber, Dist. for USA,
Grune, NY, 1956. 200p. 25cm. [LC62]

ZWEIG, Arnold, 1887- .
A bit of blood. (Ein Tropfen Blut.) Tr. Anon. Berlin:
Seven Seas, 1959. 181p. 19cm. [LC62, IT13]

A bit of blood and other stories. Tr. Anon. Berlin:
Seven Seas; (L: Collet's,) 1959. 184p. (19cm.)
[B60]

ZWEIG, Stefan, 1881-1942.
Erasmus of Rotterdam. Trs. E. and C. Paul. NY:
Viking, 1956. 247p. 20cm. [LC62, IT9]

Jeremiah, a drama in nine scenes. (Jeremias, dramatische Dichtung.) Trs. Eden and Cedar Paul. NY: Rialto Service Bureau, n. d. 1v. 28cm. [LC62]

Kaleidoscope. Trs. Eden and Cedar Paul. 2nd Hallan
ed. L: Cassel, 1955-1959. 19cm. [LC62]

Volpone. In Gassner, John. Twenty best European
plays on the American stage. Tr. Ruth Langner. NY:
Crown, 1957. 402-442p. [LC62]

ZWILLING, E. Ax. 1904- .
Jungle fever. (Steppentage-Urwaldnächte.) Tr. Mervyn
Savill. L: Souvenir, 1956. 216p. 22cm. [LC62,
B56, IT9]

Same. L: Odhams, 1958. 291-384p. [IT11]

A Glossary of Abbreviations

Anon.	Anonymous
anthol.	anthology
B	British National Bibliography
Bart	Baronet
c	copyright issued in year following designation
ca	circa
C. L. S.	College Library Series
cm.	centimeters
comp.	compiled (by), or compiler
Dan.	Danish
ed.	edited, edition, or editor
Eng.	English
enl.	enlarged
Fr.	French
fwd.	foreword (by)
Ger.	German
G. M. B. H.	Gemeinschaft mit Beschränkter Handlung
H. M. S. O.	Her Majesty's Stationery Office
H. U. C. -	
J. I. R.	from source, unknown meaning
Ill.	Illinois
illus.	illustrations, or illustrator
introd.	introduction (by)
IT	Index Translationum
J. P. S. A.	Jewish Publication Society of America
jt.	joint
L.	London
l.	leaves, (listed with numerals immediately pre ceeding.)

LC	Library of Congress Catalog
lib.	library
Md.	Maryland
M. H. L.	from source, unknown meaning
Microf. of Tw.	Microfilm copy of typewritten manuscript at location listed
Mo.	Missouri
ms.	manuscript
n. d.	no date listed in source work
NJ	New Jersey
n. p.	no publisher listed in source work
NY	New York
O. S. P.	from source, unknown meaning
orig.	original
p.	page or pages
photog.	photographer, or photographs
pr.	press
pref.	preface (by)
pseud.	pseudonym
publ.	published, or publisher
rev.	revised (by)
RUSS.	Russian
SCM	Student Christian Movement Press
sel.	selected (by), or selection
Sp.	Spanish
S. P. C. K.	Society for Promoting Christian Knowledge
tr. -trs.	translator - translators
trans.	translation
U.	University
unp.	unpaged, (no pagination listed in source work)
U. S. J. P. R. S.	United States Joint Publications Research Service
v.	volume, or volumes
Va.	Virginia
ver.	version(s)
Verb.	Verbessert.